face2face

Upper Intermediate Teacher's Book

Chris Redston & Theresa Clementson with Gillie Cunningham

CAMBRIDGE
UNIVERSITY PRESS

CAMBRIDGE UNIVERSITY PRESS
Cambridge, New York, Melbourne, Madrid, Cape Town,
Singapore, São Paulo, Delhi, Mexico City

Cambridge University Press
The Edinburgh Building, Cambridge CB2 8RU, UK

www.cambridge.org
Information on this title: www.cambridge.org/9781107629356

First published 2013

Printed in the United Kingdom by Polestar Wheatons Ltd, Exeter

A catalogue record for this publication is available from the British Library

ISBN 978-1-107-62935-6 Upper Intermediate Teacher's Book with DVD
ISBN 978-1-107-42201-8 Upper Intermediate Student's Book with DVD-ROM
ISBN 978-1-107-60956-3 Upper Intermediate Workbook with Key
ISBN 978-1-107-60957-0 Upper Intermediate Workbook without Key
ISBN 978-1-107-42203-2 Upper Intermediate Class Audio CDs (3)

Cambridge University Press has no responsibility for the persistence or
accuracy of the URLs for external or third-party internet websites referred to in
this publication, and does not guarantee that any content on such websites is,
or will remain, accurate or appropriate. Information regarding prices, travel
timetables and other factual information given in this work is correct at
the time of first printing but Cambridge University Press does not guarantee
the accuracy of such information thereafter.

Contents

Welcome to face2face Second edition!

Teaching Notes

Photocopiable Materials

Class Activities

Vocabulary Plus

Extra Reading

Study Skills

Progress Tests

Welcome to face2face Second edition!

face2face Second edition

face2face Second edition is a general English course for adults and young adults who want to learn to communicate quickly and effectively in today's world. Based on the communicative approach, it combines the best in current methodology with innovative new features designed to make learning and teaching easier. Each self-contained double-page lesson is easily teachable off the page with minimal preparation.

The **face2face** Second edition syllabus integrates the learning of new language with skills development and places equal emphasis on vocabulary and grammar. The course uses a guided discovery approach to learning, first allowing students to check what they know, then helping them to work out the rules for themselves through carefully structured examples and concept questions.

There is a strong focus on listening and speaking throughout **face2face** Second edition. Innovative *Help with Listening* sections help students to understand natural spoken English in context and there are numerous opportunities for communicative, personalised speaking practice. The *Real World* lessons in each unit focus on the functional and situational language students need for day-to-day life.

This language can now be presented using video material on the Teacher's DVD. For more on the **face2face** approach, see p20.

All new language is included in the interactive *Language Summaries* in the back of the Student's Book and is regularly recycled and reviewed. Students can also review new language in the *Extra Practice* section in the Student's Book, on the Self-study DVD-ROM and in the Workbook.

The Student's Book provides approximately 80 hours of core teaching material, which can be extended to 120 hours with the inclusion of the photocopiable materials and extra ideas in this Teacher's Book.

The vocabulary selection in **face2face** Second edition has been informed by the *English Vocabulary Profile* (see p15) as well as the *Cambridge International Corpus* and the *Cambridge Learner Corpus*.

face2face Second edition is fully compatible with the *Common European Framework of Reference for Languages* (CEFR) and gives students regular opportunities to evaluate their progress. The Upper Intermediate Student's Book completes B2 (see p14–p19).

face2face Second edition Upper Intermediate Components

Student's Book with Self-study DVD-ROM

The **Student's Book** provides 48 double-page lessons in 12 thematically linked units, each with four lessons of two pages. Each lesson takes approximately 90 minutes (see p6–p9).

The **Self-study DVD-ROM** is an invaluable resource for students with over 300 exercises in all language areas and a Review Video for each unit, *My Test* and *My Progress* sections where students evaluate their own progress (see p11–p13) and an interactive Phonemic Symbols chart. In addition there is an e-Portfolio with *Grammar Reference*, *Word List*, *Word Cards*, plus a *My Work* section where students can build a digital portfolio of their work.

You can help students to get the most out of the Self-study DVD-ROM by giving them the photocopiable user instructions on p11–p13.

Class Audio CDs

The three **Class Audio CDs** contain all the listening material for the Student's Book, including drills, *Real World* conversations and the listening sections of the *Progress Tests* for units 6 and 12.

Workbook

The **Workbook** provides further practice of all language presented in the Student's Book. It also includes a 24-page *Reading and Writing Portfolio* based on the *Common European Framework of Reference for Languages*, which can be used either for homework or for extra work in class.

Teacher's Book with Teacher's DVD

This **Teacher's Book** includes *Teaching Tips*, *Classroom Activities and Games* and *Teaching Notes* for each lesson. There is also an extensive bank of photocopiable materials (see p3): 35 *Class Activities*, 12 *Vocabulary Plus* worksheets, 12 *Extra Reading* worksheets, 4 *Study Skills* worksheets and 12 *Progress Tests*.

The **Teacher's DVD** contains video presentation material for all the *Real World* lessons in the Student's Book, as well as printable PDFs of all the Teaching Notes and photocopiable materials (see p10). The DVD by default opens the Video menu, where you will find help on how to access the PDFs.

Website

Visit www.cambridge.org/elt/face2face for bilingual Word Lists, sample materials, full details of how **face2face** Second edition covers the grammatical and lexical areas specified by the CEFR and much more!

New Features of face2face Second edition Upper Intermediate

2 **a** VIDEO ▶2 CD1 ▶20 Look at the people in the photo and watch or listen to their conversation. What are the two main topics they discuss?

NEW optional **VIDEO** presentation material for all ▶ **REAL WORLD** lessons in the Student's Book.

NEW Teacher's DVD with all the Real World video presentation material, Teaching Notes and photocopiable materials from this Teacher's Book.

NEW Help with Pronunciation sections at the end of each unit in the Student's Book enable students to improve their pronunciation and help them to communicate more effectively.

> **HELP WITH PRONUNCIATION**
> Sounds (1): final letters *se*
>
> **1** **a** Work in pairs. How do you say the final letters *se* in these words, /s/ or /z/?
> 1 promise / / house / / purse / /
>   purpose / / sense / /
> 2 advertise / / noise / / vase / /
> 3 close v. / / close adj. / / use v. / / use n. / /
>
> **b** CD1 ▶12 Listen and check. Then practise.
>
> **c** Look at the words in 1a again. Complete rules a–c with /s/ or /z/.
> a -se = / / after the sounds /ɪ/ /aʊ/ /ɜː/ /ə/ /n/
> b -se = / / after the sounds /aɪ/ /ɔɪ/ /ɑː/
> c When a verb has the same form as a noun or adjective -se = / / in verbs and / / in nouns and adjectives
>
> **2** **a** CD1 ▶13 Look at the final *se* in pink. Which sound is different? Listen and check.

Home   1   2   3   4   5   6   7   8   9   10   11   12   My Tests

face2face   Upper Intermediate DVD-ROM

NEW full-page **Extra Practice and Progress Portfolio** sections for each unit in the back of the Student's Book provide further controlled practice of all new language.

> **Extra Practice 5**   Language Summary 5 p137
>
> *(sample page showing exercises 5A p40, 5B p42, 5C p44, 5D p46 and Progress Portfolio 5)*

NEW Extra Reading photocopiable worksheets in the back of this Teacher's Book provide extended reading practice in class or for self-study.

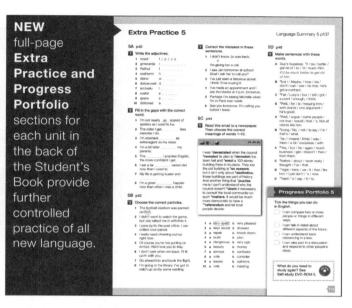

> **6** ▶ Tattoo
>
> **The art of tattooing**

NEW Self-study DVD-ROM with over 300 practice exercises, Review Video, *My Test* and *My Progress* sections, e-Portfolio and much more!

A Guide to the Student's Book

Lessons A and B in each unit introduce and practise new vocabulary and grammar in realistic contexts.

The menu lists the language taught in each lesson.

Help with Grammar sections encourage students to work out the rules of form and use for themselves before checking their answers in the interactive *Language Summary* for the unit.

2A ▶ It's bad for you!

Vocabulary expressing frequency
Grammar present and past habits, repeated actions and states

QUICK REVIEW Keeping a conversation going
Work in pairs. Take turns to tell each other what you did last weekend. Ask each other short questions and try to keep each conversation going for a minute.
A *I went camping.* **B** *Did you? Who with?*

Speaking, Reading and Listening

1 a Write a list of six types of food that are good for you and six that aren't. Then work in pairs and compare lists.

b Answer these questions.
1 Why do you think your items of food are good or bad for you?
2 In your opinion, is your national diet generally healthy? Give reasons.
3 Do you think governments should give nutritional advice? Why?/Why not?

2 Read the introduction to an article about nutritional advice. Answer these questions.
1 Why are people confused about which types of food are and aren't good for them?
2 Why do you think the writer mentions organically grown food?

3 a Look at the photos of Guy and Jasmin, two people who took part in a survey about eating habits. Who do you think says sentences 1–3 and who do you think says sentences 4–6?
1 I think I'm pretty healthy and I just **eat** what I like.
2 Most mornings **I'll have** toast with a lot of peanut butter and jam.
3 My mom's **always complaining** about my diet.
4 But **I used to be** so unfit and I **used to eat** burgers and fries all the time.
5 And **I'd get** an ice cream or something on the way home from school every day.
6 And then I **read** a lot of stuff about healthy eating and I **knew** my diet had to change.

b CD1·14 Listen and check.

c Listen again. Answer these questions.
1 What does Guy think of government advice on food?
2 Has Guy's attitude to food ever changed?
3 Who is healthier, Guy or his mother?
4 Does Jasmin ever eat things that are unhealthy?
5 Why did she decide to get fit?
6 What does she say about Japanese and American eating habits?

d Work in pairs. Compare answers. Whose attitude to food is most like yours, Guy's or Jasmin's?

Guy

Jasmin

Should I eat it or not?

Eating should be one of life's pleasures, but we are constantly bombarded with contradictory information about which foods are healthy and which aren't. It can be difficult to know what a nutritious meal consists of these days. One minute milk and red meat are good for us, the next they're not! And when you have sorted that out, then comes the question of whether we should only eat organically grown food or whether industrially farmed food is just as healthy. Government agencies are quick to advise us about what and what not to eat, but how much notice do we really take?

HELP WITH GRAMMAR Present and past habits, repeated actions and states

4 a Look at the verb forms in bold in sentences 1–3 in 3a. Complete these rules with Present Simple, *will* + infinitive or Present Continuous.
• We use the _____ to talk about present habits, repeated actions and states.
• We often use the _____ with *always* to talk about present habits and repeated actions that annoy us or happen more than usual.
• We can use _____ to talk about repeated and typical behaviour in the present. We don't usually use this verb form with state verbs for this meaning.

b Look at these sentences. Which talks about repeated and typical behaviour? Which talks about a future action?
1 Sometimes **I'll eat** junk food if I'm with friends.
2 Tonight **I'll probably have** a pizza.

c Look at the verb forms in bold in sentences 4–6 in 3a. Complete these rules with Past Simple, *would* + infinitive or *used to* + infinitive.
• We use the _____ to talk about past habits, repeated actions and states.
• We can use _____ to talk about past habits and repeated actions. We **don't** usually use this verb form with state verbs.

TIP • We don't use *used to* or *would* + infinitive for something that only happened once: *I gave up smoking in May.* not *I used to give up smoking in May.*

d Check in GRAMMAR 2.1 ▶ p130.

5 Look at these sentences. Are both verb forms possible? If not, choose the correct one.
1 Last night *I'd have/I had* two burgers for dinner and *I used to feel/I felt* a bit sick afterwards.
2 I hardly ever drink coffee now, but at one time *it'd be/it used to be* my favourite drink.
3 I don't usually pay attention to government reports about food because *they'd change/they're always changing* their advice.
4 I *walk/I'll walk* to work just for the exercise and I frequently *go/am going* to the gym.
5 I *eat/I'll* eat vegetables occasionally, but only because *I'll know/I know* they're good for me.
6 I *always worry/I'm always worrying* about my diet.
7 Once *I used to try/I tried* not adding salt to my food. It tasted awful!
8 When I was younger, *I didn't use to like/I wouldn't like* coffee.

6 a Read about Guy's parents, Bernie and Ellen. Fill in the gaps with the correct form of the verbs in brackets. Sometimes there is more than one possible answer.

Bernie and I [1] _____ (want) to buy a place before we [2] _____ (start) a family so **most days** we [3] _____ (work) 12 hours a day to earn extra money. **More often than not** when we [4] _____ (get) home from work, we [5] _____ (be) so tired that we [6] _____ (just have) a sandwich. We [7] _____ (seldom watch) TV in the evening and we [8] _____ (rarely go) to bed later than 10 p.m. However, **once in a while** Bernie [9] _____ (take) me to a local café for a treat. Bernie [10] _____ (always tell) Guy how hard life [11] _____ (be) back then, and it's true, but **most of the time** Bernie and I [12] _____ (be) happy, though **every now and again** I [13] _____ (get) upset because we [14] _____ (not have) much money. Then in 1981 we [15] _____ (buy) a small apartment and ten months later we [16] _____ (have) Guy. Now that we have more money we [17] _____ (eat out) quite often. And **every so often** we [18] _____ (go) to a restaurant we [19] _____ (love), called Sam's, even though Bernie [20] _____ (always say) we can't afford it!

b Work in pairs. Compare answers.

Vocabulary and Speaking Expressing frequency

7 a Put the words/phrases in bold in 6a into these groups. Check in VOCABULARY 2.1 ▶ p130.

lower frequency	higher frequency
seldom	most days

b Write four true and four false sentences about your eating habits. Use words/phrases from 6a.

c Work in pairs. Tell each other your sentences. Guess which of your partner's sentences are true.

Get ready … Get it right!

8 Make notes on the differences between your life five years ago and your life now. Use these ideas or your own.
• sleeping habits
• free time activities
• sport and exercise
• annoying habits
• taste in music/films/TV/books
• time with friends and family
• work or study
• places you have lived

9 Work in groups. Discuss how your life now is different from your life five years ago. Use the language from 4 and 7.

Students can learn and check the meaning of new vocabulary in the interactive *Language Summary* for the unit in the back of the Student's Book.

Reduced sample pages from the **face2face**
Second edition Upper Intermediate Student's Book

2B ▶ Life's different here

Vocabulary feelings and opinions
Grammar be used to, get used to

QUICK REVIEW Present and past habits
Choose three friends. Write a sentence about each friend's present or past habits or routines. Take turns to tell your partner about your friends. Ask follow-up questions if possible.
A *My friend Lara is always worrying about work.*
B *Oh, why's that?*

Vocabulary and Speaking
Feelings and opinions

1 a Look at the adjectives in bold. Then choose the correct prepositions. Check in **VOCABULARY 2.2** p130.

1 I'm **terrified** for/of flying.
2 I'm **fascinated** by/for other cultures.
3 I always get **excited** of/about travelling to new places.
4 I'm usually **satisfied** for/with the service I get on planes.
5 I'm **shocked** by/with how little some people know about my country.
6 I was quite **disappointed** in/of the last place I went to on holiday.
7 I was **impressed** of/by the facilities at the last hotel I stayed in.
8 I'm not **aware** to/of any dangers for travellers in my country.
9 My country is **famous** for/about its historical buildings.
10 I grew very **fond** with/of the people I met on holiday.
11 I'm not **sure** for/about the need for so many security checks at airports.
12 I'm **sick** of/at wasting time at airports because of delays or cancellations.

b Tick the sentences in 1a that are true for you.

c Work in pairs. Take turns to say the sentences you ticked. Ask follow-up questions.

> I'm terrified of flying. | Really? Why's that?

Speaking and Reading

2 a Look at the photos of Mongolia. What do you know about this country's geography, sports, food and weather?

b Read the article. What does the writer think are the hardest things to deal with in Mongolia?

Letter from abroad
by Lottie Clarkson

I've always been fascinated by exotic countries, so imagine how excited I was about having the opportunity to work as a volunteer nurse in Mongolia. Before I came here, all I knew about the country was that it was full of wide open spaces and nomadic people moving from place to place, tending their animals and living in tents, known as *gers*. My work mainly takes me to the rural parts of Mongolia and although sleeping in a *ger* seemed very strange to me at first, [1]**I'm used to staying in these wonderful tents now**.

The one thing I really wasn't prepared for was how different Mongolian food is, but [2]**I'm slowly getting used to it**. The diet is mainly milk-based in summer (yoghurt, cheese etc.) with a shift to meat in winter. It took me a while [3]**to get used to eating so much meat**, especially as it's usually served without vegetables. And [4]**I certainly wasn't used to the lumps of fat** my Mongolian friends ate with such pleasure. But this amount of fat in the diet is necessary because Mongolians have to withstand viciously cold winters. It can go as low as -40°C. [5]**I'll never get used to being outside in those temperatures!**

The highlight of my stay in Mongolia so far has been the Naadam festival, which happens every year in July. All over the country you'll see people in their spectacular traditional dress, taking part in wrestling, archery and horse racing. It's a fantastic event, particularly the horse races which are 15 to 30 kilometres long. The jockeys riding these horses are fearless children – boys and girls, aged between 5 and 13!

Oh, one more thing about Mongolia – [6]**I still haven't got used to Airag**, which is made from fermented horse's milk. It's been the Mongolian traditional alcoholic drink for 5000 years. I'm told it's an acquired taste!

3 a Read the article again. What does Lottie Clarkson say about these things?

a the way of life outside the cities
b seasonal changes in the diet
c why fat is important in the diet
d the Naadam
e horse races
f Airag

b Work in groups. Discuss these questions.

1 In what ways is Mongolia different from your country?
2 What festivals do you have in your country? What happens at these festivals?
3 Think of other countries with very different cultures from yours. Which would you most like to visit and why?

HELP WITH GRAMMAR
be used to, get used to

4 a Look at phrase 1 in bold in the article. Answer these questions.

1 When Lottie first stayed in a Mongolian tent, did it feel strange to her?
2 Does it feel strange to her now?

b Look at phrases 1 and 2 in the article. Complete these rules with *get used to* and *be used to*.

- We use _____ to talk about things that are familiar and no longer strange or difficult for us.
- We use _____ to talk about things that become familiar, less strange or less difficult over a period of time.

c Look at phrases 1–6 in the article. Choose the correct words/phrases in these rules.

- After *be used to* and *get used to* we use the **infinitive/verb+ing**.
- After *be used to* and *get used to* we **can/can't** use a noun or a pronoun.

d Match phrases 1–6 in the article to these forms of *be used to* or *get used to*.

a Present Simple
b Present Continuous
c Present Perfect Simple
d Past Simple
e *will* + infinitive
f infinitive with *to*

e What is the difference in meaning between these two sentences?

1 I used to live in Mongolia.
2 I'm used to living in Mongolia.

f Check in **GRAMMAR 2.2** p131.

5 CD1▶15 **PRONUNCIATION** Listen and practise. Copy the stress.

I'm /jʊstə/ *staying in these wonderful tents now.*

Japan

Iceland

6 a Look at the photos of Japan and Iceland. Then fill in the gaps with the correct positive or negative form of *be used to* or *get used to*. Sometimes there is more than one possible answer.

1 I _____ all the customs yet – like it's rude to blow your nose in public.
2 It was hard to _____ just eating rice for breakfast.
3 I _____ sleeping in daylight, so I find it difficult in the summer when it never gets dark.
4 I don't think I'll ever _____ the written language – it has three alphabets.
5 The summers here aren't very warm and I _____ temperatures of about 35°C in the summer.
6 I _____ finding my way around new places using a map, but I can't read the street signs here.

b Work in pairs. Compare answers. Which sentences in 6a refer to Japan? Which refer to Iceland?

▶ Get ready ... Get it right!

7 Write five of these things on a piece of paper. Don't write them in this order.

Something that you:

- are used to doing during the week
- don't think you'll ever get used to
- will have to get used to in the future
- would find it impossible to get used to
- are getting used to at the moment
- weren't used to doing at one time, but you are now

8 Work in pairs. Swap papers. Take turns to ask your partner about the things he/she has written. Ask follow-up questions if possible.

18 / 19

Reduced sample pages from the **face2face**
Second edition Upper Intermediate Student's Book

A Guide to the Student's Book

Lesson C VOCABULARY AND SKILLS lessons develop students' range of receptive skills by providing opportunities to see and hear new words and phrases in extended reading and listening texts.

Help with Listening sections focus on the areas that make spoken English so difficult to understand and teach students how to listen more effectively.

Help with Vocabulary sections encourage students to work out the rules of form and use of new vocabulary themselves, before checking in the interactive *Language Summary* for the unit.

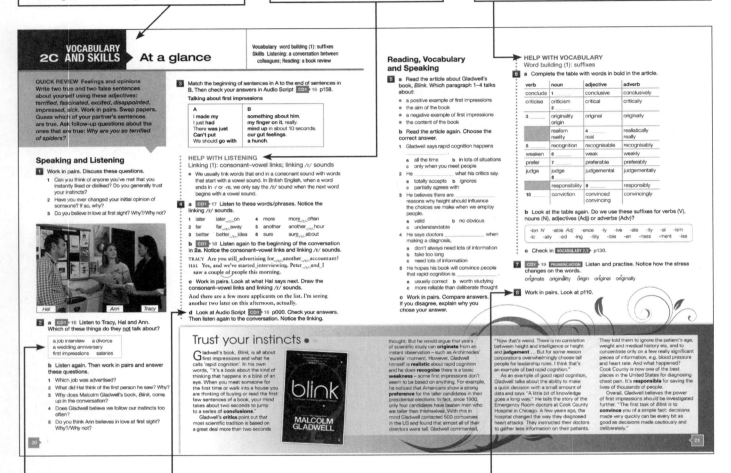

Key vocabulary in listening and reading texts is pre-taught before students listen or read.

Students are often asked to refer to the *Audio and Video Scripts* in the back of the Student's Book to help develop their ability in both listening and pronunciation.

The *Pair and GroupWork* section at the back of the Student's Book provides numerous communicative speaking practice activities.

Reduced sample pages from the **face2face**
Second edition Upper Intermediate Student's Book

Lesson D REAL WORLD lessons focus on the functional and situational language students need for day-to-day life.

Real World sections help students to analyse the functional and situational language for themselves before checking in the interactive *Language Summary* for the unit.

Help with Pronunciation sections help students with specific areas of pronunciation that they often find problematic.

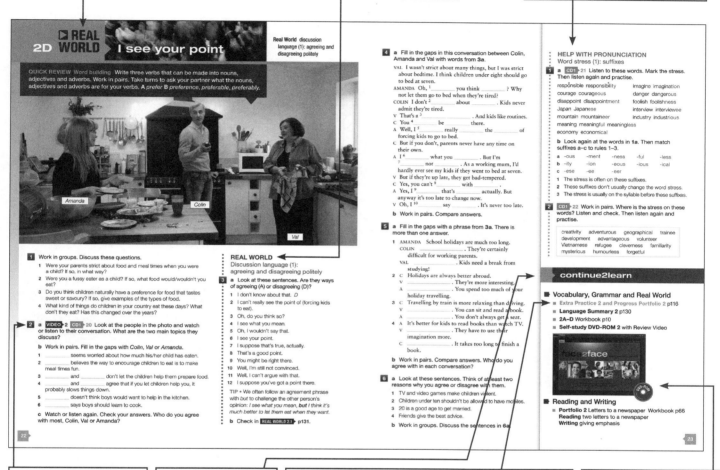

Add variety to your lessons by presenting *Real World* language visually using the new video clips on the **face2face** Second edition Upper Intermediate Teacher's DVD.

The *continue2learn* sections show students where they can continue practising and extending their knowledge of the language taught in the unit.

There is a full-page *Extra Practice* section in the back of the Student's Book, which provides revision of key language from the unit. Students can also monitor their progress by completing the *Progress Portfolio*, which is based on the requirements of the *Common European Framework of Reference for Languages*.

The Self-study DVD-ROM provides further practice activities, Review Video, drills, *My Test*, *My Progress* and e-Portfolio sections.

Reduced sample pages from the **face2face**
Second edition Upper Intermediate Student's Book

Teacher's DVD Instructions

The Teacher's DVD contains the *Real World* video presentation material as well as printable PDFs of all the Teaching Notes and photocopiable materials from this Teacher's Book.

- To play the *Real World* video presentation material you can use the DVD in a DVD player or in a computer. Insert the DVD and follow the instructions on the main menu.
- To access the PDFs on a Windows operating system, double-click **My Computer**. Right click on the CD/DVD drive and choose *Explore*. Open the "Teaching Notes and Photocopiable Materials" folder and double-click on the PDFs you want to view or print.
- To access the PDFs on a computer with a Mac operating system, double-click on the DVD icon on the desktop. Open the "Teaching Notes and Photocopiable Materials" folder and double-click on the PDFs you want to view or print.

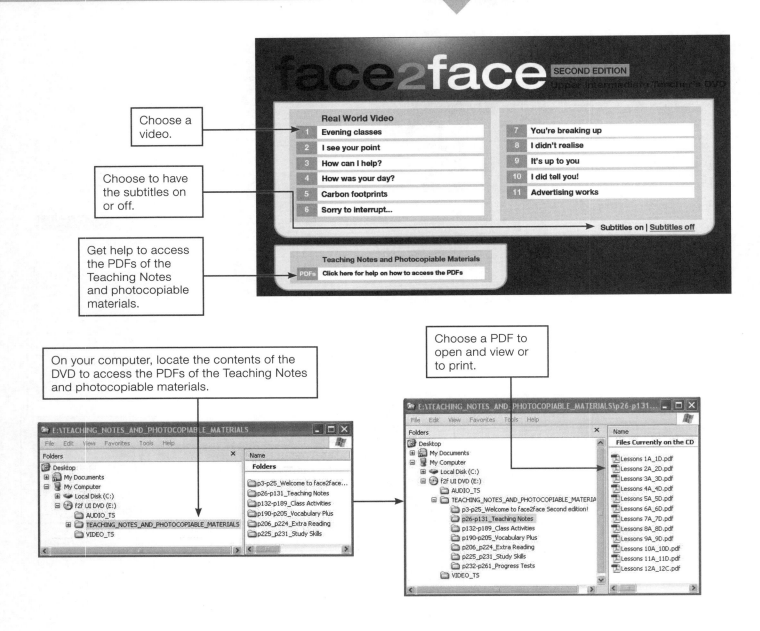

Choose a video.

Choose to have the subtitles on or off.

Get help to access the PDFs of the Teaching Notes and photocopiable materials.

On your computer, locate the contents of the DVD to access the PDFs of the Teaching Notes and photocopiable materials.

Choose a PDF to open and view or to print.

To view or print the Teaching Notes and photocopiable materials you will need a software program that can read PDFs such as Adobe® Reader®, which is free to download and install at www.adobe.com.

Self-study DVD-ROM Instructions

Installing the Self-study DVD-ROM to your hard disk

- Insert the **face2face** Second edition Upper Intermediate Self-study DVD-ROM into your CD/DVD drive. The DVD-ROM will automatically start to install. Follow the installation instructions on your screen.
- On a Windows PC, if the DVD-ROM does not automatically start to install, open **My Computer**, locate your CD/DVD drive and open it to view the contents of the DVD-ROM. Double-click on the *CambridgeApplicationInstaller* file. Follow the installation instructions on your screen.
- On a Mac, if the DVD-ROM does not automatically start to install, double-click on the **face2face** DVD icon on your desktop. Double-click on the *CambridgeApplicationInstaller* file. Follow the installation instructions on your screen.

Support

If you need help with installing the DVD-ROM, please visit: www.cambridge.org/elt/support

System requirements

Windows
- Intel Pentium 4 2GHz or faster
- Microsoft® Windows® XP (SP3), Vista® (SP2), Windows 7
- Minimum 1GB RAM
- Minimum 750MB of hard drive space
- Adobe® Flash® Player 10.3.183.7 or later

Mac OS
- Intel Core™ Duo 1.83GHz or faster
- Mac OSX 10.5 or later
- Minimum 1GB RAM
- Minimum 750MB of hard drive space
- Adobe® Flash® Player 10.3.183.7 or later

Unit menus

Choose a unit.

Practise the new language from each lesson.

Listen and practise new language. You can also record your own pronunciation.

Watch the Review Video and do the activities.

Use the navigation bar to go to different areas of the DVD-ROM.

Create vocabulary and grammar tests for language in the Student's Book.

Listen to the main recordings from the Student's Book and read the scripts.

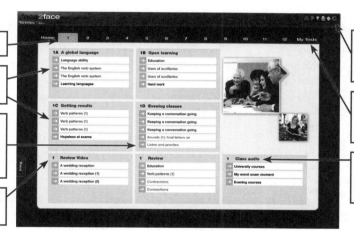

Go to the home screen.

Look at the Phonemic Symbols chart and practise the pronunciation of vowel and consonant sounds.

Check *My Progress* to see your scores for completed activities.

Explore the e-Portfolio. See p12.

Get help on using the Self-study DVD-ROM.

Go to Cambridge Dictionaries Online.

Activities

Read the instructions.

Click play ▶ to listen to the audio.

Record your own pronunciation of words and sentences. Send these recordings to the *My Work* section of the e-Portfolio. See p13.

Check your answers. Sometimes activities then give you extra help or the Audio Script.

Submit your answers when you have finished the activity. Your score is recorded in *My Progress*.

After submitting your answers, see the correct answers.

Start the activity again.

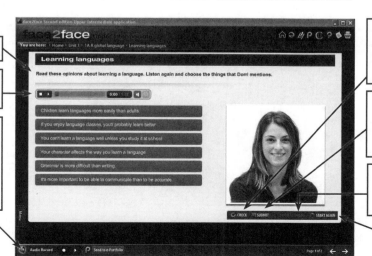

Self-study DVD-ROM Instructions

e-Portfolio

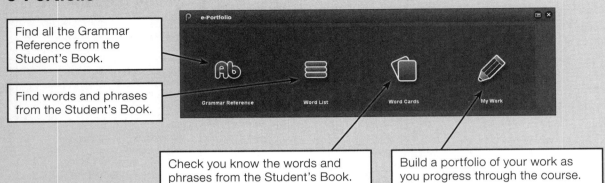

Find all the Grammar Reference from the Student's Book.

Find words and phrases from the Student's Book.

Check you know the words and phrases from the Student's Book.

Build a portfolio of your work as you progress through the course.

Grammar Reference

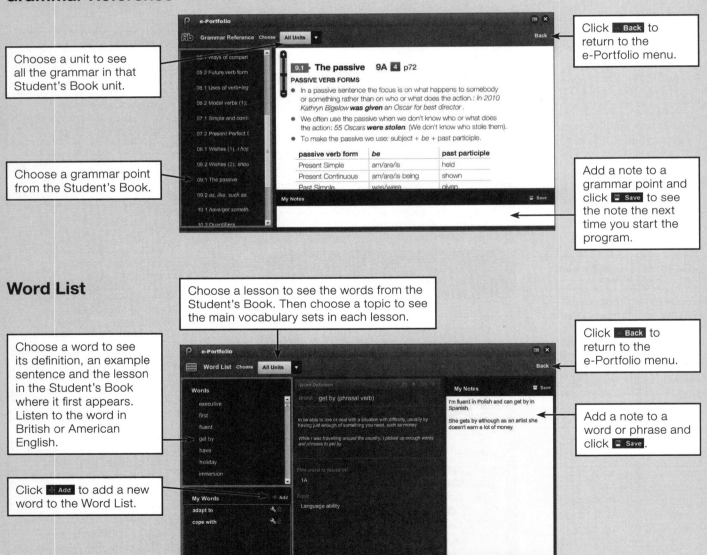

Choose a unit to see all the grammar in that Student's Book unit.

Choose a grammar point from the Student's Book.

Click Back to return to the e-Portfolio menu.

Add a note to a grammar point and click Save to see the note the next time you start the program.

Word List

Choose a lesson to see the words from the Student's Book. Then choose a topic to see the main vocabulary sets in each lesson.

Choose a word to see its definition, an example sentence and the lesson in the Student's Book where it first appears. Listen to the word in British or American English.

Click Add to add a new word to the Word List.

Click Back to return to the e-Portfolio menu.

Add a note to a word or phrase and click Save.

face2face Second edition Upper Intermediate Photocopiable

Word Cards

Choose the number of words.

Choose to have the Word Cards in alphabetical order or shuffled.

Click **Start Again** to move all the cards back to the middle pile and start again.

Choose a unit.

Click **Back** to return to the e-Portfolio menu.

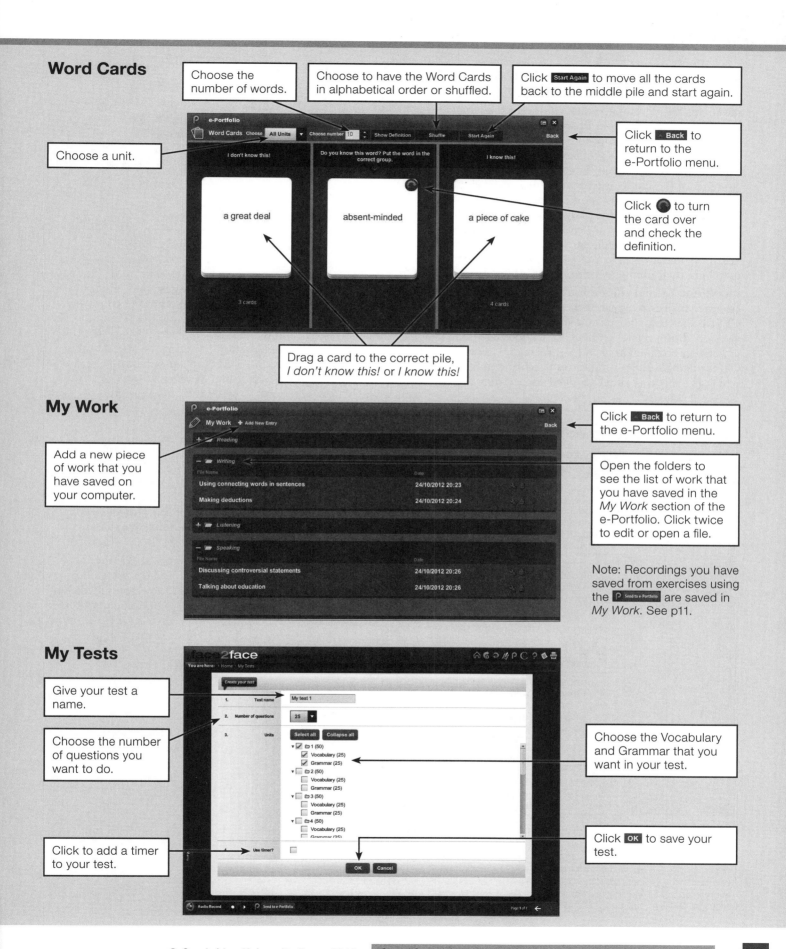

Click ● to turn the card over and check the definition.

Drag a card to the correct pile, *I don't know this!* or *I know this!*

My Work

Click **Back** to return to the e-Portfolio menu.

Add a new piece of work that you have saved on your computer.

Open the folders to see the list of work that you have saved in the *My Work* section of the e-Portfolio. Click twice to edit or open a file.

Note: Recordings you have saved from exercises using the **Send to e-Portfolio** are saved in *My Work*. See p11.

My Tests

Give your test a name.

Choose the number of questions you want to do.

Choose the Vocabulary and Grammar that you want in your test.

Click to add a timer to your test.

Click **OK** to save your test.

What is the Common European Framework (CEFR)?

Since the early 1970s, a series of Council of Europe initiatives has developed a description of the language knowledge and skills that people need to live, work and survive in any European country. *Waystage 1990*[1], *Threshold 1990*[2] and *Vantage*[3] detail the knowledge and skills required at different levels of ability. In 2001, the contents of these documents were further developed into sets of 'can do' statements or 'competences' and officially launched as the *Common European Framework of Reference for Languages: Learning, teaching, assessment (CEFR)*.[4] A related document, *The European Language Portfolio*, encourages learners to assess their progress by matching their competence against the 'can do' statements.

face2face Second edition has been developed to include comprehensive coverage of the requirements of the CEFR. The table above right shows how **face2face** Second edition relates to the CEFR and the examinations which can be taken at each level through University of Cambridge ESOL Examinations (Cambridge ESOL), which is a member of ALTE (The Association of Language Testers in Europe).

CEFR level:		Cambridge ESOL exams:
	face2face	
C1	Advanced	Advanced (CAE)
B2	Upper Intermediate	First (FCE)
B1 +	Intermediate	Preliminary (PET)
B1	Pre-intermediate	
A2	Elementary	Key (KET)
A1	Starter	

In the spirit of *The European Language Portfolio* developed from the CEFR, **face2face** Second edition provides a Progress Portfolio for each unit in the Student's Book. Students are encouraged to assess their ability to use the language they have learned so far and to review any aspects they are unsure of by using the Self-study DVD-ROM. In the Workbook there is a 24-page *Reading and Writing Portfolio* section (two pages for each unit) linked to the CEFR and a comprehensive list of 'can do' statements in the *Reading and Writing Progress Portfolio*, which allows students to track their own progress.

face2face Second edition Upper Intermediate and CEFR level B2

		B2
UNDERSTANDING	Listening	I can understand extended speech and lectures and follow even complex lines of argument provided the topic is reasonably familiar. I can understand most TV news and current affairs programmes. I can understand the majority of films in standard dialect.
	Reading	I can read articles and reports concerned with contemporary problems in which the writers adopt particular attitudes or viewpoints. I can understand contemporary literary prose.
SPEAKING	Spoken interaction	I can interact with a degree of fluency and spontaneity that makes regular interaction with native speakers quite possible. I can take an active part in discussion in familiar contexts, accounting for and sustaining my views.
	Spoken production	I can present clear, detailed descriptions on a wide range of subjects related to my field of interest. I can explain a viewpoint on a topical issue giving the advantages and disadvantages of various options.
WRITING	Writing	I can write clear, detailed text on a wide range of subjects related to my interest. I can write an essay or report, passing on information or giving reasons in support of or against a particular point of view. I can write letters highlighting the personal significance of events and experiences.

The table on the left describes the general degree of skill required at level B2 of the CEFR. Details of the language knowledge required for B2 are listed in *Vantage 1990*. The 'can do' statements for B2 are listed in the *Common European Framework of Reference for Languages: Learning, teaching, assessment*.

The Listening, Reading, Speaking and Writing tables on p16–p19 show where the required competences for level B2 are covered in **face2face** Second edition Upper Intermediate. For more information about how **face2face** covers the areas specified by the Common European Framework of Reference for Languages, see the **face2face** website: www.cambridge.org/elt/face2face.

[1]*Waystage 1990* J A van Ek and J L M Trim, Council of Europe, Cambridge University Press ISBN 978-0-521-56707-7
[2]*Threshold 1990* J A van Ek and J L M Trim, Council of Europe, Cambridge University Press ISBN 978-0-511-66717-6
[3]*Vantage* J A van Ek and J L M Trim, Council of Europe, Cambridge University Press ISBN 978-0-511-66711-4
[4]*Common European Framework of Reference for Languages: Learning, teaching, assessment* (2001) Council of Europe Modern Languages Division, Strasbourg, Cambridge University Press ISBN 978-0-521-00531-9

What is the English Vocabulary Profile?

The English Vocabulary Profile is part of English Profile, a ground-breaking and innovative programme which is shaping the future of English language learning, teaching and assessment worldwide. Endorsed by the Council of Europe, English Profile provides a unique benchmark for progress in English by clearly describing the language that learners need at each level of the Common European Framework (CEFR).

The CEFR is already widely used around the world to assess language ability. However, because it is 'language neutral' it needs to be interpreted appropriately for each language. English Profile makes the CEFR even more relevant to English language teachers by showing the specific vocabulary, grammar and functional language that students can be expected to master at each level in English. By making the CEFR more accessible in this way, it provides unparalleled support for the development of curricula and teaching materials, and in assessing students' language proficiency.

The English Vocabulary Profile shows, in both British and American English, which words and phrases learners around the world know at each level – A1 to C2 – of the CEFR. Rather than providing a syllabus of the vocabulary that learners *should* know, the English Vocabulary Profile verifies what they *do* know at each level. CEFR levels are assigned not just to the words themselves, but to each individual meaning of these words. So, for instance, the word *degree* is assigned level A2 for the meaning *temperature*, B1 for *qualification*, B2 for *amount* and C2 for the phrase *a/some degree of sth*. The capitalised guidewords help the user to navigate longer entries, and phrases are listed separately within an entry.

face2face Second edition Upper Intermediate and the English Vocabulary Profile

The vocabulary taught in **face2face** Second edition Upper Intermediate has been informed by the English Vocabulary Profile to ensure that the majority of the new words and phrases taught in the Student's Book are B2.

To find out more about the English Vocabulary Profile and the English Profile project or to get involved, visit www.englishprofile.org.

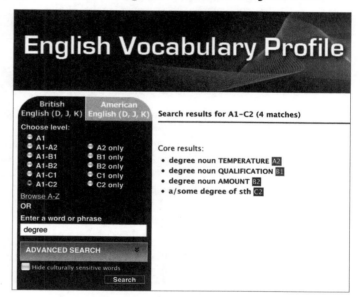

English Profile is a collaborative project between:

CEFR Tables: Listening and Reading

Listening

A language user at level B2 can:	1	2	3
understand in detail what is said to him/her in standard spoken language even in a noisy environment			
catch much of what is said around him/her by native speakers	1B 1C 1D	2C 2D	3B 3C 3D
understand the main ideas of complex speech on both concrete and abstract topics delivered in standard dialect			
follow extended speech and complex lines of argument provided the topic is reasonably familiar and the direction of the talk is signposted by explicit markers	1C	2A 2C	
understand most broadcast materials, including radio documentaries, delivered in standard dialect and can identify the speaker's mood and tone			3C
understand plays and the majority of films in standard dialect			
use a variety of strategies to achieve comprehension, including listening for main points and checking comprehension by using contextual clues	1C 1D	2C 2D	3B 3C 3D
generally follow complex lectures, talks and reports and other forms of presentation			
keep up with an animated conversation between native speakers		2D	3D

Reading

A language user at level B2 can:	1	2	3
understand articles on current problems in which the writers express specific attitudes and points of view	1A 1C WBP1	2B WBP2	3C WB3C
quickly grasp the content and significance of news, articles and reports on topics connected with his/her interests or job, and decide if closer reading is worthwhile	1C WB1C	2C	WBP3
scan quickly through long and complicated texts, locating relevant details	1A 1C	2B WB2C	3C
understand in a narrative the motives for the characters' actions and their consequences for the development of the plot			
understand reviews dealing with the content and criticism of cultural topics (films, theatre, books, concerts) and summarise the main points		2C	
read correspondence relating to his/her field of interest and readily grasp the essential meaning		WBP2	
understand in detail texts within his/her field of interest or academic and professional speciality	1C		3B
understand specialised articles outside his/her own field with the occasional help of a dictionary			
guess the meaning of single unknown words from their context*			

WB1A = **face2face** Upper Intermediate Workbook unit 1 lesson A
WBP1 = **face2face** Upper Intermediate Workbook Reading and Writing Portfolio 1
* refers to descriptors for B1
1A = **face2face** Upper Intermediate Student's Book unit 1 lesson A

4	5	6	7	8	9	10	11	12
This interactive competence is practised throughout the course.								
4C 4D	5B 5D	6B 6D	7A 7D	8A 8C 8D	9C 9D	10D	11A 11B 11C	12A 12C
	5C 5D	6C						
4A	5D		7C			10A	11D	
			7A					
This competence is practised throughout the course on the interactive CD-ROM/Audio CD.								
4A 4C 4D	5B 5C 5D	6B 6C	7A 7C 7D	8A 8C 8D	9B 9C 9D	10A 10C 10D	11A 11B 11C	12A
	5C							
4C 4D	5B 5D	6D	7C 7D	8D	9B 9D	10C 10D	11D	12C

4	5	6	7	8	9	10	11	12
		WBP6	7B 7C WB7C	8C	9C	10B 10C WBP10		12C
4C WB4C	5A 5B WB5C	WB6C	WB7C	WB8C WBP8	WBP9		WB11C	12B WB12C
WBP4	5A	6C	7B 7C	WB8C WBP8	9A 9C	10B 10C WB10C	WB11C	
WB4C					WB9C		11C	WBP12
4B 4C		6A			WBP9			
			WBP7				11C WBP11	WBP12
	5C WBP5		7C					12C
	5C	6C WBP6	7C					12C
		6C	7B	8C		10C		12C

CEFR Tables: Speaking and Writing

Speaking

A language user at level B2 can:	1	2	3
engage in extended conversation in a participatory fashion on most general topics	1B 1C 1D	2A 2B 2D	3A 3C 3D
initiate, maintain and end discourse naturally with effective turn-taking	1A 1B 1D	2B 2C 2D	3A 3B 3C 3D
exchange detailed factual information on matters within his/her field of interest	1D		
account for and sustain his/her opinions by providing relevant arguments, etc.		2A 2C 2D	3A 3C
express his/her thoughts about abstract and cultural topics such as music and films*			
take an active part in discussions, evaluate proposals and respond to hypotheses		2D	3C
help a discussion along on familiar ground, confirming comprehension, etc.		2D	
convey degrees of emotion and highlight the personal significance of events		2B	3B 3D
use stock phrases to gain time and keep the turn		2D	
carry out a prepared interview, checking information and following up replies*	1A		
take initiatives in an interview and expand and develop ideas	1C		3A 3C
summarise and give his/her opinion on a short story, article, talk, discussion or interview, and answer further questions in detail*		2C	3C
give clear detailed descriptions on subjects related to his/her field of interest			
give detailed accounts of experiences describing feelings and reactions*	1C	2B	3B
give detailed presentations and respond to a series of follow-up questions			
explain a viewpoint giving the advantages and disadvantages of various options		2C	3B
narrate a story*			3B
summarise the plot and sequence of events in an extract from a film or play			
summarise short extracts from news items, etc. containing opinions and discussion			
construct a chain of reasoned argument linking ideas logically			
speculate about causes, consequences and hypothetical situations			3A 3B 3C
use some cohesive devices to link his/her utterances into clear, coherent discourse			

Writing

A language user at level B2 can:	1	2	3
write clear and detailed texts on various subjects related to his/her field of interest	WBP1		
write about events and experiences in a detailed and easily readable way		WBP2	
write reports and essays which develop an argument, giving reasons for or against a point of view, and explaining the advantages and disadvantages of various options	WBP1	WBP2	
develop an argument, emphasising decisive points and including supporting details		WBP2	
write letters conveying degrees of emotion, highlighting the personal significance of events and commenting on the correspondent's news and views			
express news and views in writing and relate to those of others			WBP3
write a review			
convey factual information to friends/colleagues or ask for information*			
make a note of 'favourite mistakes' and consciously monitor his/her work for them			
take notes on important points during a lecture on a familiar topic			

WBP1 = **face2face** Upper Intermediate Workbook Reading and Writing Portfolio 1
* refers to descriptors for B1
1A = **face2face** Upper Intermediate Student's Book unit 1 lesson A

4	5	6	7	8	9	10	11	12
4C 4D	5A 5B 5C	6A	7A 7B 7D	8A 8C	9A 9B 9C 9D	10C 10D	11C 11D	12B 12C
4A 4B 4C 4D	5A 5B 5C 5D	6A 6B 6C 6D	7A 7B 7C 7D	8A 8B 8D	9A 9B	10A 10B 10D	11A 11B	12A 12B
	5C	6C	7B 7C	8C	9B			
	5B 5D	6A	7B	8A 8C	9B 9C	10C	11C	12C
4B					9B 9C			12B
	5C 5D					10C	11C 11D	12A
	5D				9C 9D		11C	
4C 4D		6B	7A	8A 8B	9C	10A 10C 10D	11A 11B	12C
4C	5D						11D	
			7C	8B				
4B			7D		9A		11A 11B	
	5C	6C	7B					
		6B					11C	
4D			7A	8D				
							11D	
	5A 5D							
4A 4B 4C								
					9B			
		6C	7C				11B	
		6A					11D	12C
		6B		8A 8B				12B
4C								

4	5	6	7	8	9	10	11	12
WBP4	WBP5	WBP6		WBP8		WBP10		WBP12
				WBP8	WBP9			
	WBP5				WBP9			
							WBP11	WBP12
		WBP6						
					WBP9			
			WBP7			WBP10	WBP11	WBP12
This competence is practised in all the Workbook Portfolio writing tasks.								
4C 4D	5C			8C				12C

The face2face Approach

Listening

A typical listening practice activity in most coursebooks checks students' understanding of gist, and then asks questions about specific details. The innovative *Help with Listening* sections take students a step further by focusing on the underlying reasons why listening to English can be so problematic. Activities in these sections help students by:

- focusing on the stress system in English.
- examining features of connected speech.
- preparing them for what people in public places say.
- highlighting how intonation conveys mood and feelings.
- encouraging students to make the link between the written and the spoken word by asking them to work with the *Audio and Video Scripts* while they listen.

For *Teaching Tips* on Listening, see p21.

Speaking

All the lessons in the Upper Intermediate Student's Book and the *Class Activities* photocopiables provide students with numerous speaking opportunities. Many of these activities focus on accuracy, while the fluency activities help students to gain confidence and try out what they have learned. For fluency activities to be truly 'fluent', however, students often need time to formulate their ideas before they speak, and this preparation is incorporated into the *Get ready ... Get it right!* activities.

For *Teaching Tips* on Speaking, see p21.

Reading and Writing

In the Upper Intermediate Student's Book, reading texts from a wide variety of genres are used both to present new language and to provide reading practice. Reading sub-skills, such as skimming and scanning, are extensively practised and there are also controlled writing activities to consolidate the language input of the lesson.

For classes that require more reading and writing, there is a 24-page *Reading and Writing Portfolio* in the Upper Intermediate Workbook. This section contains 12 double-page stand-alone lessons which are designed for students to do at home or in class. The topics and content of these lessons are based closely on the CEFR reading and writing competences for level B2. There are also 12 *Extra Reading* photocopiable worksheets (p213–p224), which can be used in class or given for homework.

Vocabulary

face2face recognises the importance of vocabulary in successful communication. There is lexical input in every lesson, which is consolidated for student reference in the interactive *Language Summaries* in the back of the Student's Book. In addition, each unit in the Student's Book includes at least one *Help with Vocabulary* section, designed to guide students towards a better understanding of the lexical systems of English.

For longer courses and/or more able students, this Teacher's Book also contains one *Vocabulary Plus* worksheet for each unit (p194–p205). These worksheets introduce and practise new vocabulary that is <u>not</u> included in the Student's Book.

For *Teaching Tips* on Vocabulary, see p21.

Grammar

Grammar is a central strand in the **face2face** Second edition Upper Intermediate syllabus and new grammar structures are always introduced in context in a listening or a reading text. We believe students are more likely to understand and remember new language if they have actively tried to work out the rules for themselves, rather than just being given them. Therefore in the *Help with Grammar* sections students are asked to work out the meaning and form of the structure for themselves, before checking their answers in the *Language Summaries*. All new grammar forms are practised in regular recorded pronunciation drills and communicative speaking activities, and consolidated through written practice.

For *Teaching Tips* on Grammar, see p22.

Functional and Situational Language

face2face places great emphasis on the functional and situational language that students need to use immediately in their daily lives. Each unit contains a double-page *Real World* lesson that introduces and practises this language in a variety of situations. This language can now be presented either by using the video clips on the Teacher's DVD or by using the recordings on the Class Audio CDs.

Pronunciation

Pronunciation is integrated throughout **face2face** Second edition Upper Intermediate. Drills for grammar structures and all new *Real World* language are included on the Class Audio CDs. These drills focus on sentence stress, weak forms, intonation, etc. Students also practise specific phonological features and problem sounds in the *Help with Pronunciation* sections at the end of each unit.

For *Teaching Tips* on Pronunciation, see p22.

Reviewing and Recycling

We believe that regular reviewing and recycling of language are essential to students' language development, so language is recycled in every lesson of the Upper Intermediate Student's Book. Opportunities for review are also provided in the *Quick Review* sections at the beginning of every lesson, the full-page *Extra Practice* section and the 12 photocopiable *Progress Tests* in this Teacher's Book.

For *Teaching Tips* on Reviewing and Recycling, see p23.

Teaching Tips

Listening

- Make full use of the *Help with Listening* sections in the Student's Book, which are designed to help students understand natural spoken English and develop their ability to anticipate and understand what is being said.
- Before asking students to listen to a recording, establish the context, the characters and what information you want them to listen for.
- Also give students time to read the comprehension questions in the Student's Book. Deal with any problems or new language in these questions before playing a recording.
- When you play a recording for a second or third time, you can ask students to read the *Audio and Video Scripts* at the back of the Student's Book while they listen. This helps them to 'tune in' to spoken English and connect what they hear with what they read.
- When students need to listen and write their answers, you can stop the recording after each answer in second and subsequent listenings to give them time to write.
- Encourage students to listen to the classroom recordings again on their Self-study DVD-ROM on their computer at home.

Speaking

Pair and Group Work

- Make full use of all the communicative speaking activities in the Student's Book, particularly the *Get ready ... Get it right!* sections.
- Help students with the language they need to do speaking tasks by drawing their attention to the 'transactional language' in the speech bubbles.
- Try to ensure that students work with a number of different partners during a class. If it is difficult for students to swap places in class, you can ask them to work with students in front of or behind them as well as on either side of them.
- It is often useful to provide a model of the tasks you expect students to do. For example, before asking students to talk about their family in pairs, you can talk about your family with the whole class.
- Remember that students often find speaking activities much easier if they are personalised, as they don't need to think of ideas as well as language.
- Go around the class and monitor students while they are speaking in their pairs or groups. At this stage you can provide extra language or ideas and correct any language or pronunciation which is impeding communication.
- Avoid becoming too involved in speaking activities yourself unless you see students have misunderstood your instructions or you are asked for help.
- When giving feedback on speaking, remember to praise good communication as well as good English and focus on the result of the task as well as the language used.

Correction

- When you hear a mistake, it is often useful to correct it immediately and ask the student to say the word or phrase again in the correct form. This is particularly effective if the mistake relates to the language you have been working on in the lesson.
- Alternatively, when you point out a mistake to a student you can encourage him/her to correct it himself/ herself before giving him/her the correct version.
- Another approach to correction during a freer speaking activity is to note down any mistakes you hear, but not correct them immediately. At the end of the activity write the mistakes on the board. Students can then work in pairs and correct the mistakes. Alternatively, you can discuss the mistakes with the whole class.
- You don't have to correct every mistake when students are doing a freer speaking activity, particularly when the mistake is not specifically in the language they have been asked to practise. Effective communication is often just as important as accuracy.

Vocabulary

- Give students time to work through the exercises in the *Help with Vocabulary* sections on their own or in pairs. This gives students the opportunity to work out the rules themselves before checking their answers in the *Language Summaries* in the back of the Student's Book. You can then check students have understood the main points with the whole class.
- Point out the stress marks (˙) on all new vocabulary in the vocabulary boxes in the lessons and the *Language Summaries*. These show the main stress only in each new word or phrase.
- When you write a new vocabulary item on the board, make sure students know the stress and part of speech. Give students time to copy new vocabulary into their notebooks.
- Make students aware of collocations in English (for example, *do yoga, play cards, go to festivals*) by pointing them out when they occur and encouraging students to record them as one phrase in their notebooks.
- Review and recycle vocabulary at every opportunity in class, using the *Extra Practice* sections, the *Language Summaries*, *Classroom Activities and Games* (p24) and the *Class Activities* (p132).
- Use the photocopiable *Vocabulary Plus* worksheets (p190) to introduce and practise extra vocabulary which is not included in the Student's Book. They can be used for self-study in class or as homework, or as the basis of a classroom lesson. There is one *Vocabulary Plus* worksheet for each unit in the Student's Book.
- Use the photocopiable *Study Skills* worksheets (p225) in class to help students understand other aspects of vocabulary, such as using a monolingual dictionary, how to review vocabulary and understanding spelling rules.

Teaching Tips

Grammar

- Give students time to work through the exercises in the *Help with Grammar* sections on their own or in pairs, rather than doing this with the whole class. This gives students the opportunity to try and work out the grammar rules themselves before checking their answers in the *Language Summaries* in the back of the Student's Book. You can then check students have understood the main points with the whole class.
- Teach your students useful grammatical terms (for example, *noun, verb, auxiliary, Past Simple*, etc.) when the opportunity arises. This helps students become more independent and allows them to use grammar reference books more effectively.
- Use different colour pens for different parts of speech when writing sentences on the board (for example, Present Perfect questions). This helps students see the patterns in grammar structures.
- If you know the students' first language, highlight grammatical differences between their language and English. This raises their awareness of potential problems if they try to translate. It is also useful to highlight grammatical similarities to show students when a structure in English is the same as in their own language.
- After teaching a grammatical item, use reading and listening texts as reinforcement by asking students to find examples of that grammatical item in the text. This helps students to see the language in a realistic context.

Pronunciation

- Make full use of the pronunciation drills on the Class Audio CDs. These drills are marked with the pronunciation icon **PRONUNCIATION** in the Student's Book and give standard British native-speaker models of the language being taught.
- Use the *Help with Pronunciation* sections at the end of each unit. These give extra practice of problematic sounds and aspects of connected speech.
- Point out the stress marks on all new vocabulary in the vocabulary boxes in the lessons and the *Language Summaries*. Note that only the main stress in each new word or phrase is shown. For example, in the phrase *get engaged*, the main stress on *engaged* is shown, but the secondary stress on *get* is not. We feel this is the most effective way of encouraging students to stress words and phrases correctly.
- Also point out the example sentences in the Student's Book before using the pronunciation drills. Note that in the examples of sentences in *Grammar* or *Real World* drills, all stresses in the sentences are shown.
- When using the recordings of these drills, there are usually sufficient pauses for students to repeat chorally without stopping the recording. Alternatively, you can pause the recording and ask each student to repeat individually before continuing.

- For variety, model and drill the sentences yourself instead of using the recordings.
- Point out the stress, linking and weak forms marked in some of the *Audio and Video Scripts* (Student's Book p157).
- Encourage students to listen and practise the drills again on their Self-study DVD-ROM.

Helping students with sounds

- Consider teaching your students the phonemic symbols (see the chart on Student's Book p174). This allows students to look up the pronunciation of the words and record difficult pronunciation themselves in their notebooks. It is often easier to take a 'little and often' approach to teaching these symbols, rather than trying to teach them all in one lesson.
- Encourage students to use the Phonemic Symbols chart on the Self-study DVD-ROM at home. This will help them to learn the symbols and allow them to practise the sounds they find difficult.
- Write the phonemic transcription for difficult words on the board and ask students to work out how the words are pronounced.
- For sounds students often have problems with (for example /θ/) you can demonstrate the shape of the mouth and the position of the tongue in front of the class (or draw this on the board). Often students can't say these sounds simply because they don't know the mouth position required to do so.
- Remember that many sounds in English are often the same in students' own language(s). Draw students' attention to the sounds which are the same as well as highlighting the ones that are different.

Helping students with stress and intonation

- Drill all new words, phrases and sentences, and pay particular attention to words that sound different from how they are spelt.
- When you write words or sentences on the board, mark the stress in the correct place or ask students to tell you which syllables or words are stressed.
- When you model sentences yourself it may be helpful to over-emphasise the stress pattern to help students hear the stress. You can also 'beat' the stress with your hand or fist.
- Emphasise that intonation is an important part of meaning in English and often shows how we feel. For example, a falling intonation on the word *please* can sound very impolite to a native English speaker.
- Show the intonation pattern of model sentences by drawing arrows on the board or making hand gestures.
- Hum the sentences you are focusing on. It is sometimes easier for students to hear the stress or intonation pattern when there are no words.

Drilling

- Make sure students know the meaning of new language before drilling this with the class.
- When you model a phrase or sentence, make sure that you speak at normal speed with natural stress and contractions. Repeat the target language two or three times before asking the whole class to repeat after you in a 'choral drill'.
- After choral drilling it is usually helpful to do some individual drilling. Start with the strongest students and drill around the class in random order.
- As the aim of drilling is accuracy, you should correct students when they make a mistake. However, avoid making the students feel uncomfortable and don't spend too long with one student.
- Praise students for good/comprehensible pronunciation and acknowledge weak students' improvement, even if their pronunciation is not perfect.
- Use 'mumble' drills. Ask students to say the phrase or sentence to themselves initially, then increase the volume each time until they are speaking at a normal volume. Shy students often appreciate the chance to say things quietly until they feel more confident about their pronunciation.

Reviewing and Recycling

- Use the *Quick Reviews* at the beginning of each lesson. They are easy to set up and should take no more than five to ten minutes. They are a good way of getting the class to speak immediately as well as reviewing what students learned in previous lessons.
- Exploit the *Extra Practice* sections for each unit. They can be done in class when students have finished the unit, or set for homework. Alternatively, individual exercises can be used as quick fillers at the beginning or end of a lesson, as the exercises and activities are organised in lesson order.
- After a mid-lesson break, ask students to write down in one minute all the words they can remember from the first part of the lesson. These quick *What have we just learned?* activities are very important for helping students transfer information from their short-term memory to their long-term memory.
- Start a class vocabulary box. You or the students write each new vocabulary item on a separate card and put the cards in the box. The cards can be used for various revision activities, for example *Know, Might Know, Don't Know*.
- Encourage students to use the Self-study DVD-ROM to review each lesson at home. Also encourage students to review new language by reading the *Language Summary* for the lesson.
- Set homework after every class. The **face2face** Second edition Upper Intermediate Workbook has a section for each lesson in the Student's Book, which reviews all the key language taught in that lesson.

Teaching Upper Intermediate Classes

Most students at Upper Intermediate level have reached a reasonable level of communicative competence and they often tend to be rather inaccurate, particularly in spontaneous conversation. Another problem with Upper Intermediate classes is that students often don't feel that they are making progress quickly enough. This 'plateau' can sometimes be rather demotivating for students. If this is the case for your class, try some of the following suggestions:

- Give students time to prepare what they are going to say, as in the *Get ready ... Get it right!* sections of the Student's Book. This allows students to work out what language they are going to use before they do the communicative stage of the activity, which will help them retain the accuracy that has been built up during the lesson.
- Use every opportunity for correction during the class and praise students who use new language correctly.
- Encourage students to make a list of their own typical mistakes, or collect typical mistakes for the class yourself. You can collect together the 'top ten' mistakes of the class and make a poster of these for the classroom.
- Record or video your students during communicative activities, then use the recordings for error correction later in the class or in the next class.
- Encourage students to broaden their vocabulary whenever possible, for example by using *brilliant* or *amazing* instead of *very good*. Students at this level often like to stay in their linguistic 'comfort zone' and often need to be persuaded to use more advanced language.
- Use the *Extra Practice* section in the Student's Book and the *Progress Tests* in the Teacher's Book (p232–p261). Keep a record of students' scores on the *Progress Tests* for end-of-term reports.
- Use the *Vocabulary Plus* worksheets (p190–p205) to give classes extra input of new lexical items.
- Ask students to tick the things they can do in the *Progress Portfolios* at the end of each unit to help give them a sense of progress.
- Plan which students are going to work together in pair and group work. Mix stronger students with weaker ones when they can give help, for example in a vocabulary matching activity. On other occasions, for example in freer speaking activities, it is often a good idea to place stronger students in the same group. Weaker students may feel more confident speaking with other students at their own level.
- Encourage students to read as much as possible outside class. Use authentic reading material in class where possible.
- Have ideas for extra activities to give early finishers something to do while the slower students are still working, for example an exercise from an *Extra Practice* section or the Workbook, or a *Vocabulary Plus* worksheet.
- Set weaker students extra homework from the Workbook or the Self-study DVD-ROM to help them catch up with areas of language that the rest of the class is confident with.

Classroom Activities and Games

These activities and games can be used to practise a variety of different language areas in class. The Teaching Notes (p26) suggest when they can be used alongside the lessons in the Student's Book.

Hot Seats

This revision activity revises vocabulary taught on the course through a lively, enjoyable team game.

- Place two chairs – or 'hot seats' – at the front of the classroom facing the students, one chair on each side of the classroom.
- Divide the class into two teams. Ask one confident member of each team to come and sit in the hot seats.
- Write a word/phrase that you want to revise on the board. Alternatively, prepare cards with the words/phrases written on before the class and hold them up behind the two students. The students in the hot seats are not allowed to turn round and see the words/phrases.
- Each team tries to convey the meaning of the word/phrase in any way they can (definition, mime, synonym, etc.) without saying or spelling the word/phrase.
- The first student in the hot seats who says the correct word/phrase gets a point for his/her team. Mark each team's points on the board.
- After they have tried to guess a few words, ask the students in the chairs to change places with other members of their team. The activity continues with different students in the hot seats.
- The team who gets the most words/phrases in the time available wins.

Know, Might Know, Don't Know

This activity helps you to find out what vocabulary students already know. It is a good activity for mixed-level classes, as stronger students can teach lower-level students vocabulary that they don't know.

- Before the lesson, write a worksheet containing 15–20 words or phrases you want to teach or review.
- Photocopy one worksheet for each student.
- In class, give each student a copy of the worksheet. Tell students to divide the words into three groups: (I know this word/phrase and can give an example or definition), (I think I know this word/phrase but I'm not sure) and (I don't know this word/phrase).
- Students work in pairs or groups and compare their answers. If one student knows a word, he/she should teach it to his/her partner or the other members of the group. Alternatively, students can move around the room and talk to various students.
- When they have finished, students say which words/phrases they still don't know. Encourage other groups to give definitions to help them, or give the meanings and examples yourself.
- Allow time for students to record any new vocabulary in their notebooks.

Dialogue Build

This activity focuses on grammatical accuracy as well as giving students confidence in speaking.

- Before the lesson, prepare a 6–8-line conversation based on language the students should know. Find a magazine picture of each person in the conversation (or draw two people on the board).
- In class, set the context, for example, on the telephone. Put the two speakers' pictures on either side of the board.
- Draw a speech bubble from the person who speaks first and insert a prompt, for example, *speak?*. Elicit the target sentence, for example, *Hello. Could I speak to Jill?*. Model and drill the target language with the whole class and then individually. Don't write the sentence on the board at this stage.
- Draw a reply speech bubble from the other person and insert a prompt, for example, *afraid*. Elicit the target sentence and continue as above, establishing one line each time until the conversation is complete.
- Students practise the conversation in pairs. They then change roles and practise the conversation again.
- Re-elicit the whole conversation, writing each line on the board by the appropriate prompt. Give students time to copy the conversation into their notebooks.

Running Dictation

This activity involves all four skills (reading, writing, speaking and listening) and is a good way to inject some energy into a class.

- Before the lesson, choose a short text. This text can be used to introduce a topic in a lesson, provide a context for new language, review a language area already covered or simply provide extra reading practice.
- Photocopy one copy of the text for each student.
- In class, divide students into pairs, one reporter and one secretary. Secretaries sit near the back of the class with pen and paper.
- Put one copy of the text on the board. With larger classes, put other copies on the wall at the front of the class.
- When you say *Go*, the reporters go to the board, remember as much as they can of the text, then run back to their secretaries, who must write down the exact words they hear. When a reporter has told his/her secretary all he/she can remember, he/she goes back to the board and repeats the process.
- In the middle of the activity, clap your hands and tell students to change roles.
- The first pair to complete the text wins. Continue the activity until most or all of the students have finished.
- Give a copy of the text to each student. Students then check their version of the text against the original.

Words Connected to Me

This activity practises vocabulary in a personalised way and provides a springboard to freer speaking practice.

- Ask students to draw a table with two columns on a piece of paper. They should head one column *Words connected to me* and the other *Words not connected to me*.
- Dictate a set of words/phrases that you have taught in a recent lesson. If a word/phrase (for example, *go on a package tour*) is connected to them in some way, they write the phrase in the *Words connected to me* column. If not, they write the phrase in the other column.
- Point out that the word/phrase can be connected to them in any way they like, for example, it could relate to the student's life now or in the past, people in her family, something they want to do in the future, etc.
- Students compare their lists in groups and discuss why they have written all the words/phrases in the *Words connected to me* column.

Grammar Auction

This is a fun grammar revision activity which involves the whole class.

- Before the class, prepare a worksheet with 10–12 sentences on it, based on the grammar areas you have covered with your class. Some of the sentences should be correct English and some should contain mistakes.
- Photocopy one worksheet for each student.
- In the lesson, divide the class into teams of four or five. Give one worksheet to each student. Students discuss in their groups which sentences are correct and which are incorrect. Students should speak quietly so that other teams can't hear them.
- Check that they know what an auction is and how to buy something. Tell the class each group has £20,000 to spend. Act as the auctioneer and sell the sentences one at a time.
- Students try to buy the correct sentences. They can also use tactics to persuade other teams to buy the incorrect ones, for example, bidding for incorrect sentences to put doubt into the minds of the other students.
- When a group buys a sentence, they mark that sentence on their worksheet. Students must stop bidding when they have no more money.
- When all the sentences have been sold, check which are correct with the class. The team with the most correct sentences wins. In the case of a tie, the team with the most money left wins.
- At the end of the auction, students work in their groups and correct the incorrect sentences. Check answers with the class.

Pyramid Discussion

This activity encourages students to exchange ideas and opinions in a fun, student-centred way.

- Set a context (for example, tell students they are going on a trip to the desert and need to decide what to take with them).
- Give each student a list of 10–15 items or write them on the board.
- Students work on their own and choose the five most useful items to take with them. Students should also think of a reason for choosing each one.
- Each student then shows their list of five items to a partner. Together they must agree on only five items from both their lists.
- Students work in groups of four and repeat the previous stage so that they end up with a new list of only five items. If you have a big class, you can then put students into groups of eight, and so on.
- Finally, the whole class share their ideas and try to agree on the best five answers.

Consequences

This activity gives students freer practice of collaborative writing. It allows them to be creative while practising language taught in the lesson (for example, Past Simple and Past Continuous or connecting words).

- Give each student a clean piece of paper to write on (or ask each of them to take one page from their notebooks).
- Give students a series of instructions about what to write (for example, a woman's name, a man's name, where and how they met, what they were doing when they met, what they said to each other, what they did next, when they saw each other again, what happened in the end). Check that students are writing full sentences.
- After each student has written an answer to each instruction, they fold their paper just enough to hide what they have written and pass it on to the student on their left.
- When students have finished the story, they fold the paper one more time and pass it to the person on their left. This student opens it and reads it. Ask students to read out any funny or interesting examples to the class.
- Display the stories around the class for everyone to read. Students decide which one is the best and why.

QUICK REVIEW Quick Reviews begin each lesson in a fun, student-centred way. They are short activities which review previously taught language and are designed to last about five or ten minutes. For more information on the **face2face** approach to Reviewing and Recycling, see p23.
This activity gives students the opportunity to get to know each other. Students move around the room and talk to three other students, or talk to three students sitting near them. At the end of the activity, ask students to tell the class about one of the people they spoke to.

Vocabulary and Speaking
Language ability

1 **a** Focus students on phrases 1–10. Students work on their own and choose the correct word in each phrase.
Students check their answers in **VOCABULARY 1.1** ▶ SB (Student's Book) p127. Note that in **face2face** Upper Intermediate, only the meanings of new words/ phrases are shown in the Language Summaries. These words/phrases are highlighted by an asterisk (*) and the meanings are given in a dictionary box ▤.
Also point out that only the main stress (•) in phrases is shown in Vocabulary sections and the Language Summaries.
Check answers with the class. Check students understand the meaning of the new words/phrases *bilingual*, *fluent*, *reasonably*, *get by* (in a language), *rusty* and *pick up* (a language), which are in the dictionary box in the Language Summary.
Also check students understand that their *first language* is the language they learned as a child and point out that we can also say a language is *very rusty*.
Model and drill the words, paying particular attention to *bilingual* /baɪˈlɪŋgwəl/, *reasonably* /ˈriːzənəbli/ and *rusty* /ˈrʌsti/.

2 in 3 in 4 at 5 by 6 few 7 of 8 have 9 bit 10 up

b Students do the exercise on their own. Remind students that they can choose phrases about other people they know (for example, members of their family) as well as themselves.

c Students do the activity in groups. Encourage students to ask follow-up questions if possible.
Ask students to tell the class one interesting thing they found out about their partner.

Reading and Speaking

2 Focus students on the article. Check students understand *outnumber*, *pretend* (to do something), *phenomenon* and *idioms*.
Students do the exercise on their own. Check answers with the class. Ask students to justify their answers by referring back to the article.

1d 2e 3a 4b

3 **a** Students do the exercise on their own, then compare answers in pairs. Check answers with the class.

- There are around **350 million** native speakers of English.
- The British Council predicts that in the near future about half the world's population – over **3.5 billion** people – will speak some English.
- **Dr Beneke** is from the University of Hildesheim, Germany. He says that the majority of interactions in English now take place between non-native speakers.
- About **75%** of the world's correspondence is written in English.
- At a **Toyota** factory in the Czech Republic, English was chosen as the working language.
- The national government of South Korea has been building English **immersion schools** all over the country.
- **Jean Paul Nerrière** is a former French IBM executive. He believes that the future of English belongs to non-native speakers.

b Students work in pairs and discuss the questions.

┌─ **EXTRA IDEAS** ─┐

- Students work in groups and tell each other the examples they gave for the importance of English for employment opportunities in their country. Ask students to share their ideas with the class and write a list of jobs where English is important.
- Students work in groups and think of two positive effects and two negative effects of the global spread of English. Ask students to share their ideas with the class.

HELP WITH GRAMMAR
Review of the English verb system

Help with Grammar sections help students to examine examples of language and discover the rules of meaning, form and use for themselves. Students should usually do the exercises on their own or in pairs, then check their answers in the Language Summaries. You can then check the main points with the class as necessary. For more information on the **face2face** approach to Grammar, see p20.

4 **a–d** Students do the exercises on their own or in pairs, then check in GRAMMAR 1.1 ▶ SB p128. Check answers with the class.

a Past Simple *visited*; Present Perfect Simple *has become*; Past Perfect Simple *had reached*; Present Continuous *is changing*; Past Continuous *was pretending*; Present Perfect Continuous *has been building*; Present Simple Passive *is written*; Past Simple Passive *was chosen*

- The aim of this exercise is to remind students of verb forms that they have probably studied in previous courses and to check they know the names of these verb forms. Students will study all these verb forms again in **face2face** Upper Intermediate, so you don't need to go into detail here.

b We usually use **simple** verb forms to talk about things that are permanent, repeated or completed.
- We usually use **continuous** verb forms to talk about things that are in progress, temporary or unfinished.
- We usually use **perfect** verb forms to talk about things that connect two different time periods (the past and the present, etc.).
- We usually use **passive** verb forms when we focus on what happens to someone or something rather than who or what does the action.
- Use the first three rules to introduce students to the concept of *aspect*. The English verb system has three aspects: simple, continuous and perfect. These aspects refer to how the speaker sees the situation. These aspects combine with past, present or future time to give the Present Simple, Past Continuous, Present Perfect, etc.
- The aim here is to raise students' awareness of the various aspects of meaning that all simple, continuous, perfect and passive verb forms have in common, not to review the meaning and use of every verb form. Note that similarities of form are dealt with in lesson 1B.
- The simple and continuous aspects are studied in more detail in lesson 7A. Perfect verb forms are studied further in lessons 4A, 7B and 11A, and the passive is studied further in lesson 9A.

c activity verbs: *use*; *change*
state verbs: *seem*; *believe*
- We don't usually use **state** verbs in continuous verb forms.

- Check that students remember the difference between activity verbs, which talk about activities and actions, and state verbs, which talk about states, feelings and opinions. Elicit a few examples of each type of verb from the class.
- Activity and state verbs are studied in more detail in lesson 7A.

┌─ **EXTRA IDEA** ─┐
- ✏ Write these verbs on the board in random order: *play, hit, wait, lose, learn, cook, swim, sleep, work, write, know, remember, forget, need, understand, love, hate, prefer, want*. Students work in pairs and decide which are activity verbs and which are state verbs. Check answers with the class. (The first ten verbs are activity verbs. The others are state verbs.)

5 Do question 1 with the class as an example. Students do questions 2–6 in pairs.

1 *studied* Past Simple; *'ve studied* Present Perfect Simple
a They don't study Portuguese any more.
b They started studying Portuguese three years ago and they still study it now.
2 *watches* Present Simple; *'s watching* Present Continuous
a This is a present habit.
b This is something in progress at the moment of speaking.
3 *did* Past Simple; *was doing* Past Continuous
a First I got home, then Jo did her homework.
b Jo started doing her homework before I got home and continued after I arrived.
4 *teaches* Present Simple; *'s teaching* Present Continuous
a Teaching English is her permanent job.
b Teaching English is her temporary job while she's in Berlin.
5 *started* Past Simple; *had started* Past Perfect Simple
a First we got there, then the class started.
b First the class started, then we got there.
6 *repaired* Past Simple; *was repaired* Past Simple Passive
a Antonio repaired the car himself.
b Somebody else repaired Antonio's car, probably a mechanic at a garage.

6 **a** Students do the exercise on their own, then compare answers in pairs.

b CD1 ▶ 1 Play the recording. Students listen and check their answers. Check answers with the class.

2 went **3** 'd never been **4** was travelling **5** picked up
6 was told **7** was **8** decided **9** recommended
10 've been going **11** always enjoy **12** is taught
13 think **14** 've learned **15** 'm studying

Get ready … Get it right!

There is a *Get ready … Get it right!* activity at the end of every A and B lesson. The *Get ready* stage helps students to collect their ideas and prepare the language they need to complete the task. The *Get it right* stage gives students the opportunity to use the language they have learned in the lesson in a communicative (and often personalised) context. These two-stage activities help students to become more fluent without losing the accuracy they have built up during the controlled practice stages of the lesson. For more on the **face2face** approach to Speaking, see p20.

7 Ask all students to turn to p110. Check they are all looking at the correct exercise.

a Focus students on the English learner profile. Students work on their own and make notes on points 1–8 in the second column of the table. While they are working, help students with language and ideas.

b Focus students on example questions 1 and 2. Students continue working on their own and write questions with *you* for prompts 3–8 in **a**. Check questions with the class.

> **3** Which exams have you taken in English?
> **4** Why are you studying English now?
> **5** Which English-speaking countries would you like to go to? **6** How do you feel about your level of English now? **7** What do you do to improve your English outside class? **8** What do you want to do (or do better) in English? **9** What don't you like about the English language? **10** What do you like about the English language?

c Students do the activity in pairs. Remind students to use the notes they made in **a** when answering their partner's questions. Also encourage students to ask follow-up questions where possible and to make a note of things that they have in common.

Finally, ask each pair to tell the class two things that they have in common.

EXTRA IDEA

- Students work in pairs and write down two things they like about the English language and two things they don't like about it. Put students with another pair to talk about the things they like and don't like.

WRITING

For homework, ask students to write a description of themselves as language learners, based on the notes they made in the English learner profile on p110. Ask students to include a photo of themselves on the profile if possible. These can then be displayed around the classroom for other students to read.

FURTHER PRACTICE

Ph **Class Activity** 1A My classmates p148 (Instructions p132)
Extra Practice 1A SB p115
Self-study DVD-ROM Lesson 1A
Workbook Lesson 1A p5

1B Open learning
Student's Book p10–p11

Vocabulary education
Grammar uses of auxiliaries

QUICK REVIEW This activity reviews verb forms. Students do the first part of the activity on their own. Put students into pairs. Students take turns to tell each other about the things they thought about and ask follow-up questions. Ask students to tell the class any interesting things they found out about their partner.

Vocabulary and Speaking Education

1 **a** Students do the exercise in pairs, then check the meanings of any new words/phrases in **VOCABULARY 1.2** ▶ SB p127.

Check students' answers by asking students to explain the differences between the sets of words/ phrases to the class.

Check students understand the difference between a *course* (a series of lessons in a particular subject) and a *module* (one part of a course).

Point out that we often use abbreviations to talk about university degrees: *a BSc* = a Bachelor of Science; *an MA* = a Master of Arts, etc. Note that *a PhD* originally stood for a Doctor of Philosophy, although nowadays you can get a PhD in any subject. Note that *professor* is a false friend in many languages.

Model and drill the words/phrases, paying particular attention to the pronunciation of *graduate* /'grædʒuət/, *module* /'mɒdjuːl/, *assignment* /ə'saɪnmənt/, *tutor* /'tjuːtə/, *lecturer* /'lektʃ°rə/, *tutorial* /tjuː'tɔːriəl/, *lecture* /'lektʃə/, *scholarship* /'skɒləʃɪp/ and *PhD* /piː eɪtʃ 'diː/.

Point out that *graduate* can be a noun or a verb (e.g. *I graduate next year.*), and that the verb is pronounced /'grædjueɪt/.

Note that only the main stress in words/phrases is shown in vocabulary exercises and Vocabulary sections in the Student's Book.

b Students do the first part of the activity on their own, then work in pairs to tell each other why they chose their words. Encourage students to ask follow-up questions.

Ask students to tell the class one or two things that they found out about their partner.

┌─ **EXTRA IDEA** ┐

- If you have a class of university students, you may want to do the worksheet **Vocabulary Plus 1** *Academic subjects/ professions* p194 (Instructions p190) at this point in the lesson, or alternatively give it for homework.

Speaking and Listening

2 **a** Students do the exercise in groups. Ask each group to share interesting information with the class.

b Focus students on the photos on SB p10. Tell students that they are going to listen to a conversation between Tony and his niece Jess. **CD1▸ 2** Play the recording (SB p157). Students listen and decide who talks about each thing. Check answers with the class.

Tony talks about: his computer and IT course, commitments other than studying, online support from tutors, flexible study programmes, how long his course is.
Jess talks about: her business degree, time spent with friends, her student loan.

3 Give students time to read parts of Tony and Jess's conversation 1–6, then play the recording again. Students listen and fill in gaps a–f with one word. Students compare answers in pairs. Check answers with the class.

a ages **b** Master's **c** assignments **d** everything **e** degree **f** eighty-fifth

┌─ **EXTRA IDEA** ┐

- Before playing the recording again, students predict which words are missing in the sentences in **3**. Students then listen and check their predictions.

HELP WITH GRAMMAR
Uses of auxiliaries

4 **a–d** Students do the exercises on their own or in pairs, then check in GRAMMAR 1.2▸ SB p129. Check answers with the class.

a *are you doing* Present Continuous; *was told* Past Simple Passive; *found* Past Simple; *do you manage* Present Simple; *was hoping* Past Continuous; *Do you think* Present Simple; *think* Present Simple

b All the verb forms in blue in **3** have auxiliaries except *found* and *think*.

c We make continuous verb forms with *be* + verb+*ing* (*was hoping, are doing,* etc.).
- We make perfect verb forms with *have* + past participle (*have wanted,* etc.).
- We make passive verb forms with *be* + past participle (*was told,* etc.).
- In the Present Simple and Past Simple we use a form of *do* to make questions and negatives (*do you manage ... ?,* etc.).
- Remind students that we don't use auxiliaries in the positive forms of the Present Simple and Past Simple (*I found the first ... , I think ... ,* etc.).
- Use the **TIP** in **4c** to remind students that we also use modal verbs (*will, would, can, could,* etc.) as auxiliaries: *... you'll have finished your degree by next year,* etc. Remind students that modal verbs are different from the auxiliaries *be, do* and *have* because they have their own meanings.

5 **a–b** Students do **5a** on their own or in the same pairs, then check in GRAMMAR 1.3▸ SB p129. Check answers with the class.

- **b** does get **c** No, I don't. **d** So does everyone **e** don't **f** Did it?
- Remind students that because there is no auxiliary in the positive form of the Present Simple or Past Simple, we use *do/don't, does/doesn't* or *did/ didn't* when making question tags, echo questions, etc. for these verb forms.
- For question tags, remind students that if the main verb is positive, the auxiliary in the question tag is negative, and vice versa: *You're doing an Open University course, aren't you?* not *... are you?*.
- Contrast this with the auxiliaries in echo questions to show interest, which must agree with the main verb:
Tony: *Your Aunt Gayle was hoping to do her first degree in four years – it actually took eight.*
Jess: *Did it?* not *Didn't it?*.
- Highlight that we use *So do I, So have I,* etc. to say it's the same for us after a positive sentence and *Neither do I, Neither was I,* etc. to say it's the same for us after a negative sentence.

- Point out that we can say *Nor* instead of *Neither* when saying 'it's the same for me' after a negative sentence:
  A: *I can't swim very well.*
  B: *Neither/Nor can I.*
- Check students understand what *I don't* refers to in this sentence: *Sometimes I don't (manage to do everything).*
- Highlight that when we add emphasis to a verb in the positive form of the Present Simple or Past Simple, we use the auxiliaries *do, does* or *did* and that we stress these auxiliaries: *I do understand! He does have a job. We did enjoy ourselves*, etc.
- Point out that when we add emphasis to other verb forms, we stress the uncontracted form of the auxiliary: *I am going to do it!*

HELP WITH LISTENING
Contractions

Help with Listening sections are designed to help students understand natural spoken English. They often focus on phonological aspects of spoken English which make listening problematic for students. For more information on the **face2face** approach to Listening, see p20.

This *Help with Listening* section focuses on the use of contractions in spoken English.

6 **a** Focus students on the introductory bullet and check students understand what a contraction is (*I'm, he's, she'd*, etc.).
CD1 3 Play the recording. Students listen and decide which sentence they hear first, a or b. Play the recording again, pausing after each pair of sentences to check students' answers.

1a 2b 3a 4b 5b 6a

> **EXTRA IDEA**

- Ask students to say which auxiliaries are contracted in the *a* sentences in **6a**. Check answers with the class.

  1 has 2 had 3 are 4 have 5 will 6 will not

b **CD1** 4 Play the recording (SB p157). Students listen and write the five sentences. Point out that they will hear each sentence twice.

c Students do the exercise in pairs. ✎ Check answers by eliciting the sentences from the class and writing them on the board. Ask students which auxiliaries are contracted in each sentence.

1 He **hasn't** decided which college **he's** going to yet. (*He has not*; *he is*) 2 When **I've** finished my degree, **I'd** like to do a PhD. (*I have*; *I would*) 3 **She's** waiting to hear if **she's** passed her exams. (*She is*; *she has*) 4 She **doesn't** think **she'll** go to the tutorial today. (*she does not*; *she will*) 5 **I've** started a Master's and **I'm** really enjoying it. (*I have*; *I am*)

> **EXTRA IDEA**

- **CD1** 4 With a lower-level class, use the recording to drill sentences 1–5 in **6b**. Check students copy the contractions correctly.

7 **a** Check students remember Tony and Jess. Tell students that Jess phoned Tony last night. Students do the exercise on their own. Don't check answers with the class at this stage.

b **CD1** 5 Play the recording. Students listen and check their answers. Check answers with the class.

1 were 2 is 3 Have 4 have 5 did 6 didn't 7 did
8 've 9 Is 10 is 11 wasn't 12 was 13 Did
14 didn't 15 have 16 haven't 17 do 18 Is
19 Does 20 Is 21 isn't 22 does

> **EXTRA IDEA**

- Students work in pairs and decide why each auxiliary in the conversation in **7a** is used, referring to the uses of auxiliaries in **4c** and **5a**. Check answers with the class.

8 Students do the exercise on their own, then check answers in pairs. Check answers with the class.

2 Ian didn't go to college, but his sister **did**.
3 My parents haven't been there, but we **have**.
4 Penny doesn't like golf, but her brothers **do**.
5 We're not going out tonight, but they **are**.
6 Tom enjoyed the play, but I **didn't**.

Get ready ... Get it right!

9 **a** Put students into pairs. If you have an extra student, have one group of three students.

Ask each pair to choose one of the situations or to invent their own.

Students do the exercise in their pairs. While students are working, check their conversations for accuracy and help with any problems.

b Students practise the conversation in their pairs. While they are working, monitor and help students with their pronunciation.

10 Reorganise the class so that two pairs are working together in a group of four. If you have an extra pair, have one group of six students.

Pairs takes turns to role-play their conversations. The other students guess what the relationship is between the characters.

Finally, ask the class to decide which conversation was the best.

VOCABULARY AND SKILLS

1C

Getting results

Student's Book p12–p13

Vocabulary verb patterns (1)
Skills Reading: an article;
Listening: stories about exams

QUICK REVIEW This activity reviews auxiliaries. Students do the first part of the activity on their own. Put students into pairs. Students take turns to say their sentences and respond with an echo question and a follow-up question. Ask students to tell the class one thing that they found out about their partner.

1 ✓ 2 False. The writer thinks parents put too much pressure on their children to study for exams.
3 False. The writer thinks that some exams are important.   4 False. The writer thinks our educational system discourages creativity.
5 ✓ 6 ✓ 7 ✓

Speaking, Reading and Vocabulary

1 **a** Put students into groups to make a list of positive and negative things about exams.
🖊 Ask students to share their ideas with the class and write their ideas on the board.
Don't elicit students' personal experiences of exams at this stage, as they discuss these in **8**.

b Focus students on the article and the three titles A–C. Check students understand the phrase *a necessary evil* (something that you don't like doing, but that you know you must do) and *creativity*. Students read the article and choose the best title. Check answers with the class. Ask students to give reasons for choosing a title.

The best title is B.

2 **a** Students do the exercise on their own.

b Students compare their answers in pairs. Check answers with the class.
Ask students to say if they agree with the arguments in the article and give reasons.

HELP WITH VOCABULARY
Verb patterns (1)

Help with Vocabulary sections help students to explore and understand how vocabulary works, often by focusing on aspects of lexical grammar. Students should usually do the exercises on their own or in pairs, then check their answers in the Language Summaries. Check the main points with the class as necessary. For more information on the **face2face** approach to Vocabulary, see p20.

3

a Remind students that when we use two verbs together, the form of the second verb usually depends on the first verb. Check students understand the verb patterns in the first column of the table by focusing on the examples *make, encourage, can, refuse, resent* in the article and the verb forms that follow them. Students work on their own and put the verbs in blue in the article in the correct place in the table. Remind them to write the infinitive form of the verbs.

✏️ While students are working, copy the table in **VOCABULARY 1.3** ▶ SB p127 onto the board ready for checking. Check answers with the class.

- See the verbs in blue in the table in **VOCABULARY 1.3** ▶ SB p127.
- Check students understand the meaning of the new verbs *encourage, force, resent* and *end up*.
- Model and drill *encourage* /ɪnˈkʌrɪdʒ/.

b Students do the exercise on their own or in pairs. Point out that some verbs can go in more than one place in the table. Check students understand *convince*. Students check their answers in **VOCABULARY 1.3** ▶ SB p127.

- See the table in **VOCABULARY 1.3** ▶ SB p127.
- Point out that some verbs (shown in **bold** in **VOCABULARY 1.3** ▶) have more than one verb pattern.

c–d Focus students on the verbs in pink in the article. Students do the exercise on their own, then check in **VOCABULARY 1.3** ▶ SB p127.

- 1a 2b 3d 4c 5f 6e
- Check students understand the different meanings of *remember, stop* and *try* by focusing them on the pictures in **VOCABULARY 1.3** ▶ SB p127.
- Point out that after *remember* and *stop*, verb+*ing* looks back in time from the remembering/ stopping, whereas the infinitive with *to* looks forward in time.
- Tell students that with *try*, both forms are often possible, and that we often use *and* instead of *to*: *I'll try to/and find out for you.*

4 Put students into pairs. Student As turn to SB p104 and Student Bs turn to SB p107.

a Students do the exercise on their own. If necessary, check the answers with the class. Only check the verb forms so that students in the other group doesn't hear the questions they are asked.

Student A
2 do 3 singing 4 stay 5 to study 6 to be; going
7 to give
Student B
b making c living d listening e do f to send
g to choose

b Students do the exercise in their pairs. Ask students to share any interesting answers with the class.

Listening and Speaking

5 Focus students on pictures A and B. Students work in pairs and discuss what is happening in each one. Ask students to share their predictions with the class, but don't tell them if they are correct at this stage.
CD1 ▶ 6 Play the recording (SB p157). Students listen and check their predictions. Check answers with the class.

A Henry is cheating in a history exam by looking at information he has written on his shirt cuffs.
B Yvonne is doing her French oral exam, but she can't understand anything the examiner is saying.

6 **a** Play the recording again. Students listen and write six words/phrases to help them remember each story.

b Focus students on the example questions. Students work in pairs and write five questions about each story.

c Put students into new pairs. Tell them to choose one story each. Students take turns to ask and answer each other's questions from **6b**. Encourage students to include as much detail as they can.
Ask two students to tell the stories to the class.

┌─ **WRITING** ─┐

Students write up their stories. Encourage students to use their questions from **6b** to help them remember the main points of each story.

HELP WITH LISTENING
Sentence stress and rhythm

This *Help with Listening* section develops students' understanding of sentence stress and rhythm by asking students to work out which types of word are usually stressed.

7 **a** Check students understand the introductory bullet. Then focus students on the beginning of the first exam story.
CD1 ▶ 7 Play the beginning of the first exam story. Students listen and notice the stressed words.

b ✏️ Write these parts of speech on the board: *main verb, positive auxiliary, negative auxiliary, noun, pronoun, possessive adjective, adjective, adverb, preposition, connecting word, article.* (Note that this is not a complete list of parts of speech, but only those that appear in the example sentences in **7a** and **7c**.) Elicit examples of each type of word from the class.
Focus students on the first two words of the example sentences in **7a**. Point out that the possessive *my* is unstressed and the adjective *worst* is stressed.
Students work in pairs and decide which of the parts of speech on the board are usually stressed in the example sentences in **7a**.

Check answers with the class. Note that *history* is used as an adjective in the recording (*history exam, history classes*).

Point out that these are general guidelines, not fixed rules, and that any type of word in English can be stressed if the speaker thinks that it carries important information.

Usually stressed:
adjectives (*worst, history, good*); **nouns** (*exam, moment, mum, classes, memory*); **main verbs** (*happened, caught, cheating, liked, have*); **adverbs** (*really, very*); **negative auxiliaries** (*didn't*)

---

c Focus students on the next part of the story. Students work on their own or in pairs and decide which words are stressed.

✍ While students are working, copy the paragraph onto the board ready for checking.

d CD1 8 Students listen and check their answers.

✍ Check answers by eliciting which words are stressed and marking them on the board.

So on the morning of the exam I wrote loads of important facts and figures on the insides of my shirt cuffs. I made sure that I got to the exam room really early so I could sit at the back.

---

e Play Henry's story again. Students listen and notice the sentence stress and rhythm.

8 Students discuss the questions in groups. Finally, ask each group to tell the class one interesting or funny exam story.

WRITING

For homework, ask students to write about their best or worst exam experience.

FURTHER PRACTICE

Ph **Class Activity** 1C Something circles p150 (Instructions p133)
Extra Practice 1C SB p113
Self-study DVD-ROM Lesson 1C
Workbook Lesson 1C p8

▷ REAL WORLD
1D
Evening classes
Student's Book p14–p15

Real World keeping a conversation going

QUICK REVIEW This activity reviews verb patterns. Students do the first part of the activity on their own. Put students into pairs. Students take turns to say their sentences and ask follow-up questions. Ask students to share interesting information with the class.

1 Focus students on the advert. Check students understand what it is advertising (evening classes).

Check students understand *ballroom dancing, jewellery, ceramics, carpentry* and *creative writing*. Ask students if they know what *zumba* is (a workout inspired by Latin dance). Ask students which courses are shown in the pictures (ballroom dancing, ceramics, carpentry, yoga).

Students discuss the questions in groups.

Ask the class which of the evening classes in the advert they would like to do and find out which course is the most popular.

2 **a** Tell students that they are going to watch or listen to a conversation between two friends, Chloe and Sophie.

VIDEO 1 **CD1** 9 Play the video or audio recording (SB p158). Students watch or listen and tick the evening classes that Chloe is doing on the advert. Check answers with the class. Ask students which day the conversation is taking place (Thursday).

Monday: digital photography
Wednesday: creative writing

b Give students time to read questions 1–6, then play the video or recording again.
Students compare answers in pairs. Check answers with the class.

---

1 A couple of months ago or more. **2** She had to imagine she was an animal and write a story about a typical day. **3** She got a new camera and there were lots of things she didn't know how to do. **4** Because if she forces herself to do something different in the evenings, it helps her sleep better. **5** A dance class / Zumba. **6** Two weeks.

REAL WORLD
Keeping a conversation going

Real World sections are designed to help students with functional language that they can use in real-life social situations, often by teaching common fixed and semi-fixed phrases. Students should usually do the exercises on their own or in pairs, then check their answers in the Language Summaries. Check the main points with the class as necessary. For more information on the **face2face** approach to functional language, see p20.

3 a Check students understand the introductory bullet.
Students do the exercise on their own or in pairs, then check in **REAL WORLD 1.1** SB p129.
Check answers with the class.

- **1** going **2** that **3** what **4** mean **5** like **6** else **7** as **8** come **9** way **10** sort
- Check students understand the meanings of short questions 1–10 (see **REAL WORLD 1.1** SB p129).
- Go through the first three **TIPS** in the Language Summary with the class.

b–c Students do the exercise on their own or in pairs, then check in **REAL WORLD 1.1** SB p129.

- with; for
- Use the parts of Chloe and Sophie's conversation to highlight that we often make short questions with question word + preposition. Point out that in these types of questions, both the question words and the prepositions are stressed.
- Focus on the **TIP**. Point out that we can also use echo questions and question tags to keep a conversation going.
- Go through the other **TIPS** in the Language Summary with the class.

┌─ **EXTRA IDEA** ┐
- Ask students to turn to **CD1** 9, SB p158. Play the recording again. Students listen, read and underline all the examples of ways to keep a conversation going.

4 a **CD1** 10 Play the recording. Students listen and complete the short questions with a preposition. Pause the recording after each sentence if necessary.

b **CD1** 11 Play the recording (SB p158). Students listen and check their answers. Ask students if prepositions in short questions are stressed or unstressed (they are stressed).

1 by **2** to **3** with **4** for **5** from **6** to **7** for **8** about

┌─ **EXTRA IDEA** ┐
- Ask students to close their books. Play **CD1** 10 again. Students take turns to say the correct short questions.

5 a Students do the exercise on their own. Check students understand they should only write one word in each gap.

b Students compare answers in pairs. Check answers with the class.

1 Are **2** with **3** come **4** mean **5** can't **6** else **7** Are **8** sort **9** for **10** that **11** like **12** as

6 a Focus students on the topics. Students work on their own and choose a topic. Encourage them to make notes.

b Put students in pairs. Students take turns to start a conversation with the topics from **6a**. Encourage students to use the short questions from **3** and **4a** to keep each conversation going. You can ask students to keep each conversation going for two or three minutes.
Finally, ask a few pairs to tell the class what they talked about.

┌─ **FURTHER PRACTICE** ▶
Extra Practice 1D SB p115
Self-study DVD-ROM Lesson 1D
Workbook Lesson 1D p9
Workbook Reading and Writing Portfolio 1 p64
Progress Test 1 p238

HELP WITH PRONUNCIATION
Sounds (1): final letters *se*

Help with Pronunciation sections are designed to help students with aspects of pronunciation that are often problematic for learners of English. For tips on how to help students with pronunciation, see p22.
This *Help with Pronunciation* section focuses on the two ways of pronouncing the final letters *se*.

1 a Focus students on the phonemes and the words. Put students into pairs. Students try to identify the correct sound in each group of word: /s/ or /z/.

b **CD1** 12 Play the recording (SB p158). Students listen and check. Check answers with the class.
Play the recording again. Students listen and repeat the words. Monitor and check that students pronounce the /s/ and /z/ sounds correctly.

1 all /s/ **2** all /z/ **3** /z/, /s/, /z/, /s/

c Focus on the rules a–c. Check students understand the phonemes and can identify the different sounds. Tell students to look at the three groups of words in **1a** again and complete the rules with /s/ or /z/. If necessary, play the recording again.
Check answers with the class.

a /s/ **b** /z/ **c** /z/, /s/

2 **a** Students do the exercise on their own or in pairs. Encourage students to say the words out loud to help them decide which final -*se* sound in pink is different. **CD1▶ 13** Play the recording (SB p158). Students listen and check their answers. Check answers with the class.

1 license **2** exercise **3** use

b Students work in pairs and take turns to say the sentences.

Finally, ask students to say one sentence each. Check students pronounce the final *se* correctly in each word and praise good pronunciation.

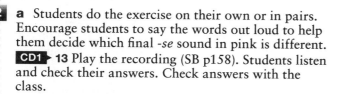

continue2learn

There is a *continue2learn* section at the end of each unit. The **Vocabulary, Grammar and Real World** section highlights where students can review and practise the language they have learned in the unit. The **Reading and Writing** section directs students to the Reading and Writing Portfolio in the Upper Intermediate Workbook. This Portfolio contains 12 stand-alone reading and writing lessons that can be done either in class or at home. For more on the **face2face** approach to writing, see p20.

Focus students on the *continue2learn* section on SB p15. Tell students that this section shows where they can practise the language from the unit.

Ask students to turn to Extra Practice 1 and Progress Portfolio 1 on SB p115. Students can do these exercises in class or for homework. For more information on this section, see the next section.

Ask students to turn to Language Summary 1 on SB p127. Remind students that the Language Summaries contain all the key language from the unit. If you are planning to give your students a Progress Test next class (see p232), tell the class that the test will only contain language that is included in the Language Summary for the unit.

If your students have the Upper Intermediate Workbook, ask them to look at WB p5. Point out that there are practice exercises for each lesson in the Student's Book.

Point out that the **face2face** DVD-ROM contains practice exercises, drills, word lists, grammar reference and tests. Encourage students to use this DVD-ROM at home to practise the language they have learned in the unit.

If your students have the Upper Intermediate Workbook, you can ask them to look at Reading and Writing Portfolio 1 WB p64. You can either do this lesson in class, or ask students to do it at home.

Extra Practice and Progress Portfolio

The Extra Practice and Progress Portfolio sections provide further controlled practice of the language taught in the unit. This can be done in class, or students can do the exercises on their own for homework. There are exercises for each lesson (1A, 1B, etc.), which can also be done at the end of each lesson as 'fillers'. For tips on Reviewing and Recycling, see p23.

Here are some ideas for exploiting the Extra Practice and Progress Portfolio section in class.

Make it a competition

Ask students to do individual vocabulary exercises (word searches, anagrams, missing letters, etc.) in pairs or groups. Give students a time limit of two or three minutes. The pair or group with the correct answers wins. Alternatively, put students into pairs and ask them to complete the whole Extra Practice section. When checking their answers, give one point for each correct answer. The pair with the most points wins. You may wish to give the winners a small prize at the end of the lesson.

Word stress

After any vocabulary exercise, ask students to mark the stress on the words. You can check the answers on the board, or students can check their answers in the Language Summaries.

Role play

After students have completed a gapfill in a conversation, put students into pairs. Ask one student to be A and the other student to be B. Students can then role play the conversation in pairs, then swap roles. You can also ask them to memorise the conversation, close their books and role play the conversation again.

Personalisation

Some exercises ask students to make questions with *you*. After checking the questions, put students in pairs. Students can then ask each other their questions and give their own answers.

Extension

After completing an exercise, ask students to write similar sentences about themselves, where they live, their family, etc. Students can then compare sentences in pairs and check their partner's work.

Extra Practice 1

1A

1 2 few 3 in 4 of 5 bit 6 by 7 up

2 2 ~~'m needing~~ need
   3 ~~'s seeming~~ seems
   4 ~~don't see~~ hadn't seen
   5 ~~was~~ has been
   6 ~~meet~~ had met
   7 ~~talked~~ was talking
   8 ~~handed~~ was handed
   9 ~~learn~~ have been learning
  10 ~~go~~ 'm going

1B

3 2 fees 3 mark 4 lecturer 5 seminar 6 degree
   7 professor 8 undergraduate 9 module
  10 assignment

4 2 didn't 3 did 4 don't 5 do 6 Do 7 Didn't
   8 didn't 9 does 10 was 11 didn't

1C

5 1 b to meet
  2 a to tell b telling
  3 a drinking b to drink
  4 a to talk b talking
  5 a to be b being
  6 a to give up b give up
  7 a trying b to try
  8 a getting up b get up
  9 a start b to start

1D

6 2 sort 3 going 4 else 5 for 6 come 7 what 8 with

QUICK REVIEW This activity reviews ways of keeping a conversation going. Students do the activity in pairs. Ask students to tell the class about any interesting things that their partner did last weekend.

Speaking, Reading and Listening

1 **a** Focus students on the lesson title and make sure they understand the meaning of the phrase *It's bad/ good for you*.
Students do the exercise on their own, then compare their lists in pairs.

b Check students understand *nutritional* /njuːˈtrɪʃənəl/. Students then answer the questions.
Ask students to tell the class about the types of food on their lists and whether they think they are good or bad for you.

2 Focus students on the introduction to a magazine article about nutritional advice. Students do the exercise on their own, then check answers in pairs. Check answers with the class.

> 1 Because we get a lot of contradictory information about which foods are healthy and which aren't.
> 2 Because generally organically grown food is considered to be healthier/better for us than industrially farmed food.

3 **a** Focus students on the photos of Guy and Jasmin. Ask students who they think is healthier.
Point out that *mom* is American English for *mum*.
Students do the exercise on their own or in pairs.

b Check students understand *high in protein/ cholesterol, a high/low fat diet, it's a killer*.
CD1▶ 14 Play the recording (SB p158). Students listen and check their answers. Check answers with the class.

> Guy says sentences 1–3. Jasmin says sentences 4–6.

┌─ **EXTRA IDEA** ─┐

• Students tick the sentences in **3a** as they hear them on the recording.

c Give students time to read questions 1–6, then play the recording again. Students listen and answer the questions.

d Students check answers in pairs. Check answers with the class.
Ask students whether their attitude to food is more like Guy's or Jasmin's.

> 1 They frequently change their minds. 2 No, it hasn't. 3 Guy, because his mother gets sick more often than he does. 4 Yes, she'll sometimes eat junk food if she's with friends. 5 Because she liked a boy in her class and she used to see him out running every morning. 6 The Japanese have a very low fat diet and they don't usually cook things in oil or fat, but her mother cooks with butter.

HELP WITH GRAMMAR
Present and past habits, repeated actions and states

4 **a–d** Elicit a few examples of state verbs from the class (*be, like, want*, etc.).
Students do the exercises on their own or in pairs, then check in **GRAMMAR 2.1** ▶ SB p130. Check answers with the class.

> **a** We use the **Present Simple** to talk about present habits, repeated actions and states.
> • We often use the **Present Continuous** with *always* to talk about present habits and repeated actions that annoy us or happen more than usual.
> • We can use *will* + **infinitive** to talk about repeated and typical behaviour in the present. We don't usually use this verb form with state verbs for this meaning.
> **b** Sentence 1 talks about repeated and typical behaviour. Sentence 2 talks about a future action.
> • This use of *will* + infinitive to talk about repeated and typical behaviour in the present often confuses students. While it is important that students recognise this use, they should be careful about using it too often themselves.
> • Highlight that to show criticism, we stress the uncontracted form of *will*: *He **will** leave the door open all the time!*
> **c** We use the **Past Simple** and *used to* + **infinitive** to talk about past habits, repeated actions and states.
> • We can use *would* + **infinitive** to talk about past habits and repeated actions. We don't usually use this verb form with state verbs.
> • Highlight that we usually make negative sentences with *used to* with subject + *didn't* + *use to* + infinitive: *I **didn't use to like** vegetables*.
> • Point out that we can also make negative sentences with *never used to*: *My brother never used to help with the washing-up*.
> • Highlight that we make questions with (question word) *did* + subject + *use to* + infinitive: *Where **did** you **use to** live?*

- Draw students' attention to the **TIP**. Point out that we don't use *used to* or *would* + infinitive for something that only happened once: *In 2011 I gave up smoking.* not ~~In 2011 I used to give up smoking.~~
- Highlight that we often use *used to* when describing past habits, then continue with *would* + infinitive: *I used to sleep until 10 a.m., then I'd get up and have breakfast in the garden. After that, I'd get the bus to work.*

5 Students do the exercise on their own. Before they begin, check students understand that both verb forms are possible in some of the sentences.

Students compare answers in pairs, giving reasons for their choices. Check answers with the class.

> **1** I had; I felt **2** it used to be **3** they're always changing **4** I walk/I'll walk; go **5** I eat/I'll eat; I know **6** I always worry/I'm always worrying **7** I tried **8** I didn't use to like

6 **a** Focus students on the photo of Guy's parents, Bernie and Ellen.

Students do the exercise on their own. Ask students to read the text quickly first for gist before they start filling in the gaps and tell them not to worry about the phrases in bold at this stage. Also encourage students to use a variety of different verb forms where possible, rather than just the Present Simple and Past Simple.

b Students compare answers in pairs. Check answers with the class.

> **1** wanted **2** started **3** worked/would work/used to work **4** got **5** were/would be/used to be **6** just had/would just have/just used to have **7** seldom watched/would seldom watch/seldom used to watch **8** rarely went/would rarely go/rarely used to go **9** took/would take/used to take **10** always told/would always tell/is always telling **11** was/used to be **12** were **13** got/would get/used to get **14** didn't have **15** bought **16** had **17** eat out/will eat out **18** go/will go **19** love **20** always says/is always saying

Vocabulary and Speaking

Expressing frequency

7 **a** Elicit some words/phrases that express frequency from the class (*always, sometimes, hardly ever, never, every week, once a month*, etc.) and write them on the board.

Focus students on the words/phrases in bold in **6a**. Use the examples *seldom* and *most days* to show that the words/phrases in bold express either lower or higher frequency.

Students do the exercise on their own, then check in **VOCABULARY 2.1** SB p130.

Check answers with the class. Note that only the main stress in words/phrases is shown in the Language Summaries.

Point out that we can also say *most mornings/days/weekends*, etc. Point out that we use the plural of countable nouns after *most*.

Also highlight that *rarely/seldom* are less common than their synonym *hardly ever*. *Rarely* and *seldom* are also more formal and can sometimes sound unnatural in spoken English. While it is important that students recognise these words, you may want to discourage them from using them too often when speaking.

Go through the word order section in **VOCABULARY 2.1** SB p130 with the class or ask them to study this for homework.

Model and drill the words/phrases, highlighting the pronunciation of *rarely* /ˈreəli/.

> **lower frequency**: seldom; rarely; once in a while; every now and again; every so often
> **higher frequency**: most days; more often than not; most of the time

b Students do the exercise on their own.

c Students do the exercise in pairs. Ask each pair to tell the class one or two things they found out about their partner.

Get ready ... Get it right!

8 Focus students on the prompts. Check students understand *taste in music/films/TV/books* (the music, films, TV or books that you like).

Students do the exercise on their own. Before they begin, remind students to make notes, not write complete sentences. If you have a class of older students, you can ask them to make notes on the differences between their lives now and ten years ago if they prefer.

9 Students do the activity in groups, using their notes from **8**. Encourage students to use a variety of verb forms from **4** in their discussion, rather than just the Present Simple and Past Simple. While they are working, monitor and help with any problems.

Finally, ask each group to tell the class about the person whose life has changed the most.

> **WRITING**
>
> For homework, ask students to write a paragraph comparing their lives now to their lives five years ago. Alternatively, students write an essay based on the discussion questions in **1b**. Encourage students to explain their arguments clearly, giving examples where necessary.

> **FURTHER PRACTICE**
>
> **Ph** **Class Activity** 2A Nightmare neighbours p151 (Instructions p133)
> **Extra Practice** 2A SB p116
> **Self-study DVD-ROM** Lesson 2A
> **Workbook** Lesson 2A p10

QUICK REVIEW This activity reviews ways of expressing present and past habits. Students do the first part of the activity on their own. Encourage them to use *used to, would* or *will* + infinitive and the Present Continuous with *always* where possible. Put students into pairs to complete the activity.

Vocabulary and Speaking
Feelings and opinions

1 **a** Students do the exercise on their own or in pairs, then check in **VOCABULARY 2.2** SB p130.

Check answers with the class. Point out that the prepositions in bold in the Language Summary are the most common for these adjectives, but we can also use the other prepositions in brackets.

Also check students understand the meaning of all the adjectives, particularly the new words/phrases *shocked, impressed, aware, fond of* and *sick of*.

Point out that we must use prepositions with *sick of* and *fond of* for these meanings, but that the other adjectives can be used without a preposition: *I was absolutely terrified.*

Highlight that we can often use *by* after adjectives that end in *-ed* because they have a passive meaning.

Remind students that prepositions are followed by a noun, a pronoun or verb+*ing*.

Model and drill the adjectives with their prepositions, highlighting the pronunciation of the *-ed* endings of the first seven adjectives. Point out that *-ed* is pronounced as an extra syllable /ɪd/ in *fascinated* /ˈfæsɪneɪtɪd/, *excited* /ɪkˈsaɪtɪd/ and *disappointed* /dɪsəˈpɔɪntɪd/ because it follows a /t/ sound; as a /t/ sound in *shocked* /ʃɒkt/ and *impressed* /ɪmˈprest/; and as a /d/ sound in *terrified* /ˈterɪfaɪd/ and *satisfied* /ˈsætɪsfaɪd/.

1 of **2** by **3** about **4** with **5** by **6** in **7** by **8** of
9 for **10** of **11** about **12** of

b Students do the exercise on their own.

c Students do the activity in pairs. Ask students to share any interesting information with the class.

┌─ **EXTRA IDEA** ┐
- ✎ Write the first six adjectives in **1a** on the board and elicit the *-ing* adjectives and the verbs for each one (*terrifying, terrify; fascinating, fascinate; exciting, excite; satisfying, satisfy; shocking, shock; disappointing, disappoint*). Also point out that we say something is *impressive* not *impressing*, and that the verb is *impress*.

Speaking and Reading

2 **a** Focus students on the photos. Ask them what they know about Mongolia's geography, sports, food and weather.

b Check students understand *volunteer, nomadic, tend* (animals), *shift, withstand, fermented* and *acquired taste*.
Students do the exercise on their own. You can set a time limit of two or three minutes to encourage students to read for gist. Check the answer with the class.

the food and the cold winters

3 **a** Students do the exercise on their own, then check answers in pairs. Check answers with the class.

a It's full of wide open spaces and nomadic people. **b** The diet is mainly milk-based in summer with a shift to meat in winter. **c** Mongolians have to withstand viciously cold winters – with temperatures as low as -40°C. **d** The Naadam is a festival which happens every year in July. **e** The horse races are 15 to 30 kilometres long and the jockeys are fearless children. **f** Airag is an alcoholic drink made from fermented mare's milk.

┌─ **EXTRA IDEA** ┐
- Put students into pairs to do **3a**. Student As read the first two paragraphs and find out about things a–c in the list. Student Bs read the second two paragraphs and find out about things d–f. Students then tell each other what Lottie Clarkson says about the things on their list.

b Students discuss the questions in groups. Ask each group to share interesting ideas and experiences with the class.

HELP WITH GRAMMAR
be used to, get used to

4 **a–f** Students do the exercises on their own or in pairs, then check in **GRAMMAR 2.2** SB p131.

Check answers with the class.

a **1** Yes, it did. **2** No, it doesn't.

b We use ***be used to*** to talk about things that are familiar and no longer strange or difficult for us (phrase 1 in the article).
- We use ***get used to*** to talk about things that become familiar, less strange or less difficult over a period of time (phrase 2).
- Check students understand that *be used to* refers to a state, whereas *get used to* refers to something that is changing.

- Point out that we can say *be accustomed to* instead of *be used to*, but this is more formal and less common: *Mr Jenkins was accustomed to working alone.*

c After *be used to* and *get used to* we use **verb+*ing*** (phrases 1, 3 and 5 in the article).
- After *be used to* and *get used to* we can use a noun or a pronoun (phrases 2, 4 and 6).

d **b2 c6 d4 e5 f3**
- Use the examples to highlight that we can use *be used to* and *get used to* in any verb form.
- Also point out that the form of *used to* in *be/get used to* doesn't change in questions or negatives: *She isn't used to it.* not ~~*She isn't use to it*~~.

e In sentence 1, the speaker lived in Mongolia in the past, but he/she doesn't live there now. In sentence 2, the speaker lives in Mongolia now and has probably lived there for some time. When he/she started living there, life was probably strange or difficult, but now it isn't.

5 Use the example to highlight the pronunciation of *used to* /ˈjuːstə/ and the sentence stress.
CD1 ▶ 15 **PRONUNCIATION** Play the recording (SB p158). Students listen and repeat the sentences. Check students copy the stress correctly.
You can also ask students to turn to **CD1 ▶ 15**, SB p158. They can then follow the stress as they listen and practise.

6 **a** Focus students on the photos on SB p19. Students do the exercise on their own.

b Students compare answers in pairs. Check answers with the class.

1 'm not used to/haven't got used to; Japan
2 get used to; Japan 3 'm not used to/haven't got used to; Iceland 4 get used to; Japan 5 'm used to/was used to/'ve been used to; Iceland 6 'm used to/'ve got used to; Japan

EXTRA IDEA
- Students work on their own and write four sentences about their family using *be used to* or *get used to*. Students then work in pairs and say their sentences to each other. Ask each pair to share interesting sentences with the class.

Get ready ... Get it right!

7 Students do the exercise on their own. Tell students to write short phrases (*commuting to work, speaking in public,* etc.), not complete sentences. Make sure students don't write the answers in the same order as the prompts.

8 Students work in pairs and swap papers. Students take turns to ask questions about the things written on their partner's paper (*Are you used to commuting to work?*, etc.).

Encourage students to ask follow-up questions if possible.

Finally, ask students to tell the class two interesting things they found out about their partner.

WRITING
Students write a paragraph about the things they chose in **7**. Encourage them to write complete sentences from the notes they made and give more information about each thing.

FURTHER PRACTICE
Ph **Vocabulary Plus** 2 Phrases with *get* p195 (Instructions p190)
Extra Practice 2B SB p116
Self-study DVD-ROM Lesson 2B
Workbook Lesson 2B p11

2C VOCABULARY AND SKILLS ▶ At a glance
Student's Book p20–p21

Vocabulary word building (1): suffixes
Skills Listening: a conversation between colleagues; Reading: a book review

QUICK REVIEW This activity reviews adjectives to describe feelings and opinions. Students do the first part of the activity on their own. Tell students to check which prepositions they should use with the adjectives in **VOCABULARY 2.2 ▶** SB p130 if necessary. Put students into pairs to complete the activity. Ask students to share any interesting information with the class.

Speaking and Listening

1 Focus students on the lesson title. Check students understand *glance* and what the expression *at a glance* means.
Students discuss the questions in pairs. Ask students to share their ideas with the class.

2 **a** Focus students on the photos. Check students understand the phrase *first impressions*.

CD1 16 Play the recording (SB p158). Students listen and decide which of the things in the list Tracy, Hal and Ann do not talk about. Check answers with the class.

> salaries; a divorce

b Play the recording again. Students do the exercise in pairs. Check answers with the class.

> 1 another accountant 2 He didn't think he was right for the company. There wasn't a particular reason, he just had a hunch. 3 Because he writes about first impressions. 4 No, he thinks we should go with our gut feelings more often. 5 Yes, she does, because it happened to her uncle and his wife.

3 Students do the exercise on their own, then check **CD1** 16 SB p158.

> made my mind up; had a hunch; was just something about him; Can't put my finger on it; go with our gut feelings

> ┌ **EXTRA IDEA** ┐
>
> • Before they do the exercise, put students in groups. Ask them to give their first impressions of Tracy, Hal and Ann. Ask groups to share their ideas with the class. Find out how many people had a similar first impression of each person.

HELP WITH LISTENING
Linking (1): consonant–vowel links; linking /r/ sounds

This *Help with Listening* section focuses on consonant–vowel linking and when we use linking /r/ sounds.

4 **a** **CD1** 17 Focus students on words/phrases 1–6, then play the recording. Students listen and notice the linking /r/ sounds. Play the recording again if necessary.
Use these examples to highlight that in British English, when a word ends in -*r* or -*re*, we only say the /r/ sound when the next word begins with a vowel sound.
Also point out that in American English, the /r/ sound is always pronounced. Note that differences between British and American accents are dealt with in lesson 8C.

b **CD1** 18 Play the beginning of the recording again. Students listen and notice the consonant–vowel links and the linking /r/ sounds.
Use the examples of consonant–vowel links to highlight that we usually link words that end in a consonant sound with words that start with a vowel sound.

c Students do the exercise in pairs.
✍ While students are working, copy the paragraph onto the board ready for checking.

d Students look at **CD1** 16 SB p158 and check their answers. ✍ Check answers with the class by eliciting each link and marking it on the board. Play this section of the recording again if necessary.
Play the whole conversation again. Students listen and notice the linking.

> And there‿/r/‿are‿/r/‿a few more‿/r/‿applicants‿on the list. I'm seeing‿another two later‿/r/‿on this‿afternoon‿actually.

Reading, Vocabulary and Speaking

5 **a** Focus students on the article and the cover of Malcolm Gladwell's book *Blink*. Establish that this is the book Tracy talked about in **2a**.
Check students understand *correlation* and *overwhelmingly*.
Students do the exercise on their own, then check answers in pairs. Check answers with the class.

> 1 the content of the book 2 a negative example of first impressions 3 a positive example of first impressions 4 the aim of the book

b Students do the exercise on their own. Don't check answers at this point.

c Students compare their answers to **5b** in pairs. Ask students to explain why they chose their answer if they disagree.

> 1b 2c 3b 4a 5b

> ┌ **EXTRA IDEA** ┐
>
> • Ask students if they agree with Gladwell's ideas. Put students into two groups – those who agree that you can trust your instincts, and those who don't. Put students into pairs, one from each group, and ask them to discuss their viewpoint, giving reasons for their ideas.

HELP WITH VOCABULARY
Word building (1): suffixes

6 **a–c** Students do the exercises on their own or in pairs, then check in **VOCABULARY 2.3** SB p130. Check answers with the class.

> **a** 1 conclusion 2 critic 3 originate 4 realistic
> 5 recognise 6 weakness 7 preference 8 judgement
> 9 responsible 10 convince
> • Check the meaning of any words students don't understand. Highlight that *conviction* in this word family means 'a strong opinion or belief': *It's my personal conviction that people should look after their parents when they get old.*

- You might want to point out that *judgement* can also be spelled *judgment* – and that both are equally correct.

b -*ence* N; -*ly* Adv; -*ive* Adj; -*ate* V; -*ity* N; -*al* Adj; -*ism* N; -*ic* Adj; -*ally* Adv; -*ed* Adj; -*ing* Adj; -*ility* N; -*ible* Adj; -*en* V; -*ness* N; -*ment* N; -*ise* V

- Point out that in British English, many verbs end with the suffix -*ise* (*criticise, recognise*, etc.), but in American English this suffix is spelled -*ize* (*criticize, recognize*, etc.).
- Also remind students that the verb and the noun are sometimes the same, for example, *plan, test, need, run*, etc.: *I **plan** to go to college next year. That's a good **plan**.*
- Highlight that if an adjective ends in -*e*, we usually replace -*e* with -*y* to make the adverb: *responsible → responsibly*. If an adjective ends in -*ic*, we add -*ally* to make the adverb: *realistic → realistically*.

7 Tell students that the stress often changes in word families. Use the examples to show that the stress on *originate, original* and *originally* is on the second syllable, but the stress on *originality* is on the fourth syllable and on the first syllable in *origin*.

CD1 ▶ 19 PRONUNCIATION Play the recording (SB p159). Students listen and repeat the words. Check students copy the word stress correctly. Don't give students more information about why the stress changes in certain words and not others. This will be covered in *Help with Pronunciation* in lesson 2D.

EXTRA IDEAS

- Students work in pairs and take turns to test each other on the word families in **6a**. For example, student A says *Responsibility* and student B says *Responsible, responsibly*.
- Students work on their own and write six sentences using words from the word families in **6a** about people they know. Put students into pairs. Students check their partner's sentences and ask follow-up questions.

8 Ask all students to turn to SB p110.

a Check students understand *on impulse*. Students do the exercise on their own.

b Students do the exercise in pairs. Encourage students to give reasons for the sentences they ticked, and to find out how many similarities there are between them.

c Finally, ask each pair to tell the class two things that they have in common.

FURTHER PRACTICE

Ph **Class Activity** 2C Where's the stress? p152 (Instructions p133)
Ph **Study Skills** 1 Spelling rules: the final -*e* p228 (Instructions p225)
Extra Practice 2C SB p116
Self-study DVD-ROM Lesson 2C
Workbook Lesson 2C p13

▷ REAL
2D WORLD **▷ I see your point**
Student's Book p22–p23

Real World discussion language (1): agreeing and disagreeing politely

QUICK REVIEW This activity reviews suffixes and word families. Students do the first part of the activity on their own. Put students into pairs to complete the activity. Remind students to stress the words correctly. Students can check answers in **VOCABULARY 2.3 ▶** SB p130. Ask each pair to tell the class one of their word families.

1 Check students understand *strict* and point out that the opposite in this context is *relaxed*. Also check understanding of *fussy eater, sweet* and *savoury*. Students discuss the questions in groups. Ask students to share interesting answers with the class.

EXTRA IDEA

- Begin the class by asking students to think of at least three things their parents made them do when they were children and three things they let them do. Students discuss their ideas in groups or with the whole class.

2 **a** Focus students on the photo. Establish where the people are (in a kitchen) and what they are doing (preparing food). Use the photo to establish the relationships between the people (daughter and parents).
VIDEO ▶ 2 CD1 ▶ 20 Students watch or listen to the conversation, then answer the questions. Students compare answers in pairs. Check answers with the class.

children's eating habits; children helping in the kitchen

b Students do the exercise in pairs.

c Play the video or audio recording again. Students compare answers in pairs. Check answers with the class.

Ask the class who they agree with most: Colin, Val or Amanda.

> 1 Colin 2 Val 3 Colin, Amanda 4 Colin, Val
> 5 Colin 6 Val

REAL WORLD
Discussion language (1): agreeing and disagreeing politely

3 **a–b** Students do **3a** on their own or in pairs, then check in **REAL WORLD 2.1** ▶ SB p131. Check answers with the class.

> • a 2D 3D 4A 5D 6A 7A 8A 9A 10D 11A 12A
> • Check students understand that *Oh, do you think so?* is a polite way of disagreeing, not a real question.
> • Draw students' attention to the **TIP**. Highlight that we often follow an agreement phrase with *but* to challenge the other person's opinion.

4 **a** Students do the exercise on their own.

b Students compare answers in pairs. Check answers with the class.

> 1 Do; so 2 know; that 3 good point 4 might; right
> 5 can't; see; point 6 see; mean 7 still; convinced
> 8 argue; that 9 suppose; true 10 wouldn't; that

5 **a** Students do the exercise on their own. Point out that sometimes there is more than one possible answer.

b Students compare answers in pairs. Check answers with the class. Ask students which person in each conversation they agree with most, giving reasons for their answers.

> **Suggested answers**
> 1 **Colin:** Well, I can't argue with that./That's a good point.; **Val:** I don't know about that./Oh, do you think so?/Oh, I wouldn't say that.
> 2 **Val:** I suppose that's true, actually./That's a good point.; **Amanda:** I don't know about that./Oh, do you think so?/Oh, I wouldn't say that.
> 3 **Val:** I see your point./That's a good point.; **Amanda:** I don't know about that./Oh, I wouldn't say that./Well, I'm still not convinced.
> 4 **Val:** You might be right there./That's a good point./I suppose you've got a point there.; **Colin:** Oh, I wouldn't say that.

EXTRA IDEA

• Put students into new pairs. Students choose one of the statements in **5a** and write an eight-line conversation between two people with opposing views on the topic. Ask one or two pairs to role play their conversation for the class.

6 **a** Students do the exercise on their own. You can ask students to make notes on their reasons.

b Students discuss the sentences in **6a** in groups. Encourage students to use the ways of agreeing and disagreeing in **3a**.

Finally, ask each group to tell the class which topic they disagreed about most and why.

FURTHER PRACTICE

Ph **Class Activity** 2D The Big Question p153 (Instructions p134)
Extra Practice 2D SB p116
Self-study DVD-ROM Lesson 2D
Workbook Lesson 2D p14
Workbook Reading and Writing Portfolio 2 p66
Progress Test 2 p240

HELP WITH PRONUNCIATION
Word stress (1): suffixes

This *Help with Pronunciation* section focuses on the changing word stress when suffixes are used.

1 **a** Focus students on the words and the suffixes in pink.

CD1 21 Play the recording (SB p159). Students listen and mark the stress on the words.

Students check answers in pairs. Check answers with the class.

Play the recording again. Students listen and repeat the words. Monitor and check that students put the stress on the correct syllable in each word.

> imagine; imagination; courage; courageous; danger; dangerous; disappoint; disappointment; foolish; foolishness; Japan; Japanese; interview; interviewee; mountain; mountaineer; industry; industrious; meaning; meaningful; meaningless; economy; economical

b Focus students on the words in **1a**. Students do the exercise on their own, then check answers in pairs. Check answers with the class.

> 1c 2a 3b

2 Students do the exercise in pairs. Encourage students to say the words out loud to help them identify where the stress is.

> **EXTRA IDEA**
>
> • With a weaker class, before students do the exercise, ask them to underline the suffix in each word.

CD1▶22 Play the recording (SB p159). Students listen and check their answers.

Play the recording again. Students listen and repeat the words.

Finally, ask students to say one word each. Check they put the stress on the correct syllable and praise good pronunciation.

creativity; adventurous, geographical; trainee; development; advantageous; volunteer; Vietnamese; refugee; cleverness; familiarity; mysterious; humourless; forgetful

continue2learn

Focus students on the *continue2learn* section on SB p23. See p35 for ideas on how to exploit this section.

Extra Practice 2

See p35 for ideas on how to exploit this section.

2A
1   3 used to have 4 ✓; ✓ 5 's always losing
    6 usually wakes up 7 was; ✓ 8 ✓; ✓
2   2 More 3 Every 4 Once 5 Most 6 seldom

2B
3   2 with 3 of 4 with 5 by/with 6 of 7 about/of
    8 for 9 by/at 10 of 11 by/with
4   2 got 3 getting 4 get 5 getting used 6 used 7 had
    to get 8 to get

2C
5   judgement; judgemental; judgementally
    recognition; recognisable; recognisably
    criticism/critic; critical; critically
    conclusion; conclusive; conclusively
    preference; preferable; preferably
    weakness; weak; weakly
    conviction; convinced/convincing; convincingly
    originality/origin; original; originally

2D
6   2 a, b   3 a, b   4 b, a

Progress Portfolio 2

• See p36 for ideas on how to exploit this section.

3A ▶ Against the law
Student's Book p24–p25

Vocabulary crime
Grammar second conditional; alternatives
for *if*

QUICK REVIEW This activity reviews ways of agreeing and disagreeing politely. Check students understand *social networking sites*, *graffiti* and *reality TV*. Give students a minute or two to make notes on their opinions of the five topics. Put students into pairs. Students discuss each topic in turn. Remind students to use the language in REAL WORLD 2.1 ▶ SB p131 in their conversations. Ask students to share any differences of opinion with the class.

Vocabulary and Speaking
Crime

1 **a** Students work in pairs and say which words they know, then check new words in VOCABULARY 3.1 ▶ SB p132. Check answers with the class.

Highlight the difference between *robbery* (stealing money from banks), *theft* (stealing money and things), *burglary* (stealing from houses and flats) and *shoplifting* (stealing from a shop while it is open).

Check students understand the meaning of the other types of crime. Point out that all these types of crime are uncountable nouns and that *robbery, theft, burglary, mugging, kidnapping* and *murder* can also be used as countable nouns: *There was a robbery last night*.

Model and drill the words, highlighting the pronunciation of *burglary* /'bɜːgləri/, *fraud* /frɔːd/, *bribery* /'braɪbəri/, *murder* /'mɜːdə/ and *terrorism* /'terərɪzəm/.

Point out that the stress on all the multi-syllable words here is on the first syllable (*shoplifting, kidnapping*, etc.).

b Students do the exercise on their own or in pairs, then check in VOCABULARY 3.2 ▶ SB p132.

📝 While students are working, draw a three-column table on the board and write the headings *crime, criminal* and *verb* at the top of each column. Then write the crimes in **1a** in the first column.

📝 Check answers with the class by eliciting the criminal and the verb for each crime and writing them in the correct columns on the board.

Point out that there is no word for a criminal who bribes someone. Also highlight that we say *commit fraud, commit arson* and *commit an act of terrorism*. Tell students that we can also say *I was burgled* to mean 'my house was burgled'.

Remind students that the plural of *thief* is *thieves* /θiːvz/ and point out that all the verbs are regular verbs, apart from *steal* (*stole, stolen*).

Model and drill the word families with the class (*robbery, robber, rob*, etc.). Highlight the pronunciation of *thief* /θiːf/, *burglar* /'bɜːglə/, *burgle* /'bɜːgəl/ and *fraudster* /'frɔːdstə/.

c Students discuss the questions in groups. If you have a multilingual class, put students from different countries in each group.

Ask each group to share interesting answers with the class.

Reading and Speaking

2 Check students understand *flout* (deliberately refuse to obey a rule or custom), *speed limit, a security guard* /gɑːd/ and the verb *pull over* (stop your car by the side of the road).

Focus students on the questionnaire and ask them to read the introductory paragraph. Elicit what the aim of the questionnaire is (to find out how honest you are).

Students do the activity on their own. Check answers to question 1 with the class.

> **1** speeding, eating, using mobiles whilst driving, not wearing seatbelts, illegally downloading music or films, smoking in non-smoking areas, dropping litter, cycling on pavements

3 **a** Students do the questionnaire on their own.

b Students compare answers in pairs. Students look at the key on SB p114 to find out how honest they are, according to the questionnaire.

Ask each student to tell the class their results. Make sure that you keep this stage light-hearted so that students don't feel that their honesty is being seriously questioned.

┌─ **EXTRA IDEA** ─┐

● Do the questionnaire as a whole-class activity. 📝 Write the question numbers and option letters (a, b, c) on the board. Read each question and answer options, while students follow the text in their books. After each option, ask students to raise their hand if they would choose that option. Keep a note of the number of students who chose each option by putting a number next to each one on the board. At the end of the questionnaire, find out which options were the most popular. Students then look at the key on SB p114 to find out how honest the class is, according to the questionnaire.

▶ 45

HELP WITH GRAMMAR
Second conditional; alternatives for *if*

4 **a–d** Students do the exercises on their own or in pairs, then check in **GRAMMAR 3.1** SB p133. Check answers with the class.

a 1 imaginary situations **2** b) the present/the future **3** *if* + subject + Past Simple, subject + *'d* (= *would*)/*wouldn't* + infinitive **4** *could*; *might*

- Ask students to identify the *if* clause and the main clause in the three example sentences in **bold** in the questionnaire. Use these examples to highlight that the *if* clause can come first or second in the sentence and that we use a comma if the *if* clause is first.
- Remind students that we can use *could* or *might* in the main clause of second conditionals instead of *would* to mean 'would perhaps'.
- Point out that *even if* = it doesn't matter whether the situation in the *if* clause exists or not: *No, I wouldn't, **even if** he/she got angry with me.*
- Also remind students that in second conditionals we can say *If I/he/she/it was …* or *If I/he/she/it were …* : *If I was/were rich, I'd buy a Ferrari.*

b 1 *Provided* and *as long as* mean 'only if (this happens)'. **2** *Assuming* means 'accepting that something is true'.

- Point out that we often use *provided, as long as, assuming, imagine* and *suppose* instead of *if* in conditionals.
- Tell students that *as long as* is usually pronounced /əzˈlɒŋəz/.

c *Imagine* and *suppose* have the **same meaning** (= form a picture in your mind about what something could be like).

- We can use *imagine* and *suppose* as an alternative for *if* in **questions**.
- Also highlight that we can say *provided* or *providing* and *suppose* or *supposing*, but that the first word in each pair is more common. Focus students on question 4 and answer 5b in the questionnaire for examples of second conditionals with *supposing* and *provided*.
- Point out that we can also use *provided, as long as, assuming, imagine* and *suppose* in other types of conditionals to talk about real situations.
- Tell students we can use *that* after *provided, imagine* and *suppose*: *Provided (that) there weren't any police cars around, of course I would.*
- Highlight that questions with *imagine* and *suppose* can also be written as two sentences: *Imagine you saw a ten-year-old boy shoplifting. Would you tell a security guard?*.

> **EXTRA IDEA**
> - As a class, choose four rules or laws different from those in the questionnaire in **3**. Put students in four groups and give one rule or law to each group. Tell students to write a questionnaire question (with three options) for their rule or law. Then as a class, students do the questionnaire.

5 **a** Students do the exercise on their own.

> **EXTRA IDEA**
> - With a lower-level class, ask students to circle *if* in each sentence before they begin. This will help them use the correct verb forms in the appropriate places.

b Students compare answers in pairs. Check answers with the class.

1 offered; would … accept **2** wouldn't take; didn't want **3** was/were; 'd/would … accept **4** might go; wasn't/weren't **5** didn't offer; wouldn't take **6** got; didn't like; 'd/would come

6 **a** Students do the exercise on their own. Before they begin, point out that sometimes both words/phrases are possible.

b Students compare answers in pairs. Check answers with the class.
Students take turns to ask each other the questions. Students answer for themselves.

1 Suppose; assuming **2** Imagine; provided **3** If/Suppose; even if **4** Imagine/If; as long as/provided

> # Get ready … Get it right!
>
> **7** Put students into two groups, group A and group B. Students in group A turn to SB p104 and students in group B turn to SB p107.
>
> **a** Check students understand *a park bench* and *drop something*.
>
> Put students into pairs with someone from the same group. Students do the exercise in pairs.
>
> If necessary, check answers with the class. Only check the verb forms students need to fill in the gaps, so that students in the other group don't hear the questions they are about to be asked.
>
> **Student A 1** hit; would … leave **2** found; would … hand **3** paid; would … keep **4** got; realised; would … take **5** borrowed; dropped; would … tell
> **Student B a** wanted; would … try **b** asked; thought; would … tell **c** found; would … give **d** gave; would … give **e** asked; would … buy
>
> **b** Reorganise the class so that a student from group A is working with a student from group B. Students take turns to ask and answer their questions, as in the speech bubbles. Tell students to make brief notes to help them remember their partner's answers, as they will need these for the next stage of the activity.

> **FURTHER PRACTICE**
>
> **Ph** **Vocabulary Plus** 3 Word pairs p196 (Instructions p190)
> **Extra Practice** 3A SB p117
> **Self-study DVD-ROM** Lesson 3A
> **Workbook** Lesson 3A p15

c Reorganise the class again so that students are working with the person they worked with in **a**. Students discuss how their partners from the other group answered each question, referring to their notes where necessary. Students decide if their answers were similar and which student from the other group is more honest.

Finally, ask each pair to share their conclusions with the class, giving reasons for their choices.

3B ▶ It shouldn't be allowed
Student's Book p26–p27

Vocabulary crime and punishment collocations
Grammar third conditional

QUICK REVIEW This activity reviews alternatives for *if*. Students work on their own and answer the questions. Put students into pairs. Students take turns to tell each other their answers to the questions. Encourage students to ask follow-up questions to find out more information.

Vocabulary

Crime and punishment collocations

1 **a** Students do the exercise in pairs, then check in **VOCABULARY 3.3** ▶ SB p132.

✍ Check answers with the class by eliciting the complete phrases and writing them on the board. Point out that the phrases are organised in a logical order, from committing the crime to types of sentence handed out in court. Check students understand the meanings of any new words/phrases.

Highlight the different prepositions in the phrases (*arrest someone for a crime,* etc.) by underlining or circling them on the board. Point out that *convict* is the opposite of *acquit*. Establish that *arrest, charge, sentence* and *fine* are also nouns, and that the opposite of *guilty* is *innocent*.

Also teach students that *a court* is a large room where lawyers formally present all the evidence about a crime: *He's appearing in court today.* Point out that we also use *a court* to refer to all the people in the courtroom: *Please tell the court what happened.*

Remind students that the process of deciding if somebody is guilty or innocent is called *a trial*: *The trial has already lasted three weeks.*
Model and drill the phrases with the class, highlighting the pronunciation of *guilty* /ˈgɪlti/ and *acquit* /əˈkwɪt/.

b Check students remember *judge* /dʒʌdʒ/, *jury* /ˈdʒʊri/ and *witness*. Point out that *judge* and *witness* are also verbs. Model and drill these words.

Focus students on the example, then ask students to do the exercise in pairs.

✍ Check answers with the class by writing *a criminal, the police,* etc. in front of the phrases written on the board in **1a**. Also establish that if there is a jury, it is the jury members' responsibility to deliver the *verdict* (say if someone is guilty or not guilty), but the judge decides on the type of punishment. If there isn't a jury, the judge (or panel of judges) decides on the verdict.

- **the police** arrest someone for a crime; charge someone with a crime; take someone to court; give evidence
- **the judge** sends someone to prison (for 10 years); sentences someone to (10 years) in prison; fines someone (£500)
- **the judge/the jury** finds someone (not) guilty; acquits/convicts someone of a crime
- **a witness** gives evidence

Listening and Speaking

2 **a** Focus students on pictures A and B. Tell students that both pictures show a real incident that took place in the US. Use picture A to teach the American English phrase *a parking lot* (UK = *a car park*). Students do the exercise in pairs. Ask students to share their ideas with the class. Don't tell students if they are correct at this stage.

b Tell students that they are going to listen to three friends talking about what happened. Also point out that both stories are true.

CD1▶ 23 Play the recording (SB p159). Students listen and check their answers from **2a**. Check answers with the class.

> **A** A woman thought four men were stealing her car, so she pulled out a gun and threatened to shoot them. After they'd run away she realised that the car wasn't hers and that her identical car was parked nearby.
> **B** A man was so annoyed by the sound of a car alarm going off at night that he shot the car's tyres.

3 **a** Students do the activity in pairs. Encourage students to use all the words/phrases in the boxes and to include as much detail as they can remember.

b Play the recording again. Students listen and check if their versions of the stories were correct.
Check any remaining comprehension problems with the class.

4 Students discuss the questions in groups. If possible, include students from different countries in each group. Ask each group to share their ideas with the class.
Alternatively, discuss the questions with the whole class.

HELP WITH GRAMMAR
Third conditional

5 **a–d** Students do the exercises on their own or in pairs, then check in **GRAMMAR 3.2▶** SB p133.
- Check answers with the class.

a 1 No, she didn't. **2** No, she didn't.
- We use the third conditional to talk about **imaginary** situations in the **past**.
- Highlight that the third conditional often describes the opposite of what really happened: *If the woman had shot the men, she'd have been in serious trouble.* (The woman didn't shoot the men, so she didn't get in serious trouble.)

b We use the Past Perfect Simple in the *if* clause. We use *'d* (= *would*)/*wouldn't* + *have* + past participle in the main clause.
- ✎ Write the form of the third conditional on the board: *if* + subject + Past Perfect Simple, subject + *'d* (= *would*)/*wouldn't* + *have* + past participle. Then also write the sentences in **5a** as an example.
- Point out that the third conditional is the same for all subjects (*I, we, he*, etc.).
- Also highlight that we don't usually use *would* in the *if* clause: *If I'd known, I'd have helped.* not *If I would have known, I'd have helped.*

c 1 *might* = 'would perhaps' and *could* = 'would be possible'
2 No, it isn't. As with other conditionals, the *if* clause can be first or second in the sentence: *I wouldn't have been too happy if the car alarm had woken me up.* Remind students that we use a comma when the *if* clause is first.
3 We make questions in the third conditional with: (question word) + *would* + subject + *have* + past participle ... *if* + subject + Past Perfect Simple: *What would he have done if he'd actually seen the owner of the car?*.
- Point out that we can also use *imagine* and *suppose* in third conditional questions: *Imagine/ Suppose he'd seen you, what would you have done?*.

HELP WITH LISTENING
Third conditional

This *Help with Listening* section helps students to understand the third conditional in natural spoken English.

6 **a** **CD1▶ 24** Focus students on sentences 1–4. Play the recording. Students listen and read the sentences. Point out how we say the contractions (*I'd, you'd,* etc.) and the weak forms of *have* /əv/ and *had* /əd/. Play the recording again if necessary.

b **CD1▶ 25** Play the recording (SB p159). Students listen and write the five sentences. Play the recording again if necessary. Students check their sentences in pairs.
✎ Play the recording again, pausing after each sentence is said the second time to elicit students' answers and write the sentences on the board. Ask students to identify the contractions and the examples of the weak forms of *have* and *had*. Circle or underline them on the board.

1 If I hadn't gone to the party, I wouldn't have met her. 2 He wouldn't have known about it if you hadn't told him. 3 If you'd been more careful, she might not have got hurt. 4 If I could have helped her, I would have done. 5 If Dave had known when your flight was, he could have picked you up.

7 **CD1 ▶ 26** **PRONUNCIATION** Play the recording and ask students to repeat. Check students copy the contractions and weak forms correctly.

> ⌐ **EXTRA IDEA** ⌐
>
> • Before doing **7**, ask students to decide which words are stressed in the sentences they wrote in **6b**. Students can then listen to **CD1 ▶ 26** and check their answers.
>   ✎ Elicit which words are stressed and mark them on the board.

8 **a** Tell students that they are going to read six sentences about Jim's terrible evening.
Students do the exercise on their own.

b Students check answers in pairs. Check answers with the class.

1 might have been; 'd/had taken 2 had told; could have asked 3 wouldn't have parked; 'd/had known 4 hadn't left; might not have stolen 5 hadn't given; would have stayed 6 would have been; hadn't come

Last night Jim drove to Juliet's party. He parked his car in the street, but he left it unlocked and it was stolen. Mary gave him a lift home.

9 **a** Focus students on the text. Tell students that it is a true story. Check students understand *cash register* and the US English phrase *gas station* (UK = *petrol station*), and check students remember the meaning of *end up* (somewhere).
Students read the text and answer the questions. Students can compare answers in pairs. Check answers with the class.

1 Eight dollars. 2 They weren't from that town and they didn't have a map. 3 At the gas station that they had robbed. 4 To get directions. 5 They were probably arrested.

b Focus students on the example. Students then do the exercise on their own. While they are working, monitor and check students' sentences for accuracy.

c Students work in pairs and check that their partner's sentences are correct.

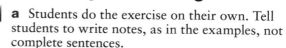

Possible answers
If they'd looked in the bag, they'd have seen that there was only $8 in it. They might not have got lost if one of them had been from Poulsbo/that town. If they'd had a map, they wouldn't have got lost. They wouldn't have driven into that gas station if they'd realised it was the same one. If they'd seen the police car, they would have driven away. They might have got away if they'd asked someone else for directions. They wouldn't have got arrested if the salesgirl hadn't called the police.

Get ready ... Get it right!

10 **a** Students do the exercise on their own. Tell students to write notes, as in the examples, not complete sentences.

b Students do the exercise on their own.

> ⌐ **EXTRA IDEA**
>
> • With a lower-level class, you can allow students to write the sentences in **10a** if they wish.

11 Students do the activity in pairs. Encourage students to ask follow-up questions if possible.

Finally, ask students to tell the class two interesting things they have found out about their partner's past.

⌐ **WRITING** ⌐
Students write a paragraph about the things that have happened to them in their life and how life would have been different if these things hadn't happened. Students use the notes they made in **10a**. Encourage students to add more information about each thing so that they write a cohesive text.

⌐ **FURTHER PRACTICE** ⌐
Ph **Class Activity** 3B The Unlucky Club p154 (Instructions p134)
Extra Practice 3B SB p116
Self-study DVD-ROM Lesson 3B
Workbook Lesson 3B p16

QUICK REVIEW This activity reviews the third conditional. Students do the first part of the activity on their own. Put students into pairs. Students take turns to tell each other their sentences. Encourage students to ask follow-up questions if possible.

Speaking and Listening

1 Students discuss the questions in groups.

2 **a** Tell students that they are going to hear a discussion about the prison population in the UK. **CD1 27** Play the recording. Students listen and do the exercise on their own, then compare answers in pairs. Check answers with the class.

> **1** Margaret Bolton is a Member of Parliament (an MP); David Gilbert is a Chief Superintendent (of Police) **2** They agree that there are too many people in prison, and that we have to stop criminals reoffending. They don't agree on the three strikes law as a deterrent. **3** It's a system where, if someone is found guilty on three different occasions, they are automatically sentenced to a minimum of 25 years to life in prison.

b Put students in pairs, A and B. Tell students A to look at the numbers in A and students B to look at the numbers in B. Play the recording again. Students listen and identify what their numbers refer to.

c Students work in their pairs and take turns to tell each other what the numbers refer to.

- £40,000 = the cost of keeping a person in prison for one year;
- £3.8 billion = the cost of keeping all the prisoners in the UK in prison for a year;
- £4,000 = the cost of keeping a person in prison for 45 days;
- 2.3 million = the prison population in the US
- 95,000 = the number of prisoners in the UK;
- 60,000 = the number of people sentenced in one year to less than a year in prison for minor crimes;
- 60% = the percentage of short-term offenders who commit another crime within a year;
- $68 billion = the amount the US spends each year on prisons

HELP WITH LISTENING
Weak forms

This *Help with Listening* section reviews common weak forms and highlights the relationship between weak forms and sentence stress.

3 **a** Focus students on the words in the box. Check students remember the difference between strong and weak forms by eliciting the strong form and the weak

form of *can* (strong /kæn/, weak /kən/). Ask students whether we usually hear strong or weak forms of these words in natural spoken English (weak forms).

b **CD1 28** Play the recording. Point out that students will hear the strong form of each word first. Students listen and check their pronunciation.
Check pronunciation with the class if necessary. Highlight that all of the weak forms contain a schwa sound (/ə/).
Point out what types of word are often pronounced in their weak forms (auxiliary verbs, the verb *be*, pronouns, prepositions, articles, etc.).

EXTRA IDEA

- Ask students to turn to **CD1 28**, SB p160 and look at the table of strong and weak forms (as shown below). Play the recording again. Students listen and notice the pronunciation of the strong and weak forms of the words. Use the table to highlight the schwa sounds /ə/ in the weak forms.

	strong	weak		strong	weak
can	/kæn/	/kən/	an	/æn/	/ən/
was	/wɒz/	/wəz/	for	/fɔː/	/fə/
were	/wɜː/	/wə/	of	/ɒv/	/əv/
has	/hæz/	/həz/, /əz/	to	/tuː/	/tə/
have	/hæv/	/həv/, /əv/	from	/frɒm/	/frəm/
are	/ɑː/	/ə/	as	/æz/	/əz/
do	/duː/	/də/	and	/ænd/	/ənd/
you	/juː/	/jə/	that	/ðæt/	/ðət/
at	/æt/	/ət/	them	/ðem/	/ðəm/
the	/ðiː/	/ðə/	your	/jɔː/	/jə/
a	/eɪ/	/ə/	but	/bʌt/	/bət/

---

c Focus students on the first part of the radio programme and highlight that *that* is a weak form. Students work in pairs and circle the other weak forms.
✎ While students are working, copy the sentences on the board ready for checking.

d Ask students to look at **CD1 27**, SB p160 to check their answers.
✎ Check answers with the class by circling the weak forms on the board.

> Government figures out today show (that) (the) cost (of) keeping (a) person in prison (for) one year (has) risen (to) £40,000. So what (can) we do (to) reduce (the) prison population?

e **CD1 27** Play the whole recording again. Students look at **CD1 27**, SB p160 and notice the relationship between the weak forms and sentence stress. Note that only the weak forms focused on in **3a** are marked in the recording. Ask students if weak forms are ever stressed (no).

Reading and Speaking

4 Focus students on the frequently asked questions. Point out that this phrase is usually shortened to *FAQ*. Check students understand *deterrent* (= something that makes you decide not to do something because you realise something horrible could happen to you) and *interpret* (= understand something in a particular way).

Students do the exercise on their own.

Students compare answers in pairs. Check answers with the class.

1c 2d 3a

> **EXTRA IDEA**

● Ask students to say why the remaining questions in **4** don't match any of the paragraphs in the text.

  b Although a particular state (California) is mentioned in paragraphs 2 and 3, there is no mention of Three Strikes Law not being an effective deterrent. **e** Although paragraph 1 mentions baseball, it is not about prisoners playing baseball.

5 **a** Put students into groups of three, A, B and C. Students A read about Leandro Andrade, students B read about Jerry Williams, and students C read about Santos Reyes. Students answer the questions for their text only.

b Students work in their groups and ask and answer the questions from **5a**.

Encourage students to give more information about each answer.

Leandro Andrade
1 California. **2** Stealing children's video tapes. **3** No, it didn't. **4** Theft and burglary. **5** Yes.
Jerry Williams
1 California. **2** Stealing a slice of pizza. **3** No, it didn't. **4** Robbery and car theft. **5** No.
Santos Reyes
1 California. **2** Taking the written part of a driving test for his cousin. **3** No, it didn't. **4** Burglary (stealing a radio) and robbery. **5** Yes, he is.

Students then discuss the questions in their groups. Ask each group to share their answers with the class.

> **EXTRA IDEA**

● Students discuss the questions as a class and try to agree on whose sentence was the most unfair. Encourage them to give reasons for their decision.

HELP WITH VOCABULARY
Verbs and prepositions

6 **a–c** Students do the exercises on their own, then check in **VOCABULARY 3.4** SB p132. Check answers with the class.

a **2** on **3** on **4** of **5** against **6** about **7** with **8** to; about **9** in **10** to **11** to; for **12** to; for
Check students understand any new words/ phrases.

b object before the preposition: *name*; *base*; *convince*; *reduce*
two prepositions: *complain*; *apologise*; *apply*

7 **a** Students do the exercise on their own. Check answers with the class.

1 protested against **2** applied for **3** apologised to; apologise for **4** cope with **5** complained about; complain to **6** named after **7** succeeded in **8** insist on **9** based on **10** reduced to **11** convince; of

b Students do the exercise in pairs. Ask students to tell the class one or two things they found out about their partner.

8 Tell students that they are going to read about four crimes that happened in the UK. Put students into groups of four. Student A in each group turns to SB p104, student B turns to p107, student C turns to p110 and student D turns to p111. If you have extra students, have one, two or three groups of three and make the strongest student in each of these groups student C. Ask these students to read about the crimes on p110 and on p111.

a Students do the exercise on their own.

b Students work in their groups and take turns to tell each other about their crimes, using the words/ phrases they wrote in **a** as prompts. After each crime, students discuss what punishment they would have given if they had been the judge. Encourage students to come to a group decision if possible.

c Students turn to SB p114 and read what happened to the criminals.

Students work in their groups and discuss the sentences each criminal actually received.

Finally, ask the class how many people agreed with the sentences for each of the four crimes.

> **WRITING**

Ask students to research a true crime story online. Students write a text about the crime, giving the important details, i.e. what the crime was, who committed the crime, whether the criminal was caught and what happened to him/her.

> **FURTHER PRACTICE**

Ph **Class Activity** 3C Preposition pelmanism p156 (Instructions p134)
Extra Practice 3C SB p117
Self-study DVD-ROM Lesson 3C
Workbook Lesson 3C p18

How can I help?
Student's Book p30–p31

Real World making, refusing and accepting offers

QUICK REVIEW This activity reviews verbs and prepositions. Students do the first part of the activity on their own. Put students into pairs. Students complete the activity with their partner. Ask each student to tell the class one of his/her sentences.

1 Students discuss the questions in groups. Ask students to share interesting ideas with the class.

2 **a** Focus students on the photos. Remind students that they first saw Chloe in lesson 1D. Elicit what has happened. (Chloe's house has been burgled.)
Give students time to read the list of topics and check they understand *fingerprints* and *home security*.
VIDEO▶ 3 **CD1▶ 29** Play the video or audio recording (SB p160). Students watch or listen then put the topics in the order in which they are first talked about. Check answers with the class.

1 the police 2 home security 3 a computer
4 fingerprints 5 Prague 6 a pet

b Play the video or audio recording again. Students make notes on the topics in **2a**.

c Students compare notes in pairs.

REAL WORLD
Making, refusing and accepting offers

3 **a–c** Students do the exercises on their own or in pairs, then check in **REAL WORLD 3.1**▶ SB p133. Check answers with the class.

a 1 Would 2 like 3 Let 4 help 5 don't 6 What
7 offering 8 better 9 manage 10 easier 11 be
12 mind 13 could 14 don't

b *Let me ...* , *Why don't I ...* and *I'd better ...* are followed by the infinitive.
• *Would it help if I ...* , *What if I ...* and *It'd be easier if I ...* are followed by the Past Simple.
• *Thanks for ...* is often followed by verb+*ing*.
• Highlight that we can also say: *It'd be great/nice/ helpful/fantastic,* etc. *if you could.*

4 **CD1▶ 30** **PRONUNCIATION** Play the recording (SB p160). Students listen and repeat. Check students copy the polite intonation correctly. Remind students that if their voices are too flat, they might sound rude or bored.

5 **a** Tell students that because of the burglary, Chloe has decided to move house. Her colleague Mark offers to help her. Students do the exercise in pairs.

b Students compare answers in pairs. Check answers with the class.

1
MARK Would you like me to help you move tomorrow?
CHLOE **Are you** sure **you wouldn't** mind?
M No, of course not.
C Thanks. That**'d be a** great help.
M Why **don't** I come over this evening and help you pack?
C It**'d be** wonderful **if you** could.
M What if I come at about seven?
C Yeah, that's good for me.
M I've got some old packing cases. Would you like me to bring some round?
C No, **it's** OK, I've got plenty. Thanks **for** offering.
2
M Let **me** help **you** pack those files.
C No, **don't** worry. I'd better do those myself.
M Well, what if **I carried** these heavy things downstairs for you?
C **As** long **as** you **don't** mind.
M Not at all. Then I'll pack up the computer and printer, if **you** like.
C Great. Then let's have something to eat and a cup of coffee.
M I'll help you make something **if you** like.
C No, it's OK, I've packed up all my kitchen stuff already. It**'d be easier if I got** a takeaway from the café.

Students practise the conversation in their pairs. Tell them to choose a role, Chloe or Mark. Encourage students to use natural sentence stress and weak forms.
Ask one or two pairs to role-play the conversations for the class.

EXTRA IDEA

• Students work in pairs, A and B. Student As write conversation A and Student Bs write conversation B. Tell students to swap papers and check each other's conversations. Then ask students to role-play their conversations.

6 Put students into pairs, Student A and Student B. Student As turn to SB p104 and Student Bs turn to SB p107.

a–b Students do the exercises on their own.
After students have been working for a few minutes, tell them to move on to **b** if they haven't already done so.

c Students work with their partner and take turns to discuss the situation in **a**. Ask Student A in each pair to begin the conversation by telling his/her partner about the situation in his/her own words. Students then continue the conversation by referring to their lists. Encourage students to use the ways of making, refusing and accepting offers from **3a** in their conversations.

Students then discuss Student B's situation in the same way. While students are working, monitor and correct students where necessary.

Finally, ask a few pairs to tell the class what they have agreed to do for their partners.

FURTHER PRACTICE

Ph **Class Activity** 3D Easy money! p157 (Instructions p135)
Extra Practice 3D SB p117
Self-study DVD-ROM Lesson 3D
Workbook Lesson 3D p19
Workbook Reading and Writing Portfolio 3 p68
Progress Test 3 p242

HELP WITH PRONUNCIATION
Stress and rhythm (1): conditionals

This *Help with Pronunciation* section focuses on the stress and rhythm in conditional sentences and reviews the pronunciation of weak forms and contractions.

1 Focus students on the sentences and the phonemes. Point out the pronunciation of *would you* (/wʊdʒə/) and *could have* (/kʊdəv/) in normal speech.

Also remind students that when a word ends in a vowel and is followed by another vowel, the words are linked by a /w/, /j/ or /r/ sound. Point out that in

the phrase *would you have, have* is a weak form, so starts with a vowel sound /ə/. The contraction of all three words therefore becomes /wʊdʒuːwəv/.

CD1 31 Play the recording. Students listen and practise the sentences. Make sure they copy the stress, weak forms and contractions correctly.

2 **a** **CD1** 32 Play the recording (SB p160). Students listen and write the answers to questions 1–4 in **1**.

b Students compare answers in pairs. Ask students to decide which words are stressed in the answers. Tell students to turn to **CD1** 32 SB p160 to check their answers.

1 I'd probably give a lot of it away to charity.
2 I think I'd choose the president of the USA.
3 I'd have chosen Alex.
4 I'd have met up with friends for coffee.

c Play the recording again. Students listen again and repeat the sentences.

3 Students work in pairs and practise the questions and answers in **1** and **2a**.

Finally, ask students to say one sentence each. Check they use the correct stress and pronounce the weak forms and contractions correctly, and praise good pronunciation.

continue2learn

Focus students on the *continue2learn* section on SB p31. See p35 for ideas on how to exploit this section.

Extra Practice 3
See p35 for ideas on how to exploit this section.

3A

2 **1** As long as the robbers couldn't hear me, I'd call the police. **2** Suppose you could work for any company in the world, which would you choose? I'd like to work for H&M, provided I could have free clothes. **3** Imagine you had the chance to learn a new skill, what would it be? If I could afford it, I'd learn to fly. **4** Supposing you were a journalist, who would you most like to interview?

I'd like to interview Prince William, providing I could ask him anything. **5** Would you live abroad if you had the chance? Yes, I'd live in Denmark if I could get a job there. **6** Do you suppose Ella would make me a jacket if I asked her? As long as you paid her for it, I think she would make you one.

3B
3 **2** commit **3** fine **4** send **5** charge **6** find **7** give **8** take
4 **2** had flown **3** could have **4** would you have got **5** wouldn't have come

3C
5 **2** on **3** about **4** to; for **5** about **6** after **7** on **8** of **9** to **10** in **11** with **12** against

3D
6 **1** b can manage c be wonderful **2** a you like b for offering c As long as **3** a it help b be better c don't mind **4** a Let me b be easier c 'd be

Progress Portfolio 3

• See p36 for ideas on how to exploit this section.

Vocabulary and Speaking
Phrasal verbs (1)

1 **a** Students work in pairs and try to guess the meanings of the phrasal verbs in bold. Tell students not to answer the questions themselves at this stage. Students check new words/phrases in **VOCABULARY 4.1** ▶ SB p134.

Check students understand the meaning of any new phrasal verbs.

Highlight that *turn out* is often followed by the infinitive with *to*, or (*that*) + clause: *The trip turned out to be rather exciting. It turns out that we went to the same school.*

Also highlight that we often use the preposition *from* with *run away* (*The man was running away from the police.*) and that *work out* is often followed by a question word (*I couldn't work out what was happening.*).

You can also point out that *turn out, go off, run away* and *come round* are type 1 phrasal verbs; *pass on, make up, run over, work out* and *knock out* are type 3 phrasal verbs; and *get away with* is a type 4 phrasal verb. Note that students studied the grammar of phrasal verbs in **face2face** Intermediate.

Phrasal verbs

There are four types of phrasal verb.

- type 1 phrasal verbs don't have an object: *Prices have gone up.*
- type 2 phrasal verbs always have an object. The object is always after the phrasal verb: *I came across some old photos. I came across them.*
- type 3 phrasal verbs always have an object. If the object is a noun, we can put it in the middle or after the phrasal verb: *I looked up the word. I looked the word up.* If the object is a pronoun, we must put it in the middle of the phrasal verb: *I looked it up.* not ~~I looked up it~~.
- type 4 phrasal verbs have three words and always have an object. The object is always after the phrasal verb: *I'm looking forward to the party. I'm looking forward to it.*

---

b Students do the activity in pairs.
Ask students to share interesting answers with the class.

Reading, Listening and Speaking

2 **a** Focus students on the pictures and the beginning of the article.

Students read the text and answer the questions. Students compare answers in pairs.

Check answers with the class. Also check that students can pronounce *urban legend* /ˈledʒənd/ correctly and explain that they are often called *urban myths* /mɪθs/.

Don't ask students to tell you any urban legends they know at this stage as students have the opportunity to do that at the end of the lesson.

An urban legend is a funny, surprising or scary story that is told again and again. People personalise them to make them sound more interesting or shocking. They are usually made up, but some of them are based on actual events.

┌─ **EXTRA IDEA** ─┐

- Students look at the pictures and predict what the urban legends are going to be. Elicit students' ideas, but don't tell them if they are correct at this stage. They can check their ideas when they listen in **3a**.

---

b Be prepared with definitions, examples, etc. to pre-teach the vocabulary or bring in a set of dictionaries for students to check the meanings themselves.

Note that the aim is to highlight which words/ phrases you need to pre-teach in order to help students understand the listening that follows. The vocabulary is not in the Language Summaries in the Student's Book.

Point out that we usually say *a bug* in American English and *an insect* in British English.

Model and drill the words.

3 **a** **CD1** ▶ 33 Play the recording (SB 161). Students listen and answer the questions.
Check answers with the class.

1a He was competing in the America's Cup yacht race. **b** No, it wasn't. **2a** Because they were a special make of cigar. **b** He smoked them. **3a** Her house was full of bugs. **b** She bought 19 'bug bombs' which are designed to spread insecticide over a wide area.

b Focus students on the prompts. Students do the activity in groups.

c Play the recording again. Students listen and check they got the details of the stories correct. Then they decide if they think the stories are true.
Students check their ideas on SB p114. Check answers with the class.

> The dead kangaroo story and the cigar story aren't true. The exploding house story is true.

HELP WITH GRAMMAR
Narrative verb forms; Past Perfect Continuous

4 **a–e** Students do the exercises on their own or in pairs, then check in **GRAMMAR 4.1** SB p135. Check answers with the class.

> **a** We use the **Past Simple** for completed actions in the past. These tell the main events of the story in the order that they happened (sentence 2).
> - We use the **Past Continuous** for a longer action that was in progress when another (shorter) action happened (sentence 3).
> - We also use the **Past Continuous** for background information that isn't part of the main story (sentence 1).
>
> **b** 4 *had been searching* Past Perfect Continuous; *bought* Past Simple 5 *made* Past Simple; *had lost* Past Perfect Simple
>
> **c** We usually use the **Past Perfect Simple** for an action that was completed before another action in the past (sentence 5).
> - We usually use the **Past Perfect Continuous** for a longer action that started before another action in the past (and often continued up to this past action) (sentence 4).
> - If necessary, go through the three diagrams in **GRAMMAR 4.1** SB p135 with the class.
>
> **d** Past Perfect Simple: subject + *had* or (*'d*) + **past participle**
> - Past Perfect Continuous: subject + *had* (or *'d*) + *been* + **verb+ing**
> - We make these verb forms negative by using *hadn't* instead of *had* or *'d*.
> - Elicit how we make the question forms of these verb forms:
> Past Perfect Simple: (question word) + *had* + subject + past participle.

> Past Perfect Continuous: (question word) + *had* + subject + *been* + verb+*ing*.
> - Go through the **TIPS** in the Language Summary with the class or ask students to read them for homework.

5 Focus on the example and highlight the weak forms of *had* /əd/ and *been* /bɪn/.
CD1 ▶ 34 PRONUNCIATION Play the recording (SB p161). Students listen and practise. Check students copy the stress and weak forms correctly.

6 Students do the exercise on their own. Note that *Monaghan* is pronounced /ˈmɒnəhən/. Students compare answers in pairs. Check answers with the class.

> 2 was crossing 3 hit 4 was getting 5 ran him over
> 6 drove 7 had been walking 8 stopped 9 called
> 10 helped 11 arrived 12 stepped 13 didn't realise
> 14 had been waiting
>
> Robert Monaghan had three accidents in one day.

7 Students do the exercise on their own, then compare answers in pairs. Check answers with the class.

> 1 I knew; had been trying (had tried) 2 called; was watching 3 hadn't been going out (hadn't gone out); proposed 4 got; realised; 'd/had left 5 arrived (had arrived); 'd/had already been waiting ('d/had already waited) 6 was walking; met; hadn't seen

Get ready ... Get it right!

8 Put students into pairs, Student A and Student B. Student As turn to SB p105 and Student Bs turn to SB p108.

a Students read their urban legends on their own. While they are working, monitor and help students with new vocabulary.

Tell students that they are going to tell their urban legend to their partners. Students write ten words/phrases from their urban legends on a piece of paper to help them remember the story.

b Ask students to close their books. Students work with their partners and take turns to tell each other their urban legends in their own words, using the words/phrases they wrote in **a** to help them.

Finally, ask students which of the urban legends in the lesson they thought was the best.

WRITING

If your students have Internet access, ask them to find another urban legend they didn't know and write about it for homework. Next class, students work in groups and take turns to tell each other their urban legends.

FURTHER PRACTICE

Ph **Class Activity** 4A Jack's story p159 (Instructions p135)
Extra Practice 4A SB p118
Self-study DVD-ROM Lesson 4A
Workbook Lesson 4A p20

4B First books
Student's Book p34–p35

Vocabulary books and reading
Grammar defining, non-defining and reduced relative clauses

QUICK REVIEW This activity reviews narrative verb forms. Write these prompts on the board: *the dead kangaroo; the cigar story; the exploding house; Robert Monaghan; the telephone bill; the dinner party.* Put students into pairs. Each pair chooses an urban legend from lesson 4A from the prompts. Students take turns to tell each other about the urban legends they have chosen.

Vocabulary and Speaking

Books and reading

1 Put students into pairs. Students say which words/phrases in bold they know, then check in **VOCABULARY 4.2** SB p134. Tell students not to answer the questions at this stage.

Check the meaning of new words/phrases with the class.

Check students understand the difference between *an author* and *a novelist*. Also check students understand *literary genre* by eliciting more types of genre from the class (science fiction, thrillers, historical novels, etc.). Explain that *chick* is a slang term for a woman that is often considered offensive when used outside the phrase *chick lit.* Highlight that *lit* is short for *literature.* Tell students that we can say *flick through* or *flip through.*

Model and drill the words/phrases, highlighting the pronunciation of *literary genre* /ˈlɪtərəri ˈʒɒnrə/, *blurb* /blɜːb/ and *browse* /braʊz/. Note that only the main stress in words/phrases is shown in vocabulary sections and the Language Summaries.

Students then ask and answer the questions in pairs. Ask students to share interesting answers with the class.

Reading and Speaking

2 **a** Focus students on the book covers. Ask if anyone in the class has read any of these books. If so, ask them to tell the class what they thought of it/them.

b Focus students on the texts on SB p34. Check students understand *walk somebody down the aisle* and *advance payment.*

Put students into pairs, Student A and Student B. Student As read about Cecelia Ahern and her first book and Student Bs read about Stephen King and his first book. All students answer questions 1–4 about their text.

c Students do the exercise in their pairs. Check answers with the class.

Suggested answers
Cecelia Ahern
1 She was born in 1981. She wrote her first book *PS, I Love You* in 2002 when she was 21. She got married in 2010. She is the daughter of a former Prime Minister of Ireland – Bertie Ahern. Her brother-in-law is Nicky Byrne, a member of the pop group Westlife. **2** *PS, I Love You* was a chick lit novel because it is about a young woman and her emotional life. **3** The main character is Holly. Her 30-year-old husband dies and leaves her a series of letters, which she has to open on the first day of each month. The letters encourage her to go on the trip of a lifetime. **4** She married her husband in 2008 in a surprise ceremony. They had been together for a long time.
Stephen King
1 He came from a very poor family and he began selling stories for 25 cents to friends at school when he was 12. His first book was published in 1973. **2** *Carrie* was a horror story because it's about someone who discovers she has psychic powers and uses them to seek revenge. **3** Carrie is a shy high-school girl who is bullied by the other students. She gets her revenge on the bullies by using her psychic powers to make them suffer. **4** His wife was responsible for getting *Carrie* published. Stephen King had thrown it away, but his wife found it in the bin and persuaded him to finish it.

EXTRA IDEA

- Students work on their own and make notes about the text they didn't read in **2b**. Put students into pairs. They cover the texts on SB p34 and take turns to tell each other about the story.

HELP WITH GRAMMAR
Defining, non-defining and reduced relative clauses

3 **a–f** Students do the exercises on their own or in pairs, then check in GRAMMAR 4.2 SB p136. Check answers with the class.

a **Defining** relative clauses give you essential information so that you know which person, thing, etc. the writer or speaker is talking about.
- **Non-defining** relative clauses add extra non-essential information.

b 1 In defining relative clauses we use *who* (or *that*) for people, *that* (or *which*) for things, *whose* for possessions, *where* for places and *when* for times. 2 We don't use commas with defining relative clauses.
- Remind students that we usually use *who* for people (but *that* is also correct) and *that* for things (but *which* is also correct).
- Point out that we can't use *what* in defining relative clauses: ~~Did you get the letter what I sent?~~. However, we can use *what* to mean 'the thing/things that': *Can you tell me what he said?*.

c In sentence 1 we must use *that* because it is the subject of the relative clause. In sentence 2 we can leave out *that* because it is the object of the relative clause (*Cecelia* is the subject).
- Focus students on the **TIPS** in the *Leaving out who, that, which, etc.* section of GRAMMAR 4.2 SB p136 or ask students to read these for homework.

d 1 No, we don't. 2 No, we can't. 3 Yes, we do.
- Point out that in non-defining relative clauses we also use *whose* for possessions, *where* for places and *when* for time.
- You can also highlight that in non-defining relative clauses *who* or *which* can also refer to a whole clause: *The book has dozens of characters, which can make the plot difficult to follow.* (*Which* refers to 'the fact that the book has dozens of characters'.)
- Point out that non-defining relative clauses are more common in written English than spoken English, particularly in stories and more formal types of writing.

e 1 Past Simple Passive: *was written* 2 Present Continuous: *are bullying*
- Establish that when a defining relative clause contains a continuous or passive verb form, we can often leave out *who, that* or *which* and the auxiliary.

4 **a** Students do the exercise on their own. Point out that they are looking for relative clauses that aren't already in blue or pink.

b Students compare answers in pairs. Check answers with the class.

Cecelia Ahern
… which is about Holly (non-defining); *… which he tells her to open* (non-defining); *… who is a former Prime Minister of Ireland* (non-defining); *who is a member of the famous pop group* (non-defining)
Stephen King
… which he sold for 25 cents (non-defining); *that has made King the most successful …* (defining); *… whose life is made miserable* (defining); *… that made King famous* (defining)

5 **a** Focus students on the book cover of *Girl with the Dragon Tattoo*. Check students understand *trilogy, anarchist, computer hacking* and that they remember *tattoo*.
Students do the exercise on their own. Ask students to read the text quickly for gist before they fill in the gaps.

b Students do the exercise in pairs. Check answers with the class.

1 which 2 who 3 whose 4 (that/which)
5 that/which 6 who 7 where 8 who 9 when

Reduced relative clause: *… Mikael Blomkvist, a journalist (who is) hired by an old man …*

> ┌ **EXTRA IDEA** ┐
> - Ask students which of the three books they would like to read (or read again), giving reasons for their answers.

6 Focus students on the example. Students do the exercise on their own, then compare answers in pairs. Check answers with the class.

2 This is the room where I wrote my first novel./ This is the room I wrote my first novel in.
3 Clive McCarthy, who was my English teacher, writes biographies now./Clive McCarthy, who writes biographies now, was my English teacher.
4 That's the woman whose first novel became a best-seller.
5 I threw out some books that/which I hadn't looked at in years.
6 I lost my copy of *Carrie*, which had been signed by the author.
7 I saw an old lady sitting outside the library./I saw an old lady who/that was sitting outside the library.
8 I found some old books in a box./I found some old books that/which were in a box.

> ┌ **EXTRA IDEA** ┐
> - Ask students which sentences contain defining relative clauses (1, 2, 4, 5), non-defining relative clauses (3 and 6) and reduced relative clauses (7 and 8).

Get ready ... Get it right!

7 Put students into two groups, Group A and Group B. Students in Group A turn to SB p105 and students in Group B turn to SB p108.

a Put students into pairs with someone from the same group. Students do the exercise in pairs. Tell all students to write the non-defining relative clauses and the ending to the story, as they will be working separately during the next stage of the activity.

EXTRA IDEA
- Ask students to take turns to read their story to their partners before doing **b**.

b Reorganise the class so that a student from Group A is working with a student from Group B. Students take turns to tell their stories to their partner.

Finally, ask one or two students to tell the class their stories. Ask the class to decide which story they think is the best.

WRITING

Students write a summary of their favourite book. Tell them to use the two texts on SB p34 as models. They should include information about the genre, the characters and the plot. Also ask them to write why they like the book.

FURTHER PRACTICE

Ph Class Activity 4B The book quiz p160 (Instructions p136)
Ph Vocabulary Plus 4 Descriptive verbs p197 (Instructions p191)
Extra Practice 4B SB p118
Self-study DVD-ROM Lesson 4B
Workbook Lesson 4B p21

4C	**VOCABULARY AND SKILLS**	**Very funny!** Student's Book p36–p37	**Vocabulary** connecting words: reason and contrast **Skills** Reading: a magazine article; Listening: an anecdote

QUICK REVIEW This activity reviews words/phrases connected to books and reading. Students do the first part of the exercise on their own. Put students into pairs to complete the activity. Ask students to tell the class one thing that they found out about their partner.

Speaking, Reading and Vocabulary

1 Check students understand *comedian* /kəˈmiːdiən/ and *a practical joke* (a joke that involves physical action rather than words).
Students discuss the questions in groups. Ask students to share interesting answers with the class.

2 a Focus students on the pictures and the first paragraph. Elicit what April Fool's Day is and when it is.

It's a day for playing practical jokes on each other; April 1st.

EXTRA IDEA
- Students work in pairs and discuss what they think the practical joke was in each picture. Elicit ideas for each picture, but don't tell students if they are correct at this stage.

b Check students understand *drip*, *whistle* and *nylon stocking*.
Students do the exercise on their own, then check in pairs. Check answers with the class.

1 Because the burger was rotated 180° so that the ketchup would drip out of the right side, not the left. 2 It would tell you when it was fully cooked. 3 It would make it possible to watch colour programmes on black and white TVs.
4 With Mental Plex, you would stare into the disc on the screen and create a mental image of what you wanted. With Gmail Motion, you would be able to control emails with body movements.

c Ask students to share any other April Fool's Day stories they know with the class.

HELP WITH VOCABULARY
Connecting words: reason and contrast

3 a–c Check students understand *expressing contrast* by telling students that *but* is an example of a connecting word that expresses contrast.
Students do the exercises on their own or in pairs, then check in **VOCABULARY 4.3** SB p134. Check answers with the class.

- **a** giving reasons *because; because of; since; due to; as*
- **expressing contrast** *however; apart from; instead of; despite; even though; whereas; nevertheless*
- Point out that we can also use these words/phrases for expressing contrast: *except for* (= *apart from*), *in spite of* (= *despite*), *although* (= *even though*).
- Check students can pronounce *although* /ɔːlˈðəʊ/ and *even though* /iːvən ðəʊ/ correctly.

b *Because, however, whereas, as, since, even though* and *nevertheless* are followed by a clause (subject + verb + ...).
- *Apart from, instead of, despite, due to* and *because of* are followed by a noun or verb+*ing*.
- Point out that after *due to* and *because of*, it is more common to use a noun than verb+*ing*.
- Establish that we use *however* and *nevertheless* to contrast two sentences. We usually put these words at the beginning of the second sentence.
- We use the other words/phrases in the table to contrast two clauses in the same sentence. We can put these words/phrases at the beginning or in the middle of the sentence.
- Point out that we can also say *in spite of/despite the fact that* + clause: *The ad fooled thousands of people, in spite of/despite the fact that it was published on April Fool's Day.*

4 **a** Students do the exercise on their own, then compare answers in pairs. Check answers with the class.

1 I've always wanted to go to Canada. However, I can't possibly afford it.
2 In spite of feeling tired, I went jogging in the park. / I went jogging in the park in spite of feeling tired.
3 Even though I'm fascinated by politics, I could never be a politician. / I could never be a politician, even though I'm fascinated by politics.
4 Whereas I love watching motor racing, my friend prefers watching basketball. / I love watching motor racing, whereas my friend prefers watching basketball.
5 I rarely stay up late as I have to get up at 7 a.m. every day. / As I have to get up at 7 a.m. every day, I rarely stay up late.
6 Due to the bad traffic, it took absolutely ages to get home last night. / It took absolutely ages to get home last night due to the bad traffic.
7 Instead of cooking, I sometimes just have a sandwich for supper. / I sometimes just have a sandwich for supper instead of cooking.

b Focus students on the connecting words in **3a** and the two example sentences. Students do the exercise on their own.

c Put students into pairs. Students take turns to tell each other their sentences. Encourage them to ask follow-up questions.

Listening and Speaking

5 **a** Be prepared with definitions, examples, etc. to pre-teach the vocabulary in the box or bring in a set of dictionaries for students to check the meanings themselves.

Point out that *tarmac* can be a noun and a verb.

b Tell students that they are going to listen to two colleagues, Gillian and Owen, discussing a funny personal story.
CD1 35 Give students time to read questions a–d, then play the recording (SB p161). Students listen and make notes.

Students compare notes in pairs. Check answers with the class.

Possible answers
a at Heathrow, going to an important meeting in Poland **b** she was reading emails on her iPad **c** she was trying to enter the plane through the door the ground crew use **d** the plane missed its slot and they had to wait another 45 minutes before take-off

c Play the recording again. Students listen, tick the true sentences and correct the false ones.

Students compare answers in pairs. Check answers with the class.

1✓ **2F** She had plenty of time. **3F** She went to the right gate number. **4✓** **5F** The door at the top was closed. **6F** She thought they were going to arrest her.

HELP WITH LISTENING
Predicting what comes next

This *Help with Listening* section focuses on words/phrases that we often use at the beginning of a sentence to prepare the listener for what we are going to say next.

6 **a** Focus students on the table. Use the example to show that when we hear a sentence that begins with *Actually*, we know that the speaker is going to correct something that the other person said.

Students do the exercise in pairs. Check answers with the class.

Point out that we can say *Luckily* or *Fortunately*, and that we often use *Unfortunately* (but not *Unluckily*) at the beginning of a sentence to prepare the listener for something bad or unfortunate.

1d 2c 3a 4b 5e 6i 7h 8f 9g

b ✍ Write the words/phrases 1–9 from the table on the board.
Students turn to **CD1** 35, SB p161. Play the recording again. Students listen and underline the words/phrases on the board when they hear them.

7 All students turn to SB p111.

a Students think of a story they can tell other students, using one of the ideas or their own. Students work on their own and make notes about the story.

b Students look at their notes from **a** and decide where they can use some of the words/phrases in the box in their story. Point out that they don't have to use all the words/phrases.

c Put students into groups. Students take turns to tell their stories.

Finally, ask students to decide which is the best story in the class.

EXTRA IDEA

- Each group decides which story is the most interesting or the funniest. Ask students to tell the class the most interesting or the funniest stories from their group.

WRITING

Students write their story for homework. These can be collected in next class and displayed around the classroom for other students to read.

FURTHER PRACTICE

Ph Class Activity 4C The island p161 (Instructions p136)

Extra Practice 4C SB p118

Self-study DVD-ROM Lesson 4C

Workbook Lesson 4C p23

▷ REAL
4D WORLD ▷ How was your day?
Student's Book p38–p39

Vocabulary ways of exaggerating
Real World saying you're surprised or not surprised

QUICK REVIEW This activity reviews connecting words. Give students a minute or two to think of a memorable evening that they have had. Put students into pairs. Students take turns to tell each other about their evening. Encourage each student to keep talking for two minutes if possible.

1 **a** Check students understand *exaggerate* /ɪɡˈzædʒəreɪt/, for example by referring to a local place and saying *I've been there millions of times*. Students do the exercise on their own or in pairs then check in **VOCABULARY 4.4** ▷ SB p134. Check answers with the class.

You can also teach the literal meanings of *stiff, starving, a fortune, a nightmare* and *a ton* /tʌn/ to help students understand the ways of exaggerating. Model and drill the sentences with appropriate intonation. Point out that our voices often rise when we are exaggerating.

1a 2f 3d 4b 5e 6c 7j 8l 9g 10i 11h 12k

b Students do the exercise on their own.

c Focus students on the examples. Students work in pairs and take turns to tell each other about their situations from **1b**.

Ask students to tell the class about any interesting or unusual situations they discussed.

2 **a** Focus students on the photo. Tell students that they are going to listen to Judy telling her husband, Martin, about her day.

VIDEO ▷4 **CD1** ▷ 36 Give students time to read the bullet points, then play the video or audio recording (SB p161). Students watch or listen and tick the things Judy talks about.

Check answers with the class. Don't go into too much detail about each point at this stage.

Judy talks about something they've bought recently; Judy's computer; a problem with their son; Judy's brother

b Play the video or audio recording again. Students watch or listen and make notes on the four things from **2a** that Judy talks about.

c Students compare notes in pairs. Check answers with the class.

something they've bought recently: Judy waited in all morning for the new TV to be delivered, but they never turned up. They didn't turn up last week either. She arranged for it to be delivered next Wednesday.

Judy's computer: Her laptop crashed while she was on the Internet. She thinks it's got a virus. She hadn't installed the anti-virus software.

a problem with their son: Jack's teacher phoned because he was caught fighting during the break. He said that the other boy started it.

Judy's brother: Her brother Eddy has found a job working in a bar in a ski resort. He hasn't been able to get an acting job.

REAL WORLD
Saying you're surprised or not surprised

3 **a–c** Students do the exercises on their own or in pairs, then check in **REAL WORLD 4.1** SB p136. Check answers with the class.

> **a** 1 believe 2 must 3 kidding 4 earth 5 news
> 6 honest 7 bet 8 no wonder 9 wouldn't
> 10 imagine
> - Point out that we can say *You're joking/kidding!* or *You must be joking/kidding!* and tell students that *kidding* is more informal.
> - Also highlight that we can also say *What/Who/ Where/How on earth ... ?*.
> - Teach students that we often use *Guess what!* to introduce surprising news.
>
> **b** 1 c and d 2 a and b
> - We often use **negative** auxiliaries in questions when we think we know the answer. The answer we expect can be *yes* or *no*, depending on the context.
> - Focus students on question a. Point out that Martin thinks the answer will be *yes* because he knows that Judy made the appointment with the TV delivery company.
> - Focus students on question b. Point out that Martin thinks the answer will be *no* because Judy thinks she has a virus on her laptop.

> **EXTRA IDEA**
> - Students turn to **CD1** 36, SB p161. Play the recording again. Students listen and underline all the ways of exaggerating and the ways of saying you're surprised and not surprised that they hear.

4 **CD1** 37 **PRONUNCIATION** Play the recording. Students listen and repeat the sentences. Check students copy the intonation correctly. Play the recording again if necessary.

5 Students do the exercise on their own, then check their answers in pairs.
Check answers with the class.

> 1 news 2 moon 3 can 4 wonder 5 kidding/joking
> 6 wasn't 7 surprised 8 honest 9 bet 10 Aren't
> 11 joking/kidding 12 fortune

6 Students do the exercise on their own, then compare answers in pairs. Check answers with the class.
The key shows the wrong responses.

> 1 I'm not surprised, to be honest. 2 Yes, I can imagine. 3 Wow, that's fantastic news. 4 Why on earth are they doing that? 5 Why on earth are you cold?

7 **a** Students do the exercise on their own. Ask students to think of at least four good or bad things that have happened to them today. Tell them to use the ideas given or their own ideas.

b Students work in pairs and take turns to tell each other about their day. Encourage students to use language from **1a** and **3a** in their conversations. Finally, ask students to tell the class the best or worst thing that happened to their partner.

> **FURTHER PRACTICE**
>
> **Extra Practice** 4D SB p118
> **Self-study DVD-ROM** Lesson 4D
> **Workbook** Lesson 4D p24
> **Workbook Reading and Writing Portfolio** 4 WB p70
> **Progress Test** 4 p244

HELP WITH PRONUNCIATION
Stress and rhythm (2): auxiliaries

This *Help with Pronunciation* section gives further practice in strong and weak forms, focusing on auxiliaries.

1 Focus students on the words.
CD1 38 Play the recording (SB p162). Students listen and repeat the strong and weak forms of the auxiliaries in the list. Point out that the strong form is said first.

> **EXTRA IDEA**
> - If students need help remembering how to pronounce each word, tell them to look at the table in **CD1** 38 on SB p162.

2 **a** Focus students on the auxiliaries in the conversation. Point out that the weak forms are in pink and the strong forms are in blue.
CD1 39 Play the recording. Students listen and notice the weak and strong forms.
Students do the exercise on their own or in pairs. Check answers with the class.

> We stress auxiliaries: in question tags; in short answers; in echo questions; to add emphasis.

b Students work in pairs and practise the conversation in **2a**.
Finally, ask students to role-play the conversation to the class. Check they use the correct strong and weak forms of the auxiliaries, and praise good pronunciation.

continue2learn

Focus students on the *continue2learn* section on SB p39. See p35 for ideas on how to exploit this section.

Extra Practice 4

See p35 for ideas on how to exploit this section.

4A

1 **2** Pass on **3** make up **4** knocked out; came round **5** went off **6** get away with **7** work out **8** turned out **9** ran over

2 I heard an explosion; I nearly called; I ran out; what was happening; got outside; saw; if he was; hadn't realised; when it hit

4B

3 **2** author **3** paperback **4** browsing **5** flick through **6** literary genre **7** novelist **8** chick lit **9** contents page

4 **2** who/that **3** whose **4** who **5** when **6** who **7** where **8** whose **9** who/that

4C

5 **2** Instead of **3** ✓ **4** ✓ **5** Despite/In spite of **6** Although

4D

6 I'm over the moon.; She's scared stiff.; I'm going out of my mind.; Their house cost a fortune.; This suitcase weighs a ton.; It takes forever.; This problem is a nightmare.

7 **2** wonder (NS) **3** earth **4** wouldn't (NS) **5** imagine (NS) **6** kidding **7** bet (NS) **8** news **9** must

Progress Portfolio 4

- See p36 for ideas on how to exploit this section.

QUICK REVIEW This activity reviews ways of saying you're surprised or not surprised. Students do the first part of the activity on their own. Put students into pairs. Students take turns to tell each other their interesting or surprising things and respond by saying they are surprised or not surprised, as in the example. Encourage students to ask follow-up questions if possible. Ask students to tell the class the most interesting or surprising thing their partners told them.

Vocabulary Common adjectives

1 Students work in pairs and check the new words in VOCABULARY 5.1 ▶ SB p137.

Point out that the opposite of *suitable* and *faithful* are *unsuitable* and *unfaithful*. Also point out that you can use *addictive* to describe somebody's personality, meaning that they are easily addicted to things.

Model and drill the words, highlighting the pronunciation of *eager* /ˈiːgə/, *enthusiastic* /ɪnθjuːzɪˈæstɪk/, *rare* /reə/, *fierce* /fɪəs/, *outrageous* /aʊˈtreɪdʒəs/, *weird* /wɪəd/ and *exotic* /ɪgˈzɒtɪk/.

Note that only the main stress in words/phrases is shown in vocabulary boxes and the Language Summaries.

Students take turns to tell each other which of the statements they agree/disagree with. Encourage them to give reasons for their answers. Ask students to share interesting information with the class.

Speaking and Reading

2 **a** Check students understand *a pool* and *jewels* /ˈdʒuːəlz/ and check students have heard of Freddie Mercury (he was the lead singer of the rock group Queen, and he died in 1991).

Focus students on the photos and ask students what type of fish they are (they are called *koi* /kɔɪ/, which is the Japanese word for *carp*). Note that *koi* is both a singular and a plural word.

Students read the article and answer the questions. Check answers with the class.

> **1** Because they're extremely beautiful and very expensive. **2** No, he didn't, because he thought they were too expensive.

b Students do the exercise on their own.
Students check answers in pairs. Check answers with the class.

> a2 b1 c5 d6 e4

EXTRA IDEA

- Ask the class if they would like to own some koi, giving reasons for their answers. Ask students how much they would be prepared to pay for a koi.

HELP WITH GRAMMAR
Ways of comparing

3 **a–d** Students do the exercises on their own or in pairs, then check in GRAMMAR 5.1 ▶ SB p138. Check answers with the class.

> **a** **a big difference:** *far (more addictive) than, nowhere near as (high) as, considerably (less) than, not nearly as (exotic) as, a great deal (cheaper) than*
> - **a small difference:** *almost as (much) as, nearly as (expensive) as, slightly (bigger) than, not quite as (enthusiastic) as*
> - **no difference:** *as (beautiful) as, not any (nicer) than, no more (time-consuming) than*
> - Point out that *considerably* and *a great deal* are more formal than the other phrases. Check students can pronounce *slightly* /ˈslaɪtli/ correctly.
> - Tell students that we can also say *not anywhere (near) as* to talk about a big difference: *The normal price isn't anywhere near as high as that.*
> - Remind students that we can also use *much/a lot* with comparatives to talk about a big difference and *a bit/a little* to talk about a small difference.
>
> **b** We use comparatives with *than*: *They're slightly bigger than the ones I've got.*
> - We use adjectives with *as … as*: *The normal price is nowhere near as high as that.*
> - Go through the other **TIPS** in GRAMMAR 5.1 ▶ SB p138 with the class or ask students to read them for homework.
>
> **c** **1** twice as big as **2** is getting more and more lucrative; was getting better and better **3** The more I learned about koi, the more interested I became; the bigger they are, the more they cost.
> - Use the example from the article to establish that we can use *twice/three times, four times,* etc. + *as … as* to compare two things: *The koi were only about **twice as big as** my goldfish.*
> - To describe something that continuously changes we can use *get + more (and more) +* adjective for long adjectives and *get + comparative + and + comparative* for short adjectives.
> - We can use *the + comparative/more … , the + comparative/more …* to say that one thing depends on the other.
> - Teach students the common phrase *the sooner, the better* (= *as soon as possible*).

4 Focus students on the example and point out the linking and the weak form of *as* /əz/.
CD2 ▶ 1 PRONUNCIATION Play the recording (SB p162). Students listen and repeat the sentences. Check students copy the linking and the weak forms correctly. Note that not all the phrases in the article are included in the recording.

You can also ask students to turn to CD2 ▶ 1, SB p162. They can then copy the sentence stress, linking and weak forms as they listen and repeat.

5 If necessary, check students understand *destructive* and *be likely to do something*.
Students do the exercise on their own, then compare answers in pairs. Check answers with the class.

1 than 2 near 3 as 4 great 5 more 6 likely 7 far
8 considerably 9 the 10 and 11 nearly 12 no
13 than

┌─ EXTRA IDEAS ─┐

- Students discuss which animals make the best pets. Encourage students to give reasons, using language from **3a** if possible.
- Alternatively, ask each student to decide which animal makes the best pet. Put students into groups. Students share ideas and try to convince the rest of the group that their pet is the best, using language from **3a**.

┌─ WRITING ─┐

Students write a text comparing two pets using the text in **5** as a model. They shouldn't write about cats and dogs.

6 Focus students on the example and check students understand what they have to do.
Students do the exercise on their own, then compare answers in pairs. Check answers with the class.

2 Looking after children is far more time-consuming than looking after animals. 3 Teenagers are nowhere near as affectionate as young children. 4 People now live twice as long as they did in the past. 5 Working for someone else isn't nearly as rewarding as being self-employed. 6 Unemployment figures are slightly higher than they were last month.

7 a Students do the exercise on their own. While they are working, monitor and check their sentences for accuracy.

b Students compare sentences in pairs and decide if they agree with their partner's sentences.
Ask each pair to share one or two of their sentences with the class.

┌─ EXTRA IDEA ─┐

- Elicit a complete sentence for 1 in **7a**, for example, *The older you get, the less you worry.* Ask students to continue the 'sentence chain' for as long as possible, for example, *The less you worry, the better you sleep. The better you sleep, the more energy you have.*, etc. Students work in pairs and make 'sentence chains' for their sentences 2–5 in **7a**.

Get ready ... Get it right!

8 a Put students into pairs. Ask each pair to choose two places, two people or two things that they both know well.

b Students work on their own and write at least five sentences comparing the places, people or things they chose in **8a**, as in the example. Encourage students to use language from **3a** in their sentences. Students are not allowed to talk to their partner during this stage of the activity.

9 a Students work with their partner from **8a**. Students take turns to say their sentences. If their partner doesn't agree, he/she must explain why not, again using language from **3a** if possible.

b Finally, ask each pair to tell the class two things that they disagreed about.

┌─ FURTHER PRACTICE ─┐

Ph **Class Activity** 5A Comparisons board game p162 (Instructions p136)
Extra Practice 5A SB p119
Self-study DVD-ROM Lesson 5A
Workbook Lesson 5A p25

5B ▶ Royal treasures
Student's Book p42–p43

Vocabulary phrasal verbs (2)
Grammar future verb forms; Future Continuous

QUICK REVIEW This activity reviews ways of comparing. Students do the first part of the activity on their own. Put students into pairs. Students take turns to say their sentences and guess if their partner's sentences are true or false. Ask a few students to tell the class something that they found out about their partner.

Vocabulary and Speaking
Phrasal verbs (2)

1 a Students work in pairs and say which words they know, then check in **VOCABULARY 5.2** ▶ SB p137. Check answers with the class.

Point out that *cheer up*, *pass by*, *talk into* and *put out* are all Type 3 phrasal verbs; *catch up with* and *fit in with* are Type 4 phrasal verbs; and *go ahead* is a Type 1 phrasal verb. If students need a reminder about the four types of phrasal verbs, go through the information on p137.

Model and drill the words, highlighting the pronunciation of *cheer* /tʃɪə/.

b Students take turns to ask and answer the questions in **1a**. Encourage students to ask follow-up questions if possible. Ask students to share interesting information with the class.

Reading, Listening and Speaking

2 **a** Focus students on photos A and B. Ask them if they know either of the places and why they think they are popular tourist destinations (A is Windsor Castle, B is Eton College). Elicit ideas, but don't confirm their answers at this point.

b Put students into pairs, A and B. Student As read text A about Windsor Castle and Student Bs read text B about Eton College. Students answer the questions about their text. Don't check answers yet.

c Students take turns to tell their partner about the place they read about. Tell them to use the answers to the questions in **2b** to help them. Check answers with the class.

Ask students to say which place they'd prefer to visit and give reasons for their answer.

Windsor Castle:
1 It's almost 1,000 years old. 2 It was the Official Residence of the Royal Family. Its purpose hasn't changed. 3 The Royal Family. 4 Almost every day of the year. Visitors should check opening arrangements before they visit because it's a working royal palace and times may change.
Eton College:
1 It's nearly 600 years old. It was founded in 1440. 2 It was a school. It was originally founded to provide free education for 70 scholars. Its purpose hasn't changed, although the education is no longer free. 3 Princes William and Harry and 19 British prime ministers. 4 Between April and October. Visitors should check that the school is open before visiting, as it is sometimes closed to visitors.

┌─ **EXTRA IDEA** ─┐

• Students work on their own and underline three words/phrases in the text that they would like to know the meaning of. Students work in pairs and help each other with the meanings of the words/phrases they chose.

3 **a** Tell students that they are going to listen to a phone conversation between two friends, Zoe and Abby.
CD2 2 Play the recording (SB p162). Students listen and answer the questions. Check answers with the class.

Zoe and Abby are friends. Rick is Zoe's husband and Alice is Zoe's daughter.

b Focus on the bullet points. Check students understand what *a cheap deal* is.
Play the recording again. Students do the exercise on their own.

c Students compare answers in pairs. Check answers with the class.

• Alice didn't do much preparation for her exams, so Zoe thinks she's going to fail some of them.
• Zoe, Rick and Alice are going to Windsor for a holiday. Rick found a cheap deal for a bed and breakfast on the Internet, which isn't easy during school holidays as Windsor is packed out.
• Rick isn't keen on visiting Windsor Castle, but he really wants to go to Eton College.
• Abby has been on a tour of Eton College before, but she'd love to go again.
• Zoe will be passing by Abby's house on the way to Eton, so they'll call by and pick her up.

HELP WITH GRAMMAR
Future verb forms; Future Continuous

4 **a–b** Students do the exercises on their own or in pairs, then check in the **Future verb forms** section of **GRAMMAR 5.2** SB p138. Check answers with the class.

a b 're staying c 'll go ahead d starts e 's going to fail f 'll enjoy

b a be going to b Present Continuous c will d Present Simple e be going to f will
• Go through the **TIPS** in the **Future verb forms** section of **GRAMMAR 5.2** SB p138 with the class or ask students to read them for homework.

c–f Students do the exercises on their own or in pairs, then check in the **Future Continuous** section of **GRAMMAR 5.2** SB p138. Check answers with the class.

c a 'll be walking b 'll be passing
• Use sentence 2 to highlight that we use the **Future Continuous** for something that will be in progress at a point of time in the future. If students are having problems with this meaning, refer them to the diagram in **GRAMMAR 5.2** SB p138.
• Use sentence 1 to show students that we also use the **Future Continuous** for something that will happen in the normal course of events, without any particular plan or intention.

- Point out that for this meaning there is often very little difference between the Future Continuous and the Present Continuous: *Don't call me in the morning, I'll be working/I'm working then.*

d We make the Future Continuous with: subject + *will* or *'ll* + *be* + verb+*ing*.

e Establish that we make the negative form of the Future Continuous with: **subject + *won't* + *be* + verb+*ing***.

- Also highlight that we make questions with the Future Continuous with: **(question word) + *will* + subject + *be* + verb+*ing***.

- Remind students that as with other continuous verb forms, we don't usually use state verbs with the Future Continuous.

5 **CD2** **3** **PRONUNCIATION** Play the recording (SB p162). Students listen and repeat the sentences. Check students copy the stress correctly.

6 **a** Remind students of Zoe, the woman who is going to Windsor with her family.
Focus students on her conversation with her husband, Rick.
Students do the exercise on their own.

b Students compare answers in pairs. Encourage students to explain why they have chosen each verb form by referring back to the rules in **4a** and **4c**.

c **CD2** **4** Play the recording (SB p162). Students listen and check their answers. Check answers with the class.

1 She's coming 2 are we going 3 I'm going to buy
4 Will you be seeing 5 I'll be seeing 6 I'll ask
7 I'll call 8 starts 9 We're going to miss 10 she'll be
11 I'll be playing 12 I'll call

7 **a** Students work on their own and write sentences about their plans and arrangements for the next few weeks, as in the examples. Encourage students to use *be going to*, the Present Continuous, the Present Simple or the Future Continuous in their sentences. While they are working, monitor and check their sentences for accuracy.

b Put students into pairs. Students take turns to tell each other their sentences and ask follow-up questions.
Ask students to tell the class about their plans and arrangements.

WRITING

Students write a longer text about their plans and arrangements for the next couple of weeks. Encourage them to use information from the follow-up questions in **7b** so that they don't just write a list of sentences.

Get ready ... Get it right!

8 Check students understand *scientific advances* (improvements and new discoveries in science).

Students do the exercise on their own.

EXTRA IDEA

- With a lower-level class you can ask students to write complete sentences instead of notes.

9 **a** Students discuss their ideas in groups, giving reasons for their opinions where possible. Encourage students to use *be going to*, *will* or the Future Continuous in their conversations.

While they are working, monitor and correct any mistakes you hear.

b Finally, ask students to tell the class two things their group agreed about.

FURTHER PRACTICE

Ph **Vocabulary Plus** 5 Geographical features p198 (Instructions p191)
Extra Practice 5B p119
Self-study DVD-ROM Lesson 5B
Workbook Lesson 5B p26

VOCABULARY
5C AND SKILLS **The nature of cities**
Student's Book p44–p45

Vocabulary guessing meaning from context
Skills Reading: a newspaper article; Listening: an interview

QUICK REVIEW This activity reviews future verb forms. Students do the first part of the activity on their own. Put students into pairs. Students take turns to tell each their sentences. Encourage them to ask follow-up questions if possible. Ask students to share interesting ideas with the class.

Speaking and Reading

1 Students do the exercise in groups.
Ask groups to present their list to the class and discuss any problems or threats the animals present to humans.

- With a lower-level class you could elicit names for wild animals and write them on the board before students do the activity. Students then use the words to help them identify wild animals that live in towns and cities.

2 **a** Put students into pairs. Focus students on the photo of David Stead and the questions. Students discuss the questions in their pairs. Ask students to share interesting ideas with the class, but don't confirm if they're correct or not at this point.

b Focus students on the article on SB p45. Students read the article and check their answers to the questions in **2a**.

Tell students not to worry if they don't understand every word in the article. They will do work on guessing meaning from context in **3**.

Check answers with the class.

> 1 The bird is a falcon. 2 David is in Dubai.
> 3 He's about to fly his falcon to scare away pigeons.

c Students work in the same pairs and add extra information to their answers from **2a**. Check answers with the class.

Possible answers
1 Falcons are bird hunters and they can reach amazing speeds of 280 kph as they dive towards their prey. They have very good eyesight and they think visually.
2 Dubai is a city in the desert. It has lots of towers of concrete, steel and glass. There are many businesses and hotels in Dubai.
3 David uses falcons to scare pigeons away from the buildings as each bird produces 12 kg of droppings a year. They would eat away at the buildings if nothing was done about the pigeons. David doesn't lose many of the birds because they have transmitters clipped to their backs.

EXTRA IDEAS

- You could do **2c** as a class activity. Write the three areas on the board: *falcon, city, David's job*. Students find information in the text about the three areas and make notes. Ask students to tell the class one piece of information for each area and write it on the board under the correct heading.
- With a lower-level class, give students more help by asking questions, for example: *Why does David use falcons to keep pigeons away? How fast can falcons fly? Why don't the falcons hurt the birds they chase? How does David make sure he doesn't lose any birds?*

HELP WITH VOCABULARY
Guessing meaning from context

3 **a–b** Discuss the importance of being able to guess meaning from context with the class.
Focus students on the words/phrases in blue in the article. Students do the exercises on their own or in pairs, then check in **VOCABULARY 5.3** SB p137.

- 1 adjective; a 2 adjective; b 3 phrasal verb; a 4 adjective; a 5 verb; a 6 verb; b 7 noun; a
- Model and drill the words/phrases. Pay particular attention to the pronunciation of *unsightly* /ʌn'saɪtli/, *flourish* /'flʌrɪʃ/ and *prey* /preɪ/.

c–d Focus students on the words in pink in the article. Students do the exercise in pairs, then check in **VOCABULARY 5.3** SB p137. Check answers with the class.

- See **VOCABULARY 5.3** SB p137 for definitions and the parts of speech of the words/phrases in pink.
- Model and drill the words/phrases. Pay particular attention to the pronunciation of *exploit* /ɪk'splɔɪt/ and *aviary* /'eɪviəri/.

Listening and Speaking

4 **a** Put students into pairs. Tell students they are going to listen to an interview with a television producer about urban foxes.
If *foxes* didn't come up in students' lists in **1**, use the photo to check students understand *urban fox*.
CD2 5 Play the recording (SB p162). Students listen and answer the questions.

> 1 She saw a pair of foxes playing with their cubs in her garden in London. 2 She was surprised as she hadn't expected to see wild animals in London. She thought they were cute. 3 Some people treated them as potential pets; others saw them as a health hazard.

EXTRA IDEA

- Students work in the same pairs. Before students listen again, ask them to make notes about Rachel and her attitude to foxes – before and after she made the documentary. Put pairs of students together into groups of four to check their notes. Then play the recording for students to listen and check.

b Play the recording again. Students listen again and tick the true sentences and correct the false ones. Check answers with the class.

> 1 ✓ 2 F Some people fed the foxes. 3 ✓ 4 F Foxes don't like the scent of lion dung. 5 ✓ 6 F Foxes have been known to occasionally go into people's homes.

HELP WITH LISTENING
Homophones

This *Help with Listening* section introduces students to homophones, which are very common in spoken English, and helps students to recognise some homophones in context.

5 **a** Focus students on the introductory bullet and check that they understand what a homophone is. Students do the exercise on their own. Check answers with the class.

> 1 Whether 2 find 3 know 4 there

b Ask students to look at the pairs of homophones 1–10. Check students understand the meanings of all the words.
Tell students that they are going to listen to ten sentences from the interview.
CD2▸ 6 Play the recording (SB p163). Students listen and choose the correct words, a or b. Check answers with the class.

> 1 saw 2 principle 3 would 4 meat 5 your 6 here
> 7 no 8 scent 9 through 10 sight

c Students do the exercise in pairs.

> ┌─ **EXTRA IDEA** ─────────────────────────┐
> • You can make this activity into a game by setting a time limit of three minutes. The pair with the most homophones wins.

🖉 Elicit students' answers and write them on the board for other students to copy.

Possible answers
ad/add; allowed/aloud; aren't/aunt; ate/eight; band/banned; be/bee; bean/been; blew/blue; board/bored; dear/deer; fair/fare; hi/high; knows/nose; lead/led; one/won; right/write; road/rode; rose/rows; steal/steel; sweet/suite; to/too/two; wait/weight

6 Students discuss the questions in groups. Finally, ask students to share interesting information with the class.

> ┌─ **WRITING** ─────────────────────────────┐
> Students choose one wild animal that lives in towns and cities. Tell them to make notes about where it lives and how it survives, and to make a list of advantages and disadvantages of having the animal in towns. They could use their answers to the questions in **6** to help them. Students then use their notes to write a short article about the animal.

> ┌─ **FURTHER PRACTICE** ────────────────────┐
> **Ph** **Class Activity** 5C Homophone snap p163 (Instructions p137)
> **Ph** **Study Skills** 2 Mind maps p229 (Instructions p225)
> **Extra Practice** 5C SB p118
> **Self-study DVD-ROM** Lesson 5C
> **Workbook** Lesson 5C p28

▷ REAL WORLD
5D WORLD ▶ Carbon footprints
Student's Book p46–p47

Vocabulary adjectives for giving opinions
Real World discussion language (2): opinions

QUICK REVIEW This activity reviews homophones. Students do the first part of the activity on their own. Put students into pairs. Students take turns to say their pairs of sentences and their partner spells each homophone. Ask students to share a few pairs of sentences with the class.

1 **a** Students do the exercise in pairs, then check in **VOCABULARY 5.4 ▶** SB p137.
Check students understand the meanings of any new words.
🖉 Also check the opposites of the adjectives in B by eliciting them from students and writing them on the board. You could also point out that the word *amoral* /eɪˈmɒrəl/ also exists, but that this means someone who doesn't care whether their behaviour is morally right or not.

Point out that the words in A don't have direct opposites. Establish that *damage* /ˈdæmɪdʒ/ and *waste* are both verbs and uncountable nouns. Model and drill the words, highlighting the pronunciation of *damaging* /ˈdæmɪdʒɪŋ/, *ethical* /ˈeθɪkəl/, *legal* /ˈliːgəl/ and *justifiable* /dʒʌstɪˈfaɪəbəl/.
Also model and drill the opposites of the words in B. Point out that the prefixes (*im-*, *un-*, etc.) aren't usually stressed.

> moral – immoral; ethical – unethical;
> legal – illegal; sustainable – unsustainable;
> justifiable – unjustifiable

b Students do the exercise in pairs.

c Focus students on the example. Students compare ideas in pairs and say whether they agree or disagree with their partner's statements, giving reasons for their opinions if possible.
Ask students to share interesting ideas with the class.

2 a Ask the class what they think a 'carbon footprint' is and what things might increase it. Elicit students' ideas. Students read the web page and check their ideas. Check the answer with the class.

> The following things increase our carbon footprint: the type of food we buy, the amount of travelling we do, the amount of rubbish we throw away, how much energy we consume.

b Students work in groups and make a list of different ways people could reduce their carbon footprints, as in the examples.

✍ Elicit ideas from the class and write them on the board in preparation for the listening activity. Students can also decide which are the most useful ideas.

3 a Tell students that they are going to watch or listen to two friends, Tony and Eddy, discussing carbon footprints.

VIDEO ▸5 CD2 ▸ 7 Play the video or audio recording (SB p163). Students watch or listen and decide which of the ideas on the board the two people talk about. Check answers with the class.

> **Tony and Eddy talk about** recycling (newspapers, packaging, etc.); saving energy (turning off the TV); buying food that is produced locally; avoiding food with too much packaging; becoming a vegetarian

b Play the video or audio recording again. Students watch or listen and do the exercise on their own. Don't check answers at this stage.

c Students compare answers in pairs. Check answers with the class.
Ask the class whether they agree with Tony's ideas, giving reasons for their answers.

> 1a 2b 3a 4c 5c 6c

REAL WORLD
Discussion language (2): opinions

4 a–b Students do **4a** on their own, then check in **REAL WORLD 5.1 ▸** SB p139. Check answers with the class.

- **a** giving opinions **b** giving the opposite opinion **c** clarifying your position **d** giving yourself time to think
- Go through the phrases with the class and check students understand them all.

EXTRA IDEA

- Students work in pairs and think of ways to agree or disagree politely with someone (these were taught in lesson 2D). Set a time limit of two minutes. Students check their ideas in **REAL WORLD 5.1 ▸** SB p139.

5 Students do the exercise on their own, then compare their answers in pairs. Check answers with the class.

> TONY I think people **should** leave their cars at home more often.
> EDDY Maybe, but **I don't** see **how** you **can** ask everyone to give up their cars.
> T No, that's **not** what **I'm trying to** say. What I **meant was** people **should** use public transport if they can.
> E Fair **enough**, but **I** still think a lot of people prefer to drive.
> T All **I'm saying is** that cars are a big environmental problem.
> E Yes, but **then** again, public transport is expensive.
> T I know, but it'd **be** better **if we thought** about how much transport costs the planet, not just ourselves.
> E That's **an** interesting point. I've never really **thought** about **that**.

6 a Check students understand the six topics. Students work on their own and think of two things to say about each topic.

b Students work in groups and discuss the topics in **6a**. Remind students to use the language in **4a** in their discussion.

c Finally, ask each group to tell the class which topic was the most controversial and why.

EXTRA IDEA

- If students have access to the Internet, ask them to work out their carbon footprint online for homework (on an English-language website if possible). Students can compare their footprints in the next class.

FURTHER PRACTICE

Ph Class Activity 5D The congestion charge p164 (Instructions p137)
Extra Practice 5B SB p118
Self-study DVD-ROM Lesson 5D
Workbook Lesson 5D p29
Workbook Reading and Writing Portfolio 5 p72
Progress Test 5 p246

HELP WITH PRONUNCIATION
Sounds (2): the letters *our*

This *Help with Pronunciation* section focuses on the different ways of pronouncing the letters *our*.

1 **a** Focus students on the words and phonemes in the chart.

CD2▸8 Play the recording. Students listen to the words and notice the pronunciation of the letters in pink, then write them in the table.
Check answers with the class.

/ɜː/ journalist	/ə/ flavour	/ʌ/ encourage
/ɔː/ courtroom	/aʊə/ our	

b Play the recording again. Students listen and repeat the words. Elicit that we use the schwa (/ə/) when *our* is not stressed.

If students are having problems with the different *our* sounds, help them with the mouth position.

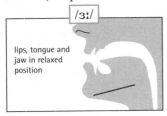

Point out that when we make the /ɜː/ sound, the lips, tongue and jaw are all in a relaxed position. It is a long vowel sound.

lips, tongue and jaw in relaxed position

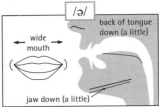

back of tongue down (a little)
wide mouth
jaw down (a little)

Remind students that /ə/ is a weak sound – it is not stressed. When we make the /ə/ sound, the tongue and lips are relaxed.

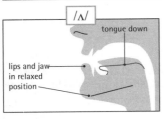

tongue down
lips and jaw in relaxed position

Point out that /ʌ/ is a short sound. When we make this sound, the lips and jaw are relaxed and the tongue is down.

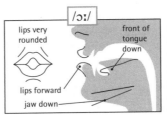

/ɔː/
lips very rounded
front of tongue down
lips forward
jaw down

/ɔː/ is a long vowel sound. When we make this sound, the lips are forward, the jaw and the front of the tongue are down, and the lips are very rounded.

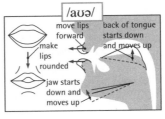

/aʊə/
move lips forward
make lips rounded
back of tongue starts down and moves up
jaw starts down and moves up

When we make the sound /aʊə/, we move from the long vowel sound /aʊ/ to a schwa sound /ə/. To make the /aʊ/ sound, we start with the mouth open, then round the lips and move them forward. The jaw and the back of the tongue start down and move up.

2 **a** Students do the exercise in pairs.

b **CD2▸9** Play the recording (SB p163). Students listen and check their answers.
Play the recording again. Students listen again and repeat the words.

/ɜː/ journey; courtesy; journal
/ə/ favour; humour; neighbour
/ʌ/ courage; flourish; nourishment
/ɔː/ course; pour; fourth
/aʊə/ flour; hour; sour

3 Students do the exercise in pairs.
Finally, ask students to say a sentence. Check students say the *our* sounds correctly, and praise good pronunciation.

continue2learn

Focus students on the *continue2learn* section on SB p47. See p35 for ideas on how to exploit this section.

Extra Practice 5

See p35 for ideas on how to exploit this section.

5A
1 2 rewarding 3 faithful 4 harmless 5 weird
6 destructive 7 lucrative 8 exotic 9 eager
10 addictive
2 2 the 3 near 4 than 5 more 6 more 7 busier 8 deal

5B
3 2 into 3 by 4 up 5 out 6 in 7 ahead 8 up on
4 2 ~~I'll see~~ I'm seeing 3 ~~I'll be buying~~ I'll buy 4 ~~I see~~ I'm seeing 5 ~~I'm seeing~~ I'll see 6 ~~I'm calling~~ I'll call

5C
5 2b 3b 4a 5b 6a 7b 8b 9a 10a

5D
6 2 Maybe, but I don't see how we can do that.
3 Fair enough, but I still think Lucy's got a point. 4 Well, one argument for keeping him is he's good with clients. 5 Well, some people would argue that's not true. 6 No, that's not what I'm trying to say. 7 What I meant was he socialises with them a lot. 8 Yes, but then again, he doesn't get much business from them. 9 I've never really thought about that before. 10 I just don't think it's right that we fire him now. 11 It's hard to say.

Progress Portfolio 5

• See p36 for ideas on how to exploit this section.

QUICK REVIEW This activity reviews language for discussion and opinions. Check students understand *cosmetic surgery* /ˈsɜːdʒəri/. Students do the activity in groups of three. You can ask students to look at REAL WORLD 5.1 ▶ SB p139 if they need reminding of the language they need for the activity. Ask students to share some of their opinions with the class.

Vocabulary and Speaking
Phrases with *take*

1 Students work on their own and say which of the phrases in **bold** they know, then check in VOCABULARY 6.1 ▶ SB p140.

Check students understand the meaning of any new phrases.

Highlight the prepositions in *take responsibility for, take someone for granted, take something out on somebody, take an interest in, take notice of* and *take advantage of*.

Point out that we can also *take something for granted*: *In this country we take clean water for granted*. Also highlight that we can also *take somebody's side* in an argument: *Whenever my mother and I argue, my father always takes her side*.

Also point out that we usually use *it* in *take it out on somebody*, but we can also use a noun and *something*, for example: *He took his frustration out on the ball*.

Model and drill the phrases, highlighting the pronunciation of *granted* /ˈɡrɑːntɪd/ and *advantage* /ədˈvɑːntɪdʒ/. Also highlight that the stress on *responsibility* is on the fourth syllable.

Students then do the activity in pairs.

Ask students to tell the class if they both agreed with any of the statements.

Speaking and Reading

2 **a** Students discuss the questions in groups.

Ask students to share interesting answers to question 1 with the class.

🖉 Elicit which adjectives the students think best describe the English and write them on the board. Ask students if they agree with other groups' choices.

┌─ **EXTRA IDEA** ─┐
- Ask students to think of five adjectives that describe people from their countries. Students can compare adjectives in pairs, giving reasons for their answers.

b Focus students on the book cover and on the cartoon. Tell students that the book is about how the English behave in social situations. Also ask students

why they think the Spanish tourist in the cartoon is looking confused (it isn't a warm day at all).

Students read the article and decide if the writer thinks English people are unfriendly.

You can set a time limit of two minutes to encourage students to read for gist.

Check the answer with the class (she doesn't think they're unfriendly, just very private people).

c Check students understand *mystify* (confuse completely) and *chilly* and check students remember *commute* and *a commuter*.

Students do the exercise on their own, then check answers in pairs.

Check answers with the class.

> 1 F English social codes aren't obvious to everyone.
> 2 F People who commute together don't often become friends. 3 ✓ 4 ✓ 5 F English people don't like talking about themselves to strangers. 6 ✓

d Focus students on the questions in **2a**. Students work in the same groups and think about what they said and whether the article has changed their opinion of the English. Encourage students to give reasons for their decision.

Also ask the class if people from their country or countries behave in a similar way. Don't go into too much detail here as students discuss this topic in detail in **7** and **8**.

┌─ **EXTRA IDEA** ─┐
- Ask students to tell the class about anything in the review that surprised them and if the ideas in the review match their own experiences of English people.

HELP WITH GRAMMAR
Uses of verb+*ing*

3 **a–c** Students do the exercises on their own or in pairs, then check in GRAMMAR 6.1 ▶ SB p141.
Check answers with the class.

- **b** spend years travelling **c** was laughing **d** avoid talking
- Point out that we always use *being* in continuous passive verb forms: *We're very uncomfortable when we're being asked questions*.
- Also highlight that we often use verb+*ing* after these verbs + object: *hear, see, watch, feel, imagine, stop, love, like, don't mind, dislike, hate*: *I often hear her **playing** the piano*.
- For verbs without an object that are often followed by verb+*ing*, see the table in VOCABULARY 1.3 ▶ SB p127.

- **e** despite feeling **f** talking to strangers
  g standing at a bus stop **h** entertaining
- If students don't remember what a reduced relative clause is, refer them to the final section in **GRAMMAR 4.2** SB p136.
- Use the answer for **f** to highlight that we don't use a form of the infinitive as a subject: *Living in London is expensive.* not ~~*Live in London is expensive.*~~ or ~~*To live in London is expensive.*~~
- Go through the **TIPS** in **GRAMMAR 6.1** SB p141 or ask students to read them for homework.
- Note that verb+*ing* can sometimes be a present participle (in continuous verb forms) or a gerund (when it acts as a noun, for example after prepositions). However, students often find this grammatical distinction confusing, so we feel it is simpler to refer to both as verb+*ing*.

4 Focus students on words/phrases 1–8 in **bold** in the article.
Students do the exercise in pairs. Check answers with the class.

1c 2a 3f 4g 5b 6d 7h 8e

5 **a** Check students understand *obey, stare* and *sarcastically*. Also check students remember *queue* /kjuː/, which is a noun and a verb.
Students do the exercise on their own. Tell students to read the article quickly for gist first before correcting the mistakes.

b Students compare answers in pairs, giving reasons for each change they have made.

c **CD2** 10 Play the recording (SB p163). Students listen and check their answers.
Check answers with the class. Ask students to explain the reason for each change to the class.

The section of Kate Fox's book **explaining** (*reduced relative clause*) the rules of queuing is interesting and the English obey these rules without **thinking** (*after a preposition*) about it. **Jumping** (*subject of a verb*) a queue will certainly annoy those people **queuing** (*reduced relative clause*) properly. However, despite **feeling** (*after 'despite'*) intense anger towards the queue-jumper, the English will often say nothing – **staring** (*subject of a verb*) angrily is more their style. Then there are the rules for **saying** (*after a preposition*) please and thank you. The English thank bus drivers, taxi drivers, anyone **giving** (*reduced relative clause*) them a service. In fact the English spend a lot of time **saying** (*after a verb + object*) please and thank you, so others don't feel they're being taken for granted. They hate not **being** (*after a verb*) thanked if they think they deserve it. Not **saying** (*subject of a verb*) thank you will often cause a person to sarcastically shout out "You're welcome!".

6 **a** Students do the exercise on their own.
While students are working, monitor and check their sentences for accuracy.

b Students do the exercise in pairs. Encourage students to ask follow-up questions if possible.
Ask students to tell the class interesting things that they found out about their partners.

Get ready … Get it right!

7 Check students understand *social codes* (how to behave in certain social situations) and *cause offence* (upset people).

Students do the exercise on their own. Remind students to use a verb+*ing* form in each tip.

While students are working, monitor and correct their sentences if necessary.

8 **a** Put students into pairs. Include students from different countries in each pair if possible.

Students take turns to tell each other their tips. If students are from the same country, they decide if they agree with their partner's tips, giving reasons why they disagree if necessary.

If students are from different countries, they decide if their partner's tips are also true for their country, giving reasons why they aren't if necessary. Students can also decide which are the three most important tips on their list.

b Finally, ask students to tell the class the three most important tips for visiting their country.

┌─ **EXTRA IDEA** ─┐
- ✎ If you have a monolingual class, ask each pair to tell you their top three tips and write them on the board. Students can then vote on which they think are the three most important tips.

┌─ **WRITING** ─┐
For homework, ask students to write a description of how people in their country behave in certain situations. Students must use at least six verb+*ing* forms in their descriptions. Next class you can collect in the descriptions and display them around the classroom for other students to read.

┌─ **FURTHER PRACTICE** ─┐
Ph **Class Activity** 6A Is this your card? p166 (Instructions p138)
Extra Practice 6A SB p120
Self-study DVD-ROM Lesson 6A
Workbook Lesson 6A p30

6B ▶ Rebel!

Student's Book p50–p51

Vocabulary compound adjectives describing character

Grammar modal verbs (1): levels of certainty about the future

---

QUICK REVIEW This activity reviews phrases with *take*. Students work on their own and write four phrases with *take*. Put students into pairs. Students swap papers and write sentences about people they know with their partner's phrases. Students then take turns to tell their partner their sentences and ask follow-up questions, as in the example. Ask students to share any interesting sentences with the class.

Vocabulary and Speaking

Compound adjectives describing character

1 Students do the exercise on their own or in pairs, then check in **VOCABULARY 6.2** ▶ SB p140. Check answers with the class.

Check students understand the meanings of the compound adjectives.

Point out that the opposite of *strong-willed* is *weak-willed*. Highlight that the opposite of *narrow-minded* is *open-minded* (or *broad-minded*). We usually use *open-minded* to talk about ideas and *broad-minded* to talk about morals and behaviour. Also point out that the opposite of *bad-tempered* is *good-tempered* (or *even-tempered*).

Model and drill the words, highlighting the pronunciation of *self-conscious* /self ˈkɒnʃəs/. Also highlight that the stress is on the second part of each adjective.

> self-conscious N; laid-back P; open-minded P; self-centred N; narrow-minded N; easy-going P; big-headed N; bad-tempered N; absent-minded N; level-headed P; self-assured P

> ┌ **EXTRA IDEA** ┐
> - Students work in pairs, Student A and Student B. Student Bs close their books and Student As look at **VOCABULARY 6.2** ▶ SB p140. Student As ask questions about the vocabulary, for example, *What do you call people who (tend to forget things)?* Student B says the correct word (*absent-minded*). After a minute or two ask students to change roles.

2 **a** Focus students on the examples. Point out that *stubborn* /ˈstʌbən/ is similar in meaning to *strong-willed*, but has a negative meaning.

Students work in pairs and make a list of all the other positive and negative character adjectives that they know. You can set a time limit of two minutes.

✍ Divide the board in half and write *Positive* on the left and *Negative* on the right. Find out which pair has the most words. Elicit the words and write them on the board. Ask if other pairs have any different words and add them to the list. Check the meaning and pronunciation of any problematic words.

b Students do the exercise on their own. Encourage them to use the words on the board as well as those in **1**.

c Students do the activity in pairs. Encourage students to ask follow-up questions if possible. Ask students to tell the class if they agreed with their partner's descriptions of people they knew about.

Listening and Speaking

3 Focus students on the photo and ask where the people are (in a hospital). Also ask students who they think Sarah and Mickey are talking about (Beatrice). Tell students they are going to listen to Sarah, Mickey and Beatrice's conversation and allow them time to read questions 1–6.

CD2▶ 11 Play the recording (SB p163). Students listen and answer the questions.

Students check answers in pairs. Check answers with the class.

> **1** It's a bit bright. **2** No, she doesn't. She thinks it suits her. **3** She's a receptionist. **4** Laurie is Beatrice's boss. **5** A lot of people are off sick, so he's unlikely to find someone to replace her. **6** He's Beatrice's boyfriend. He's pretty laid-back. **7** She's going to meet Ned's parents. She feels quite excited.

> ┌ **EXTRA IDEA** ┐
> - Put students into groups. Before students listen, ask them to predict what the conversation will be about. Tell students to use the photo to help them with their predictions. Ask groups to share interesting ideas with the class.

4 **a** Give students time to read sentences 1–10, then play the recording again. Students listen and decide who said each sentence, Sarah, Mickey or Beatrice.

b Play the recording again. Students listen and check their answers. Check answers with the class.

> 1M 2S 3M 4S 5M 6B 7B 8M 9B 10B

> ┌ **EXTRA IDEA** ┐
> - If students are finding the recording difficult, ask them to look at **CD2▶ 11**, SB p163. Play the recording again. Students listen, read and check their answers.

c Students discuss the questions in pairs. Ask pairs to share interesting answers with the class.

HELP WITH GRAMMAR
Modal verbs (1); levels of certainty about the future

5 **a–d** Students do the exercises on their own or in pairs, then check in **GRAMMAR 6.2** SB p141. Check answers with the class.

a 1C 2P 3P 4P 5C
- Use sentences 1–5 to remind students that we often use *'ll* (= *will*) and *won't* to express future certainty and *might, could* and *may* to express future possibility.
- Also remind students that modal verbs are followed by the infinitive: *I might go there later*.
- Point out that we say *I don't think he'll …* not ~~I think he won't …~~ .
- Also highlight that we often use *definitely* and *probably* with *will/won't*. Point out the difference in word order: *Jane will definitely/probably be there. Henry definitely/probably won't be there.*

b a 4, 7, 8, 9, 10 **b** 1, 2, 3, 5, 6
- Use sentences 1–10 in **4a** to highlight these rules.
- We use *be bound to do sth* and *be sure to do sth* when we think something will definitely happen.
- We use *be likely to do sth, may well do sth* and *I daresay* when we think something will probably happen.
- We use *be unlikely to do sth, I don't suppose, I doubt if* and *I shouldn't think* when we think something probably won't happen.
- We use *I can't imagine* when we think something definitely won't happen.

c *be bound to, be sure to, be likely to, may well* and *be unlikely to* are followed by the infinitive. Tell students that we can use these phrases with any subject.
- *I daresay, I don't suppose, I doubt if, I shouldn't think* and *I can't imagine* are followed by subject + *will* + infinitive. Although it is possible to use some of these phrases with other subjects, we suggest you teach these as fixed phrases with *I* for this meaning of expressing degrees of certainty about the future.
- Point out that we can also use these phrases to talk about present situations or states: *He's bound to be home by now.*
- Establish that we can also say *I'm sure (that)* + clause: *I'm sure (that) he'll be here on time.* and that *I can't imagine* can also be followed by verb+*ing*: *I can't imagine working for another company.*

6 **CD2 12** **PRONUNCIATION** Play the recording (SB p164) and ask students to repeat. Check students copy the sentence stress correctly.
Play the recording again if necessary.

7 **a** Students do the exercise on their own.
b Students compare answers in pairs. Check answers with the class.
Ask each pair to tell the class one or two sentences that are true for both of them.

2 I'm unlikely to need English for my next job. (It's unlikely that I'll need English for my next job.)
3 I'm bound to need English for my work.
4 I daresay I'll do an advanced English course at some point.
5 I can't imagine I'll be able to visit England next year.
6 I may well spend some time working on the **face2face** DVD-ROM this weekend.
7 I doubt if I'll take any more English exams.
8 I don't suppose I'll be able to watch an English DVD this weekend.

8 **a** Check students understand *property* (houses, flats, etc.) and that they remember *abroad*. Students do the exercise on their own.
While students are working, monitor and check their sentences for accuracy.

b Put students into pairs. Students take turns to tell their partners about people they know well, using the sentences they have prepared. Tell students to begin by telling their partner what their relationship is with the four people they chose. Encourage students to ask follow-up questions if possible.
When students have finished discussing the people, they decide which person's life they think will change the most in the next few years.
Ask students to tell the class about the person whose life they think will change the most.

> **WRITING**
> Students write about the four people they chose for homework. Tell students to include as much information as they can about each person, expanding on their ideas given in **8a**.

Get ready … Get it right!

9 Students do the exercise on their own. Remind students to write notes, as in the example, not complete sentences. Point out that students should only think about the next two weeks.

10 Students work in groups and take turns to tell each other their predictions, using language from **4a** and **5a** as shown in the speech bubbles. Remind students to ask follow-up questions, as in the example.
While students are working, monitor and correct any mistakes you hear.
Finally, ask students to tell the class who they think is going to have the busiest, best or worst two weeks in each group.

> **FURTHER PRACTICE**
> **Ph Class Activity** 6B Future thoughts p167 (Instructions p138)
> **Extra Practice** 6B SB p120
> **Self-study DVD-ROM** Lesson 6B
> **Workbook** Lesson 6B p31

VOCABULARY
6C AND SKILLS ▶ Dress code
Student's Book p52–p53

Vocabulary back referencing
Skills Reading: a fashion article;
Listening: interviews about style

QUICK REVIEW This activity reviews levels of certainty about the future. 🖉 Write these prompts on the board: *traffic, population, parking, public transport, local taxes, house prices, sports, pollution.* Students do the first part of the activity on their own, using the prompts on the board or their own ideas. Also remind students to use the phrases for expressing levels of certainty about the future in GRAMMAR 6.2 ▶ SB p141. Put students into pairs to compare predictions.

Speaking, Reading and Vocabulary

1 Focus students on the title and the photos. Check students understand *dress code* (rules about what you should wear in a particular place or to a particular event).
Students work in pairs and discuss the questions.
Ask students to share interesting information about designer clothes with the class.

2 **a** Students read the article quickly and do the exercise on their own or in pairs. Set a time limit of two or three minutes to encourage students to read for gist.
Check answers with the class.

part A: 2
part B: 3

EXTRA IDEAS

• Put students into pairs, A and B. Student As read part A and Student Bs read part B. Ask them to tell their partner which summary sentence they think is correct for their part of the text. Students then read the other part of the text and see if they agree with their partner's choice.
• Ask students to explain why the two sentences they didn't use were incorrect.

Sentence 1 isn't correct because Part B talks about designer labels and status, but it doesn't say whether people like them or not.
Sentence 4 isn't correct because Part A doesn't mention the age of the people targeted by fashion designers.

b Students do the exercise on their own or in pairs.

c Students compare answers in pairs. Check answers with the class.
Focus on the two underlined sentences in Part B of the article. Students work in their pairs and say whether they agree with the sentences or not. Encourage them to give reasons for their answers. Ask students to share their opinions with the class.

1 Designer labels began with Charles Frederick Worth in France, when he moved there from England in 1846. He began to sew labels into the clothes that he created.
2 They were very enthusiastic so they queued outside the shop for up to 12 hours to buy the clothes. Some people even camped outside the shop.
3 It was trying to find out whether wearing designer labels affects your status and your job prospects.
4 It concluded that designer labels are seen as signs of superior status.
5 Because male peacocks have beautiful tails that attract female peacocks, which is like somebody wearing a designer label to improve his status. Whereas the peacock can't fake his tail (therefore his status), humans can fake their status by wearing designer goods.

HELP WITH VOCABULARY
Back referencing

3 **a** Go through the introductory bullet with the class and check students understand what we mean by 'back referencing'.
Students do the exercise on their own. Do the first question as an example with the class if necessary. Students compare answers in pairs. Check answers with the class.

• 2b clothes 3a sewing labels in clothes 4a the late 19th century 5b anonymous dressmakers 6b France 7b designers 8b international high street shops 9a people 10a outside H&M, London 11b when people were camping

b–c Students do the exercise on their own, then check in VOCABULARY 6.3 ▶ SB p140. Check answers with the class. Note that back referencing in listening is focused on in lesson 11C.

• 12 *The Economist* 13 research from Tilburg University 14 labelled clothes 15 a shirt 16 a shirt 17 video 18 his shirt 19 humans 20 faking status
• Go through the TIPS in VOCABULARY 6.3 ▶ SB p140 or ask students to read them for homework.

Listening and Speaking

4 **a** Focus students on questions 1–5 and responses a–f. Check students understand *image* and *bling* (a slang word for jewellery).
Students do the exercise in pairs.

b Tell students they are going to listen to five people being asked about their image.

CD2 13 Play the recording (SB p164). Students listen and check their answers. Check answers with the class.

1c 2b 3e 4f 5a

c Play the recording again. Students work on their own and write down words to help them remember the main points from each person's response.

d Put students into pairs. Students take turns to summarise each speaker's response, using the words they wrote down in **4c**.
Find out if students agreed with each other's summaries. Ask students to add any other information they can remember about each speaker's response.

┌─ **EXTRA IDEA** ─┐

- Focus students on questions 3–5 in **4a**. Students work on their own and write their own responses to the questions. Students then work in pairs and discuss the questions. Ask pairs to share interesting answers with the class, and to say whether they had similar answers to each question.

HELP WITH LISTENING
Linking (2): /w/, /j/ and /r/ sounds

This *Help with Listening* section reviews the sounds we often use to link words together in natural spoken English.

5 **a** Go through the introductory bullet point with the class. Remind students that we use the sounds /w/, /j/ and /r/ to link words that end in a vowel sound with those that begin with a vowel sound.
Also remind students that we often pronounce the /r/ sound in words that end in -r or -re when they are followed by a word that begins with a vowel sound

(see the *Help with Listening* section in lesson 2C, SB p20). Note that this type of linking /r/ is much more common than those which follow a word that doesn't contain the letter 'r', for example *law_/r/_and order*, *India_/r/_and China*, etc.

CD2 14 Focus students on the sentences from the interviews, then play the recording. Students listen and notice the linking sounds in each sentence.

b Students do the exercise in pairs.

c Students turn to **CD2 13**, SB p164 and check their answers.

d Ask students to continue looking at **CD2 13**, SB p164. Play the first two interviews again. Students notice the extra linking sounds.

6 Check students understand *gender* (your sex, i.e. male or female) and *socio-economic group* (where you fit within your society, dependent on a number of factors such as background, income, etc.).
Students work in groups and discuss the questions. Finally, ask students to share interesting information with the class.

┌─ **WRITING** ─┐

Students choose two of the groups in question 1 in **6** (for example, a particular age group, a socio-economic group) and write a short article about things associated with those groups in their country. Students should give as much extra information as possible, and as a conclusion to the article, say whether things will change or not for those groups.

┌─ **FURTHER PRACTICE** ─┐

Ph Vocabulary Plus 6 Commonly confused verbs p199 (Instructions p191)
Extra Practice 6C SB p120
Self-study DVD-ROM Lesson 6C
Workbook Lesson 6C p33

▷ REAL
6D WORLD ▶ Sorry to interrupt ...
Student's Book p54–p55

Real World polite interruptions

QUICK REVIEW This activity reviews compound adjectives describing character. Students do the first part of the activity on their own. Put students into pairs. Students take turns to say the first part of an adjective. Their partner says the whole adjective and its meaning, as in the example.

Listening

1 **a** Check students understand *an open-plan office*. Focus students on the photos. Ask students if Judy works in an open-plan office (she doesn't). Point out the open-plan office that can be seen through the door and windows of her office.

Students work in pairs and discuss the advantages and disadvantages of working in an open-plan office.

> **Possible advantages:** cheaper for the company; easier for employees to talk to other people; creates an atmosphere of teamwork; harder for employees to avoid working
> **Possible disadvantages:** not much privacy; often noisy; phone conversations can be overheard; not enough space for files

b Check students understand *IT (= information technology) department* (the department responsible for a company's computers, phones, etc.). Also check students remember *an accountant* and *a colleague* /ˈkɒliːg/.

Tell students that they are going to watch or listen to five people having short conversations with Judy.
VIDEO 6 CD2 15 Play the video or audio recording (SB p164). Students watch or listen and match people 1–5 to their relationships with Judy. Check answers with the class.

> 1a 2d 3b 4c 5e

c Check students understand *go over* (check), *figures* (numbers) and *insurance*.

Play the video or recording again. Students watch or listen and make notes on why each person wants to speak to Judy.
Students check answers in pairs. Check answers with the class.

> **1** Amanda wants to go over some figures. **2** Martin wants to ask Judy about house insurance. **3** Chloe wants to ask Judy about the report Judy asked her to type up. **4** Tina wants to know when it would be a good time to install some new software on Judy's computer. **5** Colin wants to know if he can use Judy's office any time today.

REAL WORLD Polite interruptions

2 **a–d** Students do the exercises on their own or in pairs, then check in **REAL WORLD 6.1** SB p141. Check answers with the class.

> **a** 1c 2e 3d 4f 5a 6b
> - Highlight that *Sorry to bother you, but have you got a minute?*, *Sorry to disturb you.* and *I was wondering if I could see you for a moment.* sound more polite.
> **b** 1 time 2 against 3 tied 4 pushed 5 busy
> - Use sentences 1–5 to check students understand the phrases *be up against it* (under pressure to hit a deadline), *be (a bit) tied up* (be busy/occupied) and *be (a bit) pushed for time* (be busy/in a hurry).
> - Highlight that when we are refusing permission, we often use *I'm afraid* to sound more polite.

- Point out that if we are refused permission we often say: *Don't worry, it's not important/it can wait/it's not urgent/I'll catch you later/some other time.* or *When would be a good time/a better time/more convenient?* (*When would be convenient?* is more formal.)
- **c** When we want to give permission to the person interrupting us, we often say: *Yes, of course. What can I do for you? How can I help? What's the problem?* or *What's up?* (informal).

HELP WITH LISTENING
Intonation: being polite

This *Help with Listening* section focuses on the natural intonation patterns we use when we want to interrupt people politely.

3 **a** Focus students on the introductory bullet point. Highlight the importance of polite intonation when interrupting.
CD2 16 Play the recording. Students listen and say why the first sentence sounds impolite and why the second sentence sounds polite. Check answers with the class.

> The first time each sentence is spoken, it has a flat intonation, which sounds impolite. The second time, the speaker's voice goes up and down, which sounds more polite.

b **CD2 17** Play the recording (SB p164). Students listen and decide which sentences sound polite, a or b. Check students' answers by playing the recording again and pausing after each pair of sentences to elicit their answers.

> 1b 2a 3b 4b 5a 6b

4 **CD2 18** **PRONUNCIATION** Play the recording (SB p164). Students listen and repeat the sentences. Check students are copying the polite intonation when asking for permission to interrupt.

5 **a** Students do the exercise on their own, then check answers in pairs. Check answers with the class.

> 1 wondering 2 could 3 against 4 moment
> 5 would 6 time 7 disturb/bother 8 word 9 afraid
> 10 tied 11 worry 12 wait 13 bother/disturb
> 14 minute 15 pushed 16 time 17 catch 18 busy
> 19 time 20 urgent 21 be 22 convenient

b Students practise the conversation in pairs. While they are working, monitor and check they are using the correct polite intonation.

6 Put students into two groups, Group A and Group B. Students in Group A turn to SB p105 and students in Group B turn to SB p108.

a Put students into pairs so that they are working with someone from the same group. Students do the exercise in pairs. Remind students to invent their own endings.

b Students practise their conversations in pairs. Remind students to use polite intonation.

c Reorganise the class so that a pair from Group A is working with a pair from Group B. Students take turns to role-play their conversations. After each conversation, the other pair guesses who the people are from their list of ideas in the Student's Book. Point out that there is one extra idea before they begin.
Finally, ask a few pairs to role-play their conversations.

> **FURTHER PRACTICE**
>
> **Ph** **Class Activity** 6D Four in a line p168
> (Instructions p138)
> **Extra Practice** 6D SB p120
> **Self-study DVD-ROM** Lesson 6D
> **Workbook** Lesson 6D p39
> **Workbook** Reading and Writing Portfolio 6 p74
> **Progress Test** 6 p248

HELP WITH PRONUNCIATION
Word stress (2): compound adjectives

This *Help with Pronunciation* section focuses on the different stress patterns in compound adjectives.

1 **a** Focus students on the stress patterns and the words in the table.
CD2 19 Play the recording. Students listen and notice the stress patterns.

b Play the recording again. Students listen again and repeat the words.

c Focus students on the stress patterns in **1a** again. Check students understand *hyphenated*. Students decide whether the stress is usually on the first or second word (the second).

2 **a** Students do the exercise in pairs. Encourage students to say the words out loud to help them identify the correct stress pattern.

b **CD2 20** Play the recording (SB p165). Students listen and check their answers.
Play the recording again. Students listen and repeat the words. Finally, ask students to say words from the list. Check they use the correct stress pattern and praise good pronunciation.

> ### continue2learn

Focus students on the *continue2learn* section on SB p55. See p35 for ideas on how to exploit this section.

Extra Practice 6
See p35 for ideas on how to exploit this section.

6A
1 **2** sides **3** granted **4** time **5** responsibility **6** notice **7** out **8** answer **9** value **10** seriously
2 **2** turning up **3** keep **4** frustrating **5** being **6** to leave **7** getting **8** allowing **9** cancelled **10** to get

6B
3 **2** easy **3** strong/weak **4** laid **5** open/narrow **6** big **7** bad/good/even/level **8** self
4 **2** I can't imagine we'll have time to visit Sarah. **3** I daresay he'll disagree. **4** I doubt she'll want to come. **5** I don't suppose she'll mind if we're late. **6** They're unlikely to arrive before six. **7** I shouldn't think Tom'll care what you wear. **8** She may well leave him soon. **9** You're sure to make a good impression on them.

6C
5 **2** money **3** his parents **4** Tony **5** his parents **6** last month **7** a flat **8** Tony **9** the time when he lost his job **10** a job
6 **2** there **3** one **4** he **5** his **6** that/this/it **7** him **8** we **9** then **10** They **11** ones **12** he

6D
7 **a** **2** got a minute **3** could see **4** disturb **5** a good time **6** busy
b **2**a **3**b **4**e **5**d

Progress Portfolio 6

- See p36 for ideas on how to exploit this section.

7A ▶ At the airport
Student's Book p56–p57

Vocabulary state verbs
Grammar simple and continuous aspects;
activity and state verbs

QUICK REVIEW This activity reviews polite interruptions. Students do the first part of the activity on their own. Put students into pairs. Tell students to imagine that they are working in an office. Students complete the activity in their pairs. Encourage students to continue the conversations if possible, as in the example.

Vocabulary and Speaking

State verbs

1 **a** Students work in pairs and say which of the state verbs in **bold** they know. Tell students not to fill in the gaps at this stage. Students check any new verbs in **VOCABULARY 7.1** ▶ SB p142.
Check the meaning of any new verbs with the class.
Point out that *respect, envy* and *trust* are also uncountable nouns.
Establish that *involve* is often followed by verb+*ing* (*My course involves doing a lot of research.*) and that *deserve* is often followed by the infinitive with *to* (*He deserves to be promoted.*).
Also point out that *doubt* is often followed by *if/whether.*
Remind students that in British English we usually write *realise* and *recognise*, but that these words are spelled *realize* and *recognize* in American English.
Model and drill the verbs, highlighting the pronunciation of *envy* /'envi/ and *doubt* /daʊt/.
Point out that the stress on *recognise* is on the first syllable, not the third and that the stress on the verb *suspect* is on the second syllable, not the first.

b Students do the exercise on their own. Students then tell each other their sentences in pairs.
Ask students to tell the class one or two things they found out about their partner.

Speaking and Listening

2 Students discuss the questions in groups. Ask students to share interesting answers with the class.

3 **a** Focus students on the photo and ask students where the people are (in a departure lounge at an airport). Ask students what some of the people in the photo are doing to pass the time (reading, sleeping, shopping, etc.).
Students work on their own and circle the activities they've done to pass the time at an airport.

b Students compare ideas in pairs and find out which things they have both done.
Find out what students' most popular ways of passing the time at an airport are.

4 **a** Tell students that they are going to listen to part of a radio news programme about how people are passing the time at an airport.

CD2 ▶ 22 Play the recording (SB p165). Students listen and tick the activities in **3a** that the people talk about. Check answers with the class.

> read; do some shopping; phone family; work or study; people-watch; have a meal

b Give students time to read sentences 1–10, then play the recording again. Students listen and fill in the gaps with one word. Students compare answers in pairs. Check answers with the class.

> **1** read **2** missed **3** five **4** parents **5** ten **6** business **7** client **8** myself **9** camera **10** difficult

┌─ **EXTRA IDEA** ┐

● **CD2** ▶ 22 Play the recording again. Students listen and make notes about each person Nicole Watson interviewed. ✎ Write on the board *Woman 1, Woman 2, Man 1, Man 2*. Ask students for information about each person, for example, *Woman 1: downloads books before travelling, usually reads in an airport, nearly missed her flight once.* Students check their notes against the information on the board.

HELP WITH GRAMMAR
Simple and continuous aspects; activity and state verbs

5 **a** Students do the exercise on their own, then compare answers in pairs. Check answers with the class.

> **a** Sentence 1 describes something that is repeated. Sentence 2 describes something that is in progress at a specific point of time. **b** Sentence 3 describes something that is unfinished. Sentence 4 describes something that is completed. **c** Sentence 5 describes something that is permanent. Sentence 6 describes something that is temporary.
> ● Use sentences 1–6 in **4b** to highlight the difference between the simple aspect and the continuous aspect, which students studied in lesson 1A. We use **simple** verb forms to describe something that is repeated, completed or permanent. We use **continuous** verb forms to describe something that is in progress at a specific point in time, unfinished or temporary.

b–d Check students remember the difference between activity verbs (which talk about activities and actions) and state verbs (which talk about states, feelings and opinions).
Students do the exercises on their own or in pairs, then check in **GRAMMAR 7.1** ▶ SB p143. Check answers with the class.

b Activity verbs: *fly; travel; listen; run; work; sit; study; wait*

State verbs: *know; seem; understand; dislike; need; prefer; forget; mean; agree; cost; own; belong*

- We don't usually use state verbs in continuous verb forms: *I want a new car.* not ~~I'm wanting a new car~~.
- Focus students on the table of common state verbs in GRAMMAR 7.1 ► SB p143. Check the meanings of any verbs students don't know and encourage students to learn the verbs in the table.
- Also remind students that the verbs they studied in **1a** are also state verbs and are therefore not usually used in continuous verb forms.

c 7 *be seeing* = meeting; *see* = with my eyes
8 *have* = possess; *'m having* = experiencing
9 *'m … thinking* = considering; *think* = have an opinion 10 *is* = permanent characteristic; *'s being* = behaving
- Use sentences 7–10 in **4b** to highlight that some verbs, such as *see, have, think* and *be*, can describe both activities and states, but the meaning changes.
- You can highlight these differences in meaning by focusing students on the blue and pink words in the *verbs with two meanings* section of GRAMMAR 7.1 ► SB p143.

6 Check students understand *an engine* /ˈendʒɪn/ and *a discount*.

Tell students to read the text for gist first before filling in the gaps on their own. Students compare answers in pairs. Check answers with the class.

1 've been working 2 love 3 'm waiting 4 'm phoning/'ve been phoning/'ve phoned 5 've never had 6 were flying 7 stopped 8 happened 9 were sleeping 10 managed 11 suppose 12 'm flying/fly 13 cost 14 hate 15 've been

7 Students do the exercise on their own. Remind students to use the same verb for both sentences in each pair.
Students compare answers in pairs. Check answers with the class.

1 **a** do … think **b** 'm thinking 2 **a** was having **b** 've had 3 **a** Have … seen **b** is seeing 4 **a** 's/is **b** 's/is being

Get ready … Get it right!

8 Students do the exercise on their own. Tell students to write short phrases (*buy a laptop, my job, going to the cinema*, etc.), not whole sentences.

9 Students work in pairs and swap papers. Students take turns to ask questions about the things written on their partner's paper (*Are you thinking of visiting your brother next weekend?*, etc.). Encourage students to ask follow-up questions if possible.

While they are working, monitor and help students with any problems. Finally, ask students to tell the class two interesting things they found out about their partner.

WRITING

Students use the information from **8** and **9** to write two paragraphs, one about themselves and the other about their partner. Tell them to include as much extra information as they can in order to write a coherent text.

FURTHER PRACTICE

Ph **Class Activity** 7A My partner's life p170 (Instructions p139)
Extra Practice 7A SB p121
Self-study DVD-ROM Lesson 7A
Workbook Lesson 7A p38

7B ▸ Showpiece of China
Student's Book p58–p59

Vocabulary business and trade
Grammar Present Perfect Simple and Present Perfect Continuous

QUICK REVIEW This activity reviews simple and continuous aspects. Give students a minute or two to think of an interesting plane, train or bus journey they have been on (in a different country if possible). Put students into pairs. Students take turns to tell each other about their journeys.

Speaking and Reading

1 **a** Students work in pairs and discuss what they know about China.

b Students compare their ideas in groups or with the class. If students have compared ideas in groups, ask each group to tell the class one or two things they know about China.

2 **a** Focus students on the photo and ask them which city they think it is (Shanghai). Ask students if they would like to go there, giving reasons for their answers.

b Focus students on the title of this lesson. Elicit ideas for the meaning of *showpiece*. Don't confirm if they are correct yet.

Check students understand *exhilarated* /ɪɡˈzɪləreɪtɪd/, *a skyscraper, a hut, entire* /ɪnˈtaɪə/, *an apartment block* and *hotspots*.

Students read the article and find three ways in which Shanghai has changed since 1990. You can set a time limit of two minutes to encourage students to read for gist. Check answers with the class.

Check students' ideas for the meaning of *showpiece* (the most impressive thing of its type).

> Shanghai is now seen as the symbol of the country's new capitalist economy. There are more buildings over 450 metres than any other city in the world. There are now many western shops and restaurants, such as a huge Armani store, McDonald's and Starbucks, in the city.

c Students do the exercise on their own, then compare answers in pairs. Check answers with the class.

> 1 China is now the biggest producer of manufactured goods in the world.
> 2 Whereas the bike was once the most popular form of transport, by 2010 the Shanghai bicycle culture had all but disappeared.
> 3 ... many of China's biggest cities have become more polluted due to increased car ownership / The city authorities have become more and more concerned about pollution ...
> 4 ... business is still growing year on year
> 5 When you see Pudong's incredible collection of space-age skyscrapers up close, it's almost impossible to believe that in 1990 there was nothing there but fishermen's huts.
> 6 I've been coming to China for nearly 25 years.

> **EXTRA IDEA**
> • If appropriate, ask students for their reaction to the article and to China's growing influence on the world.

HELP WITH GRAMMAR
Present Perfect Simple and Present Perfect Continuous

3 **a** Students do the exercise on their own. Check answers with the class.

> • Present Perfect Simple *'ve visited; 've (ever) seen; 've known; have become; 've (just) got back*
> • Present Perfect Continuous *'ve been cycling; 've been coming; has been working*
> • Remind students that we use the Present Perfect Simple to talk about things that connect the past and the present.

b–d Students do the exercises on their own or in pairs, then check in **GRAMMAR 7.2** SB p143. Check answers with the class.

> **b** Present Perfect Simple **b** *'ve visited* **c** *'ve (just) got back* **d** *'ve (ever) seen* **e** *have become*
> • Present Perfect Continuous **b** *'ve been cycling* **c** *'ve been coming*

• Check students understand the difference between the uses of the Present Perfect Continuous. Point out that the result in the present in **b** is the fact that the writer is both exhausted and exhilarated. Also highlight that in **c** the writer has come to China repeatedly, not just once.

• Remind students that we make the Present Perfect Simple with: subject + *have/has* + past participle (*I've known Rob for about ten years.*) and we make the Present Perfect Continuous with: subject + *have/has* + *been* + verb+*ing* (*We've been living here since 2005.*).

• Go through the *Simple or continuous?* section of **GRAMMAR 7.2** SB p143 with the class.

• Also go through the **TIPS** in this section of **GRAMMAR 7.2** SB p143 with the class or ask students to read them for homework.

> **c** **a** sentence 1 **b** sentence 2 **c** 1 *How long has your company been building skyscrapers here?* 2 *How many new apartment blocks have you built this year?*

• Use sentences 1 and 2 to highlight that we usually use the Present Perfect Continuous to talk about **how long** something has been happening and we usually use the Present Perfect Simple to talk about **how many** things have been completed.

• Remind students to use the Present Perfect Simple with *How long* for state verbs: *How long have you had your car?* not ~~*How long have you been having your car?*~~.

• Point out that we can also make questions with the Present Perfect Simple and *how much* (+ noun): *How much time have you spent on this project so far?*

4 **a** Students do the exercise on their own.

b Students compare answers in pairs. Students should explain why they chose each verb form, referring to the meanings in **3b** as appropriate. Check answers with the class.

> 1 **a** *'ve/have called* (describes a completed action that only happened once) **b** *'ve/have been calling* (describes an action that happened repeatedly)
> 2 **a** *'s/has been writing* (describes how long something has been happening) **b** *'s/has written* (describes how many things have been completed)
> 3 **a** *'ve/have cleared out* (emphasises that the action has been completed) **b** *'ve/have been clearing out* (emphasises the action the person has been doing)
> 4 **a** *'ve/have been cutting* (describes a repeated action and how long this action has been happening) **b** *'ve/have cut* (describes a short action that has been completed)

5 a *'ve/have read* (describes an action that has been completed) **b** *'ve/have been reading* (describes an action that started in the past and hasn't been completed yet)

5 Put students into new pairs, Student A and Student B. Student As turn to SB p106 and Student Bs turn to SB p109.

a Students do the exercise on their own. Remind students to use the continuous form if possible. While they are working, monitor and check students' questions for accuracy.

Check the answers with the class if necessary.

Student A
2 How long have you been living (have you lived) in your house or flat? **3** How many phone calls have you made today? **4** How long have you been studying (have you studied) English? **5** How long have you known your oldest friend? **6** How much have you spent on food today?

Student B
b How long have you been living (have you lived) in this town or city? **c** How many novels have you read in English? **d** How long have you had your mobile? **e** How long have you been coming to this class? **f** How many times have you been/gone to the cinema this month?

┌─ **EXTRA IDEA** ─────────────────────────┐

- Before students work in pairs, model and drill the questions in **a**, highlighting the sentence stress and the weak forms of *have* /əv/ and *been* /bɪn/, for example, *How long have* /əv/ *you been* /bɪn/ *living in your house or flat?*.

└──┘

b Students do the exercise in pairs. Remind students to give natural short answers (*For two years. Three or four. Since 2008.*, etc.) and to ask follow-up questions if possible.

Ask students to tell the class one or two things they found out about their partner.

Vocabulary and Speaking

Business and trade

6 a Focus students on the words in blue in the article. Students do the exercise on their own, then compare answers in pairs.

✏ While students are working, draw a blank three-column table on the board with the headings *noun for a person*, *noun for a thing/an idea* and *adjective* as in **VOCABULARY 7.2** ▸ SB p142.

✏ Check answers with the class by eliciting the words and their parts of speech, and writing them in the correct column on the board. Check the meaning of any new words with the class.

political (adjective); *capitalist* (adjective); *economy* (noun); *developer* (noun); *investment* (noun); *industrial* (adjective); *producer* (noun); *manufactured* (adjective); *environmental* (adjective); *polluted* (adjective)
In the article, *developer* refers to a person, and *economy, investment* and *producer* refer to a thing.

b Students do the exercise in pairs, then check in **VOCABULARY 7.2** ▸ SB p142.

✏ Check the answers by eliciting the other words in each word family and writing them in the correct place in the table on the board (see the table in **VOCABULARY 7.2** ▸ SB p142).

Point out that we use *capitalism* to describe an economic system and *capital* to describe the money that we use to start a business or invest in something.

Notice the difference between *economic* and *economical*: *Government ministers met yesterday to discuss economic policy.* (= relating to the economy of a country). *This car is very economical.* (= saves you money).

Point out that *a developer* can refer to a person and a company. Also highlight that we use *industrial* for cities but *industrialised* for countries.

Tell students that *economise, develop, invest, produce, manufacture* and *pollute* are all regular verbs.

Model and drill the words in 'word family' groups. Highlight the different stress patterns in these word families: *politician, politics, political; economist, economy, economic, economical; industrialist, industry, industrial, industrialised; environmentalist, environment, environmental.* Point out that the stress doesn't change in the other word families.

┌─ **EXTRA IDEAS** ─────────────────────────┐

- ✏ Before drilling the new vocabulary, ask students to decide where the stress is on each word on the board. Elicit students' ideas and mark the correct stress on each word on the board.
- ✏ Ask students to close their eyes. Rub out six words from the table on the board. Ask students to open their eyes again. Students work in pairs and decide which words have been rubbed out. Check answers with the class. Repeat the procedure another two or three times.

└──┘

c Students do the exercise on their own.

d Students compare answers with a partner. Check answers with the class.

Students tell their partners which sentences are true for them.

Ask students to share interesting information with the class.

1 capitalist **2** economy **3** products **4** investment **5** politics **6** environmental **7** industrial **8** pollution

Get ready ... Get it right!

7 Check students understand all the prompts and teach any new words/phrases if necessary. Students do the exercise on their own. Encourage students to use the Present Perfect Simple and Present Perfect Continuous in their sentences if possible, as in the examples.

8 **a** Put students into groups. If you have a multilingual class, include students from different countries in each group if possible.

Students do the exercise in their groups. Students from the same country decide if they agree. Students from different countries find out how many of their sentences are the same. Encourage students to discuss any sentences or ideas that they find interesting.

b Finally, ask students to tell the class two interesting things that their groups discussed.

WRITING

Students write an essay based on their sentences in **7**, explaining how things have changed in their country in the last five years. Tell students to expand on their ideas, giving reasons for the changes if possible, and highlighting interesting changes.

FURTHER PRACTICE

Ph **Class Activity** 7B Foreign correspondent p171 (Instructions p139)
Ph **Vocabulary Plus** 7 Words from other languages p200 (Instructions p191)
Extra Practice 7B SB p121
Self-study DVD-ROM Lesson 7B
Workbook Lesson 7B p36

7C VOCABULARY AND SKILLS ▷ Life online
Student's Book p60–p61

Vocabulary word building (2): prefixes
Skills Reading: history of the Internet; Listening: conversations about using the Internet

QUICK REVIEW This activity reviews vocabulary connected to business and trade. Students do the activity in pairs. If students are having difficulty remembering the word families, they can check in **VOCABULARY 7.2** ▷ SB p142. Ask students to share some of their sentences with the class.

Speaking and Reading

1 Students work in pairs and make a list of positive and negative things about the Internet.
Ask students to share their lists with the class and tell them to find out how many students had the same things on their list.

EXTRA IDEA

- ✍ With a weaker class, you could elicit words connected with the Internet onto the board before beginning the activity, for example, *search engine*, *chat room*, *forum*, *blog*, *webcam*, *MP3 file*, *podcast*, *wi-fi*, etc. Students use the words to help them make their list.

2 **a** Check students understand *a handful* (a small number), *a vice president*, *claim* (say something is true, even though you can't prove it and other people might not believe it), *crash* (when a computer or computer system stops working completely) and *influential*.

Students do the exercise on their own. You can set a time limit of two minutes to encourage students to read quickly for gist. Check answers with the class.

a4 b2 c1 d5 e3

b Students do the exercise on their own.

c Students compare answers in pairs. Check answers with the class.

- In the **1980s** the Internet was only used by a handful of people.
- **ARPANET** is the old name for the Internet.
- **Social networking sites** have revolutionised global communication and have become more popular and influential.
- **Charles Kline** was the first person to try and connect to another computer via the Internet.
- Email first appeared in **1972**.
- **The World Wide Web** was invented by British scientist Tim Berners-Lee in 1989 and is the system which allows us to move from one website to another.
- The public were finally allowed access to the Internet in **1990**.

- ✍ You could alter **2b** by writing just dates or just names on the board, for example, *the 1980s, 1969, 1972, 1979, 1980s, 1990*; *Al Gore, Charles Kline, Tim Berners-Lee*; *ARPANET, email, the World Wide Web, Facebook*. Students read the article and find what it says about these dates, names or things.
- Put students into groups of four, A, B, C and D. Student As read paragraphs 1 and 2, Student Bs read paragraph 3, Student Cs read paragraph 4 and Student Ds read paragraph 5. Students make notes on their paragraph, then summarise it for the other students in their group.

HELP WITH VOCABULARY
Word building (2): prefixes

3 **a** Students do the exercise on their own, then compare answers in pairs.

✍ While students are working, draw the table from **3a** on the board ready for checking. Check answers with the class.

- Focus students on the table on the board. Elicit the meanings and examples for each prefix and write them in the correct place in the table (see the table in **VOCABULARY 7.3** SB p142).
- Point out that we always use hyphens with *pro-, anti-, ex-, self- and non-*. With the other prefixes, it depends on the word. Note that words beginning with *multi-* are often spelt with or without hyphens (*multimillionaire, multi-millionaire*, etc.).

b–c Students do **3b** in pairs, then check in **VOCABULARY 7.3** SB p142. Check answers with the class.

- Elicit answers from the class and write them in the third column of the table on the board (see the table in **VOCABULARY 7.3** SB p142).
- Alternatively, check answers by focusing students on the table in **VOCABULARY 7.3** SB p142 and going through the prefixes in turn.
- Remind students that prefixes are not normally stressed.

4 Put students into new pairs, Student A and Student B. Student As turn to SB p106 and Student Bs turn to SB p109.

a Students do the exercise on their own.
Check answers with the class. Only check the prefixes, so that the students in the other group don't hear the questions they are about to be asked.

Student A: 1 anti-social **2** self-discipline **3** postgraduate **4** pro-/anti-hunting **5** ex-/non-smokers **6** under/overrated **7** multimillionaire **8** misbehave

Student B: a multicultural **b** ex-presidents **c** redecorating **d** under/overcharged **e** misunderstand **f** under/overpaid **g** multinational **h** non-stop

b Students do the exercise in their pairs.
Ask students to tell the class one or two interesting things they found out about their partners.

Listening and Speaking

5 **a** Focus students on pictures A–D and ask them what the people are doing in each one.

A Someone is talking to friends or family via a webcam. **B** Someone is downloading a film onto their computer. **C** Someone is playing a video game. **D** Someone is shopping online.

Tell students that they are going to listen to four people discussing how they use the Internet.
CD2 **24** Play the recording (SB p165). Students listen and put pictures A–D in the order the people talk about them. Check answers with the class.

1D **2**B **3**C **4**A

b Give students time to read questions 1–6, then play the recording again. Students listen and answer the questions. Students compare answers in pairs. Check answers with the class.

1 There were over 500 emails in his inbox. **2** It's so easy and it doesn't feel like you're spending money at all. **3** Because he and Molly never have time to go to the cinema. **4** He plays a role-playing game for hours. **5** About half a million. **6** Because a lot of her family live in the States.

HELP WITH LISTENING
Recognising redundancy

This *Help with Listening* section helps students to recognise which words and phrases they can ignore when listening to natural spoken English.

6 **a** Focus students on the introductory bullet point. Remind students that we often use fillers and false starts to give us 'thinking time' when we are deciding what to say next. Also establish that fillers such as *um, you know*, etc. have no meaning.
Students do the exercise on their own, then compare answers in pairs. Check answers with the class.

1 filler: *like* **2 fillers:** *you see, sort of, like* **3 fillers:** *um, er, you know*; **false start:** *I generally* **4 fillers:** *kind of, er*; **false starts:** *Most of …, in touch …*

b Ask students to turn to **CD2** **23**, SB p165. Play the first half of the conversation. Students listen and notice the underlined fillers and false starts.

Play the second half of the conversation. Students listen and underline all the fillers and false starts. Students compare answers in pairs. Check answers with the class.

> OLIVIA That's because you're usually too busy, <u>um</u>, playing that role-playing game of yours. Honestly, <u>every time I</u> … I often come home and find that he's been sitting in the study for hours, <u>you know</u>, fighting some evil monster or something.
>
> IAN That's only when your mother comes to stay.
>
> O Ha ha, very funny.
>
> CLIVE <u>They're</u>, <u>er</u>, they're very addictive though, those role-playing games, aren't they?
>
> I Yeah, and incredibly popular too. Any number of people can play. Some of them have <u>like</u> about half a million people playing at the same time.
>
> MOLLY Really? Wow!
>
> O Well, the thing I love most about the Internet is skyping people.
>
> M Really. Do you, <u>um</u>, do you use Skype a lot?
>
> O Yeah, I do, actually. <u>Most of</u> … a lot of my family live in the States, and we <u>kind of</u>, <u>er</u>, <u>keep in touch through</u> … we skype each other a lot – it's become a weekly thing, really. It's a great way to keep in touch and it means I can see my nieces and nephews growing up.
>
> M Yes, it's wonderful. Much better than phoning people. And it's free.
>
> WAITER Excuse me, are you ready to order?
>
> M <u>Oh</u>, <u>er</u>, no, sorry, we've been chatting. <u>Can we have</u>, <u>um</u>, can you give us a few more minutes?
>
> W Of course. Let me know …

7 a Tell the class that they are going to write a survey to find out more about their class's Internet habits.

Put students into pairs. Students work with their partner and write at least four questions. Students should include three possible answers for each question, as in the example.

┌─ **EXTRA IDEA** ─
- If you used the Extra Idea in **1**, encourage students to use the vocabulary you discussed then. 🖉 If you didn't, you could brainstorm some vocabulary onto the board at this point to help students with their survey.

b Students work on their own and move around the room interviewing two other students, or interview two students sitting near them. Each student should make brief notes on their interviewees' answers.

c Students work with their partner from **7a** and compare notes. Finally, ask each pair to tell the class about the results of their survey.

┌─ **WRITING** ─
For homework, students write a paragraph about the results of their Internet surveys. In the next class these can be displayed around the room for other students to read.

┌─ **FURTHER PRACTICE** ─
Ph **Class Activity** 7C Wordbuilding squares p172 (Instructions p140)
Ph **Study Skills** 3 Silent letters p230 (Instructions p226)
Extra Practice 7C SB p121
Self-study DVD-ROM Lesson 7C
Workbook Lesson 7C p38

▷ REAL
7D WORLD ▷ You're breaking up
Student's Book p62–p63

Vocabulary on the phone
Real World problems on the phone

QUICK REVIEW This activity reviews prefixes. Students do the first part of the activity on their own. Put students into pairs. Students swap lists and complete the activity in their pairs. Ask students to tell the class one or two of their sentences.

1 a Students do the exercise on their own, then check new words/phrases in **VOCABULARY 7.4** ▷ SB p143. Tell students not to answer the questions at this stage. Check the meaning of new words/phrases with the class. Point out that we can often say *reception* or *signal*: *The reception/signal isn't very good here. I can't get any reception/signal.* Note that *reception* is

an uncountable noun. Highlight that we can say *an answerphone* or *an answering machine*.
Check students understand the difference between *a smart phone* and *a mobile phone* (you can access the Internet on a smart phone, as well as making phone calls).
Model and drill the words, highlighting the pronunciation of *feature* /ˈfiːtʃə/.

b Students do the exercise in pairs. Ask students to tell the class one thing they found out about their partners.

c Students discuss the questions in groups. Ask students to share interesting or surprising answers with the class.

2　**a** Focus students on the photos. Tell students that they are going to hear three conversations. **VIDEO** 7 **CD2** 24 Play the video or audio recording (SB p165). Students watch or listen, and find out what each person is doing next Tuesday. Check answers with the class.

b Students read questions 1–8. Play the video or audio recording again. Students watch or listen and answer the questions. Students compare answers in pairs. Check answers with the class.

1 Gstaad. 2 Tony offers to pick Eddy up at the airport. 3 Yes. 4 Eddy's father is Tony's boss and he wants to leave work early. 5 No. 6 a meeting 7 Yes. 8 He suggests going out for dinner.

EXTRA IDEA

- If your class are finding the recording difficult, ask them to look at **CD2** 24, SB p165. Play the video or audio recording again. Students watch or listen, read and check their answers.

REAL WORLD Problems on the phone

3　**a–c** Students do the exercise on their own or in pairs, then check in **REAL WORLD 7.1** SB p144. Check answers with the class.

a 1 delay 2 breaking up 3 catch 4 credit 5 line 6 speak up 7 reception 8 any 9 losing 10 cut off 11 die
- Point out that *break up* means 'lose part of the signal' and *speak up* means 'speak louder'.
- Also remind students that we can say *The reception isn't very good here.* or *The signal isn't very good here.*
- Check the meaning of any other new words/ phrases with the class.

b 1 Shall I call you back on the hotel's landline?
2 Would you like me to phone you back?
3 Do you want me to give you a ring later?

4　**a** Students do the exercise in pairs using language from **3a** and **3b**.

b Students compare their answers in pairs. Check answers with the class.

1 A Why don't we meet outside the cinema at seven?
B Sorry, I **didn't** get any **of** that. It's a **bad** line.
A I said let's meet outside the cinema at seven.
B I keep **losing** you. **Shall** I call you **back** on **your** landline?
A Yes, if you don't mind. I think **my** phone's **about to** die.

2 A The meeting's at 3.30 in Room F.
B Sorry, I **didn't** catch all **of** that. You're **breaking up** a bit.
A I said, the meeting's at 3.30 in Room F.
B OK … Oh dear, I'm **just** about **to** run out **of** credit.
A **Would** you like **me to** phone **you** back?
B That'd be great, thanks.

5　**a** Students do the activity in new pairs. Make sure that students make notes, but don't write the whole conversation.

b Students practise the conversation with their partners.

c Reorganise the class so that students are working in groups of four with another pair. Each pair takes turns to role-play their conversations. Students decide which phone problems they heard in the other pair's conversation.
Finally, ask one or two pairs to role-play their conversations for the class.

WRITING

Students write their conversation from **5**.

FURTHER PRACTICE

Extra Practice 7D SB p121
Self-study DVD-ROM Lesson 7D
Workbook Lesson 7D p39
Workbook Reading and Writing Portfolio 7 p76
Progress Test 7 p250

HELP WITH PRONUNCIATION
Stress and rhythm (3): linking

This *Help with Pronunciation* section focuses on the linking sounds we use between words in connected speech.

1 Focus students on the introductory bullet point. Check students remember the linking sounds /w/, /r/ and /j/. If necessary, remind students that we use the sounds /w/, /j/ and /r/ to link words that end in a vowel sound with those that begin with a vowel sound. Also remind students that we usually link words that end in a consonant sound with words that start with a vowel sound.

CD2 25 Focus on the news item. Play the recording. Students listen and notice the linking.

2

a Students do the exercise in pairs.

b Tell students to look at **CD2** ▶ **26** SB p166 and check their answers. Check answers with the class. Play the recording. Students listen and repeat the sentences.

> 1 Joe _/w/_ Atkins, the _/j/_ ex-transport minister, agrees with_all the protestors'_arguments.
> 2 This city _/j/_ already has_enough_airport capacity.
> 3 He said any _/j/_ airport_expansion should be _/j/_ in the north of the country where there _/r/_ are high levels_of_unemployment.
> 4 The police, who _/w/_ underestimated the number _/r/_ of demonstrators, made many _/j/_ arrests.

c Put students into pairs. Students take turns to say the sentences in **1** and **2a**. While they are working, monitor and check they are using the correct linking sounds. Finally, ask students to say one of the sentences. Check they use the correct linking sound and praise good pronunciation.

continue2learn

Focus students on the *continue2learn* section on SB p63. See p35 for ideas on how to exploit this section.

Extra Practice 7

See p35 for ideas on how to exploit this section.

7A
1 2 suspected 3 suits 4 involves 5 envy 6 realise 7 doubted 8 seemed 9 trusted 10 deserves
2 2 is; 've read 3 's working; 's thinking 4 's being; 's 5 has; 's having 6 thinks; 's thinking

7B
3 2 ~~They been~~ They've been 3 ✓ 4 ~~I've been writing~~ I've written 5 ~~I've come~~ I've been coming 6 ~~Lyn's having~~ Lyn's had 7 ✓ 8 ✓
4 2 's been studying 3 've had 4 've never been 5 's won 6 've been going 7 has become 8 's been working 9 've been looking
5 economy (economist/economic/economical); polluted (polluter/pollution); capitalist (capitalism/capital); environment (environmentalist/environmental); product (producer/production/productive); investment (investor/invested); industrial (industrialist/industry/industrialised)

7C
6 2 decorate 3 smoker 4 hunting 5 valued 6 understand 7 stop 8 qualified
7D
7 2 run out 3 get 4 speak 5 reception 6 losing 7 cut off 8 die 9 line

Progress Portfolio 7

• See p36 for ideas on how to exploit this section.

QUICK REVIEW This activity reviews phrases for talking about problems on the phone. Students do the first part of the activity on their own. Put students into pairs to have a phone conversation about arranging to meet up. Make sure they include the four phrases they wrote in their conversation. Ask pairs to role-play their conversations to the class.

Vocabulary Dealing with money

1 a Focus students on the example. Students work on their own and do as much of the exercise as they can before checking new words/phrases in **VOCABULARY 8.1** SB p145. Check answers with the class.

Check the meaning of any new words/phrases with the whole class.

Teach students that in informal English, we often say *in the red* to mean overdrawn and *in the black* to mean *in credit*: *Oh no! I'm in the red again!*.

Point out that *debt* can be a countable or an uncountable noun, and that we can also say *be in debt*: *Lorna's terrible with money – she's always in debt*.

Also establish that we often use *interest* to talk about the amount of money we have to pay when we borrow money, or that we earn from a bank account: *I have to pay a lot of interest on this loan.*

Point out that in more formal situations we often use *withdraw money* (= take money out of your account) and *deposit money* (= put money into your account): *I'd like to withdraw £100. I deposited £100 into your account yesterday.*

You can also teach students that the piece of paper that tells you how much money you have in your bank account is called *a bank statement* and the amount of money you have in a bank account at any point of time is called *a (bank) balance*.

Model and drill the words/phrases, highlighting the pronunciation of *overdrawn* /əʊvə'drɔːn/, *debt* /det/ and *loan* /ləʊn/.

Note that only the main stress in words/phrases is shown in vocabulary sections and the Language Summaries.

> be in credit – be overdrawn; get into debt – get out of debt; buy/get something on credit – pay cash for something; get a loan – repay a loan; have a good credit rating – have a bad credit rating; get a high interest rate – get a low interest rate; have a current account – have a savings account; be well off – be short (of money); take/get money out of an account – put money into an account

b Give students one minute to memorise the opposites in **1a**.

Put students into pairs, Student A and Student B. Ask Student As to close their books. Student Bs say a phrase and Student Bs say the opposite.

After a couple of minutes, ask students to change roles.

> ### EXTRA IDEA
> - Students work on their own and choose five phrases from **1a** that are connected to their life in some way. Put students into groups. Students take turns to tell each other why they have chosen these phrases. Note that money can be a sensitive subject, so only do this activity if you feel your students know each other well.

Speaking and Listening

2 Check students remember *advantage* /əd'vɑːntɪdʒ/ and *disadvantage* /'dɪsədvɑːntɪdʒ/. Drill these words with the class.

Students do the exercise in pairs. Ask students to share their ideas with the class.

3 a Focus students on the photo of Briony and her father. Ask students to speculate on what they might be talking about.

CD2 ▶ **27** Play the recording (SB p166). Students listen and answer the questions.

Students compare answers in pairs. Check answers with the class.

> **1** some money (£250) **2** She owes her flatmate £100 and her rent's due. **3** No, she doesn't. She gets £150.

b Give students time to read sentences 1–6, then play the recording again. Students listen and tick the correct answers and correct the false ones.

Students compare answers in pairs. Check answers with the class.

> **1** ✓ **2** F She hasn't put petrol in the car. **3** ✓ **4** ✓
> **5** F He hasn't had dinner yet. **6** F He doesn't know where she is or when she'll be home.

> ### EXTRA IDEA
> - Ask students if they think Briony's father should give her the money. Put students into pairs. Ask students to discuss the question, and decide whether they would give her the money or not. Ask students to share their ideas with the class.

HELP WITH GRAMMAR

Wishes (1); *I hope ...* ; *It's time ...*

4 **a–e** Students do the exercises on their own or in pairs, then check in **GRAMMAR 8.1** SB p146. Check answers with the class.

> **a** **1** imaginary situations in the present or the future
> **2 a** *would* + infinitive **b** *knew* (Past Simple)
> **c** *were coming* (Past Continuous) **d** *could* + infinitive

- Point out that we often use *I wish ...* to talk about the opposite to what is true or real: *I wish I had my own car.* (I don't have my own car, but I would like to).
- Highlight that we use *wish* + **Past Simple** to make wishes about states (sentence b).
- We use *wish* + **Past Continuous** to make wishes about actions in progress now or to refer to a future event (sentence c).
- We use *wish* + *could* + **infinitive** to make wishes about abilities or possibilities (sentence d).
- Point out that we can say *I wish ...* or *If only ... .*

> **b** **1** Stop talking about the accident. **2** No, she doesn't. **3** Yes, she is.

- Use sentence a to highlight that we use *wish* + *would* + **infinitive** to make wishes about things other people, organisations, etc. do that we would like to change. This is often used to show annoyance or impatience about things that are outside our control.
- Point out that we can't use *wish* + *would* + infinitive to talk about ourselves: *I wish I had a job.* not ~~I wish I would have a job.~~
- Go through the **TIPS** in the *Wishes in the present* section in **GRAMMAR 8.1** SB p146 with the class and check students understand them.

> **c** **1**b **2**a

- Point out that in sentence 1, the speaker thinks she might come home. This is a real possibility. In sentence 2, the speaker doesn't think she will come home. This is an imaginary situation.
- Use sentence 1 to highlight that we use *I hope ...* to talk about things that we want to happen in the future: *I hope she comes home soon.*
- Point out that *I hope ...* is followed by a clause (subject + verb + ...): *I hope they enjoy themselves.*

> **d** We often use *It's (about) time* + subject + **Past Simple** to say that we are frustrated or annoyed that something hasn't happened yet. We use *about* to add emphasis.

- We use *It's time* + **infinitive with** *to* to say that something should happen now.
- Go through the **TIPS** in the *I hope ...* section in **GRAMMAR 8.1** SB p146 with the class and check students understand them.

EXTRA IDEA

- Focus students on sentences a–d in **4a**. Ask students to say who said each sentence (Briony or her father), and to put them in the order they heard them.
- **CD2** 27 Play the recording again. Students listen and check their answers. Check answers with the class.

> **a** father **b** Briony **c** Briony **d** Briony
> Order: d, c, b, a

5 **a** Students do the exercise on their own, then compare answers in pairs. Check answers with the class.

> **1** pay **2** had **3** thought **4** would come **5** could
> **6** found **7** didn't have to **8** weren't rehearsing

b Students do the exercise on their own.

c Students compare answers in pairs and decide who said each sentence 1–8 and replies a–h, Briony or her dad.
Check answers with the class. Use sentences a and h in **5b** to highlight that we often use second conditionals to give reasons for wishes.

> **1**f (Briony's dad, Briony)
> **2**d (Briony, her dad)
> **3**g (Briony's dad, Briony)
> **4**c (Briony, her dad)
> **5**b (Briony, her dad)
> **6**a (Briony's dad, Briony)
> **7**h (Briony, her dad)
> **8**e (Briony, her dad)

6 **a** Students do the exercise on their own.
While students are working, monitor and check their sentences for accuracy.

EXTRA IDEA

- ✏ Write these prompts on the board: *work, studies, money, lifestyle, languages, relationships, abilities, where you live, home life, health, free time, holidays.* Students can use these ideas or their own when writing their wishes.

b Put students into pairs. Students take turns to tell each other their wishes.
Encourage students to give reasons for their wishes, as in the example, and to ask follow-up questions.
Ask students to tell the class one or two of their partner's wishes.

Get ready ... Get it right!

7 Check students understand all the prompts.

Students work on their own and think of five things that annoy them. Students should make notes, not write complete sentences.

8 Students do the activity in groups.

Remind students to use *wish* + *would* + infinitive and *It's (about) time* + subject + ... where possible. Also encourage students to give reasons for their ideas.

While students are working, monitor and correct any mistakes you hear.

Finally, ask students tell the class about things that annoy everybody in their group. Ask the class to decide what the three most annoying things are.

WRITING

Students write a short text about their six wishes from **6a** and the things that annoy them from **7**. Encourage students to use the answers from the follow-up questions to add interesting information to their text.

FURTHER PRACTICE

Ph Class Activity 8A Life isn't perfect p173 (Instructions p140)
Extra Practice 8A SB p122
Self-study DVD-ROM Lesson 8A
Workbook Lesson 8A p40

8B — Every little helps
Student's Book p66–p67

Vocabulary phrasal verbs (3): money
Grammar wishes (2): *should have*

QUICK REVIEW This activity reviews wishes in the present, *I hope* ... and *It's time* ... . Students do the first part of the activity on their own. Put students into pairs. Students complete the activity with their partner. Ask a few pairs to share interesting sentences with the class.

Vocabulary Phrasal verbs (3): money

1 **a** Students do the exercise on their own, then check any new words/phrases in **VOCABULARY 8.2** SB p145. Students compare answers in pairs. Check answers with the class.

Check the meaning of any new words/phrases with the whole class.

Point out that you can *pay someone back* or *pay something back*.

Also highlight that you *come into* some money or property when a relative dies and leaves it to you in his/her will.

Establish that *rip someone off* is an informal verb and the noun is *a rip-off*: *£5 for a cup of tea? What a rip-off!*.

Point out that *go down* is a Type 1 phrasal verb; *come to* and *come into* are Type 2 phrasal verbs; *pay back, pay off, take out, put down, take off* and *rip off* are Type 3 phrasal verbs for these meanings. *Save up (for sth)* is either a Type 1 phrasal verb (*save up*) or a Type 4 phrasal verb (*save up for something*). For more information about the different types of phrasal verbs, see lesson 4A SB p32.

1 the money/my brother 2 mortgage/student loan 3 mortgage/loan 4 Mortgage rates/House prices 5 bill/meal 6 a deposit/£25,000 7 some money/some property 8 £20/15% 9 new bike/holiday 10 hotel/shopkeeper

b Students work in pairs and take turns to test each other on the collocations in **1a**, as shown in the speech bubbles.

EXTRA IDEAS

- Students work in pairs and take turns to say a noun from **1a**. Their partner says which phrasal verb(s) can go with each noun.
- Students write six sentences about their life, using the phrasal verbs and other words/phrases from **1a**. Three should be true and three should be false. Students work in pairs, swap sentences and guess which of their partner's sentences are false.

Speaking and Reading

2 **a** Students do the exercise in pairs. Ask students to share their ideas with the class. Students can decide which is the best (or worst!) money-making idea.

b Focus students on the article and the pictures. Students read the article and decide which is the best way to earn some extra money and which is the worst.

Elicit students' ideas and ask them to give reasons if possible. Find out which money-making scheme they think is the best and which they think is the worst.

3 **a** Students do the exercise on their own.

b Students compare answers in pairs, then check on SB p114. Check answers with the class.

Ask students if they would like to do any of the things in the article, giving reasons for their answers. You can also ask students to tell the class about any other interesting or unusual jobs they have done to make some extra money.

- **Pose as a live model:** the usual rate is £8–12 an hour.
- **Be a mystery shopper:** £8–10 a visit, but could be as high as £100 a day.
- **Rent out a room:** up to £450 a month.
- **Let out your home for film and TV shoots:** on average about £1,000 a day.
- **Do some dog walking:** on average you can make £10–15 an hour.
- **Sleep research:** £25 a night.

4 Students work on their own and match the speech bubbles to the people in the pictures. Check answers with the class.

A Anna **B** Louise **C** Charlie **D** Lee **E** Tom **F** Lucy

HELP WITH GRAMMAR
Wishes (2): *should have*

5 **a–d** Students do the exercises on their own or in pairs, then check in GRAMMAR 8.2 SB p146. Check answers with the class.

a They are talking about the past.

b **1** Anna **took** five dogs for a walk at the same time. She **regrets** that. **2** Louise **didn't start** doing this work years ago. She **regrets** that.

c **1** Past Perfect Simple **2** past participle
- Use speech bubbles A, C and E to highlight that we use *wish* + Past Perfect Simple to make wishes about the past. These wishes are used to express regret and are often the opposite of what really happened.
- Use speech bubbles B, D and F to highlight that we can also use *should/shouldn't have* + past participle to talk about regrets in the past.

- Point out that we can also use the third conditional for regrets: *If I'd known about this before, I'd have done it years ago.*
- Highlight that we can use *I wish ...* or *If only ...* to make wishes about the past: *I wish I'd been there. = If only I'd been there.*
- Establish that we can also make sentences in the past with *wish* with *you/he/she/we/they: They wish they hadn't moved house.*

HELP WITH LISTENING Wishes

This *Help with Listening* section helps students to hear the difference between different types of wishes in the present and the past.

6 **a** Focus students on the sentences in 1. Ask students which sentence talks about the past (the second sentence) and what *'d* is short for in the second sentence (*had*, as it's followed by the past participle).

Focus students on the sentences in 2. Ask students whether both sentences talk about the present or the past (the present) and what *'d* is short for in the second sentence (*would*, as it's followed by the infinitive).

CD2 28 Play the recording. Students listen and notice the difference between the verb forms in each pair of sentences.

Play the recording again if necessary, highlighting the contraction *'d* in the second sentence in each pair.

b **CD2** 29 Play the recording (SB p166). Students listen and write the six sentences. Point out that they will hear each sentence twice.

Students compare sentences in pairs.

✎ Check answers by eliciting each sentence and writing it on the board. Highlight the verb forms in each sentence and ask students which sentences express wishes in the past (2 and 5).

1 I wish she lived a bit nearer. **2** I wish he'd bought chocolate instead. **3** I wish she'd visit more often. **4** I wish he worked for us. **5** I wish I'd had enough time to finish. **6** I wish I earned a bit more money.

7 **CD2** 30 **PRONUNCIATION** Play the recording (SB p166). Students listen and repeat the sentences. Check students copy the weak forms and contractions correctly.

8 **a** Check students remember *insist on something* and *jewellery* /'dʒuːəlri/.
Students do the exercise on their own.

b Students compare answers in pairs and guess which person in the pictures said each sentence. Check answers with the class.

1 I wish I **hadn't put** him in the room next to ours. (Charlie)
2 I wish **I'd met** the actors and actresses. (Lucy)
3 I shouldn't have **gone** to bed so early. (Tom)
4 I should **have** insisted on a break after an hour so I could move around. (Lee)
5 I loved the jewellery I bought. I wish I hadn't **had** to give it back. (Louise)
6 The owner should **have** told me Sammy liked to chew everything. (Anna)

9 Students do the exercise on their own, then compare answers in pairs. Check answers with the class.

2 I wish you'd/you had told me that your brother was on TV last night. 3 I shouldn't have stayed out too late last night. 4 I wish I hadn't eaten too much at lunch. 5 My sister should have paid me back the money she owed me. 6 I wish the interest rate had gone down last month. 7 You should have told me you needed a lift this morning.

Get ready … Get it right!

10 Students do the exercise on their own.

When students have written five things that they regret, they must decide how to express their regrets using *I wish/If only* + Past Perfect Simple, *should(n't) have* or the third conditional.

EXTRA IDEA

- Students work in groups and think of other phrases for each category. ✎ Write these on the board, check meaning with the class and give students time to copy the phrases into their notebooks.

With a lower-level class, you can ask students to write sentences expressing their regrets instead of making notes.

11 Students work in pairs and take turns to tell each other about the things they regret. Encourage students to ask follow-up questions if possible, as in the speech bubbles. Also tell students to find out what their partner regrets most.

Finally, students tell the class about the thing that their partners regret the most, giving reasons if possible.

WRITING

Ask students to write a paragraph about their regrets for homework.

FURTHER PRACTICE

Ph Class Activity 8B Money snakes and ladders p175 (Instructions p141)
Extra Practice 8B SB p122
Self-study DVD-ROM Lesson 8B
Workbook Lesson 8B p41

8C VOCABULARY AND SKILLS ▶ A bit extra
Student's Book p68–p69

Vocabulary synonyms
Skills Reading: a travel article; Listening: a conversation about tipping

QUICK REVIEW This activity reviews phrases and phrasal verbs connected to money. Students do the first part of the activity on their own. Put students into pairs to do the second part of the activity. Ask students to share correct sentences with the class.

Speaking and Reading

1 Check students remember *tip* and point out that this is a verb and a noun.
Students discuss the questions in groups. If you have a multilingual class, include students from different countries in each group if possible.
Ask students to share their ideas with the class and find out how much they agree or disagree with each other.

2 **a** Check students understand *a tipping custom, a hotel porter* (US = *a bellhop*) and *a service charge*.
Ask students to cover the article. Students do the exercise on their own. Students can compare answers in pairs. Don't tell students the answers at this stage.

b Students read the article and check their answers to **2a**. Check answers with the class.

1 quite different 2 often disagree 3 don't give
4 $1 5 sometimes 6 most countries

c Students do the exercise on their own then compare answers in groups. Include students from different countries in each group if possible.
Ask students to share interesting answers or disagreements with the class.

HELP WITH VOCABULARY Synonyms

3

a Remind students that we often use synonyms (words that mean the same, or almost the same) to avoid repeating words or phrases when we are speaking or writing.

Check students know the meanings of all the words/phrases in pink in the article.

b Focus students on the words/phrases in blue in the article. Students work on their own and match them to their synonyms in pink and write them in the table. Remind students to write the infinitive forms of the verbs.

✏ While students are working, draw the table on the board ready for checking. Check answers with the class.

Model and drill the words, highlighting the pronunciation of *precise* /prɪˈsaɪs/, *obligatory* /əˈblɪgətəri/ and *pursue* /pəˈsjuː/. Point out that the stress on *offended* is on the second syllable, not the first.

exact – precise; problem – dilemma; appropriate – acceptable; compulsory – obligatory; certainly – definitely; insulted – offended; chase – pursue; discover – find out; simply – just

c–d Students do the activity on their own or in pairs, then check in **VOCABULARY 8.3** ▶ SB p145. Check answers with the class. Check the meaning of any new synonyms.

Model and drill the words, paying particular attention to *especially* /ɪˈspeʃəli/, *customary* /ˈkʌstəməri/ and *vary* /ˈveəri/.

Point out that many synonyms in English have small differences in meaning or use, for example, *customary* is more formal than *normal*. Encourage students to use synonyms when they are speaking and writing where possible.

b particularly **c** generally **d** customary **e** odd **f** observe **g** additional **h** vary **i** complicated **j** such as

4

Give students a minute or two to memorise the synonyms in **3b** and **3c**.

Put students into pairs, Student A and Student B. Ask Student As to close their books. Student Bs say a word/phrase and Student As say the appropriate synonym. After a couple of minutes ask students to change roles.

Listening and Speaking

5

a Discuss the question with the class and elicit students' ideas. Don't tell them if they are correct at this stage.

b Focus students on the photo. Tell the class that they are going to listen to Graham, an Englishman, and Ruth, an American, having a conversation at the end of their meal.

CD2▶ 31 Give students time to read questions 1–4, then play the recording. Students listen and answer the questions. Check answers with the class.

1 The USA. **2** Because they get much bigger tips if they introduce themselves. **3** bartenders/bar staff; taxi drivers; bellhops/hotel porters; people who provide room service **4** The USA.

c Put students into pairs, Student A and Student B. Play the recording again. Student As listen and make notes about tipping in the UK, while Student Bs make notes about tipping in the USA.

d Students do the exercise in their pairs.
Check the tipping customs in the UK and the USA with the class.

The UK: Restaurants: about 10% (half the average tip in the USA). Bar staff: British people never tip bar staff, but they might offer them a drink. Taxi drivers: some people tell taxi drivers to keep the change, while others give 10%. Hotel porters: a pound or two. Room service: a couple of pounds.

The USA: Restaurants: 20% (maybe more if the waiters/waitresses introduce themselves); 15% is the absolute minimum. Bartenders: a couple of dollars a drink or if you pay at the end of the evening for everything, 15% or 20% of the total. Taxi drivers: 15 to 20% and never less than a couple of dollars. Bellhops: a dollar a bag and two dollars for every journey he makes to your room. Room service: a couple of dollars.

┌─ WRITING ┐

Students write an essay comparing and contrasting tipping in the UK and the USA. Encourage them to use the notes they made in **5c**.

HELP WITH LISTENING
British and American accents

This *Help with Listening* section helps students to hear the difference between British and American accents.

6

a Focus students on the sentences. Tell students they will hear each sentence twice, once with a British accent and once with an American accent.

CD2▶ 32 Play the recording. Students listen and notice the different accents.

b Focus students on the letters in blue in groups of words 1–5 and point out that British and American people often say these letters differently.

Before students begin, point out that they will hear the British accent first.

Highlight that the letter 'r' is usually pronounced in American English (as in 1), whereas the letter 'r' isn't usually pronounced in British English (unless it is followed by a vowel sound). Also highlight that in American English, a 't' between two vowel sounds is pronounced more like a /d/ (as in 2).

Highlight that the vowel sounds in 3–5 are usually said differently in British English (UK) and American English (US): 3 *staff* UK /stɑːf/, US /stæf/; 4 *dollar* UK /ˈdɒlə/, US /ˈdɑːlər/; 5 UK *bought* /bɔːt/, US /bɑːt/.

CD2 33 Play the recording. Students listen and notice the differences.

If necessary, play the recording again to allow students to hear these differences.

c Tell students they are going to hear four sentences said twice, once by a British person and once by an American person.

CD2 34 Play the recording (SB p167). Students listen and decide which they hear first, a British accent or an American accent.

Play the recording again, pausing after each pair of sentences to check students' answers. Ask students which words in each sentence helped them decide.

Check answers with the class.

1 US 2 UK 3 UK 4 US

d Ask students to look at **CD2 31**, SB p166. Play the recording again.

Students listen and notice the difference between Graham's British accent and Ruth's American accent.

7 **a** Check students remember *deserve*.
Students do the activity in pairs. Point out that students can include **any** groups of people in their list

(for example, bus drivers, dentists, cleaners, teachers, etc.), not just those who usually get tips. Remind students not to include waiters/waitresses and taxi drivers in their lists.

> **EXTRA IDEA**
>
> • ✍ Write these groups of people on the board: *hotel porters, hotel receptionists, bar staff, toilet attendants, cleaners, cloakroom attendants, bus drivers, tour guides, hairdressers, mechanics, plumbers, fast-food delivery people, street cleaners, flight attendants, teachers.* Students can choose from this list or their own ideas when doing **7a**.

b Put students into groups of four so that two pairs are working together.

Students compare lists and decide on the five groups of people from both lists who deserve tips the most. Encourage students to give reasons for including people on their lists.

c Either put groups together so that students are working in groups of eight or do the final stage of this activity with the whole class.

Ask students to agree on a final list of five groups of people who deserve tips the most.

✍ If students have done this stage of the activity in groups, elicit their final lists and write them on the board for other groups to comment on.

Finally, ask students to decide which group of people deserves tips the most.

> **FURTHER PRACTICE**
>
> **Ph Class Activity** 8C Bingo! p176 (Instructions p141)
> **Ph Vocabulary Plus** 8 British and American English p201 (Instructions p192)
> **Extra Practice** 8C SB p122
> **Self-study DVD-ROM** Lesson 8C
> **Workbook** Lesson 8C p43

▷ REAL WORLD

8D I didn't realise
Student's Book p70–p71

Real World apologising

QUICK REVIEW This activity reviews synonyms. Students do the first part of the activity on their own. Put students into pairs. Students complete the activity with their partner. Ask students to tell the class some of their pairs of synonyms.

1 **a** Students do the exercise in pairs.

b Students compare ideas in new pairs and find out which of the things on their lists they have had to apologise for recently.

Ask students to share their ideas with the class.

> **EXTRA IDEA**
>
> • ✍ Alternatively, elicit students' reasons for apologising from **1a** and write them on the board. Students work on their own and decide which of these things they have done, or other people have done to them, in the last three months. Students then compare ideas in groups, explaining the situation that required each apology if appropriate.

2 **a** Focus students on photos A–C. Ask students who the man is (Eddy) and what they remember about him (he's an actor, but he hasn't had a job for ages).

> **EXTRA IDEA**
>
> • Students look at the photos and try to predict what Eddy is talking to the people about. Don't check answers at this stage.

VIDEO►8 CD2► 35 Play the video or audio recording (SB p167). Students watch or listen and do the exercise.
Check answers with the class.

> **A**2 **B**1 **C**2, 3

b Give students time to read sentences 1–9.
Play the video or audio recording again. Students watch or listen, tick the true sentences and decide why the other sentences are false.

c Students compare answers in pairs. Check answers with the class.

> 1 ✓ 2 F Eddy is auditioning for the part of a bad guy. 3 ✓ 4 F Eddy hadn't met Roger before. 5 ✓ 6 F Eddy didn't break Roger's nose. 7 F Eddy got the part in the TV drama. 8 ✓ 9 ✓

REAL WORLD Apologising

 3 **a–c** Students do the exercises on their own or in pairs, then check in **REAL WORLD 8.1►** SB p146.
Check answers with the class.

> • 2b 3c 4b 5c 6b 7c 8c 9b 10a 11c 12a 13b 14b 15c 16a
> • Point out the difference between *I didn't mean it.* (= I didn't mean something that I said) and *I didn't mean to.* (= I didn't mean to do something).
> • Also use sentence 13 to highlight that we can use *should/shouldn't have* to be self-critical.
> • After *I'm sorry (that) …* we use **a clause.**
> • After *I'm sorry about …* we usually use **a noun.**
> • After *I'm sorry for …* we usually use *(not)* **verb+*ing*.**
> • Point out that after *I'm sorry about …* we can also use *it, this, that* or *what happened: I'm really sorry about it/this/that/what happened.*

4 **a** Students do the exercise on their own.

b Students compare answers in pairs. Check answers with the class.

> 2 believe 3 about 4 mean 5 about 6 shouldn't 7 need 8 idea 9 for/about 10 worry 11 matter

5 **a** Put students into pairs. Students choose situation 1 or 2 then write a conversation between the people. Remind students to use language for apologising from **3a** in their conversations.

> **EXTRA IDEA**
>
> • Tell half the pairs in the class to use situation 1 and the other half to use situation 2. Ensure that students swap papers in **5b** with a pair who wrote the other conversation.

b Students swap papers with another pair. Students then read the other pair's conversation and correct any mistakes they find. If students have problems understanding the other pair's conversations, they can discuss them in groups of four. While students are working, monitor and help students with any problems.

c Students work with their partner and practise the other pair's conversation.

d Reorganise the class so that students are working in groups of four with the pair they swapped papers with in **b**. Students take turns to role-play the conversation for the pair that wrote it. Students can decide which conversation they think is better.
Finally, ask students to role-play one or two conversations for the class.

> **FURTHER PRACTICE**
>
> **Extra Practice** 8D SB p122
> **Self-study DVD-ROM** Lesson 8D
> **Workbook** Lesson 8D p44
> **Workbook** Reading and Writing Portfolio 8 p78
> **Progress Test** 8 p252

HELP WITH PRONUNCIATION
Sounds (3): same stress, different sound

This *Help with Pronunciation* focuses on words from the same word family, where the stress is on the same syllable, but the sound is different.

 1 **a** Focus students on the pairs of words and the phonemes.
CD2► 36 Play the recording. Students listen and notice how the sounds in pink change in the stressed syllable.

b Play the recording again. Students listen again and repeat the words. Remind students that in each pair one sound is long and the other short.
If students are having problems remembering how to pronounce these sounds, help them with the mouth position.

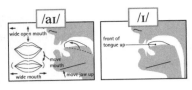

Remind students that /aɪ/ is a long vowel sound and /ɪ/ is a short vowel sound.

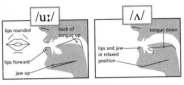

Remind students that /uː/ is a long vowel sound and /ʌ/ is a short vowel sound.

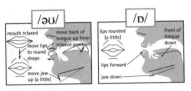

Remind students that /əʊ/ is a long vowel sound and /ɒ/ is a short vowel sound.

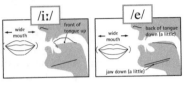

Remind students that /iː/ is a long vowel sound and /e/ is a short vowel sound.

c CD2 37 Play the recording (SB p167). Students listen and do the exercise on their own.
Students check answers in pairs. Check answers with the class.

secure / security S offend / offensive S
precise / precision D

2 a Students do the exercise in pairs. Encourage them to say the words out loud to help them identify if the sounds in pink are the same or different.

b CD2 38 Play the recording (SB p167). Students listen and check their answers.
Play the recording again. Students listen and repeat the words.
Finally, ask students to say one pair of words. Check they pronounce the short and long vowel sounds correctly, and use the correct word stress and praise good pronunciation.

2D 3S 4D 5D 6D 7D 8D 9S 10D 11S 12D

continue2learn

Focus students on the *continue2learn* section on SB p71. See p35 for ideas on how to exploit this section.

Extra Practice 8

See p35 for ideas on how to exploit this section.

8A
1 2 I took £20 out of my account. 3 He's well off. 4 Do you get a high interest rate? 5 I managed to repay that loan. 6 The company got out of debt. 7 My account is overdrawn. 8 Dan has a bad credit rating.
2 2 were thinking/thought 3 weren't sitting 4 could 5 bought 6 can 7 wouldn't keep 8 didn't have to 9 stops 10 passes 11 would stop 12 listened

8B
3 2 into 3 off 4 off 5 down 6 off 7 to 8 for 9 out 10 back
4 2 had told 3 'd/had bought 4 n't/not have shouted 5 'd/had had 6 n't/not have lent 7 'd/had studied 8 have mentioned

8C
5 2 compulsory 3 figure out 4 generally 5 appropriate 6 just 7 find out 8 customary 9 precise 10 additional

8D
6 2 I can't believe I said that. 3 I didn't mean to upset you. 4 Sorry for losing your keys. 5 Sorry I didn't invite you. I thought you were away for some reason. 6 I shouldn't have said that to you. 7 Sorry. I had no idea you were busy. 8 Don't worry about it. 9 I'm really sorry, but I'm afraid I broke/have broken your plate. 10 I'm sorry I haven't phoned you sooner. I'm afraid I lost my mobile.

Progress Portfolio 8

- See p36 for ideas on how to exploit this section.

QUICK REVIEW This activity reviews language for apologising. Students work on their own and write two things that people should apologise for. Put students into pairs and ask them to swap papers. Students complete the activity in their pairs.

Vocabulary and Speaking
The cinema

1 Students do the exercise in pairs, then check new words/phrases in **VOCABULARY 9.1** ▶ SB p147. Tell students not to answer the questions at this stage. Check the meaning of any new words/phrases with the class.

Check students understand the difference between *a review* and *a critic*, which is a false friend in many languages.

Teach student that the noun from *subtitled* is *subtitles* (*Does this DVD have subtitles?*) and that we can say a film is *dubbed into* another language (*The film was dubbed into Chinese.*).

Also point out that we use *be set in* to refer to both the place and the period of time where a film takes place: *This film is set in New York in the 1930s.*

Also check students remember *a plot* and *a character* from lesson 4B.

Model and drill the words/phrases, highlighting the pronunciation of *subtitled* /ˈsʌbtaɪtld/, *dubbed* /dʌbd/ and *sequel* /ˈsiːkwəl/. Highlight that the stress on *subtitled*, *subtitles* and *remake* is on the first syllable of each word, not the second, and that *dubbed* is one syllable, not two.

Note that only the main stress in words/phrases is shown in vocabulary boxes and the Language Summaries.

Students ask and answer the questions in their pairs. Ask students to tell the class one or two interesting or surprising things they found out about their partner.

Note that students have the opportunity to discuss a film they have seen recently at the end of lesson 9B, so don't spend too long discussing individual films at this stage.

> **EXTRA IDEA**
> • Students work in pairs, Student A and Student B. Student As close their books and Student Bs look at **VOCABULARY 9.1** ▶ SB p147. Student As read out definitions of the words and Student Bs have to say the word. After a few minutes, ask students to change roles.

Speaking and Reading

2 a Check students know *an Academy Award ®* (= an Oscar ®). Check students understand *ceremony* and *nominate (somebody for an award)*. Students discuss the questions in groups. Ask students to share interesting answers with the class.

b Check students understand *postponed, solid gold, televise* /ˈtelɪvaɪz/, *assassination* and *vanish*, and that they remember *a flood* /flʌd/. Students do the exercise in pairs. Don't tell students the correct answers at this stage.

c Focus students on the article on SB p73. Ask students what they know about the people in the photos.

> **Kathryn Bigelow** is an American director, famous for her 2008 film *The Hurt Locker* about a bomb disposal team in Iraq. The film won six Oscars in 2010 including Best Director and Best Picture.
> **Javier Bardem** is a Spanish actor who has starred in many successful films such as *Vicky Cristina Barcelona* and *Love in the Time of Cholera*. In 2008 he won an Oscar for Best Supporting Actor for his role in the film *No Country for Old Men*.

Students read the article and check their answers to **2b**. Check answers with the class.

> 1 March 2 before 3 sometimes 4 aren't 5 2010 6 aren't

3 Students do the exercise on their own, then compare answers in pairs. Check answers with the class. Ask students what they thought was the most interesting or surprising piece of information in the article.

> • The first Academy Awards ceremony to be televised was in **1953**.
> • The Oscar show has been broadcast internationally since **1969**.
> • The Oscar show reaches movie fans in more than **180** countries.
> • The ceremony had to be postponed in **1981** after the assassination attempt on President Reagan.
> • In **1939** the *Los Angeles Times* printed the names of the winners before the ceremony.
> • Kathryn Bigelow became the first woman to win an Oscar for best director for *The Hurt Locker* in **2010**. Before 2010, only three other women had been nominated for this award.
> • 52 of the Oscars that were stolen in 2000 were found in some rubbish by a man called Willie Fulgear.
> • Each Oscar costs around **$400** to make.

HELP WITH GRAMMAR
The passive

4 **a–d** Students do the exercises on their own or in pairs, then check in **GRAMMAR 9.1** SB p148. Check answers with the class.

a In the **passive** sentence, the focus is on what happens to someone or something rather than on who or what does the action.
- We often use the passive when we **don't know** who or what does the action.
- To make the passive we use: subject + **be** + past participle.
- Remind students that in passive sentences we can use '*by* + the agent' to say who or what does the action. We only include the agent when it is important or unusual information: *52 of the Oscars were found in some rubbish **by a man called Willie Fulgear.***

b **2** is being shown **3** was given **4** were being driven **5** has been broadcast **6** had been nominated **7** are going to be awarded
- Point out that we don't use the Present Perfect Continuous and Past Perfect Continuous in the passive.

c After certain verbs (e.g. *enjoy*) we use *being* + past participle: *Everyone enjoys being told they are good at what they do.*
- After certain verbs (e.g. *want*) we use *to be* + past participle: *Most of us want to be rewarded in some way.*
- After prepositions we use *being* + past participle: *Every actor dreams of being nominated for an Oscar.*
- After *the first/second/last* (+ noun) we use *to be* + past participle: *The first (Academy Awards ceremony) to be televised was in 1953.*
- After *have to* and *used to* we use *be* + past participle: *The ceremony had to be postponed in 1938 because of a flood. Newspapers used to be given the winners' names in advance.*
- After modal verbs we use *be* + past participle: *The names wouldn't be published until afterwards.*
- Point out that we can use all modal verbs (*can, must, will, could, might,* etc.) in passive verb forms: *He can't be trusted.*

EXTRA IDEA
- Focus students on the text on p73. ✍ Write these questions on the board: *1 Where is the Academy Awards ceremony held? 2 How many times has the ceremony had to be postponed? 3 What did newspapers use to be given before the ceremony? 4 Why was Willie Fulgear invited to the ceremony in 2000? 5 Why can't an Oscar be sold?* Students read the article again and do the exercise on their own. Check answers with the class.

1 in Hollywood **2** three times **3** the winners' names **4** Because he found the missing Oscars in some rubbish. **5** Because the Academy didn't want the awards to end up in the hands of private collectors.

5 Ask students if they have ever seen any Bollywood films and if so, what they thought of them.
Students do the exercise on their own. Remind students to read the text quickly for gist first before choosing the correct verb forms.

EXTRA IDEA
- Before doing **5**, elicit things that students would like to know about the Indian film industry and write them on the board. Students then read the text to find out which of their questions are answered. Check answers with the class.

1 is **2** are watched **3** include **4** last **5** to be produced **6** were being made **7** produce **8** can be seen **9** spends **10** is being forced **11** being transported **12** should go

6 Go through the example with the class. Point out that the rewritten sentences must begin with the words in brackets and that students must use a passive verb form in each sentence.
Students do the exercise on their own, then compare answers in pairs. Check answers with the class.

2 The pills should be taken with food. **3** She doesn't like being told what to do. **4** I hope to be promoted next year. **5** He was the first to be invited. **6** She had to be taken to hospital. **7** The parcel will be delivered to me tomorrow. **8** The boss needs to be told immediately.

Get ready ... Get it right!

7 Put students into two groups, Group A and Group B. Students in Group A turn to SB p106 and students in Group B turn to SB p109. Check they are all looking at the correct exercise.

a Put students into pairs with someone from the same group. Students work with their partner and write questions 1–6, as in the example. Remind students to use the correct passive verb form in each question.

While they are working, check their questions for accuracy. Early finishers can check their questions with another pair in the same group.

> **Student A: 2** How many Oscars **have been refused** so far? **3** Which of these films **hasn't been awarded** an Oscar for best movie? **4** Approximately how many Oscars **are made** each year? **5** Which actress **has been nominated** for the most best actress awards? **6** At what time of day in the USA **are** the nominations **announced**?
>
> **Student B: 2** In which year **was** the first Oscar **awarded** for special effects? **3** How many Oscars **was** the film *The Lord of the Rings* **nominated** for in 2003? **4** How many people **are told** the results before the ceremony? **5** Which country **has been awarded** the most Oscars for best foreign film? **6** How many Oscars **have been awarded** since the Academy Awards began?

b Reorganise the class so that a pair from Group A is working with a pair from Group B. Students take turns to ask and answer their questions, saying the three possible answers after each question. The correct answers are in **bold**.

c Students work out which pair got most answers right. Finally, ask the class if any pair answered all six questions correctly.

WRITING

Ask students to research information about another awards ceremony or film festival, for example the BAFTA (British Academy of Film and Television Arts) awards in the UK, the Cannes Film Festival, The Golden Globe Awards, etc. Students write an article about the event, giving information about when it started, where it is held and any particular stories associated with it.

FURTHER PRACTICE

Ph **Class Activity** 9A Passive dominoes p177 (Instructions p142)
Extra Practice 9A SB p123
Self-study DVD-ROM Lesson 9A
Workbook Lesson 9A p45

9B ▶ What was it like?
Student's Book p74–p75

Vocabulary entertainment adjectives
Grammar *as, like, such as, so, such*

QUICK REVIEW This activity reviews words/phrases connected to the cinema. Students do the first part of the activity on their own. Put students into pairs for the second part of the activity. Ask students to share a few of their example sentences with the class.

Vocabulary and Speaking
Entertainment adjectives

1 **a** Students do the exercise on their own, then check new words in **VOCABULARY 9.2** SB p147. Note that only new words are in the Language Summary.
Check the meaning of new words with the class.
Elicit these opposite adjectives from the class and write them on the board: *believable – unbelievable*;

predictable – unpredictable; *sentimental – unsentimental*; *overrated – underrated*; *realistic – unrealistic*. Remind students that prefixes aren't usually stressed and point out that the other adjectives in **1a** don't have direct opposites.
Remind students that we can say *absolutely hilarious*, but not ~~very hilarious~~.
Also teach students the phrases *easy to follow – difficult to follow* (easy/difficult to understand the plot of a film, play, etc., either because it is too complicated or because it is hard to understand what the actors say): *The film was very difficult to follow because all the actors spoke so fast*.
Model and drill the words, highlighting the pronunciation of *far-fetched* /fɑːˈfetʃt/, *scary* /ˈskeəri/, *weird* /wɪəd/ and *hilarious* /hɪˈleərɪəs/. Also point out that *memorable* is three syllables, not four.

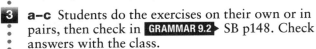

EXTRA IDEA

- Students work in pairs and decide if the words in **1a** are positive or negative qualities of a film. Check students' ideas with the class. Note that some adjectives, such as *sentimental*, *scary* and *weird*, could be considered positive or negative qualities, depending on the type of film and the speaker's attitude to it.

b Check students understand *a play* and *a TV drama*. Students do the exercise on their own. Make sure students don't write the adjectives on their paper – just the name of the film, play or TV drama.

c Put students into pairs and ask them to swap papers. Students take turns to ask their partners why they chose the films, plays or TV dramas on their list. Encourage students to ask follow-up questions where possible.
Ask students to tell the class about one or two films, plays or TV dramas on their partner's list.

Listening and Speaking

2 **a** Focus students on the photo of Ritika and Gloria talking to their friend Nathan.
CD3 1 Give students time to read questions 1 and 2, then play the recording (SB p167). Students listen and answer the questions.
Check answers with the class.

1 Ritika and Gloria have just been to see a musical called *Dream Train*. **2** They didn't enjoy it because it was weird – 'more like a bad dream'. It was very disappointing, even though it had a good cast, the music wasn't very good, the plot was 'far-fetched' and the ending was 'completely unrealistic'.

EXTRA IDEA

- To reinforce the answer to question 2 in **2a**, ask students what title Ritika says would have been better for the musical (*Nightmare Train*). Ask students why she chooses this title.

b Give students time to read sentences 1–10, then play the recording again. Students listen and choose the correct words/phrases.
Students compare answers in pairs. Check answers with the class.

1 bad **2** Critics **3** quite like **4** actors **5** great
6 train compartments **7** cast **8** far-fetched
9 loved **10** attention

EXTRA IDEA

- **CD3** 1 Before students listen again, ask them to work in pairs and try to choose the correct words/phrases in **2b**. Play the recording again so students can check their answers.

3 **a–c** Students do the exercises on their own or in pairs, then check in **GRAMMAR 9.2** SB p148. Check answers with the class.

a We use *like* + clause to say that things happen in a similar way (sentence 5).
- We use *like* + noun (or pronoun) to say that something is similar to something else (sentence 4).
- We use *as* + noun to say that somebody has a particular job (sentence 3).
- We use *such as* or *like* to introduce examples (sentences 2 and 4).
- We also use *as* + noun to say what something is used for (sentence 6).
- Point out that we can also use *as* + clause to say that things happen in a similar way, but this is less common: *Peter Harris was great, as he usually is.*
- You can also highlight that we use *as* in certain fixed phrases: *as well, as you know, as I said earlier, as well as,* etc.

b We use *so* + adjective (sentence 8 in **2b**).
- We use *such* (+ adjective) + noun (sentence 7).
- We use *so* + *much* or *many* + noun (sentences 10 and 9).
- Check students understand that we use *so* and *such* to give nouns, adjectives and adverbs more emphasis.
- Also point out that with *so* and *such* we often use '(*that*) + clause' to say what the consequence is: *The play was so slow (that) I actually fell asleep.*
- Highlight that we often use *a lot of* with *such*: *There was such a lot of noise.*
- Point out the word order when we use *such* with singular countable nouns: *It's such a nice restaurant.* not *It's a such nice restaurant.*

4 **a** Check students understand *an extra* (a person in a film who doesn't have a speaking part and is usually in the background).
Students do the exercise on their own, then compare answers in pairs.

1 such as **2** as **3** so **4** like **5** such **6** as **7** like **8** so

b Put students into pairs. Students take turns to ask each other the questions in **4a**. Encourage students to ask follow-up questions if possible.

5 **a** Check students understand *a model* by eliciting names of famous models from the class.
Students do the exercise on their own.

b Students compare answers in pairs. Check answers with the class.

1 so **2** such **3** like (as) **4** so **5** so **6** so **7** like (as)
8 such **9** as **10** such as/like **11** so **12** like **13** as
14 so **15** such **16** like

Get ready ... Get it right!

6 **a** Put students into new pairs. Each student chooses a film, play or TV drama they have seen recently, but their partner hasn't seen.

b Students work on their own and write five sentences with *as, like, such as, so* and *such* about their film, play or TV drama, based on the prompts or their own ideas.

While students are working, check their sentences for accuracy and help students with new vocabulary.

7 Students work with the same partner as in **6a**. Students take turns to tell each other about the film, play or TV drama that they chose, based on the prompts in **6b** or their own ideas. Students should include the sentences they prepared where appropriate. Encourage students to ask follow-up questions to find out more about the film, play or TV drama if possible.

While they are working, monitor and correct students where necessary.

Finally, ask students to tell the class two things they remember about their partner's film, play or TV drama.

9C VOCABULARY AND SKILLS

Is it art?
Student's Book p76–p77

Vocabulary homonyms
Skills Listening: discussing art; Reading: an article about an exhibition

QUICK REVIEW This activity reviews *as, like, such as, so* and *such*. Students complete the sentences on their own. Put students into pairs. Students take turns to tell each other their sentences and ask follow-up questions. Ask students to share interesting sentences with the class.

Speaking and Listening

1 Check students understand *sculpture* /ˈskʌlptʃə/ and *performance artist*. Students discuss the questions in pairs.

Focus students on works of art A–C and ask students their opinion of them in turn. Find out which is the most popular work of art in the class and which is the least popular.

Doris Salcedo (1958–) is a sculptor. She was born in Colombia and studied in both Colombia and New York. She now teaches at the Universidad Nacional de Colombia.

Tate Modern is a large modern art gallery in London. It regularly commissions artists to produce a piece of work to go in the large entrance hall. The piece Doris Salcedo presented here was called *Shibboleth* – a 167-metre-long crack in the floor. It was meant to represent the movement of immigrants across Europe.

Henri Rousseau (1844–1910) was a French post-Impressionist painter. He didn't start painting seriously until he was in his 40s and his work was considered by some people to be quite child-like. He is most well-known for his paintings of jungle scenes.

The 4th Plinth is an empty plinth (a base for a statue) in Trafalgar Square in London. It was designed in 1841 to display a statue of a horse, but the statue was never completed and the plinth remained empty until 1998. At that time, four contemporary statues were put on temporary display on the plinth. The project was a big success and the Mayor of London began the Fourth Plinth Programme, which commissions work to appear on the plinth.

Anthony Gormley (1950–) is a British sculptor, best-known for his work involving the human body. His fourth Plinth project in 2009 was called *One & Other*. It was a live project in which 2,400 people occupied the plinth for 60 minutes each, over 100 days. The people were picked at random from nearly 35,000 people who applied to be part of the project.

Hazel Imbert is a textile artist and actress. She was one of the people who took part in the *One & Other* project in 2009. She used her 60 minutes on the plinth to show something about what it is to be a woman and an artist. She wanted people watching to 'reflect peacefully on how and why women nurture others, and why this creativity is unsung'.

EXTRA IDEA

- Begin the class by asking students to work in groups and tell each other about the last time they went to visit an art gallery or an exhibition.
---

2 **a** Tell students that they are going to listen to two friends, Graham and Hannah, talking about art. **CD3 2** Play the recording (SB p168). Students listen and decide which of the art in pictures A–C each person saw. Ask them to find out who doesn't like modern art.
Check answers with the class.

> Graham saw the Henri Rousseau painting (A).
> Graham saw *Shibboleth* at Tate Modern (C).
> Hannah saw Hazel Imbert on the fourth plinth (B).
> Graham doesn't like modern art.

EXTRA IDEA

- **CD3 2** Before students do **2a**, play the recording and ask students to put the works of art A–C in the order they hear them on the recording. Check answers with the class.
---

b Put students into pairs. Give students time to read the prompts, then play the recording again. Students listen, then try to remember as much as they can from the conversation. Encourage students to add as much extra information as they can about each person and what they said.
Ask students to share any extra information they talked about with the class.

HELP WITH LISTENING
Missing words, reduced infinitives

This *Help with Listening* section shows students that we often miss out words in informal spoken English when the meaning is clear.

3 **a** Students read the beginning of Graham and Hannah's conversation and notice the missing words. Ask students what kind of words we often miss out (subject pronouns, the verb *be*, auxiliaries, prepositions).

b Students do the exercise on their own. Check answers with the class. Point out that these reduced infinitives are very common in informal spoken English.

> I was going to (apply for that job). I didn't want to (apply for that job).

c Ask students to turn to **CD3 2**, SB p168. Play the recording again. Students listen, notice the missing words and decide what the reduced infinitives in bold refer back to. Check answers with the class.

> HANNAH I **meant to** (see the Henri Rousseau exhibition).
> HANNAH (I) **really wanted to** (see the work by Doris Salcedo at the Tate).
> GRAHAM Well, maybe it's **supposed to** (make us think about life).
> HANNAH I'm **not trying to** (compare Rousseau's painting with a crack in the floor).

Speaking, Reading and Vocabulary

4 Students discuss the questions in groups. Ask students to share interesting answers with the class.

5 **a** Focus students on the photo of Michael Landy and tell students that he is a Young British Artist. Ask students what they think he is doing in the photo.

> **Young British Artists** (YBAs) is the name given to a group of artists, including Tracey Emin, Rachel Whiteread, Michael Landy and Damien Hirst, who are based in the UK.

Students read the article and write a title for it. Set a time limit of two or three minutes to encourage students to read for gist.
Then put students into pairs to do the second part of the activity.
Ask the class to choose the best title for the article.

b Students do the exercise on their own, then compare answers in pairs. Check answers with the class.

> 1F It took Landy three years to plan the *Break Down* exhibition. 2 ✓ 3F He destroyed everything he'd ever owned. 4 ✓ 5F When he had finished he felt an incredible sense of freedom. 6F He didn't give them the facts. 7 ✓

103

HELP WITH VOCABULARY Homonyms

6 a Focus students on the introductory bullet and check students understand what a *homonym* /'hɒmənɪm/ is. Elicit one or two more examples of homonyms from the class (*right, match, play,* etc.). You can contrast *homonyms*, which have the same spelling and pronunciation, with *homophones*, which have the same pronunciation, but are spelt differently (*flu/flew, through/threw, wore/war, buy/by,* etc.). Note that students studied homophones in lesson 5C. Focus students on the words in pink in the article. Students do the exercise on their own.

b Students compare answers in pairs. Check answers with the class. Ask students to explain the differences in meaning between the homonyms in each pair of sentences (see the first dictionary box in **VOCABULARY 9.3** SB p147).

1 state 2 handle 3 case 4 point 5 last

c–d Focus students on the words in blue in the article. Students do the exercise in the same pairs, then check in **VOCABULARY 9.3** SB p147. Check answers with the class by referring to the second dictionary box in **VOCABULARY 9.3** SB p147. Point out that the first meaning of each word in the Language Summary is the meaning of the word as it appears in the article and the second is an alternative meaning. Elicit any other meanings of the words that students have thought of and check if they are correct.

7 Students do the exercise on their own. Point out that the meaning of the words as they appear in these sentences is the second meaning in the dictionary box in **VOCABULARY 9.3** SB p147. Check answers with the class.

1 change 2 sense 3 examination 4 mind 5 sack

8 Put students into pairs. Ask all students to turn to SB p112.

a Students do the exercise with their partner. Encourage students to give reasons for their ideas for each photo.

b Reorganise the class so that two pairs are working together. Students discuss their ideas about each photo in their groups, again giving reasons for their opinions.

c Ask students to check their ideas on SB p114 and see how many works of art they identified correctly. Finally, ask students to share their opinions on each real work of art.

WRITING

Students choose two works of art from the photos on SB p112–p113. Tell students to describe the pieces and give their opinion of each one, giving reasons for their opinion. Encourage students to write balanced arguments, rather than just saying that they don't like something.

FURTHER PRACTICE

Ph Vocabulary Plus 9 Compound nouns p202 (Instructions p192)
Ph Study Skills 4 Homonyms p231 (Instructions p226)
Extra Practice 9C SB p123
Self-study DVD-ROM Lesson 9C
Workbook Lesson 9C p48

▶ REAL
9D WORLD
It's up to you
Student's Book p78–p79

Real World making and responding to suggestions

QUICK REVIEW This activity reviews homonyms. Students work on their own and write four homonyms. Put students into pairs and ask them to swap lists. Students finish the activity in their pairs. Ask students to share some of their pairs of sentences with the class.

1 Students discuss the questions in groups.
Ask a few students to tell the class about the last time they went out with friends.

2 a Focus students on pictures A–D.
If necessary, point out that *The Rocket* is the name of a music venue and *Blue Orchid* is the name of a club.
Students work in pairs and decide what each place is advertising. Check answers with the class.
Ask students which they would like to go to, giving reasons for their answers.

> **A** a film **B** a rock concert / a gig **C** a Mexican restaurant **D** a club

b Check students remember Chloe and Tina from lesson 6D.
Tell students that they are going to watch or listen to Chloe and Tina discussing what to do for a night out. **VIDEO▸9 CD3▸3** Play the video or audio recording (SB p168). Students watch or listen and put pictures A–D in the order Chloe and Tina talk about them, then find out what they decide to do in the end.
Check answers with the class.

> **1D 2A 3C 4B**
> In the end they decide to go to The Rocket on Sunday to see Tina's brother's new band.

c Check students understand *pour with rain*.
Give students time to read sentences 1–6, then play the recording again.
Students listen and complete the sentences.
Students compare answers in pairs.
Check answers with the class.

> **1** ... she's got to do a lot of things tomorrow. **2** ... she's seen it quite a few times already. **3** ... she's had curry a lot lately. **4** ... it's pouring with rain out there. **5** ... it's her mum's birthday. **6** ... her youngest brother's new band is playing there.

REAL WORLD
Making and responding to suggestions

3 a–c Students do the exercises on their own or in pairs, then check in **REAL WORLD 9.1▸** SB p148. Check answers with the class.

a a asking if the person is free **b** making a suggestion **c** politely refusing a suggestion **d** saying you have no preference
- Highlight that *What are you up to ... ?* is an informal way to say *What are you doing ... ?* and point out that we also use *be up to* to talk about the present: **A** *Hi, what are you up to at the moment?* **B** *I'm watching TV.*
- Remind students that *Do you fancy ... ?* is an informal way to say *Do you want to ... ?*
- Also establish that *I don't feel up to ...* means 'I don't feel well enough or have enough energy to ...' and that *It's up to you.* means 'You decide'.
- Check students also remember these ways of asking if a person is free: *What are you doing on (Saturday)?* and *Are you free on (Saturday)?*.
- ✐ Elicit ways to accept a suggestion and write them on the board, for example, *Yes, that'd be great.; That's/That sounds a good/great idea.; Yes, why not?; Yes, I'd love to.*

b *I'd rather ...* can't be followed by verb+*ing*.
- Point out that *wouldn't mind, feel like, fancy* and *feel up to* are followed by verb+*ing*, a noun or a pronoun: *I wouldn't mind **going** to that.*
- Also highlight that *I'd rather* is followed by the infinitive: *I'd rather **give** that a miss, if you don't mind.*

> ┌─ **EXTRA IDEA** ─┐
> - Ask students to turn to **CD3▸3**, SB p168. Play the recording again. Students listen and underline all the sentences for making and responding to suggestions when they hear them. Students can then check answers in pairs.

4 a Tell students that Tina's brother Ben wants his friend Penny to come to his gig at The Rocket. Focus students on Ben's half of the conversation. Students work on their own and write Ben's sentences using language from **3a**, as in the example.
Students can compare answers in pairs. Check answers with the class.

> **BEN** Do you fancy **coming** to see my new band?
> **B** Great. So, what **are** you **up** to today?
> **B** Well, I **wouldn't** mind **going to** see *The Matrix*. How **about** you?
> **B** I **don't** mind which one we go to. It's **up** to you.
> **B** OK. 8.20's fine. **Do you** feel like **having** something to eat first?
> **B** I'm easy. **Whatever** you like.

b Students work in pairs and write Penny's half of the conversation in **4a**. Again remind students to use language from **3a** where possible. Also point out that there is more than one possible way of completing the conversation.

While students are working, check their sentences for accuracy and help with any problems.

c **CD3** 4 Play the recording (SB p168). Students listen to Ben and Penny's conversation and decide how similar it is to theirs.

5 **a** Students do the exercise on their own. Ask students to write when people can do the things on their lists if appropriate.

b Put students into groups of three. Students take turns to tell each other about the places to go and things to do on their lists. Each group should then agree on some things to do and when they plan to do them. Encourage students to use the language in **3a** in their conversation.

Finally, ask each group to tell the class what they have decided to do and when, then ask if other students would like to join them.

EXTRA IDEA

- Before the class, find some adverts for places to go and things to do in the town/city you are in now. Cut out the adverts, stick them on a piece of paper and make enough photocopies for each student. Instead of asking students to make their own lists in **5a**, distribute the photocopies to the class. Students then choose which things they would like to do from the adverts.

FURTHER PRACTICE

Ph **Class Activity** 9D Giveaway! p179
(Instructions p142)
Extra Practice 9D SB p123
Self-study DVD-ROM Lesson 9D
Workbook Lesson 9D p49
Workbook Reading and Writing Portfolio 9 p80
Progress Test 9 p254

HELP WITH PRONUNCIATION
Sounds (4): the letters *ie*

This *Help with Pronunciation* focuses on the different ways we pronounce the letters *ie*.

1 **a** Focus students on the words and the phonemes.
CD3 5 Play the recording. Students listen and say how the letters in pink are pronounced, then write them in the table. Check answers with the class.

/iː/ niece   /ɪ/ accessories   /ə/ efficient
/ɪə/ twentieth   /aɪ/ die   /aɪə/ diet

b Play the recording again. Students listen and repeat the words. If students are having problems remembering how to pronounce these sounds, help them with the mouth position.

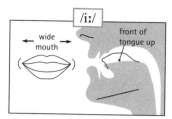

Remind students that /iː/ is a long vowel sound.

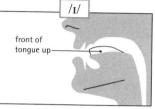

Remind students that /ɪ/ is a short vowel sound.

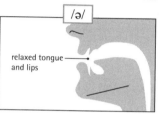

Remind students that /ə/ is a weak vowel sound, so it is always unstressed.

Point out that /ɪə/ is a long vowel sound and that it moves from /ɪ/ to /ə/.

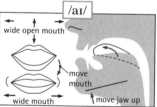

Remind students that /aɪ/ is a long vowel sound.
Point out that for the sound /aɪə/, students move from /aɪ/ to an unstressed vowel sound /ə/.

2 **a** Students do the exercise in pairs.

b **CD3** 6 Play the recording (SB p169). Students listen and check their answers. Play the recording again. Students listen and repeat the words.

/iː/ relief; achieve; piece; field
/ɪ/ series; accompanied; apologies
/ə/ ancient; conscience; impatient
/ɪə/ convenient; fierce; experience
/aɪ/ pie; lie
/aɪə/ anxiety; science; society

c Students do the activity in pairs. While they are working, monitor and check they are saying the words correctly. Finally, ask students to say a sentence from **2c** or a word from **2a**.

continue2learn

Focus students on the *continue2learn* section on SB p79. See p35 for ideas on how to exploit this section.

Extra Practice 9

See p35 for ideas on how to exploit this section.

9A

1 2 dub 3 subtitles 4 released 5 remake 6 sequel
   7 costumes; plot 8 trailer 9 soundtrack 10 rave

2 2 surprised 3 had been accepted 4 ✓ 5 wouldn't
   be offered 6 I'd expected to be asked 7 ✓ 8 ✓
    9 was the first to be asked
   10 hate being laughed at 11 ✓ 12 ✓ 13 ✓ 14 was
   accepted

9B

3 2 predictable 3 moving 4 sentimental 5 scary
   6 gripping 7 believable 8 hilarious

4 2 like 3 so 4 like 5 so 6 as 7 so 8 such

9C

5 1 round 2 case; change 3 handle 4 state 5 change
   6 handle 7 round 8 state; case 9 point

9D

6 2 What are you up to on/next Saturday? 3 Have
   you got anything on next Friday? 4 Do you fancy
   going for a drink? 5 I thought we could give that
   new club a try. 6 Do you feel like going to Pat's
   barbecue this/next weekend? 7 I wouldn't mind
   going to the cinema tonight. 8 I'm sorry, but I
   don't feel up to it this evening. 9 I'd rather give
   that a miss if you don't mind. 10 Perhaps some
   other time. 11 I'm easy. Whatever you like.
   12 I'm not bothered either way. 13 It's all the same
   to me.

Progress Portfolio 9

- See p36 for ideas on how to exploit this section.

10A ▶ How practical are you?
Student's Book p80–p81

Vocabulary household jobs
Grammar *have/get something done,*
get somebody to do something,
do something yourself

QUICK REVIEW This activity reviews ways of making and responding to suggestions. Put students into groups and ask them to imagine they are spending tomorrow evening together. Students do the activity in their groups. Remind them to use language from REAL WORLD 9.1 ▶ SB p148 in their conversations before they begin. Ask groups to tell the class about their plans for tomorrow evening. The class can then decide which group has the most interesting plan.

Vocabulary and Speaking

Household jobs

1 **a** Focus students on the example. Students work on their own and do as much of the exercise as they can before checking new words/phrases in VOCABULARY 10.1 ▶ SB p149.

Check answers with the class. Note that only new words/phrases are included in the Language Summary.

Point out that that we can say *a light bulb* or *a bulb*. You can also teach the phrase *The bulb's gone.* (= stopped working/broken).

Highlight that *leak* is also a verb (*Oh no! The roof is leaking!*) and that the singular of *shelves* is *a shelf*.

Check students understand the difference between *put something up* (= put on the wall or build) and *put something in* (= install in your home) by highlighting the nouns that go with each verb. You can also point out that these are phrasal verbs.

Also point out that we can say *fix, repair* or *mend*: *I've just fixed/repaired/mended the roof.*

Establish that *DIY = do it yourself* (making or repairing things yourself instead of buying them or paying somebody else to do them): *My husband is very good at DIY.*

Remind students that the shop where you take clothes to be dry-cleaned is called *a dry cleaner's.* Also note that the verb *dry-clean* and the adjective *dry-cleaned* are sometimes spelt without the hyphen (*dry clean, dry cleaned*).

Point out that *service* is also a noun: *When did your car last have a service?*

Model and drill the words, paying particular attention to *shelves* /ʃelvz/, *a burglar* /ˈbɜːɡlə/ *alarm*, *a duvet* /ˈduːveɪ/, *DIY* /diːaɪˈwaɪ/, *tyres* /taɪəz/ and *clothes* /kləʊðz/.

Note that only the main stress in words/phrases is shown in vocabulary boxes and the Language Summaries.

1 a leak **2** a lock **3** a duvet **4** a key **5** DIY
6 a bath **7** a flat **8** the floor **9** a window **10** clothes

b Students do the exercise in pairs.

✍ While students are working, write the verbs on the board. To check answers, elicit students' ideas for each verb and write correct collocations on the board for other students to copy.

Possible answers
change the sheets, a wheel; **put up** a picture, a poster; **put in** a new boiler, a new kitchen; **fix** the central heating, the shower; **check** the battery, the brakes; **decorate** the front room, the bedroom; **replace** the cooker, a door; **dry-clean** a skirt, the curtains; **cut** the hedge, the lawn; **service** a scooter, a washing machine

┌─ **EXTRA IDEA** ┐
• Students work in pairs and take turns to test each other on the collocations. One student says a noun, for example, *the roof*, and his/her partner says a verb that goes with the noun, for example, *fix the roof.*

2 **a** Students do the exercise on their own.

b Students compare ideas in pairs to see if any are the same.

Ask students to share interesting similarities or differences with the class. Discuss whether some of the household jobs in **1a** are thought of as 'women's jobs' and some as 'men's jobs', and if so, why.

Listening

3 **a** Check students understand *practical* (= good at repairing or making things).

Focus students on the people in the photos and the list of things they can do.

CD3 ▶ 7 Play the recording (SB p169). Students listen and do the exercise on their own.

Check answers with the class.

Charlotte: decorate a flat, put new tiles up. She's quite practical.
Rick: fix leaks, service a washing machine, do a basic car service. He's very practical.
Jason: none of the things. He isn't at all practical.
Pam: change light bulbs and batteries. She's not very practical.

b Students do the exercise in pairs.

c Play the recording again. Students listen and check their answers to **3b**.

b Pam **c** Pam **d** Rick **e** Jason **f** Jason **g** Jason
h Rick **i** Charlotte

- Put students into groups of four, A, B, C and D. Tell Student As to make notes about Charlotte, Student Bs to make notes about Rick, Student Cs to make notes about Jason and Student Ds to make notes about Pam. Encourage students to write down as much as they can remember, then tell the other members of their group about their person.

   CD3 7 Play the recording again. Students listen and check they included all the relevant information.

HELP WITH GRAMMAR

have/get something done, get somebody to do something, do something yourself

4 **a–f** Students do the exercises on their own or in pairs, then check in **GRAMMAR 10.1** SB p150. Check answers with the class.

a 1a, c 2b 3d
- Use sentences a and c in **3b** to highlight that we use *have/get something done* when we pay somebody else to do the job.
- Use sentence b to highlight that we use *get somebody to do something* when we ask somebody that we know to do the job. If it's a friend or family member, we probably don't pay them.
- Use sentence d to highlight that we use *do something myself, yourself*, etc. when we do the job without any help from other people.
- Point out that *get something done* is usually more informal than *have something done*.
- Highlight that we can also say *pay somebody to do something*: *I usually pay somebody to do the garden.*

b We make the positive form of *have/get something done* with: subject + *have* or *get* + something + **past participle**.
- We make the positive form of *get somebody to do something* with: subject + *get* + somebody + **infinitive with *to*** + something.

c 2e 3f 4h 5i
- Use sentences e–i in **3b** to establish that we can use *have/get something done* and *get somebody to do something* in any verb form by using the correct form of *have* or *get*.

d 1 Rick doesn't have his car serviced at a garage. Does Rick have his car serviced at a garage? 2 Jason didn't have his bathroom painted last week. Did Jason have his bathroom painted last week? 3 Charlotte isn't getting her boiler replaced. Is Charlotte getting her boiler replaced?
- Use the answers to **4d** to highlight that we make the negative and question forms of *have/get something done* and *get somebody to do something* by using the correct form of *have* or *get*.

- Point out that *have* is a main verb in *have something done*, not an auxiliary verb. This means that in the Present Simple and Past Simple we use *don't, doesn't* and *didn't* to make negatives and *do, does* and *did* to make questions.
- Also highlight that we never contract *have* in *have something done*: *I have my car serviced every year.* not ~~I've my car serviced every year.~~

e *myself; yourself; himself; herself; itself; ourselves; yourselves; themselves*

5 **CD3** 8 **PRONUNCIATION** Play the recording (SB p169). Students listen and practise the sentences in **3b**. Check students copy the sentence stress correctly. Play the recording again if necessary.

6 Check students remember *dye your hair*. Students do the exercise on their own, then compare answers in pairs. Check answers with the class.

1 A How much do you pay to get your duvet dry-cleaned?
  B I'm not sure. I haven't had it cleaned for ages.
2 A Did you do the decorating yourself?
  B Yes, but I got my sister to help me.
3 A Did you dye your hair yourself?
  B No, I got my friend to do it for me.
4 A Have you had some new lights put in round the pool?
  B Actually, I put them in myself.
5 A When did you last get your car serviced?
  B I haven't had it done recently.

- Students practise the conversations in **6** in pairs until they can remember them. Ask students to close their books. Students practise the conversations again.

7 **a** Focus students on the photo of Lucy and tell them that she is married to one of the men in the photos on SB p80. Students do the exercise on their own.

b Students compare answers in pairs. Check answers with the class.
Ask students which man in the photos they think Lucy is married to, giving reasons for their answers.

2 haven't had ... done 3 to get ... to help 4 to get/to have ... painted 5 get ... to come 6 have ... x-rayed 7 have/get ... mended 8 to have/to get ... resprayed 9 get ... to repair 10 getting/having ... done

Get ready … Get it right!

8 Check students understand all the prompts in the box. If necessary, check students understand *print*, *nails* and *iron* /ˈaɪən/.

Students do the exercise on their own. Remind students that they can include any words/phrases from **1a** in their lists, as well as the prompts in the box.

While they are working, monitor and check students are compiling their lists correctly. Encourage students to include at least four things on each list.

9 Put students into groups of three or four. Students take turns to tell each other about the things on their lists. Encourage students to ask follow-up questions if possible. Students also decide who is the most practical person in the group.

While they are working, monitor and correct any mistakes that you hear.

Finally, ask each group to tell the class who is the most practical person in each group, giving reasons for their choice.

You could also ask the class to decide who is the most practical person in the class.

> **WRITING**
>
> For homework, ask students to write a paragraph about themselves based on their lists from **8**.

> **FURTHER PRACTICE**
>
> **Ph** **Class Activity** 10A Having things done p181 (Instructions p143)
> **Extra Practice** 10A SB p124
> **Self-study DVD-ROM** Lesson 10A
> **Workbook** Lesson 10A p50

10B ▶ The youth of today
Student's Book p82–p83

Vocabulary adjectives for views and behaviour
Grammar quantifiers

QUICK REVIEW This activity reviews household jobs. Students do the first part of the activity on their own. Put students into pairs. Students finish the activity in their pairs. Ask students to tell the class a few of their verb–noun collocations.

Vocabulary and Speaking

Adjectives for views and behaviour

1 **a** Students work in pairs and say which words they know. Ask them to try to identify which adjectives are positive and which are negative. Students check any new words in **VOCABULARY 10.2** ▶ SB p149.

✎ While they are working, draw a blank two-column table on the board ready for checking. Write *positive* and *negative* at the top of each column.

✎ Check answers with the class by eliciting the words from students and writing them in the table on the board in the correct column.

Point out the opposites of *fair* (*unfair*) and *reasonable* (*unreasonable*). *Biased* and *disciplined* also use the prefix *un-* to make the opposite (*unbiased*, *undisciplined*), and we can use it to make the opposite of *threatening*, although we more usually say *non-threatening*. Point out that the opposite of *unruly* is not ~~ruly~~, and that we use words like *well-behaved*, *obedient*, etc. instead.

Establish that we use *subjective* to say something is based on feelings and beliefs rather than facts, but it isn't a direct opposite of *objective*.

Highlight that *abusive* can also mean harmful in a physical way, not only using rude and offensive words.

Establish that we use the preposition *against* after *prejudiced*, but we can also just say somebody is prejudiced, without saying what it is they are prejudiced against.

Model and drill the words/phrases, highlighting the pronunciation of *biased* /ˈbaɪəst/, *disciplined* /ˈdɪsəplɪnd/, *prejudiced* /ˈpredʒʊdɪst/ and *unruly* /ʌnˈruːli/.

Positive: fair; reasonable; disciplined; objective
Negative: biased; threatening; abusive; unfair; resentful; prejudiced; unruly

b Students work in the same pairs and say which statements in **1a** they agree/disagree with. Encourage them to give reasons for their answers.
Ask students to share interesting information with the class.

Reading

2 **a** Focus students on the photos. Ask students what their initial reaction is to each person in the photos. Ask students to share their reactions with the class and find out how many people agree.

 109

Focus students on the article and on the statements in **1a**. Check students understand the phrase *my blood boils*. Point out that we often say *It makes my blood boil.* when we are very angry about something.

Students do the activity on their own.

Students compare answers in pairs. Check answers with the class.

Maggie Dawson would agree with statements 1, 3, 4, 7 and 9.

b Students do the exercise on their own, then compare answers in pairs. Check answers with the class.

1 F Maggie Dawson believes young people suffer more discrimination than elderly people. 2 F The CRAE survey showed that just less than half (49%) of the young people interviewed thought they had experienced prejudice. 3 ✓ 4 ✓ 5 F The police don't have a good relationship with groups of young people in the streets, often ordering them to move on. 6 F Barbara Hearn believes that equality is for everyone – so all people deserve the same rights.

EXTRA IDEA

- Students make notes about how the following things or groups of people react to young people: TV programmes, the CRAE survey, shopkeepers, bus drivers, the police. Put students into groups to discuss whether they agree or disagree with these points of view. Encourage students to give reasons for their answers.

HELP WITH GRAMMAR
Quantifiers

3 **a–b** Focus students on the quantifiers in bold and the underlined quantifiers in the article.

Students do **3a** and **3b** on their own or in pairs, then check in the *Differences in meaning* section in GRAMMAR 10.2 SB p151. Check answers with the class.

a *Both of* and *either of* refer to two things or people.
- *Everyone, every, any of, anyone, all of* and *anything* refer to more than two things or people.
- *Each* can refer to two or more things or people.

b Point out that *no one, neither of, none of* and *no* refer to a zero quantity.
- *Neither of* refers to two things or people.
- *No one, none of* and *no* refer to more than two things or people.
- Remind students that we don't usually use 'double negatives' in English. We say *I don't like any of them.* not *I don't like none of them.* and *I haven't done anything.* not *I haven't done nothing.*
- Remind students we can say *everyone* or *everybody, anyone* or *anybody* and *no one* or *nobody*.

c–e Focus students on the words/phrases in pink and the verbs in blue in the article.

Students do the exercises on their own or in pairs, then check in the *Differences in form* section in GRAMMAR 10.2 SB p151. Check answers with the class.

c *Every* and *each* are followed by a **singular** countable noun.
- *Both of, neither of, either of, any of, all of* and *none* are followed by *the, my,* etc. + a **plural** countable noun (or the pronouns *you, us* or *them*).
- *No* is always followed by a **noun**. Point out that this noun can be singular, plural or uncountable.

d *Everyone, every, no one, each* and *anything* are followed by a **singular** verb form.
- *All of, both of, neither of, either of* and *none of* are followed by a **plural** verb form.
- Point out that we can also use a singular verb form after *neither of, either of* and *none of,* although in spoken English, a plural verb form is now more common.
- Draw students' attention to the rest of the information in GRAMMAR 10.2 SB p151 and ask them to study this for homework.
- If you have a monolingual class, you may want to focus on one or two typical mistakes your students make with quantifiers.
- Note that this is a very complex area of language that students always have problems with. The aim of this lesson is to raise students' awareness of the rules governing use of quantifiers and to help them get a feel for what is correct. However, don't expect students to absorb all these rules immediately.

4 **a** Students do the exercise on their own.

b Students compare answers in pairs. Check answers with the class.

Ask students to tell the class some of the sentences that they think are true for them or the class.

1 have 2 None 3 room 4 no 5 every 6 Both of 7 all of 8 is 9 travels

5 **a** Remind students of Maggie Dawson from the article, and explain that Gavin and Bradley are the sons she talked about in the article.

Students do the exercise on their own.

b Students compare answers in pairs.
CD3 9 Play the recording (SB p169). Students listen and check their answers.

Check answers with the class.

1 all 2 every 3 no 4 None of 5 anything 6 every 7 neither 8 both of 9 either of 10 everyone 11 no one 12 all of

Get ready ... Get it right!

6 Students do the exercise on their own. Point out that students should use a quantifier in each sentence, as in the examples.

7 Put students into pairs. If possible, ask students to work with someone that they haven't worked with so far in this lesson.

Students take turns to tell each other their sentences. Encourage students to ask follow-up questions if possible.

If you have a monolingual class, find out if all the students in your class agree about young people in the country.

If you have a multilingual class, put students from different countries together if possible. Ask each pair to share their ideas with the class.

> **EXTRA IDEA**
>
> • Focus students on the photos again. Ask students if they would now have a different initial reaction to these photos after reading the article and discussing young people.

> **WRITING**
>
> Students write an essay comparing young people in two different countries. If you have a multilingual class, students can make notes while working with their partner in **7**. If you have a monolingual class, encourage students to find out information about young people in another country on the Internet.

> **FURTHER PRACTICE**
>
> **Ph** **Class Activity** 10B Going, going, gone! p182 (Instructions p143)
> **Extra Practice** 10B SB p124
> **Self-study DVD-ROM** Lesson 10B
> **Workbook** Lesson 10B p51

VOCABULARY 10C AND SKILLS

Battle of the sexes
Student's Book p84–p85

Vocabulary compound nouns and adjectives
Skills Reading: a quiz; Listening: a discussion about gender roles

QUICK REVIEW This activity reviews quantifiers. Students do the activity in pairs. If you have a lower-level class, give students a minute or two to prepare sentences on their own first before putting them into pairs. Ask students to share interesting sentences with the class.

Reading and Speaking

 a Focus students on the quiz. Students do the exercise on their own.

b Students compare their answers in pairs. Encourage them to give reasons for their choices.

c Focus students on the text. Students read the text and check their answers to **1a**. Check answers with the class.
Ask students to share surprising information with the class.

1T 2F 3F 4T 5F 6T 7T 8F 9F 10T

> **EXTRA IDEA**
>
> • Students do the quiz in groups. Before they read what psychologists and sociologists say, ask students to discuss their answers and come to an agreement about whether each statement is true or false. Encourage students to give reasons for their choices.

HELP WITH VOCABULARY
Compound nouns and adjectives

 a–c Students do the exercises on their own or in pairs. Students can check any new compound words in **VOCABULARY 10.3** SB p149. Check answers with the class.

a Check the meaning of any new compound words with the class.
• *breakdown, attention span, problem solving, drawback, the workplace* and *daydreaming* are **nouns**.
• *self-obsessed, good-humoured, widespread, high-powered, far-fetched* and *downhearted* are **adjectives**.
• Highlight that the verb for *a breakdown* is *break down* and the verb for *daydreaming* is *daydream*.

b Compound **nouns** are usually made from noun + noun (for example, *workplace*) or verb + preposition (for example, *breakdown*).
• Compound **nouns** are usually written as one word (for example, *drawback*) or two words (for example, *attention span*).
• Compound **adjectives** are usually spelt with hyphens (for example, *self-obsessed*).
• Elicit examples of compound nouns and adjectives in the text to illustrate each rule.

 a Students do the exercise on their own. The words they choose can be connected to their life now or in the past, or to friends or family members.

b Students do the exercise in pairs. Ask students to tell the class why they have chosen one or two of their words.

> **EXTRA IDEA**
>
> • 📝 Write *good-humoured* on the board and ask students to make another compound adjective by changing one part of the word (e.g. *bad-humoured*). Ask students to continue the word chain in a similar way (e.g. *bad-humoured – bad-tempered – even-tempered*, etc.). Students work in pairs and play the same game with the other compound adjectives.

Listening and Speaking

4 **a** Focus students on the book cover of *Why Men Lie and Women Cry* and ask if any students have read this book (or the first book written by the same authors, *Why Men Don't Listen and Women Can't Read Maps*). If so, ask students to tell the class what they remember about the book(s).

Tell students that they are going to listen to three friends, Naomi, Polly and Matt, discussing the roles of men and women.

Check students understand *sexist*, *sympathy* and *exaggerate*, and check students remember *solve a problem* and *gorgeous*.

Give students time to read a–e and check students understand all the points.

CD3 ▶ 10 Play the recording (SB p169). Students listen and put points a–e in the order the people first talk about them. Check answers with the class.

1b 2d 3e 4a 5c

b Give students time to read questions 1–6, then play the recording again. Students listen and answer the questions. Students compare answers in pairs. Check answers with the class. Ask students whether they were surprised by any of the information in the recording.

1 Naomi. **2** He thinks it isn't bad and he agreed with some of it. **3** Men like to sort out their own problems. They only talk about problems when they want solutions. Women talk about problems over and over again, but want sympathy rather than solutions. **4** Women use three times more words in a day than men. **5** Men exaggerate about things like how powerful their car is and how gorgeous their latest girlfriend is. **6** Women say things like: 'I'll *never* speak to you again.' or 'You *never* think about other people.'.

> **EXTRA IDEA**
>
> • Put students into pairs. Students make notes on what each person (Naomi, Polly and Matt) thinks about the roles of men and women. **CD3 ▶ 10** Play the recording again if necessary. Tell students to say who they agree with most. Ask pairs to tell the class what they thought. Which person do most of the students agree with?

HELP WITH LISTENING Contradicting

This *Help with Listening* section focuses on how we contradict people in spoken English.

5 **a** Check students understand *contradict* by asking a student his/her opinion of something and then contradicting it yourself.

CD3 ▶ 11 Play the recording. Students listen and notice the words that Matt stresses when he contradicts Polly and Naomi.

Students choose the correct words in the rules. Check answers with the class.

- When we want to contradict someone, we often stress the **auxiliary**.
- We **sometimes** repeat the main verb.
- Use the parts of the conversation in **4a** to point out that we often use short answers (e.g. *No, we don't.*) to contradict people. Sometimes we use these short answers without *Yes* or *No* (e.g. *They do.*).
- Also highlight that when we want to use a positive form of the Past Simple to contradict people, we often include the auxiliary *did* to add emphasis (e.g. *I did agree with it.*). Note that students studied this use of auxiliaries in lesson 1B.
- Remind students that when we want to use a positive form of the Present Simple to contradict people, we often use the auxiliaries *does* or *do* to add emphasis: A *I don't know Bob.* B *You do know him.* (or *Yes, you do./You do.*); A *He doesn't work here.* B *He does work here.* (or *Yes, he does./He does.*).

b Tell students that they are going to listen to five pairs of sentences from the conversation between Naomi, Polly and Matt.

CD3 ▶ 12 Play the recording (SB p170). Students listen and write the auxiliary that the second speaker stresses when he/she contradicts the first speaker. Play the recording again, pausing after each conversation to check students' answers.

1 have **2** isn't **3** don't **4** do **5** don't

> **EXTRA IDEA**
>
> • Ask students to turn to **CD3 ▶ 12**, SB p170. Play the recording again. Students listen and notice the ways that the speakers contradict each other in context.

6 **a** Students discuss the questions in groups. If possible, include men and women in each group. While they are working, monitor and help students with any new language.

b Finally, ask students to tell the class two of the things their group disagreed about.

▷ REAL
10D WORLD ▶ I did tell you!
Student's Book p86–p87

Real World adding emphasis

QUICK REVIEW This activity reviews compound nouns and adjectives. Students do the activity in pairs. You can also ask students to make sentences using their partner's compound words to check that they understand the meaning of each word.

1 Students discuss the questions in groups. Ask students to share interesting answers with the class.

2 **a** Focus students on the photo. Tell students that the two people in the photo are Judy and Martin, who they last saw together in a video in lesson 6D.
VIDEO ▶10 **CD3** ▶ 13 Give students time to read sentences 1–6, then play the video or audio recording (SB p170). Students watch or listen and do the exercise on their own.
Students compare answers in pairs. Check answers with the class.

> 1 ✓ 2 ✓ 3F Judy wants Martin to buy the salad because he forgot to get it earlier. 4 Martin's parents haven't got a Satnav. 5F ✓ 6 ✓

b Give students time to read sentences 1–6, then play the video or audio recording again. Students watch or listen again and fill in the gaps with one or two words.

c Students compare answers in pairs and decide who said each sentence.
Check answers with the class.

> 1 store things (Judy) 2 my jokes (Martin)
> 3 a map (Harry) 4 look at (Val) 5 house (Val)
> 6 everywhere (Martin)

REAL WORLD Adding emphasis

3 **a–b** Focus students on the introductory bullet point and check students understand it.
Students do **3a** on their own, then check in
REAL WORLD 10.1 ▶ SB p151. Check answers with the class.

- **Pattern A:** sentences 1, 2, 5
  Pattern B: sentences 3, 4, 6
- Check students understand the verbs *admire* and *upset*.
- Use the tables to highlight the word order in each pattern. Point out that we usually use a noun, a pronoun or verb+*ing* after *about* ... in both patterns.
- Also point out that *is* ... in both patterns is usually followed by a clause (subject + verb + ...), as shown in the sentences in **2b**.
- Focus students on pattern B and point out that we can also say:
  What bothers/irritates me about ... is ... .
- You can also tell students that we often use *the fact that* after *is* ... in both patterns: *What I don't like about this place is the fact that the food is so expensive.*

4 **CD3** ▶ 14 **PRONUNCIATION** Play the recording (SB p170). Students listen and practise. Check students copy the sentence stress and intonation correctly. Play the recording again if necessary.

5 **a** Go through the example with the class. Students do the exercise on their own.

b Students compare answers in pairs. Check answers with the class.

> 2 The thing I like about the food Judy cooks is it's really healthy.
> 3 One thing that amazes me about Judy is she never gets angry.
> 4 The thing that worries me about Martin is he drives so fast.
> 5 One thing I love about Martin is his sense of humour.
> 6 What I don't like about Val is the way she interrupts me.
> 7 What annoys me about Harry is he never remembers my birthday.

6 **a** Students do the exercise on their own.

b Students compare answers in pairs.

> What I like about Sundays is
> Well, one thing that upsets me about you is
> The thing that annoys me about you is
> **1** 've **2** is **3** haven't **4** have **5** were **6** wasn't **7** was
> **8** don't **9** do **10** 're **11** 'm **12** are **13** have **14** don't

7 **a** Students do the exercise on their own. Tell students to use a different introductory phrase for each sentence.

b Students do the exercise in pairs. While students are working, monitor and correct any mistakes you hear. Finally, ask students to tell the class a few of their sentences.

> **FURTHER PRACTICE**
>
> **Ph** **Class Activity** 10D Love it or hate it p183 (Instructions p144)
> **Extra Practice** 10D SB p124
> **Self-study DVD-ROM** Lesson 10D
> **Workbook** Lesson 10D p54
> **Workbook** Reading and Writing Portfolio 10 p82
> **Progress Test** 10 p256

HELP WITH PRONUNCIATION
Word stress (3): compound nouns

1 Focus students on the compound nouns in the box.

CD3 15 Play the recording. Students listen and decide which part of the compound nouns is stressed.

Students compare answers in pairs. Check answers with the class.

> attention span   lost property   family doctor
> loudspeaker   problem-solving

2 **a** Check students understand all the words in the box. Focus students on the stress patterns and the example words.
Students do the exercise in pairs.

b **CD3** 16 Play the recording (SB p170). Students listen and check their answers.
Play the recording again. Students listen and repeat the words.
Finally, ask students to say words from 1 and 2. Check they are using the correct stress pattern and praise good pronunciation.

> **1** breakdown, nightclub
> **2** hairdryer, coffee shop, motorbike
> **3** double room, civil war, cotton wool
> **4** public transport, central heating

continue2learn

Focus students on the *continue2learn* section on SB p87. See p35 for ideas on how to exploit this section.

Extra Practice 10
See p35 for ideas on how to exploit this section.

10A

1

```
S O G R O O F M I
H S B O I L E R N
E Q R C L B A J T
L I G H T B U L B
V M R F T I L E S
E D U V E T K A O
S R E L L O C K I
T Y R E S G H I B
```

Possible answers
service a boiler; change a light bulb; put up some tiles; dry-clean a duvet; replace a lock; check the tyres; put up shelves, check the oil; fix a leak

2 **2** I got ... to help **3** I got ... to alter **4** 's having/'s going to have ... put in **5** I got ... to check **6** Has (Sue) had ... fixed **7** do (you) get ... serviced **8** Did ... put up

10B

3 **2** abusive **3** prejudiced **4** unruly **5** resentful **6** threatening **7** unfair **8** biased

4 **2** person's **3** speaks **4** is/are **5** wears **6** have/has **7** work/works **8** want/wants **9** seems **10** has **11** can

10C

5 **a/b** self-obsessed (adj); attention span (n); good-humoured (adj); problem solving (n); breakdown (n); day dreaming (n); high-powered (adj); drawback (n); downhearted (adj); widespread (adj); workplace (n); far-fetched (adj)

10D

6 **2** One thing I like about my brother is his taste in music. **3** One thing I love about Ted is the way he dances. **4** The thing that annoys me is that Linda never phones me./The thing that annoys me about Linda is that she never phones me. **5** What upsets me is that Dan always has to control everything./ What upsets me about Dan is that he always has to control everything. **6** The thing I admire about Pam is her generosity. **7** What amazes me (about her) is that she's always calm. **8** The thing I don't like (about him) is his sense of humour.

Progress Portfolio 10

- See p36 for ideas on how to exploit this section.

11A ▶ Meeting up
Student's Book p88–p89

Vocabulary work collocations
Grammar describing future events;
Future Perfect

Vocabulary and Speaking
Work collocations

 a Students do the exercise on their own, then check in **VOCABULARY 11.1** SB p152. Tell students not to answer the questions at this stage. Check answers with the class.

Check the meaning of new words/phrases with the class.

Point out that we can say *make a living* or *earn a living*.

Also highlight that we usually use *do something for a living* in questions: *What does your brother do for a living?*.

Remind students that we can also say *a freelance writer/journalist/photographer*, etc.

Check students understand the difference between *be made redundant* and *be fired/sacked*. Point out that in informal English we often say *get made redundant: I got made redundant last year.*

Also point out that we often use *always* or *all the time* with *be on the go: She's always on the go.*
= She's on the go all the time.

Establish that we can say *get down to work* or *get down to things*. We often use these phrases when the task we have to do is difficult or we don't want to do it: *I'm finding it hard to get down to work/things at the moment.* Tell students that we can give *a talk, a lecture* or *a presentation.*

Model and drill the words/phrases, highlighting the pronunciation of *redundant* /rɪ'dʌndənt/ and *project* /'prɒdʒəkt/.

Note that only the main stress in words/phrases is shown in vocabulary sections and the Language Summaries.

---
1 make 2 do 3 works 4 made 5 is 6 have 7 is
8 get 9 working 10 given
---

b Students do the activity in pairs. Ask students to tell the class one or two things that they found out about their partner.

EXTRA IDEA

• Students work in pairs and take turns to test each other on the collocations. One student says a word/phrase in **bold** from **1a**, for example, *a living*, and his/her partner says the whole collocation, for example, *make a living*.

Listening

 a Focus students on the photos. Tell the class that Rob is talking to his friend Mike, an advertising executive (he works for an advertising agency).

Ask students to read questions 1–4 and point out that Southampton is a city on the south coast of England.

CD3 17 Play the recording (SB p170). Students listen and answer the questions.

Students can compare answers in pairs. Check answers with the class.

---
1 Mike probably isn't happy with his job. He says that he's been finding it hard to get down to things recently and agrees that maybe it's time for a change.
2 He wants to arrange a meeting so that he can talk to Mike about a new project he's working on.
3 He's giving a talk at a conference there.
4 At 7.30 on Wednesday evening.
---

b Give students time to read sentences 1–6, then play the recording again. Students listen and correct one word in each sentence. Check answers with the class.

---
1 I'm having lunch with my **boss** tomorrow.
2 Sorry, I'll be interviewing people for our **graduate** trainee programme then.
3 No, sorry, I'll be in the middle of a **meeting** at four.
4 No, I'll be on my way to Southampton at **eleven**.
5 Well, I'll have arrived by **lunchtime**.
6 I'll have finished giving the talk by **three** thirty.

HELP WITH GRAMMAR
Describing future events; Future Perfect

 a–e Students do the exercises on their own or in pairs, then check in **GRAMMAR 11.1** SB p153. Check answers with the class.

---
a a sentence 1 b sentence 2 c We make the Present Continuous with: subject + *am/is/are* + verb+*ing*. We make the Future Continuous with: subject + *'ll* (= *will*) + *be* + verb+*ing*.
• Use sentences 1 and 2 in **2b** to highlight that we use the Present Continuous to talk about an arrangement in the future and we use the Future Continuous to talk about something that will be in progress at a point of time in the future.

b a sentence 4 b sentence 3
• Use sentence 3 in **2b** to highlight that we can use *will be in the middle of something* to describe an action that will be in progress at a point of time in the future.

- Use sentence 4 in **2b** to highlight that we can use *will be on my, his*, etc. *way to somewhere* to say that a person will be travelling at a point of time in the future.
- Point out that we can also use *be in the middle of something* and *be on my, his*, etc. *way to somewhere* to talk about the present: *I can't talk now, I'm in the middle of cooking.*

c We use the Future Perfect to talk about something that will be completed **before** a certain time in the future: *I'll have arrived by lunchtime.* (= some time before lunchtime).
- If necessary, focus students on the diagram in **GRAMMAR 11.1** SB p153 to check meaning.

d We make the **positive** form of the Future Perfect with: subject + *will* or *'ll* + *have* + past participle: *I'll have done it by midday.*
- We make the **negative** form of the Future Perfect with: subject + *won't* + *have* + past participle: *I won't have done it by ten o'clock.*
- We make **questions** in the Future Perfect with: (question word) + *will* + subject + *have* + past participle: *What time will you have finished?.*
- Point out that we often use *by* with the Future Perfect to mean 'before this time': *I'll have left the office by six o'clock.*
- We also use *by the time + clause, by this time next week, month*, etc. and *by the end of the day, week*, etc. with the Future Perfect: *Hurry up! The film will have started by the time we get there.*
- Also highlight that we often use these verbs with the Future Perfect: *do, start, finish, arrive, leave, get (somewhere).*

> **EXTRA IDEA**
>
> - Put students into pairs.
>   ✍ Write on the board: *tomorrow morning, tomorrow lunchtime, tomorrow afternoon, tomorrow evening, Wednesday morning, Wednesday lunchtime, Wednesday afternoon, Wednesday evening.* **CD3** 17 Play the recording again. Students listen again and say what Mike will be doing at each of these times. Check answers with the class.
>
> tomorrow morning: He'll be interviewing people for their graduate trainee programme.; tomorrow lunchtime: He'll be having lunch with his boss.; tomorrow afternoon: He'll be in a meeting.; tomorrow evening: He'll be looking after his children.; Wednesday morning: He'll be on his way to Southampton.; Wednesday lunchtime: He'll be having lunch with some clients.; Wednesday afternoon: He'll be chatting to lots of people.; Wednesday evening: He'll be having dinner with Rob.

HELP WITH LISTENING
Future Perfect and Future Continuous

This *Help with Listening* section helps students to hear the difference between the Future Perfect and the Future Continuous.

4 a **18** Play the recording. Students listen and notice the contractions and the weak form of *have* in the Future Perfect.

b **CD3** 19 Play the recording (SB p171). Students listen and write six sentences. Before they begin, point out that they will hear each sentence twice. Play the recording again if necessary.
✍ Check answers by eliciting the sentences and writing them on the board. Highlight the contractions and the weak forms of *have* in each sentence.

5 **19** **PRONUNCIATION** Play the recording (SB p171). Students listen and practise. Check students copy the stress, the contractions and the weak form of *have*. Play the recording again if necessary.
You can also ask students to look at the sentences on the board or turn to **CD3** **19**, SB p171. They can then follow the sentence stress, contractions and weak form of *have* as they listen and practise.

6 a Students do the exercise on their own.

b Students compare answers in pairs.
Check answers with the class. Ask students to explain the differences between pairs of sentences 1 and 4.

> **1** Different. In sentence a, the homework will be completed by nine o'clock. In sentence b, the homework will be in progress at nine o'clock. **2** The same. **3** The same. **4** Different. In sentence a, Jake has an appointment to see the doctor on Thursday. In sentence b, he is going to see the doctor some time before Thursday. **5** The same.

7 a Ask students when Mike is planning to meet Rob (on Wednesday). Then focus students on Mike's appointments for Thursday on his personal computer. Students do the exercise on their own.

b Students compare answers in pairs and decide in which sentences we could also use *in the middle of* or *on the way to*.
Check answers with the class.

> **1** will be having **2** will have finished **3** 'll/will have interviewed **4** 'll/will be talking **5** 'll/will have left **6** 'll/will be travelling **7** 'll/will be giving **8** 'll/will have had
> We can use *in the middle of* in sentences 1, 4 and 7. We can use *on the way to* in sentence 6.

> **EXTRA IDEA**
>
> - Students use Mike's appointments in **7a** as a model and write their own appointments for tomorrow. Encourage them to include at least six different appointments for the day. Then put students into pairs. Students ask and answer about the appointments and try to arrange a meeting.

Get ready … Get it right!

8 Students do the exercise on their own. Remind students to use the Future Perfect or the Future Continuous in their sentences. While students are working, monitor and check their sentences for accuracy.

9 Students do the activity in pairs. Encourage students to ask follow-up questions if possible.

While they are working, monitor and check students' pronunciation of the future verb forms.

Finally, ask students to tell the class the most interesting thing they found out about their partner.

┌─ **WRITING** ┐

Students take one of the sentences from **8** and write a paragraph explaining what they will have done or will be doing at that time. Encourage students to give as much extra information as possible.

┌─ **FURTHER PRACTICE** ┐

Ph **Class Activity** 11A The photoshoot p184 (Instructions p144)
Extra Practice 11A SB p125
Self-study DVD-ROM Lesson 11A
Workbook Lesson 11A p55

11B ▶ Going into business
Student's Book p90–p91

Vocabulary business collocations
Grammar reported speech

QUICK REVIEW This activity reviews the Future Perfect and the Future Continuous. Students do the first part of the activity on their own, as in the example. Put students into groups. Students take turns to tell each other their sentences and decide if any are the same. Also encourage students to ask follow-up questions if possible. Ask each group to share any interesting sentences with the class.

Vocabulary and Speaking

Business collocations

1 Students do the exercise on their own or in pairs, then check in **VOCABULARY 11.2** SB p152. Check answers with the class. Check the meaning of any new words/phrases with the whole class. Highlight that *take sth over* and *set sth up* are Type 3 phrasal verbs.
Teach students that the adjective from *profit* is *profitable* and its opposite is *unprofitable*.
Point out that we can also say *go into business together*: *My two sisters are going into business together*. Establish that *import* and *export* are also nouns. Point out that the stress on the verb is on the second syllable, but the stress on the noun is on the first syllable: *Brazil exports most of its coffee. Coffee is one of Brazil's biggest exports.*
Model and drill the phrases if necessary.

take over a company; go out of business; make a profit or a loss; expand the business; go into business with someone; do business with someone; set up a new company; go bankrupt; import products from another country; export products to another country; run a chain of restaurants

2 a Students do the exercise on their own. Check answers with the class.

2 go 3 chain 4 branch 5 exports 6 profit
7 gone out of 8 set up

b Students do the exercise in pairs.
Ask students to tell the class one or two things they found out about their partner.

Listening

3 a Focus students on the photo on SB p90 and ask them who the man is (Mike). Ask students what they remember about him from lesson 11A (he's an advertising executive, he's not very happy in his job, his friend Rob wanted to talk to him about a new project, etc.). Tell students that the woman in the photo is Mike's wife, Daisy, and that it is now Thursday evening.
CD3 20 Give students time to read questions 1–4, then play the recording (SB p171). Students listen and answer the questions.
Students compare answers in pairs. Check answers with the class.
Point out that Brighton is a popular tourist city on the south coast of England.

1 Rob is planning to open a coffee shop in Brighton.
2 He wants Mike to invest in the business.
3 £25,000.
4 She's not very sure about the idea and makes Mike promise to discuss it with her before he does anything.

b Check students understand *location* and *come up with some money* (find or get some money from somewhere).

Give students time to read sentences 1–8, then play the recording again. Students listen and fill in the gaps with two words.

Check answers with the class.

---

1 interesting 2 own business 3 since August
4 into business 5 other half 6 a profit
7 on Saturday 8 anyone else

EXTRA IDEA

- Put students into groups. Ask students to discuss whether they would invest money in a business like this. Encourage students to draw up a list of advantages and disadvantages, and to note down everything they know about the business at this point. Ask students to share their ideas with the class, and see how many students would invest their own money in the business.

HELP WITH GRAMMAR
Reported speech

4 **a–d** Students do the exercises in pairs, then check in GRAMMAR 11.2 SB p153. Check answers with the class.

a **a** 1 "I have something interesting to tell you."
2 "I'm planning to set up my own business."
3 "I've been looking for a good location since August." **b** We usually change the verb form in reported speech to one that is further in the past (this is sometimes referred to as 'backshifting').

- Focus students on the table in GRAMMAR 11.2 SB p153 to illustrate typical verb form changes in reported speech.
- Go through the five **TIPS** below the table in GRAMMAR 11.2 SB p153 with the class.

b **a** 4 "Do you want to go into business with me?"
5 "Can you come up with the other half?" 6 "How long will it take for the business to make a profit?" **b** In reported questions the word order is the same as in positive sentences: *I asked where he was.* not *I asked where was he*. **c** We use *if* or *whether* when we report questions without a question word. **d** We don't use the auxiliaries *do, does* and *did* in reported questions: "*What do you think?*" – *He asked me what I thought.* not *He asked me what I did think*.

- Point out that we make reported questions with: *(He) asked (me)/(He) wanted to know* + question word/*if* or *whether* + subject + verb.
- Remind students that the changes in verb forms are the same as in reported sentences.
- Also highlight that we sometimes use an object with *ask*: *He asked …* or *He asked me …* .

c **a** sentence 8 **b** sentence 7 **c** infinitive with *to*

- Point out that to report imperatives, we use: *told* + object + (*not*) + infinitive with *to*.
- To report requests, we use: *asked* + object + (*not*) + infinitive with *to*.
- Remind students that it is also correct to report the complete request: *He asked me if I could meet him in Brighton on Saturday.*
- Highlight the position of *not* when we report negative imperatives and requests.

5 **a** Focus students on the photo on SB p91. Tell the class that it's now Saturday afternoon and that Mike is phoning Daisy to tell her about his meeting with Rob in Brighton.

Check students understand *an interior designer* and *an investor*.

Focus students on the example and elicit who the pronouns in the reported sentence refer to (*He* – Rob; *me* – Mike; *you* – Daisy).

Students work on their own and put sentences 2–10 into reported speech using the words in brackets. Remind students that Mike is reporting all these sentences to Daisy.

b Students compare answers in pairs.

c CD3 21 Play the recording (SB p171). Students listen to Mike and Daisy's phone conversation and tick their reported sentences when they hear them. Check students' sentences with the class.

Ask students what Mike and Daisy decide to do (they decide to go into business with Rob and invest money in the coffee shop).

---

2 Rob asked me what I thought of his business plan.
3 He told me (that) the plan had already been approved by the bank.
4 He said (that) he'd been talking to an interior designer.
5 He wanted to know if/whether I'd help with the advertising.
6 I told him (that) I couldn't say yes or no until I talked/talk to you.
7 I said (that) I'd be talking to the bank on Tuesday.
8 I asked (Rob) when he needed a decision by.
9 I asked (him) if/whether he was talking to any other investors.
10 I told him (that) he had to name the coffee shop after you!

EXTRA IDEA

- Ask students to look at CD3 21, SB p171. Play the recording again. Students listen and check their answers to **5a**.

6 **a** Students do the exercise on their own.

b Students compare answers in pairs. Check answers with the class.

> 3 He asked me what **my last job was**. 4 She asked if I **had/have** any children. 5 He asked me **not to** tell anyone. 6 She said ~~me~~ that she wasn't coming./She **told** me that she wasn't coming. 7 ✓ 8 He asked his brother **if/whether** he could phone back later./He asked his brother **to phone** back later. 9 He told his cousin not **to be** late. 10 ✓

Get ready … Get it right!

7 **a** Students do the exercise on their own. Encourage students to think of interesting or unusual questions if possible.

> ┤ **EXTRA IDEA** ├
>
> • Before students do **7a**, write these prompts on the board to help them think of ideas for questions: *likes and dislikes, best and worst life experiences, things you did last year, plans for the future, free time activities, how long you've been doing things, past and present habits, unusual abilities.*

b Students move around the room asking each other their questions. If your students aren't able to move around the room, they should ask as many people as they can who are sitting near them. Tell students that they must try to remember all the questions that they are asked and that they can write one word to help them remember each question.

8 Students do the activity in pairs, as shown in the speech bubbles. Remind students to use reported questions and sentences.

While students are working, monitor and correct their reported questions and sentences if necessary.

Finally, ask students to tell the class two things that they told other students.

> ┤ **EXTRA IDEA** ├
>
> • To check the reported questions, focus on each student in turn and ask someone else in the class to tell you what this person asked them and the answer they gave, using reported speech.

> ┤ **WRITING** ├
>
> Put students into pairs. Tell them to write ten questions that they'd like to ask each other, for example, *Where do you live? Do you like learning English?*, etc. Students ask and answer their questions, making a note of their partner's answers. For homework, students then write a short text reporting what their partner told them about themselves.

> ┤ **FURTHER PRACTICE** ├
>
> **Ph** **Class Activity** 11B Reported board game p185 (Instructions p145)
> **Ph** **Vocabulary Plus** 11 Stress on nouns/verbs p204 (Instructions p193)
> **Extra Practice** 11B SB p125
> **Self-study DVD-ROM** Lesson 11B
> **Workbook** Lesson 11B p56

VOCABULARY
11C AND SKILLS ▶ The coffee shop
Student's Book p92–p93

Vocabulary verb patterns (2): reporting verbs
Skills Reading: a problem at Daisy's; Listening: decision time

QUICK REVIEW This activity reviews work and business collocations. Students do the first part of the activity on their own. Remind students that they studied work collocations in lesson 11A and business collocations in lesson 11B. Put students into pairs for the second part of the activity. Ask students to share interesting sentences with the class.

Speaking, Reading and Vocabulary

1 Students discuss the questions in groups. Ask students to share their ideas with the class.

> ┤ **EXTRA IDEA** ├
>
> • Elicit students' ideas for question 3 in **1** and write them on the board. Then ask the class to decide the three most important things for a good coffee shop to have from the list on the board.

2

a Focus students on the photo. Ask who the man is (Rob) and where he is working (in the coffee shop that he and his friend Mike set up in Brighton). Also ask students why the coffee shop is called 'Daisy's' (Mike's wife is called Daisy).

Tell students that the coffee shop has been open for a year and ask students how well they think it is doing.

┌─ **EXTRA IDEA** ─────────────────────────────┐

- Alternatively, put students into pairs or groups and ask them to tell each other everything they can remember about Rob, Mike and Daisy from lessons 11A and 11B. Ask students to compare ideas with the class.

└──┘

b Focus students on Mike's email to his wife, Daisy. Students read the email and find out what decision they have to make.

You can set a time limit of two minutes to encourage students to read for gist.

Check the answer with the class.

> Mike and Daisy have to decide whether to accept an offer for the coffee shop from a company called Café Pronto (a big coffee shop chain).

c Students do the exercise on their own. Check answers with the class.

> **1F** The coffee shop **is** making money at the moment (profits were up 20% last month). **2✓ 3✓ 4F** Rob's bank thinks selling the coffee shop is a **good** idea. **5✓ 6F Mike** has been invited to Rob's place this weekend.

HELP WITH VOCABULARY
Verb patterns (2): reporting verbs

3

a Focus students on the reporting verbs in blue in the email. Students work on their own and tick the verbs they know.

Students can check the meanings of any verbs that they don't know with you or in a dictionary. Be prepared with definitions, examples, etc. to pre-teach any verbs you think might be new to students or bring in a set of dictionaries for students to check the meanings themselves.

b–c Focus students on the first column of the table and highlight the six reporting verbs (*mention, agree, remind, deny, apologise, blame*). Ask students to find these reporting verbs in the email and to underline the verb form that follows each one.

Use these examples to check students understand the verb patterns in the second column of the table.

Students then work on their own or in pairs and complete the table with the infinitive forms of the other verbs in blue in the email. Students check in **VOCABULARY 11.3** SB p152.

✎ While they are working, draw the table from **3b** on the board ready for checking. Check answers with the class.

b ✎ Focus students on the table on the board. Elicit which reporting verbs from the email go in each row and complete the table (see the table in **VOCABULARY 11.3** SB p152).

- Point out that the reporting verbs in blue in the table in **VOCABULARY 11.3** SB p152 show the form of the verbs in blue in the email. Also note that some reporting verbs can have more than one verb pattern (these are shown in **bold** in the table).
- Highlight the prepositions we use with *apologise (for)*, *insist (on)*, *blame (sb for)* and *accuse (sb of)*.
- Establish that we often don't have to report every word people say. It is more important to report the idea: "*I really think you should leave your job.*" – *She advised him to leave his job.* "*It's your fault that we got lost.*" – *He blamed her for getting lost.*
- Remind students that *deny* has a negative meaning. We say *He denied stealing the money.* not ~~*He denied not stealing the money.*~~
- Also point out that we often use *not* with *warn*: *He warned me not to come.*

4 Focus students on sentences 1–12 and establish that these are things that Mike and Rob said to each other during their phone call. Go through the example with the class.

Students do the exercise on their own, then compare their sentences in pairs. Check answers with the class.

> **2** Rob apologised for going behind Mike's/his back. **3** Rob promised not to do it again./Rob promised (that) he wouldn't do it again. **4** Rob pointed out (that) the coffee shop was his idea. **5** Mike claimed (that) Rob/he was only interested in the money. **6** Mike threatened to take Rob/him to court if he closed the shop. **7** Rob agreed to work until the end of the month./Rob agreed that he'd work until the end of the month. **8** Rob insisted on being paid for every hour he (had) worked./Rob insisted that he was (to be) paid for every hour he (had) worked. **9** Rob advised Mike/him to sell his half of the business. **10** Mike warned Rob/him not to talk to the people at Café Pronto again. **11** Mike suggested seeing a lawyer./Mike suggested that they should see a lawyer. **12** Rob reminded Mike to bring his copy of the contract.

Listening

5

a Students discuss the questions in pairs.

b Check the answer to question 1 with the class (Rob wants to sell the coffee shop to Café Pronto, a coffee shop chain). ✎ Then elicit students' ideas for questions 2 and 3 and write them on the board in separate columns.

6 a Tell students that they are going to listen to a conversation between Mike and Daisy later that day. **CD3 ▸ 22** Play the recording (SB p171). Students listen and decide which options Mike and Daisy talk about and what they decide to do. Check answers with the class.

Mike and Daisy discuss three options.
Option 1: Go along with Rob's plan and sell the coffee shop.
Option 2: Refuse to sell the coffee shop.
Option 3: Buy Rob's share of the coffee shop and take over the business. They decide to do option 3.

b Give students time to read questions 1–6, then play the recording again. Students listen and answer the questions. Students compare answers in pairs. Check answers with the class.

1 She felt shocked. **2** He doesn't want their coffee shop to become another branch of Café Pronto because they're all the same. **3** Rob said he'd shut down the coffee shop if they refused to sell it. **4** He's always going on about how bored he is there and how he can't wait to leave. **5** They can sell the house and move to Brighton. **6** Maybe they'll be running their own chain of coffee shops and Daisy's can start buying branches of Café Pronto.

c Students discuss the questions in groups or with the whole class, giving reasons for their ideas.

HELP WITH LISTENING
Back referencing

This *Help with Listening* section focuses on how we use back referencing in natural spoken English.

7 a Check students remember that we use back referencing to refer back to people, places or things that we have mentioned earlier. Note that students studied back referencing in lesson 6C.
Students do the exercise in pairs.
Check answers with the class.

That = the fact that branches of Café Pronto are all the same
the place = the coffee shop

there = the coffee shop
it = the coffee shop
it = all that work they did getting the coffee shop ready

b **CD3 ▸ 22** Ask students to turn to **CD3 ▸ 22**, SB p171. Play the recording again. Students listen and notice what the words/phrases in bold refer to.

8 a Check students understand all the prompts. Students do the activity with a different partner from their partner in **7a** if possible. Tell students to make notes on their ideas in preparation for **8b**. Students should also decide which ideas they are each going to talk about.

┌─ **EXTRA IDEA** ─────────────────────────────┐
• Give students some 'rehearsal time' by asking them to practise describing their new business with their partner before they work in groups.
└──┘

b Reorganise the class so that three or four pairs are working together in groups of six or eight. If this isn't possible, put two pairs together and ask them to work in a group of four.
Students take turns to tell each other about their new business. Each group decides which new business is the best.
Finally, ask students to decide which is the best new business in the class.

┌─ **WRITING** ─────────────────────────────────┐
For homework, ask students to write a description of their new business, with an illustration if possible. These can be collected in next class and displayed around the classroom for other students to read.
└──┘

┌─ **FURTHER PRACTICE** ────────────────────────┐
Ph **Class Activity** 11C Business partners p186 (Instructions p145)
Extra Practice 11C SB p125
Self-study DVD-ROM Lesson 11C
Workbook Lesson 11C p58
└──┘

▷ REAL 11D WORLD ▶ Advertising works
Student's Book p94–p95

Vocabulary advertising
Real World discussion language (3)

QUICK REVIEW This activity reviews reporting verbs. Students do the first part of the activity on their own. Put students into pairs. Students take turns to say their sentences and guess if their partner's sentences are true or false. Ask students to tell the class one or two of their true sentences.

1 a Students work on their own and tick the words/phrases they know, then check new words/phrases in **VOCABULARY 11.4 ▶** SB p152.
Check students understand the difference between *advertising* and *publicity*, which is a false friend in many languages.

Also check students understand *a slogan* by eliciting some famous slogans from advertising campaigns from the students.

Highlight that we say *the press/media* not ~~a press/media~~. Note that we often use the phrase *new media* to describe companies that give information or advertise products on the Internet: *Roberto works in new media.*

Ask students what other things we can *launch* (a book, a campaign, a ship, a rocket, etc.).

Point out that we can say *an advertisement, an advert* or *an ad*. In British English *advertisement* is pronounced /əd'vɜːtɪsmənt/. In American English it is pronounced /'ædvərtaɪzmənt/.

Highlight that something can go *viral* online when it is taken up by people on social networks or is shown in an online video.

Model and drill the words/phrases, highlighting the pronunciation of *publicity* /pʌ'blɪsɪti/, *logo* /'ləʊgəʊ/, *campaign* /kæm'peɪn/, *budget* /'bʌdʒɪt/, *media* /'miːdɪə/, *design* /dɪ'zaɪn/, *launch* /lɔːntʃ/ and *viral* /vaɪrəl/.

b Students do the exercise in pairs. If students don't agree with their partner's explanations, they should check in **VOCABULARY 11.4** SB p152.

2 Check students understand *a brand* (a type of product made by a particular company) and elicit some examples of famous brands from the students.

Students discuss the questions in groups.

Ask students to share interesting answers to each question with the class.

3 **a** Focus students on the photo of a meeting at Target Advertising, the advertising agency where Mike (from lessons 11A–11C) used to work. Tell students that the people are discussing the launch of a new product called *Go!*.

VIDEO 11 **CD3 23** Play the recording (SB p172). Students listen and decide what kind of product *Go!* is. Check the answer with the class (*Go!* is a fruit juice drink).

b Check students remember *a disadvantage, a celebrity* and *a commuter*.

Give students time to read questions 1–4, then play the recording again.

Students can compare answers in pairs. Check answers with the class.

1 use viral marketing; a press campaign with full-page colour ads in all magazines with a healthy living section (women's magazines, Sunday supplements, sports magazines, etc.); having a celebrity advertising the product; a TV ad; giving away free samples to commuters in the morning; giving away a free glass with the *Go!* logo on.
2 If you can't stand the person, you probably won't buy the product and you never know what the media might find out about their private lives in the future.

3 Because they need some kind of TV ad, but they're incredibly expensive and their budget isn't very big.
4 Because everyone likes free samples, and in the summer everyone's thirsty, especially if they're travelling.

REAL WORLD Discussion language (3)

4 **a–b** Check students understand *react to something, summarising* and *recapping*.
Students do **4a** on their own, then check in **REAL WORLD 11.1** SB p154.
Check answers with the class.

- 1 could 2 wonder 3 know 4 about 5 like 6 try 7 makes 8 work 9 rather 10 avoid 11 problem 12 such 13 what 14 right 15 saying 16 over
- Point out that we can say *Can we just go over this again?* or *Can we just go through this again?*.
- With a lower-level class you may want to model and drill the phrases, focusing on stress and natural rhythm.

┌─ **EXTRA IDEA** ─┐

- Ask students to turn to **CD3 23**, SB p172. Play the recording again. Students listen and underline all the phrases in **4a** when they hear them.

5 **a** Remind students of Amanda and Colin in the photo. Students work on their own and write their conversation using the prompts, as in the example.

b Students check their answers in pairs.
Check answers with the class.

AMANDA I know! Why don't we use cartoon characters?
COLIN I'm not sure **that's** such **a good** idea. I think we need some real people.
A Yes, maybe you're right.
C **One thing** we **could** do **is** show someone drinking the product.
A Yes, **that makes** sense. **How** about **using** some attractive models?
C Personally **I'd rather** we **didn't** use models. They always look so false.
A So **what** you're **saying** is **that** you want ordinary-looking people.
C Yes, exactly. The kind of people who might actually go out and buy *Go!*.
A Well, it's worth **a try**.
C **I wonder if** it'd be a good idea **to** show how much fruit is in it?
A Yes, that **could** work. OK, **can we just** go **over** this again?

6 **a** Check students understand the prompts. Students do the activity in groups of three or four.
Remind students to use language from **4a** in their discussions.

Tell all students to make notes on the decisions they make, as they will be presenting their campaigns separately. While students are working, help them with ideas and new vocabulary.

EXTRA IDEA

- Ask students to tick the phrases in **4a** when they use them. Students should try to use at least five different phrases in the discussion.

b Reorganise the class so that three or four students from different groups are working together. Students take turns to present their campaigns to each other. Students then decide which campaign is the best. Ask students to tell the class about the best campaign in their group.
Finally, students can decide which is the best campaign in the class.

EXTRA IDEA

- If you have a small class, ask each group to present their ideas to the whole class instead of in groups.

FURTHER PRACTICE

Extra Practice 11D SB p125
Self-study DVD-ROM Lesson 11D
Workbook Lesson 11D p59
Workbook Reading and Writing Portfolio 11 p84
Progress Test 11 p258

HELP WITH PRONUNCIATION
Stress and rhythm (4): emphasis and meaning

1 **a** Focus students on the sentences and the words in capital letters. Point out that these are the words with extra stress.
CD3 24 Students listen and notice how the extra stress on one word affects the meaning.
Make sure students understand the two different meanings.

EXTRA IDEA

- To further reinforce the idea, write the sentence on the board twice. Underline a different word in each sentence: *1 I thought Ann would come. 2 I thought Ann would come.* Say each sentence once or twice as necessary. Students work in pairs and say what the meaning is each time.

1 I thought she would come, but other people didn't.
2 I thought Ann would come, but I was wrong, she didn't.

b Play the recording again. Students listen and repeat the sentences.

2 **a** Focus students on the sentence in pink and the responses and meanings. Check students understand that each sentence 1–5 is a response by somebody else to the sentence in pink.
Students do the exercise on their own.

b **CD3** 25 Play the recording (SB p172). Students listen and check their answers.

1b 2a 3c 4e 5d

c Play the recording again. Students take turns to say the sentence in pink and responses 1–5 and a–e. Finally, ask students to say one of the sentences from **1a** or **2a**. Check they stress the important word correctly, and praise good pronunciation.

continue2learn

Focus students on the *continue2learn* section on SB p95. See p35 for ideas on how to exploit this section.

Extra Practice 11
See p35 for ideas on how to exploit this section.

11A
1 2 do 3 work 4 has 5 gave 6 'm working 7 made 8 get 9 make
2 2 'll be 3 won't have 4 be doing 5 be staying 6 have been

11B
3 2 expanded 3 exporting 4 ran/was running 5 went 6 importing 7 made/was making
4 2 You can't use my car. 3 What do you think? 4 Don't wait for me. 5 Do you want to stay?

6 What's your next job going to be? 7 Where have you been staying? 8 You must/have to leave.
11C
5 2a refused b insisted on 3a admitted b blamed 4a reminded b mentioned 5a invited b suggested 6a denied b advised
11D
6 2f 3d 4e 5h 6a 7b 8g

Progress Portfolio 11

- See p36 for ideas on how to exploit this section.

QUICK REVIEW This activity reviews discussion language. Check students understand *raise money for charity*. Students do the activity in groups. Remind students to use language from **REAL WORLD 11.1** ▶ SB p154 in their discussions. Ask each group to share interesting ideas with the class.

Speaking and Vocabulary
Colloquial words/phrases

 a Students do the exercise on their own or in pairs, then check in **VOCABULARY 12.1** ▶ SB p155.

Check students understand the colloquial words/phrases in bold by saying each word/phrase and eliciting the meanings from the class. Point out that these are all British English colloquial words/phrases.

Remind students that we can also say *drive someone crazy*: *Waiting in queues drives me crazy*.

Highlight that we can also say *pop out* (= go out) and *pop over/round* (= go and visit somebody): *I'm just popping out. Tom's just popped over to say hello.*

Note that we can say *mess something up* or *make a mess of something*: *I really made a mess of that exam.*

Note that we say *on telly* or *on the box*: *What's on telly/the box tonight?*.

Point out that the plural of *quid* is *quid* not ~~quids~~: *Can you lend me twenty quid?*.

Also establish that in American English people usually say *the bathroom*, not ~~the loo~~: *Excuse me, where's the bathroom?*.

Highlight that we also use *guys* to address a group of people of both sexes: *What are you guys doing tonight?*.

Note that in informal British English, we also use *a bloke* /bləʊk/ to mean a man: *Who's that bloke over there?*.

Teach students the phrase *What a hassle!*: *I had to go to three different banks. What a hassle!*

Model and drill the words/phrases if necessary. Note that only the main stress in words/phrases is shown in vocabulary boxes and the Language Summaries.

b Students do the exercise on their own.

c Students do the exercise in pairs. Ask students to tell the class one or two of their sentences.

Listening

 a Students discuss the questions in new pairs.

b Focus students on photos A–D of Louise and Angie. Elicit where the women are in each photo. **CD3** 26 Play the recording (SB p172). Students listen and put photos A–D in the order they happened.

Check answers with the class. Ask students what Louise thinks happened to her mobile phone.

> **1B 2A 3B 4C**
> Louise thinks that the guy in the club stole her mobile phone (the man in the background in photo C).

 Give students time to read sentences 1–10, then play the recording again. Students listen and fill in the gaps in each sentence with one word.
Students can compare answers in pairs. Check answers with the class.

> **1** bathroom **2** off **3** bag **4** Australia **5** cloakroom **6** drink **7** table **8** bar **9** steal **10** club

┌─ **EXTRA IDEAS** ─┐

- Ask students to turn to **CD3** 26, SB p172. Play the recording again. Students listen and underline all the examples of colloquial language that they hear.
- ✎ Write these questions on the board: *1 Why is Louise stressed out? 2 What really bugs Louise? 3 Why does Angie tell Louise to chill out? 4 Who called Louise when she left work? 5 What does Angie say about Louise and the taxi driver?* Students answer the questions on their own, then check answers with a partner. Play the recording again. Check answers with the class.

> **1** Because she can't find her mobile. **2** losing things **3** Because Louise is starting to panic and imagining that somebody is using her phone to call Australia (which would be very expensive). **4** her mate Josie **5** She says that Louise really fancied the taxi driver.

HELP WITH GRAMMAR
Modal verbs (2): deduction in the present and the past

a–d Students do the exercises on their own or in pairs, then check in **GRAMMAR 12.1** ▶ SB p156. Check answers with the class.

- **a 1 a** Sentences 1, 2 and 4 **b** Sentences 3, 7, 8, 9 and 10 **2** Sentences 5 and 6
- Use sentences 1–10 in **3** to highlight that we often use the modal verbs *must, could, might, may* and *can't* to make deductions in the present and the past.
- Use sentences 5 and 6 to show that when we know something is definitely true or is definitely not true, we don't use a modal verb.
- **b** When we believe something is true, we use *must*.

- When we think something is possibly true, we use *could*, *might* or *may*.
- When we believe something isn't true, we use *can't*.
- Point out that we don't use *can* or *mustn't* to make deductions: *It must be true.* not ~~It can be true.~~ *He can't have gone home yet.* not ~~He mustn't have gone home yet.~~

c To make deductions about a state in the present we use: modal verb + infinitive (sentences 1 and 2 in **3**).
- To make deductions about something happening now we use: modal verb + *be* + verb+*ing* (sentence 4).
- To make deductions about a state or a completed action in the past we use: modal verb + *have* + past participle (sentences 3, 7, 8 and 10).
- To make deductions about a longer action in the past we use: modal verb + *have* + *been* + verb+*ing* (sentence 9).
- Point out that we can also use *couldn't* instead of *can't* to make deductions in the past: *You couldn't have left it in the bar.*

HELP WITH LISTENING
Modal verbs in the past

This *Help with Listening* section helps students to understand how we say modal verbs in the past in natural spoken English.

5 **a** **CD3** 27 Play the recording. Students listen and notice the weak forms of *have* /əv/ and *been* /bɪn/ in sentences 1 and 2.
Play the recording again. Ask students to decide which words in each sentence are stressed. Check answers with the class. Point out that we usually stress the modal verbs when we are making deductions.

> 1 Someone could have taken it from your bag.
> 2 He might have been waiting for a chance to steal my phone.

b **CD3** 28 Play the recording (SB p172). Students listen and write six sentences. Before they begin, point out that they will hear each sentence twice. Play the recording again if necessary.
Students check sentences in pairs.
✍ Check students' answers by playing the recording again, pausing after each sentence is said the second time to elicit students' answers and write them on the board.

> 1 I think I must have left it at home. 2 He could have been talking to someone else. 3 We might have locked the keys in the car. 4 She can't have been working all night. 5 I may have sent it to the wrong address. 6 Your father must have been trying to call you.

6 **CD3** 28 **PRONUNCIATION** Play the recording again. Students listen again and repeat the sentences. Check that students copy the sentence stress and weak forms correctly. Play the recording again if necessary. You can also ask students to look at the sentences on the board or turn to **CD3** 28, SB p172. They can then follow the sentence stress and weak forms as they listen and practise.

7 **a** Check students remember what problem Louise has (she's lost her mobile phone).
Students do the exercise on their own.

b Students compare answers in pairs and try to think who the note might be from.

> 2 must be having 3 must have delivered 4 could be 5 can't be 6 must have found 7 might have written

c **CD3** 29 Play the recording (SB p173). Students listen and check their answers. Check answers with the class.

> The note is from Patrick, the taxi driver who drove them home from the club (see photo A on SB p96).

8 Students do the exercise on their own. While they are working, monitor and check their sentences for accuracy.
Ask students to compare sentences in pairs. If they have different sentences, they should check that both are correct.
Ask students to share some of their sentences with the whole class.

> **Possible answers**
> 2 She might have been shopping. / She might have been at the doctor's. 3 She may/might/must have forgotten. 4 He might have asked her to go out with him. 5 Patrick must have asked Louise to marry him. 6 Patrick and Louise may/might be going on honeymoon to Jamaica.

Get ready ... Get it right!

9 Put students into pairs. Ask all students to turn to SB p111.

a Check students remember who Patrick is (the taxi driver who drove Louise and Angie home from the club). Focus students on pictures 1–4. Tell the class that these people were also in Patrick's taxi yesterday.

Students work with their partner and make at least two deductions about the present or the past for each picture, as shown in the speech bubbles. While they are working, help students with any problems and new vocabulary.

b Reorganise the class so that students are working in groups of four with another pair. Students take turns to tell the other pair their deductions about the people in each picture and find out if any are the same.

c Finally, ask students to tell the class their deductions about one of the pictures.

WRITING

Students choose one of the pictures from SB p111. For homework, tell students to write a story about the person or people in the picture, using the deductions they made in **9a**, and adding more information. Next class, ask students to read out their story.

FURTHER PRACTICE

Ph **Class Activity** 12A The diamond mystery p188 (Instructions p146)
Extra Practice 12A SB p126
Self-study DVD-ROM Lesson 12A
Workbook Lesson 12A p60

12B ▶ A great inheritance
Student's Book p98–p99

Vocabulary vague language expressions
Grammar verbs (3): modal past forms and related verbs

QUICK REVIEW This activity reviews colloquial words/ phrases. Students do the first part of the activity on their own. Put students into pairs and ask them to swap lists. Students take turns to make sentences about people they know with words/phrases from their partner's list. Ask students to share a few of their sentences with the class.

Vocabulary Vague language expressions

1 **a** Focus students on sentence 1 and check students understand the exercise.

Students work on their own and do as much of the exercise as they can before checking new words/ phrases in **VOCABULARY 12.2** SB p155. Check answers with the class.

Point out that when we can't or don't want to be precise about a number, size, distance, time, etc. we use certain expressions to show what we are saying is <u>not</u> an exact number, time, etc.

Highlight that we use the preposition *of* after *in excess*, *in the region* and *tons*.

Establish that we use a comparative adjective after *far*.

Also point out that we often use *-ish* as a way of saying *about* in many instances, as well as when we are talking about time, for example, *He's sixtyish* (= he's about sixty). We can also use *-ish* after adjectives, for example, *Yes, I'm happy-ish*. (= I'm quite happy, but I could be happier.). Make sure students realise this is only used in spoken, colloquial English and that in spoken English we would probably pause before we added the *-ish*.

Highlight that we can say *tons of*, *loads of* or *a load of*. These expressions are less formal than saying *a lot of/lots of*.

Point out that we can also use *approximately* to mean *about*, but it is more formal.
Model and drill the new words/phrases if necessary.

1b 2a 3a 4b 5a 6b 7a 8a 9b 10b 11a 12a

b Students do the exercise on their own.

c Students work in pairs and take turns to tell each other their sentences. Encourage students to ask follow-up questions where possible.

EXTRA IDEA

• Put students into pairs to ask and answer about the words/phrases. Student A says a sentence from **1a** and Student B says whether it means more than, about, a small amount or a large amount.

Speaking and Reading

2 **a** Students discuss the questions in pairs. Ask students to share interesting information with the class.

b Focus students on the article. Ask students if they know who Leona Helmsley, Bill Gates and Anita Roddick are. They can check their answers by reading the first line of each text.

Students do the exercise on their own. Set a time limit of three minutes to encourage students to read for gist.

Students check answers in pairs. Check answers with the class.

1 The story about Leona Helmsley is different from the others because she left most of her money to her dog. **2** The stories about Bill Gates and Anita Roddick are similar because they both decided to give away most of their wealth to charities, rather than leaving it to their children. **3** The stories about Bill Gates and Anita Roddick are different because Bill Gates' children will inherit some money, but Anita Roddick's children didn't inherit any of their mother's money.

┌─ **EXTRA IDEA** ─────────────────────────┐

- Put students into groups of three, Student A, B and C. Student As read about Leona Helmsley, Student Bs read about Bill Gates and Student Cs read about Anita Roddick. Students make notes, then take turns to tell each other about the person they read about. Students then discuss what is similar and different about each story.

└──────────────────────────────────────┘

3 **a** Focus students on the cartoon. Ask students which person the cartoon relates to (Leona Helmsley). Students do the exercise on their own, then compare answers in pairs. Check answers with the class.

1 The money for the dog was left in the hands of Leona's brother, Alvin Rosenthal.
2 ... but amazingly he received $2m less than the dog!
3 It will be a minuscule portion of my wealth.
4 They will be given an unbelievable education and that will be paid for. And certainly anything related to health issues we will take care of.
5 I told my kids they would not inherit one penny.
6 ... to their great credit, Anita's daughters supported their mother's decision.

b Students discuss the questions in groups. Encourage students to share interesting answers with the class.

HELP WITH GRAMMAR
Verbs (3): modal past forms and related verbs

4 **a–d** Students do the exercises on their own or in pairs, then check in **GRAMMAR 12.2** SB p156. Check answers with the class.

a We use *could have* + past participle to say something was possible in the past, but didn't happen: *They could have left at least some of that money to her, but they haven't.*
- We use *should have* + past participle to criticise people's behaviour in the past: *... some people felt she should have left at least some of that to her children.*
- We use *would have* + past participle to imagine something in the past that didn't happen: *Many people would have reacted differently.*

- You can point out that we can also say *ought to have* + past participle to criticise people's behaviour in the past: *You ought to have told me you were going to be late.*

b 1 No, she didn't. 2 Yes, she did. 3 We usually use *didn't need* + infinitive with *to* to talk about things people didn't do in the past because they weren't necessary: *She decided that her daughters would be alright and she didn't need to leave them her money.* (= she didn't leave them her money because she thought it wasn't necessary).
- We use *needn't have* + past participle to talk about things people did in the past that weren't necessary: *She needn't have given it all away.* (= she did give it all away, but this wasn't necessary).

c We usually use **could** to talk about a general ability in the past: *My sister could speak ten languages before she was ten.*
- We usually use **was/were able to** to talk about ability at one specific time in the past: *Due to her vast wealth, Leona Helmsley was able to leave £12 million to her dog.*
- Highlight that we usually use *could* with verbs of the senses (*see, hear,* etc.): *We could see the lake out of our hotel window.*
- Go through the **TIPS** in each section of **GRAMMAR 12.2** SB p156 with the class or ask students to study them for homework.

5 **CD3 30** **PRONUNCIATION** Play the recording (SB p173). Students listen and repeat the sentences. Check that students copy the stress and the weak form of *have* correctly.
Play the recording again if necessary.
You can also ask students to turn to **CD3 30**, SB p173. They can then follow the sentence stress and weak forms as they listen and repeat.

6 Students do the exercise on their own, then compare answers in pairs.
Check answers with the class.

1 would have 2 should have 3 could have; would have 4 should have 5 didn't need to go 6 needn't have 7 was able to 8 shouldn't have

Get ready ... Get it right!

7 Students do the exercise on their own. Tell students to write short phrases (*paid the phone bill, gone out for dinner,* etc.), not whole sentences. Make sure students don't write the answers in the same order as the prompts.

8 Students work in pairs and swap papers. Students take turns to ask each other questions about the things their partner has written. Encourage students to ask follow-up questions if possible.

While they are working, monitor and help students with any problems.

Finally, ask students to tell the class two things they found out about their partner.

EXTRA IDEA

- ✎ While students are doing **7**, write your own answers to the prompts on the board in random order. To demonstrate **8**, draw students' attention to your answers on the board and elicit questions from the class for each of them. Students then do **8** in pairs.

WRITING

Students use the ideas they wrote in **7** and write about what they should have done/needn't have done/would have done, etc. Encourage them to expand each phrase and write a complete text, including any information they gave to their partner in answer to follow-up questions.

FURTHER PRACTICE

Ph **Class Activity** 12B What would you have done? p189 (Instructions p147)
Extra Practice 12B SB p126
Self-study DVD-ROM Lesson 12B
Workbook Lesson 12B p61

VOCABULARY 12C AND SKILLS

Spooky!
Student's Book p100–p101

Vocabulary idioms
Skills Reading: an article about a themed weekend; Listening: a conversation about a haunted flat

QUICK REVIEW This activity reviews past forms of modal verbs. Students do the first part of the exercise on their own. Put students into pairs. Students take turns to say their sentences and ask follow-up questions. Ask students to tell the class one or two interesting things they found out about their partner.

Speaking and Reading

1 Students discuss the questions in groups.
Ask students to share answers with the class. Find out how many students believe in ghosts and if anyone thinks he/she has seen a ghost.

2 **a** Be prepared with definitions, examples, etc. to pre-teach the vocabulary in the box or bring in a set of dictionaries for students to check the meanings themselves. Point out that *sceptical, haunted* and *spooky* are adjectives, *vanish* is a regular verb and *proof* is an uncountable noun.
Model and drill the words, highlighting the pronunciation of *sceptical* /'skeptɪkəl/, *haunted* /'hɔːntɪd/ and *werewolves* /'weəwʊlvz/.
Also teach students that we call a sceptical person *a sceptic* /'skeptɪk/, the verb from *haunted* is *haunt* /'hɔːnt/ and that the singular of *werewolves* is *a werewolf*.

b Focus students on the article. Students do the exercise on their own. Make sure students notice there is one more heading than they need.
You can set a time limit of two minutes to encourage students to read for gist. Check answers with the class.

1c 2a 3e 4b 5d

c Students do the exercise on their own, then compare answers in pairs.
Check answers with the class.

1 ✓ 2 ✓ 3 F The writer thought most of the other ghost-hunters were **normal enough**. 4 F The ghosts who haunt the castle are **two brothers who died in a fire over 200 years ago**. 5 ✓ 6 F The writer **hasn't changed** her mind about the existence of ghosts.

d Students discuss the questions in pairs.
Ask students to share their ideas with the class and find out how many people would like to go on a ghost-hunting weekend.

HELP WITH VOCABULARY Idioms

3 **a–b** Focus students on the introductory bullet and check they remember what an idiom is. Students do **3a** on their own, then check in 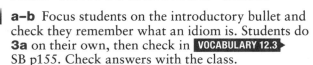 **VOCABULARY 12.3** SB p155. Check answers with the class.

- 2 keep an eye out for sb/sth 3 take sth with a pinch of salt 4 pull sb's leg 5 be a piece of cake 6 recharge sb's batteries 7 in the middle of nowhere 8 out of the blue 9 give sb food for thought 10 break the ice 11 make sb's day 12 sleep like a log
- Highlight that the words in idioms are in a fixed order and you can't change any words for synonyms, e.g. we say *in the middle of nowhere* not ~~*in the centre of nowhere*~~.

- Note that idioms are extremely common in informal spoken English. Although it can often be hard for students to use idioms correctly in context, it's important that they recognise and understand them when they see or hear them.

4 Put students into pairs, Student A and Student B. Student As turn to SB p106 and Student Bs turn to SB p109.

a Students do the exercise on their own, then check in **VOCABULARY 12.3** SB p155.

Student A: 1 nowhere 2 recharge 3 leg 4 cry 5 log 6 day
Student B: 1 cake 2 food 3 blue 4 eye 5 salt 6 ice

b Students do the exercise with their partner.

Student A: a1 b4 c6 d3 e2 f5

c Students do the exercise with their partner.

Student B: a2 b5 c1 d6 e4 f3

Listening

5 **a** Tell students that they are going to listen to a conversation between three friends, Laura, Chris and Mark.
CD3 31 Play the recording (SB p173). Students listen and answer the questions. Check answers with the class.

Laura thinks that her flat is haunted.
Chris is quite sympathetic and thinks that the flat might be haunted.
Mark is very sceptical and doesn't believe that the flat is haunted at all.

b Play the recording again. Students listen and make notes on the reasons why Laura thinks that her flat is haunted.

c Students compare notes in pairs, then discuss what they think Laura should do.
Check students' answers with the class. Ask students what advice they would give Laura.

Laura's old cat refuses to go into her bedroom and it used to sleep on the end of her bed every night. The other night she heard footsteps outside her room, but there was nobody there and the people next door were away. One night she saw a woman, about forty years old, dressed in clothes from the fifties. She stood there staring at Laura, then vanished into thin air. A couple of days later Laura saw the ghost again. She was standing in the corner holding her hands out, as though she was asking for help. There's a part of the kitchen that's always freezing cold.

HELP WITH LISTENING
Natural rhythm: review

6 **a** Focus students on the introductory bullet and check students understand it. Focus students on the extract from the conversation and highlight the examples of stressed words, weak forms and linking. Put students into pairs, Student A and Student B. Student As mark the stressed words and circle the weak forms. Student Bs mark the linking and extra sounds (/w/, /j/, /r/).

b Students compare answers with their partner.

c Ask students to look at **CD3** 31, SB p173. Students check their answers to **6a**. Note that the weak forms are in pink in the Audio Scripts.

LAURA Well, first_of_all, my_/j/_old cat refuses to go_/w/_into my bedroom. In my last flat she slept_on the_/j/_end_of my bed_every night, so_/w/_I thought that was rather_/r/_odd.
MARK Well, the previous_owners' cat might have slept_in that room. Or they could have had_a dog.
LAURA They didn't have_a cat_or_/r/_a dog.

d **CD3** 31 Play the recording again. Students read how stress, weak forms, linking and extra sounds give spoken English its natural rhythm.

7 **a** Go through the prompts with the class and check students understand them all.

b Put students into groups, if possible with people they haven't worked with so far. Students take turns to discuss their opinions of the things in **7a**, giving reasons for their opinions if possible.
Finally, ask each group to tell the class about anything that they all believe in or don't believe in.

┌─ **WRITING** ─┐

Put students into pairs. Tell them to think of ideas for a ghost story and make notes about the characters, the plot, etc. Students write their ghost story for homework. In the next class, ask pairs of students to read out their stories and see how different the stories are.

┌─ **FURTHER PRACTICE** ─┐

Ph Vocabulary Plus 12 Idioms about feelings/ opportunities p205 (Instructions p193)
Extra Practice 12C SB p126
Self-study DVD-ROM Lesson 12C
Workbook Lesson 12C p63
Workbook Reading and Writing Portfolio 12 p86
Progress Test 12 p260

HELP WITH PRONUNCIATION
Word stress (4): word families

1 **a** Focus students on the introductory bullet and check students understand it.
Focus students on the words. Check students understand all the words.
Go through the example with the class.
Students do the exercise in pairs.

b **CD3 32** Play the recording. Students listen and check their answers. Check answers with the class.
Play the recording again. Students listen and repeat.

2 photography photographic photographer
3 economics economical economist
4 philosophy philosophical philosopher
5 environment environmental environmentalist
6 politics political politician
7 analysis analytical analyst
8 universe universal universally

EXTRA IDEA
- Ask students to look at **CD3 32** SB p173. Play the recording again. Students can listen and check their answers.

2 **a** Students practise the conversations in pairs. While they are working, check students are putting the stress on the correct words.

b **CD3 33** Play the recording. Students listen and check. Tell students to swap roles and practise the conversations in **2a** again.
Finally, ask pairs to role-play a conversation. Check they are putting the stress in the correct place on words and praise good pronunciation.

continue2learn

Focus students on the *continue2learn* section on SB p102. See p35 for ideas on how to exploit this section.

Extra Practice 12
See p35 for ideas on how to exploit this section.

12A
1 2 stressed out 3 chucked out 4 messed up 5 chill out; telly 6 trendy 7 bugs; mates 8 pop in 9 quid
2 3 I might **have left** it in the café. 4 ✓ 5 ✓ 6 He can't **have been** ill yesterday. 7 They might **have been** playing football. 8 ✓ 9 I don't know, someone must **have eaten** it. 10 It might **be** there.
3 **Possible answers** 2 He might be asleep. 3 She must be a vegetarian. 4 He/She may be going on a camping holiday. 5 He must be quite well off. 6 He might have forgotten. 7 She might have changed jobs.
8 She must have got divorced.

12B
4 2 both 3 both 4 take 5 ish 6 both 7 or so 8 great 9 vast majority 10 both
5 2 shouldn't have stayed 3 needn't have bought 4 could have driven 5 would have called 6 didn't have to queue

12C
6 2 cake 3 eye 4 leg 5 log 6 blue 7 middle 8 day 9 ice 10 cry

Progress Portfolio 12
- See p36 for ideas on how to exploit this section.

End of Course Review
Student's Book p102–p103

The aim of this activity is to review language that students have learned throughout the course in a fun, student-centred way. The activity takes about 30–45 minutes.

Check students remember *a counter, throw a dice, land on a square* and *move forward/back.*

Give students time to read the rules on SB p102 and answer any questions they may have.

Check students have understood that when a student lands on a Grammar or Vocabulary square, they only need to answer question 1.

Ask what happens when a second student lands on the same square (they answer question 2).

Also check what happens when a third or fourth student lands on the square (they can stay there without answering a question).

Put students into groups of four and give a dice and counters to each group (or students can make their own counters).

Ask a student with a watch in each group to be the time-keeper for the group. He/She should time students when they land on a Talk About square and have to talk about a topic for 40 seconds.

Students take turns to throw the dice and move around the board.

If a student thinks another student's answer to a question on a Grammar or Vocabulary square is wrong, he/she can check in the Language Summaries in the Student's Book or ask you to adjudicate.

While students are working, monitor and help with any problems.

The first student to get to FINISH is the winner. Students can continue playing until three students have finished if you wish.

If one group finishes early, ask them to look at all the squares they didn't land on and answer the questions.

1 1 We can say *used to have*, but not *'d have.*
   2 Yes, they are.
2 1 convince sb **of** sth; cope **with** sb/sth; succeed **in** sth
   2 insist **on** sth; base sth **on** sth; protest **against** sth
4 1 If he **had** a car, he'd drive to work.
   2 I'd **have gone** out last night if I hadn't been so tired.
6 1 See **VOCABULARY 4.2** SB p134.
   2 See **VOCABULARY 7.4** SB p143.
8 1 shocked **by** (at); sick **of**; sure **about** (of); excited **about** (by, at)
   2 fascinated **by** (with); famous **for**; fond **of**; disappointed **in** (by, with)
10 1 He/She asked/wanted to know what I thought of his/her new coat.
   2 He/She asked/wanted to know if/whether I could let him/her know by Sunday.

12 1 written 2 've been playing
14 1 criticism, critical; origin, original; conviction, convinced/convincing; judgement, judgemental
   2 weakness, weak; preference, preferable; conclusion, conclusive; recognition, recognisable
15 1 In the first sentence, I fixed my car myself. In the second sentence, I paid someone (probably a mechanic) to fix it for me.
   2 In the first sentence, it was possible for me to go, but I didn't. In the second sentence, I didn't go and now I regret it.
16 1 *persuade* + object + infinitive with *to* (*persuade somebody to do*); *refuse* + infinitive with *to* (*refuse to do*); *let* + object + infinitive (*let somebody do*); *finish* + verb+*ing* (*finish doing*)
   2 *end up* + verb+*ing* (*end up doing*); *manage* + infinitive with *to* (*manage to do*); *force* + object + infinitive with *to* (*force somebody to do*); *had better* + infinitive (*had better do*)
18 1 It's twice as big **as** my car, but not any **harder** to drive. 2 The **older** they are, **the** more they cost.
20 1 and 2 See **VOCABULARY 7.3** SB p142.
22 1 theft, thief; burglary, burglar; shoplifting, shoplifter; robbery, robber
   2 mugging, mugger; smuggling, smuggler; murder, murderer; vandalism, vandal
23 1 so; like 2 such; as
25 1 In the first sentence I watched TV until six, then I stopped. In the second sentence I stopped doing something I'd been doing before and watched the news.
   2 In the first sentence I have a memory of buying milk. In the second sentence I didn't forget to buy milk.
26 1 Lee is being interviewed at the moment.
   2 The computer might be fixed tomorrow.
28 1 and 2 See **VOCABULARY 6.2** SB p140.
33 1 See **VOCABULARY 8.2** SB p145.
   2 See **VOCABULARY 12.1** SB p155.
34 1 That's the shop **where** I bought the food.
   2 My dad, **who** is 50, is unemployed.
36 1 He warned me not **to walk** across the park.
   2 They accused him **of** stealing the diamond.
37 1 *claim* + *that* + clause (*claim that*); *warn* + object + infinitive with *to* (*warn somebody to do*); *blame* + object + preposition + verb+*ing* (*blame somebody for doing*); *agree* + infinitive with *to* (*agree to do*)
   2 *accuse* + object + preposition + verb+*ing* (*accuse somebody of doing*); *point out* + *that* + clause (*point out that*); *deny* + verb+*ing* (*deny doing*); *advise* + object + infinitive with *to* (*advise somebody to do*)
38 1 be driving 2 have written

Class Activities

Instructions

There are 35 Class Activities worksheets (p148–p189). These worksheets give extra communicative speaking practice of the key language taught in the Student's Book. Each activity matches a lesson in the Student's Book, e.g. 1A *My classmates* matches lesson 1A, etc. There are three activities for units 1–11 and two activities for unit 12.

The Class Activities can be used as extra practice when you have finished the relevant lesson or as review activities in the next class or later in the course.

Many of the activities involve students working in pairs or groups. When you have an odd number of students, you can:

- ask two lower-level students to share a role card.
- give two role cards to a stronger student.
- vary the size of the groups.

1A ▸ My classmates p148

Language
The English verb system

Activity type, when to use and time
'Find someone who' activity. Use any time after lesson 1A. 15–25 minutes.

Preparation
Photocopy one worksheet for each student.

Procedure
- Give a copy of the worksheet to each student. Students work on their own and choose the correct verb form for each sentence in the first column. Check answers with the class.
- Explain that students are going to try and find someone in the class who matches each sentence in the first column. Elicit the questions that students will need to ask for each sentence, e.g. *1 Do you like buying birthday presents for other people?*, etc.
- Point out the follow-up questions in the third column of the worksheet and elicit some of these from the class, e.g. *What was the last present you brought? Who did you buy it for?*, etc. Also tell students that they will need to decide which verb form to use in each question. With a lower-level class you may want to check these follow-up questions with the class before they begin.
- Students move around the room and ask questions 1–10. If students aren't able to leave their seats, they should ask as many students as they can sitting near them. Encourage students to talk to as many people as possible. Point out that they only need to find one person who answers *yes* to each question. When they

find a student who answers *yes* to a question, they should write his/her name in the second column on the worksheet. Then they should ask him/her the follow-up questions based on the prompts in the third column.
- Finally, ask students to tell the class interesting things they have found out about their classmates.

1 likes 2 did 3 has been living 4 was interviewed
5 is staying 6 does 7 has been 8 goes 9 was watching
10 went

1B ▸ Auxiliary dominoes p149

Language
Uses of auxiliaries

Activity type, when to use and time
Dominoes. Use any time after lesson 1B. 15–25 minutes.

Preparation
Photocopy one set of dominoes for each pair of students. Cut into sets and shuffle each set.

Procedure
- Put students into pairs. Give one set of dominoes to each pair. Students share out the dominoes equally. Students are not allowed to look at their partner's dominoes.
- One student puts a domino on the table. His/Her partner puts another domino at either end of the first domino so that the two dominoes match. Encourage students to pay particular attention to the verb forms and auxiliaries in **bold** when trying to match up the dominoes. Also ask students to check that the punctuation on each pair of matching dominoes is correct.
- Students continue taking turns to put dominoes at either end of the domino chain. If a student thinks that the dominoes don't match, he/she can challenge his/her partner. If the match is incorrect, the student must take back his/her domino and the turn passes to his/her partner. If students can't agree, they should ask you to adjudicate.
- When a student can't put down a domino, the turn automatically passes to his/her partner. The game continues until one student has put down all his/her dominoes, or until neither student can make a correct match. The student who finishes first, or who has the fewer dominoes remaining, is the winner.
- When students have finished, ask them to choose three sentences from the dominoes that are true for them and three questions that they would like to ask their partner. Students then take turns to tell each other the sentences and ask each other the questions they have chosen.

1C ▶ Something circles p150

Language
Verb patterns (1)

Activity type, when to use and time
Personalised guessing game. Use any time after lesson 1C. 20–30 minutes.

Preparation
Photocopy one worksheet for each student.

Procedure
- Give a copy of the worksheet to each student. Students work on their own and fill in the gaps in the prompts with the correct form of *do*.
- Students continue working on their own and write short answers to ten of the prompts in the circles. Students should write single words or short phrases, for example, *find a part-time job, smoking, call Daniela*, etc. They can write their answers in any order they want, but not in the same order as the prompts.
- Students work in pairs and swap worksheets with their partner. Students then take turns to guess why their partners have written the things in the circles. For example, if a student has written *find a part-time job*, his/her partner might ask: *Are you trying to find a part-time job at the moment?* or *Have you managed to find a part-time job this year?*, etc. Tell students to ask follow-up questions if possible.
- Finally, ask each student to tell the class the most interesting thing they found out about their partner.

2 doing 3 to do 4 doing 5 doing 6 to do 7 to do
8 to do 9 doing 10 doing 11 do/to do 12 to do
13 do 14 to do 15 doing 16 to do

2A ▶ Nightmare neighbours p151

Language
Present and past habits, repeated actions and states

Activity type, when to use and time
Pairwork role play. Use any time after lesson 2A. 20–35 minutes.

Preparation
Photocopy one worksheet for each pair of students. Cut into separate role cards.

Procedure
- Check students understand *bark* (for a dog), *chase, dig something up, the drums, a car alarm* and *go off*.
- Put students into pairs, A and B. Give each student a copy of the appropriate role card. Give students a minute or two to read the paragraph at the top of their worksheet and check they understand the situation.
- Students work on their own and decide how to express the information about their neighbours on their worksheets.

- Encourage students to use *used to* + infinitive, *would* + infinitive and the Present Continuous with *always* where possible, rather than using the Present Simple or the Past Simple for every sentence.
- Students work with their partner and discuss their situations. Also encourage students to have a natural conversation, rather than just reading out sentences.
- Finally, ask each pair to tell the class who they think has the worst neighbours and why.

2C ▶ Where's the stress? p152

Language
Stress on word families

Activity type, when to use and time
Matching activity. Use any time after lesson 2C. 10–20 minutes.

Preparation
Photocopy one set of cards for each pair of students. Cut the vocabulary cards into sets and shuffle each set. Cut out the two stress pattern cards.

Procedure
- Put students into pairs. Give each pair the two stress pattern cards. Ask them to put these cards face-up next to each other at the top of their table.
- Give each pair of students a set of the vocabulary cards. Students put the cards on the table face-down in a pile.
- Student A turns over a vocabulary card from the top of the pile and places it under the correct stress pattern, saying the word at the same time with the correct stress. If student B thinks that the stress pattern is correct, student A gets one point.
- If student B thinks that student A has placed the word under the wrong stress pattern, he/she can challenge his/her partner. If students can't agree, they should ask you to adjudicate. If student A has put the word in the wrong place, student B can try to match the card to the correct stress pattern. If he/she is correct, he/she gets a bonus point.
- Students take turns to turn over the cards from the pile and match them to the correct stress pattern until the pile is finished. The student with the most points wins.
- Finally, ask each pair to organise all the cards into word families and decide whether each word is a verb, noun, adjective or adverb.

●• really; weaken; weakness; critic; judgement
•● prefer; convince; convinced; conclude
●•• preference; preferably; origin; criticise; critical; recognise
•●• conclusion; conclusive; conviction; convincing; judgemental
●••• preference; criticism
•●•• conclusively; originate; original; reality; responsible; responsibly
••●• realistic; recognition
••●•• recognisable; recognisably

2D ▶ The Big Question p153

Language
Agreeing and disagreeing politely

Activity type, when to use and time
Debate. Use any time after lesson 2D. 30–40 minutes.

Preparation
Photocopy one set of role cards for every four students.
Cut into four separate cards.

Procedure
- Check students understand *compulsory*, *optional*, *aggressive*, *a psychologist* /saɪˈkɒlədʒɪst/ and *tease somebody*. Also check students understand what *a parents' association* is.
- Divide the class into four groups: head teachers, parents, psychologists and presenters. If you have extra students, add them to the first three groups. Arrange the class so that each group is sitting together. If this is not possible, students can do the Preparation stage on their own.
- Give each student in the four groups the appropriate role card. Students work with other people in their groups and do the tasks written on their cards.
- ✍ While students are preparing their roles, copy the table from **REAL WORLD 2.1** ▶ SB p131 onto the board.
- Rearrange the class so that students are sitting in groups of four, with one head teacher, parent, psychologist and presenter in each group. Focus students on the language on the board and ask them to use it during the debate.
- Ask each presenter to start their debate. You can set a time limit of 15 minutes.
- Finally, ask each presenter to share their group's conclusions with the class.

3B ▶ The Unlucky Club p154–p155

Language
Third conditional

Activity type, when to use and time
Information gap. Use any time after lesson 3B.
20–30 minutes.

Preparation
Photocopy one set of role cards for every ten students. Cut into separate cards. Photocopy one worksheet for each student.

Procedure
- Check students understand *lightning*, *sink (sank, sunk)*, *burn down*, *the summit (of a mountain)*, *slip*, *an audition*, *a jackpot*, *a role* and *a compass*.
- Explain to the class that they are all members of The Unlucky Club – a club whose members have all been unlucky in the past in some way. Give each student a role card. If you have more than ten students in the

class, you can give out duplicate role cards without affecting the outcome of the activity. Students are not allowed to look at each other's cards.
- Give students time to read their role cards and encourage them to add more detail to their roles, for example, what they did or said afterwards, etc.
- Also ask each student to make a third conditional sentence to explain what would, could or might have happened to them if they hadn't been so unlucky. Tell students to memorise their sentences. While they are working, monitor and check their sentences for accuracy.
- Students then move around the room and have conversations with each other to find out why each person is a member of The Unlucky Club. Students should explain what happened in their own words and finish their explanation with the third conditional that they have prepared. Before they begin, tell students that they must remember what happened to each person.
- Put students into pairs. Give each student a copy of the worksheet. Students work with their partner and try to fill in the names and complete the third conditionals for each person on the worksheet.
- Check the sentences with the class. Finally, ask the class to decide which student is the unluckiest.

Possible answers 1 … his/her boat hadn't sunk.
2 … his/her house hadn't burnt down. 3 … his/her brother hadn't slipped and fell. 4 … he/she hadn't lost his/her voice. 5 … the taxi driver hadn't broken his/her fingers. 6 … his/her parents' dog hadn't eaten the lottery ticket. 7 … he/she hadn't got food poisoning. 8 … his/her compass hadn't broken. 9 … the letter had arrived earlier. 10 … he/she hadn't broken his/her wrist.

3C ▶ Preposition pelmanism p156

Language
Verbs and prepositions

Activity type, when to use and time
Pelmanism. Use any time after lesson 3C. 10–20 minutes.

Preparation
Photocopy one worksheet for each group of three students. Cut into sets. Shuffle each set.

Procedure
- Put the class into groups of three. Give each group a set of cards. Ask them to spread the cards out face-down on the table in front of them, with the small cards on the left and the large cards on the right.
- Students take turns to turn over one small card and one large card. If a student thinks that the two cards match, he/she makes a sentence that includes the verb and the preposition(s) on the cards. If the two cards match and the sentence is correct, the student keeps the pair of cards and has another turn. If the two cards don't match, the student puts both cards back on the table face-down **in exactly the same place**.

- If a student thinks that another student's cards don't match or that the sentence is not correct, he/she can challenge him/her. If students can't agree, they can ask you to adjudicate. If the cards don't match or the sentence is incorrect, the student puts the cards back and the turn passes to the next student.
- The activity continues until all the cards are matched up. The student who collects the most cards wins.
- If a group finishes early, students can take turns in testing each other on the prepositions by saying the verbs on the small cards.

3D ▶ Easy money! p157–p158

Language
Review of lessons 1A–3D

Activity type, when to use and time
Board game. Use any time after lesson 3D.
20–30 minutes.

Preparation
Photocopy one board, one set of Vocabulary cards and one set of Grammar cards for each group of four students. Cut the Vocabulary cards and Grammar cards into sets. Shuffle each set. Each group also needs a dice and counters.

Procedure
- Put students into groups of four. Give each group a copy of the board, a set of Vocabulary cards, a set of Grammar cards, dice and counters (or students can make their own counters). Students place the cards face-down in two separate piles in the middle of the board.
- Check students understand that they can go round the board as many times as they like and that they collect £500 every time they pass the *START* square. Students will need a pen and paper to keep a record of how much money they have during the game. Tell students that they all start the game with £1,000.
- Students take turns to throw the dice and move around the board. When a student lands on a square that says Vocabulary card or Grammar card, he/she turns over the top card of the appropriate pile and reads out the question to the group. He/She must then answer the question himself/herself. If he/she answers the question correctly, he/she **wins** the amount of money on the square. If he/she doesn't answer the question correctly, he/she **loses** the amount of money on the square. He/She then puts the card at the bottom of the appropriate pile.
- Students always stay on the square they land on, whether they win or lose money. Students don't have to leave the game if they have a negative amount of money. They should keep playing to try and win more money.
- If a student thinks that another student's answer is wrong, they can ask you to adjudicate.
- The game can continue as long as you wish. Alternatively, students can continue playing until they've answered all the Grammar and Vocabulary cards. The student with the most money when the game finishes is the winner.

Vocabulary cards
1 in; of **2** preference, preferable; conclusion, conclusive; criticism, critical **3** See VOCABULARY 1.2 ▶ SB p127. **4** of; on **5** getting; to come **6** in sentence 1, first I stopped, then I talked to Rob. In sentence 2, I was talking to Rob, then I stopped. **7** in; now; often **8** robbery, robber; burglary, burglar; smuggling, smuggler; kidnapping, kidnapper **9** originate, origin; weaken, weakness; recognise, recognition **10** of; about **11** He's fluent **in** French. I picked **up** some Spanish on holiday. **12** arrest sb for sth; charge sb with sth; convict sb of sth **13** See VOCABULARY 1.2 ▶ SB p127. **14** thief, steal; shoplifter, shoplift; murderer, murder; vandal, vandalise **15** to, for; with **16** to pass; sending

Grammar cards
1 is spoken; go **2** hadn't; have **3** doesn't; does **4** provided; was **5** If I didn't have children, I'd go out a lot. **6** I'll never get used to **living** here. I can't **get** used to the noise. **7** Don't you?; Hasn't he?; Did they? **8** If Mike's car hadn't broken down, he wouldn't have missed the meeting. **9** Sentence 1 is correct. Sentence 2: She **had/used** to have a flat there. **10** Suppose; would **11** has been; was working **12** did; was **13** In sentence 1 I worked at the weekend in the past, but I don't now. In sentence 2, I work at the weekend now and it's familiar or no longer strange to me. **14** don't; did **15** If I hadn't left home late, I wouldn't have missed the train. **16** go; called; asking

4A ▶ Jack's story p159

Language
Narrative verb forms; Past Perfect Continuous

Activity type, when to use and time
Story ordering. Use any time after lesson 4A.
20–35 minutes.

Preparation
Photocopy one worksheet for each pair of students. Cut out the Outline story card. Cut the Extra information cards into sets. **Do not shuffle the cards.** Organise each set **in number order**, with card 1 at the top and card 20 at the bottom.

Procedure
- Check students understand *a lane, the boot of a car, briefcase* and *porch*.
- Put students into pairs. Give a copy of the Outline story card to each pair. Allow students time to read the story. You can ask students to speculate about what is happening, but don't give them any more information at this stage. Students then place the card on the left-hand side of the table.
- Give each pair a set of Extra information cards. Ask students to place the cards face-down in a pile. Students take turns to turn over the cards one at a time, starting with card 1. They should try to fit each card into the story by placing them in an appropriate place to the

right of the Outline story card. Tell students to look at the punctuation on the cards as well as the narrative verb forms. Also point out that some cards can be put in more than one place in the story.

- When students have finished, they can compare stories with another pair near them. If some cards are in different places, students can discuss if both places are possible. Check answers with the class.

- Students work in their pairs and discuss what they think was in the briefcase, who the man in the kitchen was, what had happened before the story began and how the story ended.

- Finally, ask some pairs or groups to share their ideas with the class. You can also ask students to write the end of the story for homework.

Possible answers
A 2; 9 B 5; 14 C 3; 8 D 1; 7; 12; 17
E 4; 11; 19 F 13; 18 G 15 H 6; 10 I 16 J 20

4B The book quiz p160

Language
Defining and non-defining relative clauses

Activity type, when to use and time
Pairwork quiz. Use any time after lesson 4B.
15–20 minutes.

Preparation
Photocopy one worksheet for each pair of students. Cut into two separate worksheets.

Procedure
- Put students into groups of four. Divide each group into two pairs, pair A and pair B. Give each student a copy of the appropriate quiz. Students are not allowed to show their quizzes to the other pair in their group.

- Students work in their pairs and fill in the gaps in each question with *who, that, which, whose,* or *where.* Check answers with the class. Note that both quizzes have the **same** answers. Only check the missing words so that the other pair doesn't hear the questions they are about to be asked. Each pair gets one point for each correct answer and one bonus point if all the answers are correct.

- Students work in their groups of four. Each pair takes turns to read out a sentence and the three possible answers from their quiz. If the other pair guesses the correct answer, they get two points. Before they begin, point out that the words/phrases in **bold** are the correct answers.

- Each pair adds up their points from both parts of the activity. The pair with the most points wins.

Quizzes A and B
1 who 2 that/which/– 3 whose
4 which 5 where 6 who/that

4C The island p161

Language
Connecting words: reason and contrast; narrative verb forms

Activity type, when to use and time
Story-telling. Use any time after lesson 4C.
30–45 minutes.

Preparation
Photocopy one worksheet for each student.

Procedure
- Give each student a copy of the worksheet. Ask students to read all the information on the worksheet and find out what happened to Steve and his family, and where they are now. Tell students not to write anything at this stage. Check answers with the class.

- Tell students that they are going to invent a story about what happened to Steve and his family. Students work in pairs and decide how to complete each sentence in the story. Both students in each pair should write their sentences on their worksheets. Before they begin, point out the connecting words/phrases in **bold**.

- When students have finished, they write the end of the story in their pairs on the back of their worksheet. Alternatively, students can finish the story for homework.

- Finally, students read each other's stories and decide which one they think is the best.

5A Comparisons board game p162

Language
Ways of comparing

Activity type, when to use and time
Board game. Use any time after lesson 5A.
20–30 minutes.

Preparation
Photocopy one board for every three or four students. You will also need a dice for each group and a counter for each student.

Procedure
- Put students into groups of three or four. Give each group a copy of the board, a dice and counters (or students can make their own counters). Ask a student with a watch in each group to be the timekeeper.

- Students take turns to throw the dice and move around the board. When they land on a sentence square, they must rephrase the sentence using the word(s) in brackets so that it has the same meaning.

- If a student thinks another student's sentence is incorrect, he/she can challenge him/her. If the students can't agree, they should ask you to adjudicate. If a student gets the sentence wrong, he/she must move back to his/her previous square.

- When a student lands on a *Compare* square, he/she must talk about the topic for at least 30 seconds. If he/she stops talking before 30 seconds are up, he/she must move back to his/her previous square.
- The first student to reach the FINISH square wins. If groups finish early, students can go through the squares in order and take turns to rephrase the sentences. They can also discuss the topics in the *Compare* squares that they didn't land on during the game.

1 My brother is slightly taller than me/I am. 3 The more exercise I do, the healthier I feel. 4 Our house isn't nearly as nice as Tony's. 5 I'm not quite as good at tennis as Nick (is). 8 The last book I read is/was far better than this one. 11 I've been here nearly as long as him/he has. 13 The harder I work, the more stressed I get. 14 Sarah's laptop was a bit cheaper/less expensive than mine. 16 Petrol keeps getting more and more expensive. 17 Your garden isn't any nicer than Tony's. 19 Mark's mobile is nowhere near as big as Chris's. 20 The older I get, the more I worry about my health. 21 My brother earns twice as much as me/I do. 24 The club was less crowded than I expected. 26 My sister earns much more than me/I do. 27 My new flat is no larger/smaller than my old one. 29 Learning English/German is just as hard as learning German/English. 30 You're a little slimmer than her/she is. 32 My old camera is/was almost as good as my new one. 33 That TV was a great deal more expensive than mine.

5C ▶ Homophone snap p163

Language
Homophones

Activity type, when to use and time
Snap card game. Use any time after lesson 5C. 15–25 minutes.

Preparation
Photocopy the worksheet for each group of three students. Cut into separate cards and shuffle.

Procedure
- Put students into groups of three. Give each group a set of cards. Make sure they are shuffled. Elicit a homophone from the class and point out that many of the words in the game are from lesson 5C in the Student's Book.
- Demonstrate the card game with one group of students. Point out that it should be a quick game, with students taking their turn quickly and being the first to notice if two matching cards (homophones) have been laid in the middle.
- Tell students to deal the cards out between the three members of the group. Students put their cards face down in front of them so they can't see the words.

They take turns to put a card face up in the middle so everyone can see the word clearly. If two consecutive words are placed in the middle which are homophones (i.e. they have the same sound but different spelling and meaning), then the first student to say the words correctly wins that pair of cards. Play continues with the next student placing a card from their pile in the middle.

- When students have placed all their cards in the middle, they shuffle the discarded cards, deal again and continue playing until all the homophones have been won.
- Once all the homophones have been won, there is a further stage to the game in which students have a chance to convert their cards to points or lose them to another player.
- Students take turns to turn over the pairs of homophones they have won. One of the words will be bold (for example, *wood*, **would**). Each student should write a sentence using the bold word correctly in a sentence (e.g. *Would you like a cup of tea?*).
- Students then take turns to say their sentence to the group. If the student who originally won the cards says a correct sentence, they can keep their cards. But if their sentence is incorrect, the cards should go to the first person to make a correct sentence in the group. Students should judge each other's sentences, but monitor while they are playing and help if there are any doubts or disagreements, or check the winning sentences at the end of the game.
- The winner is the player who has the most homophones at the end of the game.

5D ▶ The congestion charge p164–p165

Language
Discussion language (2): opinions

Activity type, when to use and time
Debate. Use any time after lesson 5D. 30–45 minutes.

Preparation
Photocopy one set of six role cards for each group of six students. Cut into separate role cards.

Procedure
- Check students understand *the mayor* /meə/, *congestion* /kən'dʒestʃən/, *raise money, economy, a resident* and *a scheme* /skiːm/.
- Introduce the idea of a congestion charge (an amount that people have to pay if they want to drive into a town or city centre, usually during the day on weekdays).
- Divide the class into six groups A–F. Give each student in group A a copy of the Student A role card, etc. Try to choose confident students to be the chairpeople.
- **Extra students:** If you have one or two extra students, put them in group E. If you have three extra students, put one each in groups A, B and E. If you have four extra students, put one each in groups A, B, C and D. If you have five extra students, put one each in groups A, B, C, D and E. Note that students A and B are for the congestion charge, students C and D are against the congestion charge, while student E is undecided.

- Give students time to read the introduction on their cards. Check they understand the situation. Students then work in their groups and follow the instructions on their role cards.
- ✏ While students are working, write the discussion language from REAL WORLD 5.1 ▶ SB p139 on the board.
- Rearrange the class so that students are sitting in groups of six, with one student A, one student B, etc. in each group. If you have extra students, distribute them equally among the groups. Try to ensure that each group contains an equal number of A/B students and C/D students so that the debate is balanced. Focus students on the language on the board and remind them to use this during the meeting.
- Ask the chairpeople to start their meetings. Allow about 15 minutes for this stage.
- At the end of the meetings, each chairperson conducts a vote on whether the congestion charge should be introduced or not. Finally, ask each chairperson to share his/her group's conclusions with the class.

6A ▶ Is this your card? p166

Language
Uses of verb+*ing*

Activity type, when to use and time
Sentence completion and mingle. Use any time after lesson 6A. 15–20 minutes.

Preparation
Photocopy Worksheet A and B so that there are enough cards for everyone in the class to have one sentence beginning or ending each. Cut into separate cards. Photocopy worksheet A so that each student has a copy to complete.

Procedure
- Give half the class cards from Worksheet A and half the class cards from Worksheet B. Tell students someone in the class has the other half of their sentence. (As are sentence beginnings, Bs are the endings.) They mingle to find their 'other half'. Then pairs brainstorm different true endings for their sentence beginning.
- Give each student a copy of Worksheet A. Tell students that they must complete the sentences with true information about themselves, using a verb+*ing* form in each sentence and any other words they need. Students are not allowed to look at each other's sentences.
- Collect all the papers, place them in a bag and mix them up. Ask students to pick out one of the papers each from the bag. If they pick their own paper, they should put it back in the bag and take a different one. Explain that they are going to try and find the person in the class who wrote the sentences on their paper.
- Students then prepare questions to find out who wrote the sentences on their card.

- Students move around the room asking their questions. Point out that some students may have written similar endings. Students should therefore check they have found the correct person by asking about all the sentences on the paper.
- If students find the person who wrote their paper quickly, they should take another paper and do the activity again.

6B ▶ Future thoughts p167

Language
Modal verbs (1); levels of certainty about the future

Activity type, when to use and time
Personalised guessing game. Use any time after lesson 6B. 15–25 minutes.

Preparation
Photocopy one worksheet for each student.

Procedure
- Give a copy of the worksheet to each student. Tell students to read the prompts in the box and then write short answers to ten of the prompts in the thought bubbles. Students should write single words or short phrases, for example, *Rome, scuba-diving*, etc. They can write their answers in any bubble they want, but not in the same order as the prompts.
- Students work in pairs and swap worksheets with their partner. Students then take turns to say why they think their partners have written the things in the thought bubbles. For example, if a student has written *Rome*, his/her partner might say: *I think you're likely to visit Rome before the end of the year.* or *I think you're sure to go back to Rome one day.*, etc. His/Her partner should say if the sentences are true or false. Students should ask follow-up questions if possible.
- Finally, ask each student to tell the class the most interesting thing they found out about their partner.

6D ▶ Four in a line p168–p169

Language
Review of lessons 4A–6D

Activity type, when to use and time
Puzzle game. Use any time after lesson 6D. 20–35 minutes.

Preparation
Photocopy one Board 1/Team A question sheet for half the number of students in your class and one Board 2/Team B question sheet for the other half. Cut each worksheet into separate boards and question sheets.

Procedure

- Put students into groups of four or six. Give each group a copy of Board 1.
- Divide each group into two teams: team A and team B. Give each student in each team a copy of the appropriate question sheet. Students are not allowed to look at the other team's question sheet.
- Focus students on Board 1. Tell students that G = grammar, V = vocabulary and M = a mystery question. Explain that the first team to get four squares in a line on any part of the board, either down or across (but **not** diagonally), wins the game. When students choose a square, they should consider if it is better to block the other team's line or to build their own line.
- Students toss a coin to decide who starts. The teams then take turns to choose a square on the board. When a team lands on a square, the other team reads out a question from the relevant section on their question sheets. If a team answers correctly, they win the square and mark it in a suitable way, for example by colouring in the square. If the answer is incorrect, the square remains available (the other team **doesn't** get the square). Point out that students must read out the questions in number order and the answers are in brackets on the question sheets.
- When a group has finished playing, you can give them a copy of Board 2 and ask them to play again. If students run out of questions in a particular category, they can ask questions from the other categories instead.
- Groups that finish early can ask each other the unanswered questions on their question sheets.

7A ▶ My partner's life p170

Language
Simple and continuous aspects; activity and state verbs

Activity type, when to use and time
Personalised information gap. Use any time after lesson 7A. 15–20 minutes.

Preparation
Photocopy one worksheet for each pair of students. Cut into two separate worksheets.

Procedure
- Put students into pairs, A and B. If possible, put students with someone they don't know very well. Give each student a copy of the appropriate worksheet. Students are not allowed to look at each other's worksheets.
- Students work on their own and choose the correct verb form in sentences 1–10 on their worksheets. Check answers with the class. Only check the verb forms so that students don't hear the questions they will be asked. Note that the answers are the same on both worksheets.

- Students continue to work on their own and write a *T* in the second column on the worksheet if they think the sentence is true or an *F* if they think it is false. Students are not allowed to speak to their partner during this stage of the activity.
- Students work with their partners and take turns to ask and answer questions about the sentences on their worksheets. With a lower-level class, ask students to prepare the questions they are going to ask before they work in their pairs.
- For each prediction a student gets right, he/she gets a point. Encourage students to ask follow-up questions where possible. The student with the most points wins.
- Finally, students tell the class two things they found out about their partner.

1 goes 2 is thinking 3 trusts 4 thinks 5 was studying 6 had 7 is reading 8 wants 9 is having 10 has bought

7B ▶ Foreign correspondent p171

Language
Present Perfect Simple and Present Perfect Continuous

Activity type, when to use and time
Pairwork role play. Use any time after lesson 7B. 20–30 minutes.

Preparation
Photocopy one worksheet for each pair of students. Cut into separate role cards.

Procedure
- Check students remember *a foreign correspondent*.
- Divide the class into two groups, A and B. Give each student a copy of the appropriate role card. If you have an extra student, make him/her an interviewer.
- Ask students to read the review at the top of the role cards to find out what the radio programme is about. Check the answer with the class.
- Students work on their own and follow the instructions on their role cards. Encourage the foreign correspondents to use their imagination when preparing their roles. Also check the interviewers' questions for accuracy and help them with any problems. With a lower-level class, interviewers can prepare questions in pairs.
- Reorganise the class so that one student from group A is sitting with one student from group B. Students do the role play in pairs. Encourage the interviewer to welcome his/her guest before beginning the interview.
- Finally, ask the interviewers to tell the class a few interesting things they found out about 'Pat Cook'.

7C ▶ Wordbuilding squares p172

Language
Prefixes

Activity type, when to use and time
Card matching game. Use any time after 7C.
15–25 minutes.

Preparation
Photocopy one worksheet for each pair of students. Cut into separate cards. Shuffle each set.

Procedure
- Put the students into pairs. Give each pair a set of cards. Ask each pair to divide the cards equally between them. Students put their cards face-down in a pile in front of them.
- One student turns over the first card in his/her pile and puts it on the table. His/Her partner then turns over the first card in his/her pile and tries to make a word by placing it next to the first card. If it isn't possible to make a word, he/she puts the card at the bottom of his/her pile. The turn then passes to his/her partner.
- Students can place their cards above, below, to the left or to the right of **any** card on the table. However, all the arrows on the cards must be pointing upwards and students are not allowed to rotate the cards. If more than one edge of a card is in contact with other cards, then each edge must make a word.
- If a student thinks that one of his/her partner's words isn't correct, they can ask you to adjudicate. If the word isn't correct, the student takes back the card, places it at the bottom of his/her pile and the turn passes to his/her partner. The first student to put down all of his/her cards wins.
- Finally, students can write any new words they have made in their vocabulary notebooks.

8A ▶ Life isn't perfect p173–p174

Language
Present wishes

Activity type, when to use and time
Role play and sentence completion activity. Use any time after lesson 8A. 20–30 minutes.

Preparation
Photocopy one set of role cards for every twelve students and one *What did they wish?* worksheet for each student. Cut the role cards into twelve separate cards. Shuffle the cards.

Procedure
- Begin the activity by asking the class what they think the advantages and disadvantages of being famous are.
- Tell students that they are all famous people and that they have been invited to a very exclusive party. Give out the cards in random order. If you have more than 12 students, you can give out duplicate cards without affecting the outcome of the activity. If you have fewer than 12 students, omit the later role cards and delete the corresponding sentences from the *What did they wish?* worksheet.
- Students read their role cards, then write a sentence beginning with *I wish ...* for the sentence in **bold** on their cards. Students should think of reasons for their wishes and also invent answers to the question prompts in brackets on their cards.
- 🖉 While students are working, write these questions and prompts on the board: **Questions:** *What do you do exactly? What are you working on/doing at the moment? Do you enjoy being famous?* Advice prompts: *Maybe it's time you ... ; Why don't you ... ?; Perhaps you should ... ; Have you tried ... ?; Well, I hope you ... .*
- Explain that students must talk to all of the other guests and find out as much as they can about them. Remind students to start each conversation naturally, not by reading out the information on their card. During the conversations students must tell each other the wishes that they have prepared, giving reasons for them if possible. Also tell students to remember the other guests' wishes as they will need them after the party.
- Students move around the room and talk to the other guests. Encourage students to ask the questions on the board when they meet new people and to respond to each other's wishes by using the advice prompts on the board.
- When students have finished, put them into pairs and give each student a copy of the *What did they wish?* worksheet. Students fill in the gaps at the beginning of each sentence with a student's name, then complete the sentence with that person's wish.
- Check answers with the class. Finally, ask students which character they thought had the biggest problem.

a ... all the critics didn't hate his/her work. **b** ... he/she didn't have to work on his/her own all the time. **c** ... photographers wouldn't (didn't) follow him/her around every day. **d** ... the newspapers wouldn't (didn't) write about his/her private life all the time. **e** ... he/she could eat the same food as everyone else. **f** ... people wouldn't (didn't) ask him/her to tell jokes all the time. **g** ... he/she didn't get so nervous before big matches. **h** ... he/she wasn't/weren't under so much pressure all the time. **i** ... department stores wouldn't (didn't) keep stealing his/her designs. **j** ... he/she didn't have to start filming at 6 a.m. **k** ... people wouldn't (didn't) stop him/her in the street all the time. **l** ... he/she didn't have to be away from home most of the year.

8B ▶ Money snakes and ladders p175

Language
Money vocabulary and phrasal verbs

Activity type, when to use and time
Board game. Use any time after lesson 8B.
15–25 minutes.

Preparation
Photocopy one worksheet for each group of three or four students. You also need a dice for each group and a counter for each student.

Procedure
- Check students understand *a cashpoint, the stock market, a plasma TV* and *scratched*.
- Put students into groups of three or four. Give each student a copy of the snakes and ladders board, a dice and counters (or students make their own counters).
- Students take turns to throw the dice and move around the board. When they land on a square, they must say the complete sentence, including the missing word or phrase. Point out that there is one space for each letter and that an oblique (/) indicates a new word.
- If a student gets the sentence wrong or can't remember the correct word or phrase, he/she must move back to his/her previous square. Note that all the vocabulary practised in the activity is from **VOCABULARY 8.1** and **VOCABULARY 8.2** ▶ SB p145.
- If students land at the bottom of a ladder, they must complete the sentence correctly before they are allowed to go up it. They don't have to complete the sentence at the top of the ladder.
- If they land on the head of a snake, they must always go down the snake to its tail. They don't have to complete the sentence at the bottom of a snake.
- If a student thinks another student's answer is wrong, he/she should ask you to adjudicate.
- If a student lands on a square that has already been answered, he/she must say the completed sentence again to check that he/she has been listening!
- The first student to reach the *FINISH* square is the winner.
- If groups finish early, they can go through the squares in order and take turns to say the missing words/phrases.

1 loan 2 mortgage 3 get … out 4 interest 5 well off
6 saving up for 7 rip … off 8 credit 9 invest … in
10 going down 11 deposit 13 savings 14 short of
money 15 spend … on 16 pay … back 18 comes to
19 getting … debt 20 overdrawn 22 credit 23 credit
rating 24 took … off 26 taking out 27 pay cash
28 low interest rate 29 came into 30 repay
31 pay off 33 get out of

8C ▶ Bingo! p176

Language
Synonyms

Activity type, when to use and time
Bingo game. Use any time after lesson 8C.
15–20 minutes.

Preparation
Photocopy one worksheet for every four students in the class. Cut into four separate bingo cards.

Procedure
- Give each student a bingo card. Allow students a few minutes to check they know the synonyms for all the words/phrases on their card. Students can check any words they don't know in **VOCABULARY 8.3** ▶ SB p145. Students are not allowed to write the synonyms on their cards.
- Explain that you are going to say some words/phrases. When students hear a word/phrase which has the same meaning as a word/phrase on their card, they cross it out. The first student to cross out **all** the words on his/her card shouts *Bingo!*.
- Read out the words/phrases in **bold** in the tables below slowly in random order. When you say a word/phrase, put a tick next to it so that you don't say it twice. Continue until a student shouts *Bingo!* and wins the game. If necessary, check his/her card against the tables.
- If you want to play the game again, distribute new cards and read out the synonyms in **bold** again in random order. Alternatively, students work in pairs and read out their words to each other. Their partner says the synonyms.

work out	figure out	simple	straightforward
exact	precise	especially	particularly
problem	dilemma	usually	generally
appropriate	acceptable	normal	customary
compulsory	obligatory	strange	odd
certainly	definitely	watch	observe
insulted	offended	extra	additional
chase	pursue	differ	vary
discover	find out	difficult	complicated
simply	just	for example	such as

9A ▶ Passive dominoes p177

Language
The passive

Activity type, when to use and time
Dominoes. Use any time after lesson 9A. 15–25 minutes.

Preparation
Photocopy one set of dominoes for each pair of students. Cut into sets and shuffle each set.

Procedure
- Put students into pairs. Give one set of dominoes to each pair. Students share out the dominoes equally. Students are not allowed to look at their partner's dominoes.
- One student puts a domino on the table. His/Her partner puts another domino at either end of the first domino so that the two dominoes make a sentence. Encourage students to pay attention to the words/phrases in **bold** when trying to match up the dominoes.
- Students continue taking turns to put dominoes at either end of the chain. If a student thinks the dominoes don't make a sentence, he/she can challenge his/her partner. If the sentence is incorrect, the student takes back the domino and the turn passes to his/her partner. If students can't agree, they should ask you to adjudicate.
- When a student can't put down a domino, the turn automatically passes to his/her partner.
- The game continues until one student has put down all of his/her dominoes, or until neither student can make a correct match. The student who finishes first, or who has the fewer dominoes remaining at the end of the game, is the winner.

9B ▶ Entertainment crossword p178

Language
Entertainment adjectives; the cinema

Activity type, when to use and time
Paired crossword. Use any time after lesson 9B. 15–25 minutes.

Preparation
Photocopy one worksheet for each pair of students. Cut into two separate worksheets.

Procedure
- Divide the class into two groups, A and B. Give each student a copy of the appropriate worksheet. Point out that all the words/phrases in the crossword are from lessons 9A and 9B.
- Students work in pairs with a student from the same group and check they know the meanings of all the words/phrases on their worksheet. Students can check any words/phrases they don't know in **VOCABULARY 9.1** and **VOCABULARY 9.2** SB p147. With a lower-level class, you may want to ask students to prepare clues for each of their words/phrases.

- Put students into pairs so that a student from group A is working with a student from group B. Students are not allowed to look at each other's worksheets.
- Students then take turns to give clues for the words/phrases on their crossword, e.g. *1 down : a film that continues the story of an earlier one.* Students should also tell their partner if an answer is more than one word.
- Finally, students check their completed crossword and their spelling with their partner.

9D ▶ Giveaway! p179–p180

Language
Review of lessons 7A–9D

Activity type, when to use and time
Mingle (**Procedure A**) or group card game (**Procedure B**). Use any time after lesson 9D. 25–35 minutes.

Preparation
Procedure A: photocopy one set of cards for the whole class. Cut into separate cards. Shuffle the cards.
Procedure B: photocopy one set of cards for every four students in the class. Cut into separate cards. Shuffle each set.

Procedure A
- Distribute all the cards to the class. Try to give each student the same number of cards, but it doesn't affect the outcome of the activity if some students have one more card than others. Students are not allowed to look at each other's cards.
- Tell students to answer the questions on their cards. Students **mustn't** write the answers on the cards, but they can make a note of the answers on a piece of paper. Point out that the relevant Language Summary reference for each question is in the top right-hand corner of the card if students want to check their answers.
- Tell students that the aim of the activity is to give away all their cards. Students move around the room and take turns to ask each other the questions on the cards. For example, student A reads out the question from one of his/her cards to student B. If student B answers the question correctly, student A keeps the card. If student B gets the answer wrong, student A gives the card to student B and tells him/her the correct answer. Students must answer **all** parts of the question correctly to avoid being given a card. Set a time limit of 10 or 15 minutes. Demonstrate this part of the activity before they begin.
- When a student has given away all his/her cards, he/she must remain standing and can still be asked questions by other students. The student with the fewest cards when the activity finishes is the winner.

Procedure B

- Put students into groups of four. Give each group a set of cards. Students divide the cards between them. Students are not allowed to look at each other's cards.

- Tell students to try and answer the questions on their cards (see Procedure A).

- Tell students that the aim of the activity is to give away all their cards. Students work in their groups and take turns to ask the person on their left the question on one of their cards. For example, student A asks student B the question. If student B answers the question correctly, student A keeps the card. If student B gets the answer wrong, student A gives the card to student B and tells him/her the correct answer. The turn then passes to the next student. Students must answer **all** parts of the question correctly to avoid being given a card.

- Students continue playing until they have asked all the questions on the cards. The student with the fewest cards at the end of the game wins.

10A▶ Having things done p181

Language
have/get something done, get somebody to do something, do something yourself

Activity type, when to use and time
'Find someone who' activity. Use any time after lesson 10A. 15–25 minutes.

Preparation
Photocopy one worksheet for each student.

Procedure

- Check students understand *remove something from somewhere, read somebody's palm, paint somebody's portrait* and that they remember *shave*.

- Give each student a copy of the worksheet. Focus students on the questions in the first column. Students work on their own and put the verbs in brackets in the correct form. Check answers with the class.

- Explain that students are going to try and find someone in the class who answers yes to each question. Point out the follow-up questions in the third column of the worksheet and elicit some of these from the class, for example, *Where/When did you have your photo taken?*, etc. Tell students that they will need to decide which verb form to use in each question. With a lower-level class you may want to check all the follow-up questions with the class before they begin.

- Students move around the room and ask each other questions 1–10. If students are not able to leave their seats, they should ask as many students as they can sitting near them. Encourage students to talk to as many people as possible and point out that they only need to find one person who answers yes to each question. When they find a student who answers *yes* to a question, they write his/her name in the second

column on the worksheet. Then they should ask him/her the follow-up questions based on the prompts in the third column.

- Finally, ask students to tell the class two interesting things they have found out about their classmates.

1 Have … had … taken 2 Do … get … to check
3 Do … do 4 Have … had … made 5 would … get
… to cook 6 Did … choose 7 would … get … to
remove 8 Have … had … read 9 Would … get …
shaved 10 Have … had … painted

10B▶ Going, going, gone! p182

Language
Quantifiers

Activity type, when to use and time
Auction game. Use any time after lesson 10B. 20–30 minutes.

Preparation
Photocopy one worksheet for each pair of students.

Procedure

- Check students understand *an auction* /ˈɔːkʃən/ and how an auction works.

- Put students into pairs. Give a copy of the worksheet to each pair. Tell students that some sentences are correct and some are incorrect. Point out that the incorrect sentences can have one or two mistakes.

- Students work in their pairs and decide if the use of quantifiers and related language (articles, verb forms, etc.) in each sentence is correct. If they think a sentence is wrong, they must decide how to correct it. Tell students not to share their ideas with other pairs, as they will be competing against each other later.

- Tell students that they can now bid for these sentences at an auction and that they should try to buy as many sentences as possible. Explain that each pair has £5,000 to spend and that they can only bid in multiples of £50 (£50, £100, etc.). Auction the sentences to the class by inviting bids for each sentence in number order. When you have no further bids, you can say *Going, going, gone!*.

- When a pair buys a sentence, they must say whether they think the sentence is correct, or tell you the correct version of the sentence, before they are allowed to own it. If a pair gets the sentence wrong, they lose the money they have bid, but **don't** get the sentence. You can then auction the same sentence again.

- When a pair buys a sentence, they deduct the price from the £5,000 on their worksheet. If they tried to buy a sentence, but didn't get the sentence correct, they must still deduct the money they spent from their total. Students can only spend £5,000 during the whole auction. The pair that buys the most sentences wins.

1 I haven't seen **any of** my friends from university for ages. 2 ✓ 3 All of **the** people in my office work very hard, but I don't really like **any** of them. 4 All of the rooms in my house **are** quite big, but **none of** them are very tidy! 5 ✓ 6 ✓ 7 I've got all of his books, but I haven't read **any** of them. 8 Everyone in my family **has** got a mobile and all **of** them text me quite a lot. 9 ✓ 10 Sam bought both of these laptops last year, but **neither** of them works any more. 11 I work hard every **day**, so I don't usually do **anything** on Sundays. 12 I've got two digital cameras, but neither **of** them **works** properly. 13 ✓ 14 Tom's got five sisters, but **none** of them live in the same town as him. 15 I know lots of Americans, but I've never met **anyone** from Canada. 16 The guests ate all of **the** food and **everyone** had a wonderful time.

10D ▶ Love it or hate it p183

Language
Adding emphasis

Activity type, when to use and time
Discussion activity. Use any time after lesson 10D. 10–20 minutes.

Preparation
Photocopy one worksheet for each pair of students. Cut into separate worksheets.

Procedure
- Divide the class into two groups, A and B. Give each student a copy of the appropriate worksheet.
- Students work on their own and write the words in the ovals in the correct order below each oval, as in the example. Ask students to check their answers with another student in their group.
- Students work on their own and complete the sentences in any way they like. While they are working, monitor and check their sentences for accuracy.
- Rearrange the class so that a student from group A is working with a student from group B. Tell students that they must talk for at least one minute about each of the nine different topics on their worksheets.
- Students should take turns to begin each conversation by saying one of their sentences from the worksheet. For example, student A says: *What I love about the Internet is being able to send photos to people.* Student B should respond by agreeing or disagreeing and asking follow-up questions, for example, *Yes, me too. Who do you send photos to?*, etc. When they have finished discussing that particular aspect of the topic, student B says the sentence that he/she has prepared to continue the discussion, for example, *The thing that amazes me about the Internet is how fast it is.*

- To help students keep talking on each topic, you can time each conversation and tell students to move on to a new topic when one minute has passed.
- Finally, ask each pair to tell the class one thing they agreed or disagreed about.

Student A
2 The thing that annoys me about mobile phones is …
3 One thing I enjoy about staying in hotels is …
4 The thing I like most about weddings is …
5 One thing that annoys me about going to the cinema is … 6 What I like about the English language is … 7 The thing that irritates me about travelling by plane is … 8 One thing that depresses me about the modern world is …
9 What I love about living in this town is …

Student B
b What I like most about mobile phones is …
c What irritates me about staying in hotels is …
d The thing that annoys me about weddings is …
e What I like about going to the cinema is …
f One thing I don't like about the English language is … g What I really enjoy about travelling by plane is … h One thing I love about the modern world is … i The thing that annoys me about living in this town is …

11A ▶ The photoshoot p184

Language
Future Perfect and Future Continuous

Activity type, when to use and time
Information gap. Use any time after lesson 11A. 15–25 minutes.

Preparation
Photocopy one worksheet for each pair of students. Cut into separate role cards.

Procedure
- Check students understand *a photoshoot* (a time when a photographer takes photos of someone, for example, a famous person, band, etc.).
- Put students into pairs, A and B. Give each student a copy of the appropriate role card. Focus students on the text at the top of the role card and allow them a minute or two to read the information. Check they understand their roles, what they have to do (arrange a time for a photoshoot) and what time of day it is now (5.30 p.m. on Tuesday).
- Focus students on the diary pages and allow them time to read the information. Point out that they need at least an hour for the photoshoot and that they should try to make the appointment as soon as possible. Tell students that they are not allowed to cancel any of the appointments in their diaries or make an appointment before 8 a.m. Students work on their own and make a note of possible times for the photoshoot on each day.

- ✏ While students are working, write these prompts on the board: *I'm afraid I'll/She'll be …ing then. I'll/She'll have (finished/left/gone) … by … . I/She won't have (finished) … by then. I'm sorry, I'll/She'll be in the middle of (a meeting) then. I'll/She'll be on her way to … then.*
- Students work with their partners and role play the situation. The photographers should begin the role play by phoning the managers and introducing themselves. Before they begin, tell students to use the prompts on the board during the conversation where appropriate.
- Finally, ask students what time they have arranged the photoshoot for.
  The only available time for the photoshoot is between 3.00 and 4.30 on Friday afternoon.

11B ▶ Reported board game p185

Language
Reported speech

Activity type, when to use and time
Board game. Use any time after lesson 11B. 15–25 minutes.

Preparation
Photocopy one board for every three or four students. You also need a dice for each group and a counter for each student.

Procedure
- Put students into groups of three or four. Give each group a copy of the board, a dice and counters (or students can make their own counters).
- Students take turns to throw the dice and move around the board. When they land on a square, they must put the sentence or question in the speech bubble into reported speech using the verb at the bottom of the square. Tell students that they must change the verb form of the sentence in the speech bubble if possible (Present Simple → Past Simple, *will* → *would*, etc.). Students should also look at the people on the square, and use the correct pronouns and possessive adjectives.
- If a student thinks another student's sentence is incorrect, he/she can challenge him/her. If students can't agree, they should ask you to adjudicate. If a student gets the sentence wrong, he/she must move back to his/her previous square.
- If a student lands on a square that another student has already landed on, he/she must report the sentence again to show that he/she has been listening!
- The first student to reach the *FINISH* square wins. If groups finish early, students can go through the squares in order and take turns to put the sentences and questions into reported speech.

1 He asked her what she'd/she had been doing. 2 She told him not to worry about it. 3 He asked her to call him later./He asked her if she could call him later. 4 She said (that) she had to go home. 5 He asked her if/whether Tom had a car. 6 She said (that) she was going to buy a flat. 7 He asked her what she was doing. 8 She told him (that) she'd/she would email him later. 9 He asked her what she'd/she had done on Sunday. 10 She told him (that) she was living in London. 11 He said (that) he'd been waiting for ages. 12 She asked him to give her his address./She asked him if he could give her his address. 13 He told her (that) he'd been watching TV. 14 She asked him not to tell anyone. 15 He told her (that) he'd/he had been living in Italy for a year. 16 She said (that) she'd been there before. 17 He told her to try and relax a bit more. 18 She asked him if/whether he'd/he had been waiting long. 19 He told her not to tell anyone else about it. 20 He asked her if/whether she needed a new computer. 21 He told her (that) he'd/he had just finished work. 22 She asked him not to say anything. 23 He said (that) he couldn't ride a bike. 24 She asked him if/whether he could play the guitar. 25 He told her not to be late. 26 She said (that) she couldn't understand it. 27 He asked her if/whether she was going to call Tim. 28 She told him (that) she might leave her job. 29 He asked her if/whether she'd/she had ever been sailing. 30 She told him to stop worrying. 31 He asked her who she worked for. 32 She said (that) she had to read her emails. 33 He asked when she would make a decision.

11C ▶ Business partners p186–p187

Language
Verb patterns (2): reporting verbs; reported speech

Activity type, when to use and time
Role play. Use any time after lesson 11C. 30–45 minutes.

Preparation
Photocopy one copy of the newspaper article for each student in the class. Photocopy two Journalist role cards, one Vicky Robinson role card and one Mark Clarke role card for each group of four students in the class. Retain any extra Journalist cards in case you have extra students.

Procedure
- Check students understand *the founder* (of a company), *innovators/innovation, cosmetics, press conference, a rumour, tabloids, a board meeting, go public* (tell the media what you know about a particular situation) and *exclusive* (only in one newspaper).
- Give each student a copy of the newspaper article. Ask students to read the article and find out what problems the company Pure has. Check answers with the class.
- Divide the class into two equal groups, A and B. Note that you need an even number of students in group B. If there are extra students, put them in group A.

- Give students in group A a copy of the Journalist role card. Students work in pairs and prepare questions based on the prompts. Tell both students in each pair to write the questions, as they will be interviewing Vicky and Mark separately.
- Divide the students in group B into pairs. Give one student in each pair a copy of the Vicky Robinson role card and his/her partner a copy of the Mark Clarke role card.
- Students work on their own and prepare their roles by answering the questions on their role cards. Students in each pair are not allowed to talk to each other or look at each other's role cards.
- ✏ While they are working, write these reporting verbs on the board: *say, tell, ask, mention, explain, point out, admit, claim, agree, offer, promise, threaten, refuse, advise, warn, suggest, insist, blame, accuse, deny, apologise.*
- Rearrange the class so that one journalist from each pair in group A is sitting with either 'Vicky' or 'Mark' from the **same** pair in group B. If possible, put the pairs in different parts of the room so that they can't hear what the other pair is saying.
- The journalists conduct their interviews separately. Remind journalists to make brief notes of their interviewee's answers. Before they begin, encourage the students in group B to use the reporting verbs on the board when answering questions.
- When they have finished, swap the journalists in each group of four so that the journalist who has been interviewing 'Vicky' is interviewing 'Mark' and vice versa. During this interview journalists should use reporting verbs to tell their new interviewee what their business partner has just said, for example, *When I asked Vicky if there were financial problems in the company, she accused you of stealing £1 million from the company. Is that true?*, etc. Again point out the reporting verbs on the board before they begin.
- **Optional stage:** When students have finished, journalists work in their original pairs and compare what Vicky and Mark have said using the reporting verbs on the board where possible. Also ask the students who have been 'Vicky' or 'Mark' to work in pairs with students who have the same role. These students tell each other the questions that the journalists have asked them and what their business partners have said about them, again using the reporting verbs on the board where possible.
- Ask journalists to tell the class some interesting facts they have found out about Vicky and Mark and to say who they think is telling the truth.
- Finally, you can ask journalists to write the article for the newspaper and the businesspeople to write a letter to their lawyers! Alternatively, this stage can be done for homework.

12A ▶ The diamond mystery p188

Language
Modal verbs: deduction in the present and the past

Activity type, when to use and time
'Whodunnit' deduction puzzle. Use any time after lesson 12A. 20–30 minutes.

Preparation
Photocopy one worksheet for each pair of students in the class. Cut into separate cards. Organise each set of clue cards 1–20 into piles so that card 1 is at the top and card 20 is at the bottom of the pile when the cards are placed face-down.

Procedure
- Check students understand *a will, a suspect, a safe, a combination* (for a safe), *a corridor, a purse, a washbasin* and *inherit*.
- Tell students that they are going to solve a crime. Put students into pairs. Give each pair a copy of the Crime report card. Allow students time to read the information on the card. Check that students have understood the situation and know how all the suspects are connected to Sir Thomas Breen.
  ✏ If necessary, you can elicit the Breen family tree from the class and draw it on the board.
- Give each pair a set of clue cards 1–20. Ask students to put the cards face-down in a pile with card 1 at the top and card 20 at the bottom. Then ask students to turn over card 1 only. Students read the information on the card and make deductions in the present or the past, for example, *The diamond must have been stolen during dinner., Arthur might be the thief.*, etc.
- Students continue turning over the cards **in number order** and making deductions about each clue. Encourage both students in each pair to make at least one deduction about each card. The aim of the activity is to find out who stole the diamond and how he/she/they managed to steal it.
- When students have finished, ask pairs to work together in groups of four and compare their ideas.
- Finally, ask students who the thief is and why.

The diamond was stolen by Caroline Breen. She was angry that she didn't inherit anything when her father died and felt that the diamond was rightfully hers. When she went to the bathroom, she came across Lady Mary's purse. She picked up the purse, opened it, then took out the notebook and memorised the combination to the safe. Then, as she is left-handed, she put the purse down on the left-hand side of the washbasin, not the right. After that she went into the study, unlocked the safe and stole the diamond. Next she unlocked the window (using the key she found on the desk) and threw the diamond under a nearby bush, hoping to collect it at the end of the evening. Finally, she returned to the dinner party.

12B What would you have done? p189

Language
Past forms of modal and related verbs

Activity type, when to use and time
Discussion activity. Use any time after lesson 12B.
15–25 minutes.

Preparation
Photocopy one worksheet for every three students in the class. Cut into three separate Story cards.

Procedure

- Check students understand *a hoax*, *a stream*, *a care worker* (someone who looks after elderly people), *a verbal agreement*, *the Loch Ness monster*, *an electronic tag* (a device for monitoring the movements of newly-released prisoners, usually fastened to the prisoner's leg), *artificial* and *crutches*.

- Divide the class into groups of three. Give each student in each group a copy of one of the Story cards. Students are not allowed to look at each other's cards.

- Students read the stories quickly and check they understand them. Tell the class that all the stories are true. Then explain that they are going to tell their stories to the other people in their group in their own words. Allow students time to memorise their stories. They can write six words/phrases for each story on a piece of paper to help them remember their stories.

- While students are working, write these prompts on the board: *He/She should have …* ; *He/She could have …* ; *He/She needn't have …* ; *If that had been me, I would(n't) have …* ; *I (don't) think I'd have …* ; *I might have …* .

- Ask students to cover their Story cards. Students then work in their groups and take turns to tell each other their stories in their own words, using the words/phrases they have written as prompts. After each story, the group should discuss what the people should have done, could have done, etc. and what they would have done if they'd been in that situation. Before they begin, point out the prompts on the board and encourage students to use them during this part of the discussion. Also tell students to consider the point of view of everyone involved in the story, not just the person who the story was about.

- Finally, ask students to share their ideas about each story with the class.

Find someone who ...	Name	Follow-up questions
1 ... *is liking/likes* buying birthday presents for other people.		What / be / last present / buy? Who / buy it for?
2 ... *did/was doing* a lot of sport when he/she was at school.		What / be / favourite sport? / do any sport now?
3 ... *lives/has been living* in this town or city for over a year.		Whereabouts / live? Who / live / with?
4 ... *interviewed/was interviewed* for a job last year.		Which job / be / it for? What kind of questions / ask?
5 ... *stays/is staying* with friends or family at the moment.		Who / stay / with? How long / be / there?
6 ... *does/is doing* quite a lot of shopping online.		What kind of things / buy? What / be / last thing / buy?
7 ... *went/has been* to more than six countries in his/her life.		Which countries / go / to? Which / be / most interesting?
8 ... *goes/is going* to the cinema quite a lot.		When / last go? What / see?
9 ... *watched/was watching* TV at 9 o'clock last night.		What / watch? What / think of it?
10 ... *went/has been* somewhere exciting on holiday last year.		Where / go? What / do there?

Yes, I do.	One of my friends **is**
didn't you?	I've never **been** to the USA,
Did you? What did you do?	How many hours of TV **do**
thinking of getting herself a new computer.	**Have** you ever **tried** to write a novel?
started a new job.	You're **coming** to the next class,
but I **have**.	My best friend can't cook, but he/she **does**
asked where his family comes from.	I **do** quite a lot of exercise.
So do I. I prefer hot, sunny days.	At 8 p.m. last Saturday Tim **was**
you **like** when you were 13?	You **don't speak** any other languages,
but I **do**.	I didn't like maths at school, but I **did**
love getting up late when I'm on holiday!	I **never watch** TV in the evening.
Neither do I. I'm too lazy!	Lots of people **think** science is boring,

looking for a place to live at the moment.	You **came** to this school last year,
but one of my friends **has**.	I **had** a great time last weekend.
you **watch** every week?	Jane **has been**
No, I haven't.	My sister **has** just
aren't you?	Most people I know **haven't been** to England,
like coming round to my place for dinner.	My husband **is** often
Do you? What do you do exactly?	I really **hate** winter.
getting ready to go out with his friends.	Which bands or singers **did**
do you?	My best friend **doesn't like** football,
enjoy art and music classes.	I **do**
Don't you? What do you do instead?	I **don't do** much exercise these days.
but I **don't**.	Do you **check** your email every day?

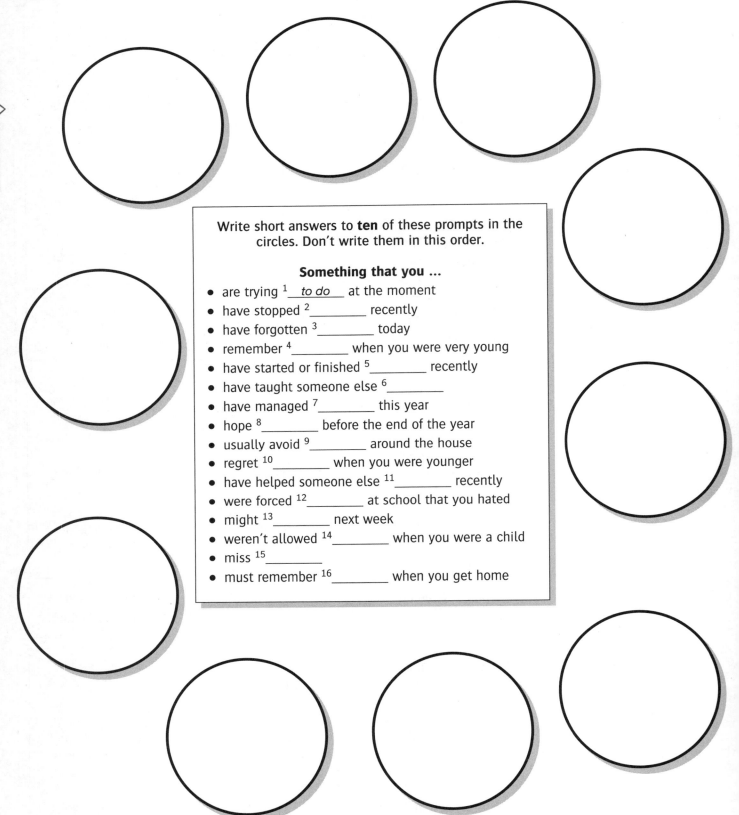

Write short answers to **ten** of these prompts in the
circles. Don't write them in this order.

Something that you ...
- are trying [1] *to do* at the moment
- have stopped [2]_____ recently
- have forgotten [3]_____ today
- remember [4]_____ when you were very young
- have started or finished [5]_____ recently
- have taught someone else [6]_____
- have managed [7]_____ this year
- hope [8]_____ before the end of the year
- usually avoid [9]_____ around the house
- regret [10]_____ when you were younger
- have helped someone else [11]_____ recently
- were forced [12]_____ at school that you hated
- might [13]_____ next week
- weren't allowed [14]_____ when you were a child
- miss [15]_____
- must remember [16]_____ when you get home

2A Nightmare neighbours present and past habits, repeated actions and states

Student B

You live in a fashionable area in the centre of town. You used to get on very well with your old neighbours, but they moved out a few months ago. Now you have some new neighbours – and they're making your life impossible! You're meeting an old friend today and you want to tell him/her about your situation.

Look at this information and decide how to express these present and past habits and states. When you meet your friend, try to convince him/her that your new neighbours are worse than his/hers!

Your old neighbours were a young married couple with no children.

- They (be) out at work all day.
- They (go) out most evenings.
- They (ask) you in for coffee every now and again.
- They (know) lots of interesting people.
- They (lend you) their car every so often.
- They (have) great parties at the weekend and (invite) you and all their other neighbours.

Your new neighbours are a married couple with three children.

- They (make) a lot of noise early in the morning.
- They (complain) about you playing music in the evening.
- Their baby (always cry) and it (wake) you up.
- Their daughter (play) the trumpet – very badly!
- Their car alarm (always go off) in the middle of the night.
- Last week you think their son (break) your window.

Now think of two more things about your past and present neighbours that you can tell your friend.

Student A

You live in a quiet street in a small town. You used to get on very well with your old neighbours, but they moved out a few months ago. Now you have some new neighbours – and they're making your life impossible! You're meeting an old friend today and you want to tell him/her about your situation.

Look at this information and decide how to express these present and past habits and states. When you meet your friend, try to convince him/her that your new neighbours are worse than his/hers!

Your old neighbours were a nice retired couple in their seventies.

- They (be) very quiet.
- They (spend) a lot of time in their garden.
- They (invite) you round for dinner every now and again.
- They (feed) your cat when you were away.
- They (babysit) for you most weekends.
- They (have) barbecues in the summer and (invite) you and all their other neighbours.

Your new neighbours are three students at the local college.

- They (always play) loud music at night.
- They (throw) rubbish into your garden.
- They (have) two big dogs that (bark) all the time.
- Their dogs (always chase) your cat and (dig up) your garden.
- One student (play) the drums!
- Last week you think one of them (steal) your bicycle.

Now think of two more things about your past and present neighbours that you can tell your friend.

prefer	preference	preferable	preferably
conclude	conclusion	conclusive	conclusively
originate	origin	original	reality
really	realistic	convince	conviction
convinced	convincing	responsible	responsibly
weaken	weakness	judgement	judgemental
criticise	critic	criticism	critical
recognise	recognition	recognisable	recognisably

Head teacher

Your name is Sam Smith and you are the head teacher of a secondary school. You are going to appear on a TV programme called *The Big Question*. This week's topic is: **Should competitive sports be compulsory in schools?**

You think competitive sports should be compulsory. Look at these reasons to support your point of view. Think what you can say about them. Then add one or two more reasons of your own.

- Competitive sports improve children's health and fitness.
- They teach children how to work as part of a team.
- They give children self-confidence and a sense of achievement.

Look at these reasons why other people are against the idea. Decide what you can say about them.

- Competition makes children more aggressive.
- Girls aren't as interested in sports as boys.
- Sport takes up school time that could be spent on other things.

Parent

Your name is Robin Hill and you are head of a local school's parents' association. You are going to appear on a TV programme called *The Big Question*. This week's topic is: **Should competitive sports be compulsory in schools?**

You think competitive sports should be optional, not compulsory. Look at these reasons to support your point of view. Think what you can say about them. Then add one or two more reasons of your own.

- Competition makes children more aggressive.
- Girls aren't as interested in sports as boys.
- Sport takes up school time that could be spent on other things.

Look at these reasons why other people are in favour of the idea. Decide what you can say about them.

- Competitive sports improve children's health and fitness.
- They teach children how to work as part of a team.
- They give children self-confidence and a sense of achievement.

Psychologist

Your name is Dr Chris Robertson and you are a child psychologist. You are going to appear on a TV programme called *The Big Question*. This week's topic is: **Should competitive sports be compulsory in schools?**

You have opinions for and against competitive sports being compulsory. Look at these reasons to support each point of view. Decide what you can say about them. Then add one or two more reasons of your own.

Reasons in favour:

- Competitive sports can help children's self-confidence.
- Many children enjoy doing sports.
- Being physically fit helps children feel better about themselves.

Reasons against:

- Competitive sports make some children more aggressive.
- Children who are bad at sports might be teased.
- They teach children that winning is the only thing that matters.

Presenter

Your name is Max Williams and you are the presenter of a TV programme called *The Big Question*. This week's topic is: **Should competitive sports be compulsory in schools?**

On this week's programme there are three guests: Sam Smith, the head teacher of a secondary school; Robin Hill, head of a local school's parents' association, and Dr Chris Robertson, a child psychologist.

Prepare a short introduction to the TV programme. Welcome the audience, say who the guests are and what the programme is about.

Then write some questions to ask the guests. Use these ideas and your own.

- the positive and negative effects of competitive sports
- health problems children have now
- the guests' experiences of school sports
- whether the school or the parents should decide
- how sport can help children cope with life

During the debate, make sure everyone speaks and has the opportunity to give his/her opinion.

CLASS ACTIVITIES: Photocopiable

STUDENT A

A couple of years ago you set off to sail around the world on your own. The journey took you three months, but unfortunately when you were just 500 metres from land your boat was hit by lightning. The boat sank and you had to swim to safety.

STUDENT B

You spent eight years writing a novel that you were sure would become a best-seller. Unfortunately the day you finished writing it, your house burnt down. Your computer and all your back-up copies of the novel were completely destroyed in the fire.

STUDENT C

Last year you set off to climb Everest with your brother. Unfortunately ten metres from the summit your brother slipped and fell. You were tied together, so you both fell over 1,000 metres. Your brother broke his leg and you both had to be rescued.

STUDENT D

A few years ago you won a local singing competition. The prize was an appearance on a popular live TV show. Unfortunately on the day of the show you completely lost your voice and couldn't even speak, so you missed your chance to appear on the show.

STUDENT E

You used to play the guitar. A few years ago you were on your way to an audition to become the Rolling Stones' new guitarist. Unfortunately while you were getting out of the taxi, the driver closed the door too quickly and broke two of your fingers.

STUDENT F

Two months ago you picked the winning lottery numbers. The jackpot that day was over £10 million. Unfortunately while you were celebrating with your parents, their dog ate your lottery ticket – so you didn't win anything at all.

STUDENT G

You used to be an actor/actress. A few years ago you were asked to audition for a major role in *The Lord of the Rings* films. Unfortunately on the day of the audition you got food poisoning and were too ill to go, so somebody else got the part.

STUDENT H

Last December you set off to walk to the South Pole alone. Unfortunately just a few miles from the Pole your compass broke and you didn't know which way to go. You got completely lost and had to be rescued by helicopter.

STUDENT I

Last June you won a travel competition. The prize was an all-expenses-paid trip around the world leaving on July 1st. Unfortunately the letter telling you that you had won got lost in the post and you didn't get it until July 2nd.

STUDENT J

You used to be a fantastic tennis player, and you won the junior championship at Wimbledon when you were 16. Unfortunately one day you fell off your scooter and broke your wrist. You haven't been able to play tennis since.

1 _____ would have sailed around the world if _____ .

2 _____ might have written a best-seller if _____ .

3 _____ would have climbed Everest if _____ .

4 _____ have become a famous singer if _____ .

5 _____ might have joined the Rolling Stones if _____ .

6 _____ would have become a millionaire if _____ .

7 _____ might have been in *The Lord of the Rings* if _____ .

8 _____ would have walked to the South Pole if _____ .

9 _____ could have gone round the world last year if _____ .

10 _____ would have become a famous tennis player if _____ .

name	sb/sth **after** sb/sth	apply	**to** sb/sth **for** sth
insist	**on** sth	complain	**to** sb **about** sth
convince	sb **of** sth	base	sth **on** sth
worry	**about** sb/sth	protest	**against** sth
cope	**with** sb/sth	apologise	**to** sb **for** sth
succeed	**in** sth	reduce	sth **to** sth
arrest	sb **for** sth	acquit	sb **of** sth
charge	sb **with** sth	sentence	sb **to** sth

face2face Second edition Upper Intermediate Photocopiable © Cambridge University Press 2012 Instructions p134

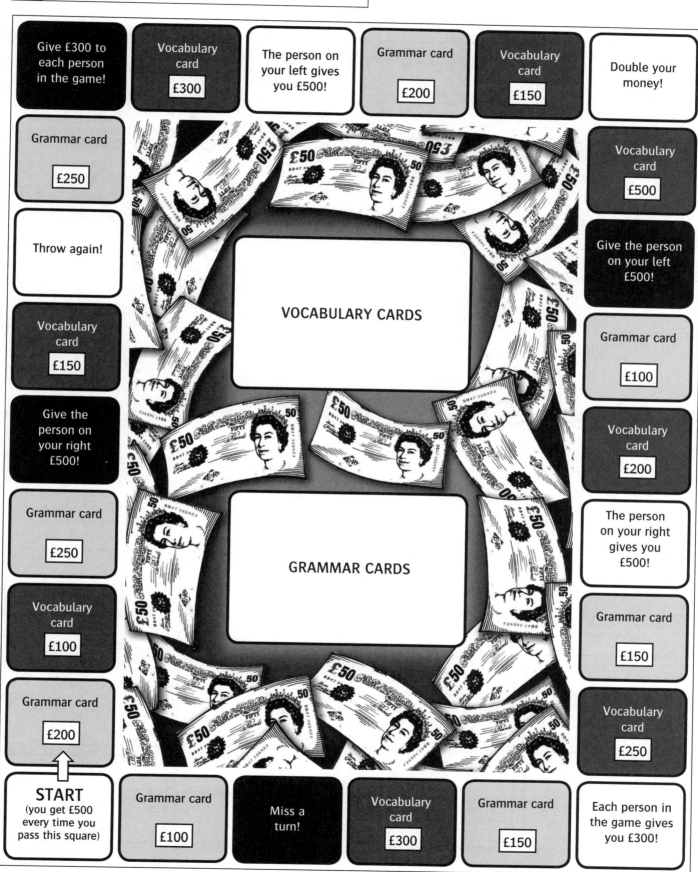

Give £300 to each person in the game!

Vocabulary card £300

The person on your left gives you £500!

Grammar card £200

Vocabulary card £150

Double your money!

Grammar card £250

Vocabulary card £500

Throw again!

Give the person on your left £500!

Vocabulary card £150

VOCABULARY CARDS

Grammar card £100

Give the person on your right £500!

Vocabulary card £200

Grammar card £250

GRAMMAR CARDS

The person on your right gives you £500!

Vocabulary card £100

Grammar card £150

Grammar card £200

Vocabulary card £250

START
(you get £500 every time you pass this square)

Grammar card £100

Miss a turn!

Vocabulary card £300

Grammar card £150

Each person in the game gives you £300!

CLASS ACTIVITIES: Photocopiable

Vocabulary cards

V1 Fill in the gaps with a preposition. He has succeeded _____ everything he has done. She's terrified _____ mice.	**V2** Say the nouns and adjectives for these verbs. prefer, conclude, criticise	**V3** What is the difference? an undergraduate, a postgraduate a lecturer, a professor	**V4** Fill in the gaps with a preposition. I'm sick _____ working so hard. He insisted _____ coming.
V5 Say the correct forms of the verbs. I ended up (get) a taxi. He persuaded me (come).	**V6** What is the difference? 1 I stopped to talk to Rob. 2 I stopped talking to Rob.	**V7** Fill in the gaps in these frequency expressions. once _____ a while every _____ and again more _____ than not	**V8** Say the crimes and criminals for these verbs. rob, burgle, smuggle, kidnap
V9 Say the verbs and nouns for these adjectives. original, weak, recognisable	**V10** Fill in the gaps with a preposition. I'm aware _____ the problem. Joe's excited _____ the trip.	**V11** Correct these sentences. He's fluent for French. I picked out some Spanish on holiday.	**V12** Match the verbs to the prepositions. arrest sb ⸻ with sth charge sb ⸻ of sth convict sb ⸻ for sth
V13 What is the difference? a tutorial, a seminar a student loan, a scholarship	**V14** Say the criminals and verbs for these crimes. theft, shoplifting, murder, vandalism	**V15** Fill in the gaps with a preposition. I apologised _____ my neighbour _____ the noise. I can't cope _____ it.	**V16** Say the correct forms of the verbs. I managed (pass) the test. I regret (send) that email.

Grammar cards

G1 Which verb form? English *speaks/is spoken* here. I *go/am going* to the gym every day.	**G2** Fill in the gaps in this third conditional. If you _____ sent me that email, I wouldn't _____ known it was her birthday.	**G3** Fill in the gaps with an auxiliary. I like golf, but she _____ . He _____ love this place – he comes here every day.	**G4** Choose the correct words. I'd steal some paper from work *imagine/provided* no one *is/was* looking.
G5 Say a second conditional for this situation. I don't go out a lot because I have children.	**G6** Correct these sentences. I'll never get used to live here. I can't be used to the noise.	**G7** Say echo questions for these sentences. I don't like cheese. He's never been abroad. They left early.	**G8** Say a third conditional for this situation. Mike missed the meeting because his car broke down.
G9 Which sentence is correct? Correct the wrong sentence. 1 Liz used to live in Rome. 2 She'd have a flat there.	**G10** Choose the correct words/phrases. *Suppose/As long as* you were rich, *would/do* you continue working?	**G11** Which verb form? Ian *was/has been* a doctor since 2003. I *worked/was working* when you called.	**G12** Fill in the gaps with an auxiliary. What _____ you do last night? When _____ he arrested?
G13 What's the difference? 1 I used to work at the weekend. 2 I'm used to working at the weekend.	**G14** Fill in the gaps with an auxiliary. You live here, _____ you? We _____ enjoy ourselves last night.	**G15** Say a third conditional for this situation. I left home late so I missed the train.	**G16** Say the correct verb forms. I'd better (go). Would it help if I (call) him? Thanks for (ask).

Outline story ✂

A Jack turned off the main road and drove down a narrow lane.
B 20 minutes later, he parked in front of an old wooden house by a river.
C He got out of the car and looked around.
D He opened the boot of the car
E Jack walked up the wooden steps to the front door
F He unlocked the door and went inside.
G He smiled to himself.
H He walked into the kitchen to make some coffee.
I "Hello, Jack," said the man. "What's in the briefcase?"
J He put the briefcase on the table and pushed it towards him.

Extra information cards ✂ ✂

1 and took out a small backpack and a brown leather briefcase.	**2** Almost there, he thought. He'd been driving all night
3 The sun was already rising behind the old house	**4** and lifted up one of the plant pots on the porch.
5 Nobody had lived in this house since his father died	**6** A man in a dark blue suit was sitting at the kitchen table.
7 Seeing the briefcase again made Jack think	**8** and the birds were already singing in the trees by the river bank.
9 and was trying not to fall asleep at the wheel.	**10** He was smoking a cigarette and had obviously been sitting there for some time.
11 Underneath the pot was the front door key	**12** about what he'd done in Chicago the previous evening
13 The room was just how he'd left it three months earlier,	**14** and Jack thought he'd be safe here. For a while, anyway.
15 The plan had worked perfectly.	**16** "Take a look for yourself," said Jack.
17 and he wondered how long to wait before it was safe for them to leave the country.	**18** before he'd gone to work as a security guard at the Chicago Bank.
19 that he had put there last time he was there.	**20** The man opened the briefcase and looked inside

CLASS ACTIVITIES: Photocopiable

4B ▶ The book quiz defining and non-defining relative clauses

Quiz A

1 Dan Brown, _____ is best known for his novel *The Da Vinci Code*, usually writes …
   a horror stories. b science-fiction. c **thrillers.**

2 The first play _____ Shakespeare wrote was …
   a *Romeo and Juliet.* b **Henry VI, Part One.** c *Hamlet.*

3 Mario Puzo, _____ novel The Godfather became an Oscar-winning film, was born in …
   a Italy. b **the USA.** c Spain.

4 *The Guinness Book of Records,* _____ was first published in 1955, has sold about …
   a 30 million copies. b 60 million copies. c **90 million copies.**

5 The imaginary place _____ the novel *The Lord of the Rings* is set is called …
   a **Middle Earth.** b Central Earth. c Middle Land.

6 *Dracula*, the story of a vampire _____ drank the blood of his victims, was originally written in …
   a **English.** b Romanian. c Russian.

Quiz B

1 J K Rowling, _____ wrote the Harry Potter books, used to be …
   a an actress. b **an English language teacher.** c a journalist.

2 The first James Bond novel _____ Ian Fleming wrote was called …
   a *Goldfinger.* b *The Spy Who Loved Me.* c **Casino Royale.**

3 Rudyard Kipling, _____ children's story *The Jungle Book* was made into a Disney film, was born in …
   a the USA. b the UK. c **India.**

4 *War and Peace,* _____ is one of the longest novels ever written, takes place in Russia in …
   a the 18th century. b **the 19th century.** c the 20th century.

5 The London flat _____ the famous detective Sherlock Holmes lived was in …
   a Oxford Street. b Regent Street. c **Baker Street.**

6 *Frankenstein*, the story of a mad scientist _____ created a monster, was written by …
   a **Mary Shelley.** b Bram Stoker. c Sir Arthur Conan Doyle.

face2face Second edition Upper Intermediate Photocopiable © Cambridge University Press 2012 ⟨ Instructions p136

On June 4th 2003, a South African engineer called Steve Nicholson set off to sail from Cape Town to Perth, Australia, in his 12-metre yacht. Travelling with him were his wife, Alice, and their two children, James (17) and Penny (15). Unfortunately they never arrived at their destination ...

Steve had always wanted to sail to Australia **because** _____ .

He managed to persuade his family to come with him, **even though** _____ .

At first everyone was having a great time, **apart from** _____ , who _____ .

Then one day there was a terrible storm. **During** the storm Steve and his family _____

_____ .

All of a sudden the boat started filling up with water **because** _____ .

Steve discovered that they couldn't radio for help **as** _____ .

Luckily, Penny spotted an island close by, **so** _____ .

All of the family were OK, **except for** _____ , who _____ .

Despite their situation, everyone _____ .

The next day Steve tried to repair the boat and the radio. **However,** _____

_____ .

Meanwhile, Alice and James began searching the island, looking for _____ .

Penny couldn't _____ **due to** _____ , so she _____ instead.

Since they didn't have any _____ , they survived on _____ .

And in the evenings **instead of** _____ , they _____ .

James was enjoying life on the island, **whereas** _____ .

And **although** Alice _____ , she was becoming very concerned about _____

_____ .

After the family had been living on the island for a few days, Steve found _____

_____ .

He realised that they had to get off the island as soon as possible, **because** _____

_____ .

30 She's not quite as slim as you. (a little)

31 MOVE BACK THREE SQUARES

32 My new camera is slightly better than my old one. (almost)

33 That TV wasn't nearly as cheap as mine. (a great deal more)

FINISH

29 Learning English is no harder than learning German. (just as)

28 Compare your life now to your life five years ago.

27 My new flat is just as large as my old one. (no)

26 I don't earn nearly as much as my sister. (much more)

25 Compare the last two holidays you've had.

20 I worry about my health more as I get older. (the older)

21 I earn about half as much as my brother. (twice)

22 MOVE FORWARD THREE SQUARES

23 Compare life in your country now to how it was 10 years ago.

24 The club wasn't as crowded as I expected. (less)

19 Mark's mobile is much smaller than Chris's. (nowhere near)

18 Compare this school to another school you've studied at.

17 Tony's garden is just as nice as yours. (isn't any)

16 Petrol keeps going up. (more and more)

15 MOVE BACK THREE SQUARES

10 MISS A TURN

11 He's been here a little longer than I have. (nearly)

12 Compare two cities that you've been to.

13 I get more stressed when I work harder. (the harder)

14 Sarah's laptop was nearly as expensive as mine. (a bit)

9 Compare two of your best friends.

8 This book is nowhere near as good as the last one I read. (far)

7 MOVE FORWARD TWO SQUARES

6 Compare two houses or flats that you know well.

5 Nick's a bit better at tennis than me. (not quite)

START

1 I'm almost as tall as my brother. (slightly)

2 Compare two people in your family.

3 I feel healthier when I do more exercise. (the more)

4 Tony's house is much nicer than ours. (isn't nearly)

wood	**would**	**meet**	meat
their	there	**sore**	saw
your	**you're**	sent	**scent**
site	**sight**	weather	**whether**
principle	**principal**	threw	**through**
hear	**here**	find	**fined**
seen	scene	**know**	no
blue	**blew**	write	**right**

Student A: Mayor

You live in the historic city of Barchester. The city's population has grown rapidly recently and traffic in the city centre is getting worse and worse. The Mayor of Barchester wants to introduce a congestion charge of £8 for cars during the day on weekdays. Barchester has a good bus service, but buses are often delayed because of traffic. There's also a train service, but the trains are often crowded, particularly at rush hour. There's a public meeting today to discuss the council's proposal.

You are the Mayor of Barchester and you want to introduce the congestion charge.
Think of the effect the charge would have on these things.

- current traffic problems
- journey times
- public transport
- local businesses
- the environment
- employment

Also think of answers to questions you may be asked and how you are going to spend the money that you raise.

Student B: Environmentalist

You live in the historic city of Barchester. The city's population has grown rapidly recently and traffic in the city centre is getting worse and worse. The Mayor of Barchester wants to introduce a congestion charge of £8 for cars during the day on weekdays. Barchester has a good bus service, but buses are often delayed because of traffic. There's also a train service, but the trains are often crowded, particularly at rush hour. There's a public meeting today to discuss the council's proposal.

You are the leader of the local Green Party and you are in favour of the congestion charge.
Think of the effect the charge would have on these things and people.

- current traffic problems
- people who live in the centre
- public transport
- climate change
- public health
- employment

Also think of other advantages of the charge and how the money that is raised could be spent.

Student C: Local businessperson

You live in the historic city of Barchester. The city's population has grown rapidly recently and traffic in the city centre is getting worse and worse. The Mayor of Barchester wants to introduce a congestion charge of £8 for cars during the day on weekdays. Barchester has a good bus service, but buses are often delayed because of traffic. There's also a train service, but the trains are often crowded, particularly at rush hour. There's a public meeting today to discuss the council's proposal.

You are head of the Barchester Business Association and you are against the congestion charge.
Think of the effect the charge would have on these things and people.

- businesses in the city centre
- people with young children
- public transport
- the cost of living
- tourism
- employment

Also think of other disadvantages of the charge and alternative ways to deal with the city's traffic problems.

face2face Second edition Upper Intermediate Photocopiable © Cambridge University Press 2012
Instructions p137

Student D: Local politician

You live in the historic city of Barchester. The city's population has grown rapidly recently and traffic in the city centre is getting worse and worse. The Mayor of Barchester wants to introduce a congestion charge of £8 for cars during the day on weekdays. Barchester has a good bus service, but buses are often delayed because of traffic. There's also a train service, but the trains are often crowded, particularly at rush hour. There's a public meeting today to discuss the council's proposal.

You are the leader of the local opposition party and you are against the congestion charge. Think of the effect the charge would have on these things and people.

- businesses in the city centre
- people who drive to work
- unemployment
- tourism
- the city's economy
- public transport

Also think of other disadvantages of the charge and alternative ways to deal with the city's traffic problems.

Student E: Local resident

You live in the historic city of Barchester. The city's population has grown rapidly recently and traffic in the city centre is getting worse and worse. The Mayor of Barchester wants to introduce a congestion charge of £8 for cars during the day on weekdays. Barchester has a good bus service, but buses are often delayed because of traffic. There's also a train service, but the trains are often crowded, particularly at rush hour. There's a public meeting today to discuss the council's proposal.

You are head of the Barchester Residents' Association and you aren't sure if the congestion charge is a good idea or not. Think of the positive and negative effects the charge would have on these people and things.

- current traffic problems
- business in the city centre
- local residents
- the environment
- public transport
- the city's economy

Also think of one or two questions to ask the mayor about the charge.

Student F: Chairperson

You live in the historic city of Barchester. The city's population has grown rapidly recently and traffic in the city centre is getting worse and worse. The Mayor of Barchester wants to introduce a congestion charge of £8 for cars during the day on weekdays. Barchester has a good bus service, but buses are often delayed because of traffic. There's also a train service, but the trains are often crowded, particularly at rush hour. There's a public meeting today to discuss the council's proposal.

You work for the local government planning department and you are going to be the chairperson at the meeting.

- Write an introduction to the meeting. Welcome everyone, introduce yourself and say what the meeting is about. Then ask everyone to introduce themselves.
- Think of questions to ask the people at the meeting about the congestion charge, e.g. *How much will the scheme cost?*
- During the meeting, make sure everyone has a chance to speak.

CLASS ACTIVITIES: Photocopiable

Worksheet A

I usually ask for recommendations before …	For most people, I think it's a waste of time …
When I first meet someone, I usually avoid …	At home, I don't like doing the …
At the weekend, I spend a lot of time …	I enjoy going out with my friends, despite …
I often hear my neighbours …	In the future, I can imagine myself …
At 9.00 p.m. last night, I was …	Next Saturday, I'm …

Worksheet B

… writing an essay.	… washing up but I enjoy cooking.
… going out to celebrate my birthday.	… talking to friends and sleeping.
… playing awful music at night.	… worrying about the future.
… talking about how much I earn.	… trying a new restaurant.
… living in another country.	… not having much money to spend.

Write ten of these people, places and things in the thought bubbles. Don't write them in this order.

- a place you're likely to visit before the end of the year
- someone who's bound to phone or email you today
- something you've done that you're unlikely to ever do again
- a relative who might come and visit you later this year
- a place in this town/city that you may well go to this weekend
- someone in another town/city that you're sure to speak to soon
- something you'll probably be given on your next birthday
- someone who you may end up celebrating the next New Year with
- a place you've been to that you're sure to go back to one day
- something that you may well buy before the end of the month
- a place you've been to that you might never go to again
- something you can't ever imagine doing
- the place where you're likely to be celebrating your next birthday
- a close friend that you're unlikely to see (or see again) this year
- something that you'll definitely keep for the rest of your life

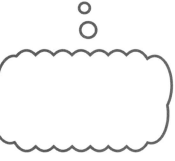

CLASS ACTIVITIES: Photocopiable

Board 1

G	V	M	V	G	V
V	V	G	M	V	G
G	M	V	G	V	M
M	G	M	V	M	G
V	G	V	G	V	M

Team A question sheet

G Grammar

1 Which verb form is correct? *I'll see/I'm seeing* the doctor at 3.30. (*I'm seeing*)
2 Which word is correct? The *much/more* I do, the better I get. (*more*)
3 Say the correct verb form: **This time tomorrow I (work).** (*I'll be working*)
4 Which word is correct? **He's no *tall/taller* than me.** (*taller*)
5 How do you make the **Past Perfect Continuous?** (*subject + had/'d + been + verb+ing*)
6 Correct this sentence: **Alan, that lives next door, is a doctor.** (*Alan, who lives ...*)
7 Say four phrases that mean something **will definitely or probably happen.** (See G6.2 SB p129.)
8 Which verb form is correct? **I don't like people *watch/watching* me.** (*watching*)
9 Say the correct verb form: **I met Jack while I (walk) home.** (*was walking*)
10 Correct this sentence: **My first book, that I wrote in 2003, is a best-seller.** (*My first book, which I ...*)

V Vocabulary

1 Fill in the gap: **That's not true, you've made it ....** (*up*)
2 Say a way of exaggerating that means: **It's very painful.** (*It's killing me.*)
3 Which word is correct? **It can become *addictive/destructive* collecting exotic pets.** (*addictive*)
4 Fill in the gap: **She takes me .... granted.** (*for*)
5 In 30 seconds say eight words connected to **books and reading.** (See V4.2 SB p122.)
6 Say a way of exaggerating that means: **I'm very frightened.** (*I'm scared stiff.*)
7 Fill in the gap: **I hit him very hard and knocked him ....** (*out*)
8 Which word is correct? **He always tries to help, even if it puts him *up/out*.** (*out*)
9 Fill in the gap: **Don't take any .... of him.** (*notice*)
10 Which word is correct? **I went out, *although/despite* I was tired.** (*although*)

M Mystery

1 How did Aurelia Oliveras destroy her house? (*She used 19 bug bombs at the same time.*)
2 What is the title of Kate Fox's book about English people? (*Watching the English*)
3 What problem can cause serious damage to the buildings of Dubai? (*pigeons*)
4 What industry is Charles Frederick Worth (1825–95) considered to be the father of? (*fashion design*)
5 For which British school is the uniform a black tailcoat, a waistcoat and pinstriped trousers? (*Eton*)
6 What did author Stephen King do with the manuscript of his most famous book, *Carrie*? (*He threw it in the bin.*)
7 How did Freddie Mercury's koi die? (*Someone turned off the electricity to their pool.*)
8 What is the official residence of the British Royal Family? (*Windsor Castle.*)

Board 2

V	M	G	M	V	G
M	G	M	V	G	M
G	V	V	G	M	V
V	G	V	M	V	G
G	M	G	V	G	V

Team B question sheet

G Grammar

1 Which verb form is correct? **I didn't know he was ill.** *I'll call/I'm calling* **him.** (*I'll call*)
2 Which word is correct? **I'm nowhere near as rich** *as/than* **him.** (*as*)
3 How do you make the **Future Continuous**? (*subject* + *will/'ll* + *be* + verb+*ing*)
4 Correct this sentence: **I've lost the key what opens this door.** (*I've lost the key that/which opens …*)
5 Which word is correct? **I'm twice as** *old/older* **as her.** (*old*)
6 Which verb form is correct? **He avoids** *talk/talking* **about it.** (*talking*)
7 Say the correct verb form: **The match (start) at 7.30 this evening.** (*starts*)
8 Correct this sentence: **That's the man which son is famous.** (*That's the man whose son …*)
9 Say the correct verb form: **When I got there, Liz already (leave).** (*had already left*)
10 Say four phrases that mean **something probably or definitely won't happen.** (See G6.2 SB p129.)

V Vocabulary

1 Say a way of exaggerating that means: **It's very expensive.** (*It costs a fortune.*)
2 Fill in the gap: **It's important not to take family members ……. granted.** (*for*)
3 Which word is correct? **a** *self-conscious/centred* **person is shy and easily embarrassed.** (*conscious*)
4 Fill in the gap: **I can't work ……. the answer.** (*out*)
5 Fill in the gap: **He's taking advantage ……. you.** (*of*)
6 Say the opposites: **moral, ethical, legal.** (*immoral, unethical, illegal*)
7 Say the word for something that earns you a lot of money: a) **rewarding** b) **lucrative** c) **outrageous.** (*lucrative*)
8 Which word is correct? **I like tennis,** *as/whereas* **Joe hates it.** (*whereas*)
9 Fill in the gap: **When my sister's angry, she really takes it ……. on me.** (*out*)
10 Say a way of exaggerating that means: **I'm very hungry.** (*I'm starving.*)

M Mystery

1 How many British prime ministers have been educated at Eton College? (*19*)
2 How many koi did Freddie Mercury have? (*89*)
3 Which female Irish writer wrote *PS I Love You*? (*Cecilia Ahern*)
4 Which clothing company has started selling cut-price clothes by high-fashion designers? (*H&M*)
5 After insuring and smoking 24 cigars, what did the man say happened to the cigars? (*They were lost in a series of small fires.*)
6 Describe three of the April Fool's Day jokes in the article in lesson 4C. (See SB p34.)
7 How often is Windsor Castle open to the public? (*almost every day*)
8 Name three things the kangaroo stole from the sailor. (*jacket, passport, three credit cards, $1,000 in cash*)

Student A

		T or F?
1	He/She *goes/is going* to football matches every so often.	
2	He/She *thinks/is thinking* of changing jobs or courses in the next few months.	
3	He/She *trusts/is trusting* people only after he/she's known them for a long time.	
4	He/She *thinks/is thinking* that most men take sport a bit too seriously.	
5	He/She *studied/was studying* English this time last week.	
6	He/She *had/was having* a pet when he/she was a child.	
7	He/She *reads/is reading* a book in English at the moment.	
8	He/She *wants/is wanting* to live in this town/city for the next ten years.	
9	He/She *has/is having* a party or a barbecue in the next few weeks.	
10	He/She *has bought/has been buying* a plane ticket recently.	

Student B

		T or F?
1	He/She *goes/is going* to art galleries every so often.	
2	He/She *thinks/is thinking* of buying something for his/her home.	
3	He/She automatically *trusts/is trusting* everyone that he/she meets.	
4	He/She *thinks/is thinking* that most women spend too much on clothes.	
5	He/She *studied/was studying* English this time yesterday.	
6	He/She *had/was having* a scooter when he/she was a teenager.	
7	He/She *reads/is reading* a good book at the moment.	
8	He/She *wants/is wanting* to go and live in a different country.	
9	He/She *has/is having* a few friends round to his/her house this weekend.	
10	He/She *has bought/has been buying* a mobile phone or a digital camera recently.	

Student B: Foreign correspondent

Pat Cook, who is one of the country's most famous foreign correspondents, has lived and worked in more famous cities than most other people have visited. In this week's **A Life Worth Living (9.00 a.m. Radio 6)** Pat, who is retiring next month, talks to Sam Baker about a lifetime in journalism. Not to be missed.

You're Pat Cook. Make notes on these things.

• how long you've been working as a foreign correspondent

• how many different newspapers or magazines you've worked for

• how many different cities you've lived in

• the most exciting city you've lived in and why you liked it so much

• two historic events you have reported on

• two famous people you've interviewed

• the most interesting or difficult person you've interviewed

• the number of books you've written in your life

• the city you're living in at the moment and how long you've been living there

• the strangest or funniest thing that has ever happened to you

• what your latest book is about and how long you've been writing it

• what you're planning to do when you retire

When you have finished, think of other things you can say about each topic.

Student A: Interviewer

Pat Cook, who is one of the country's most famous foreign correspondents, has lived and worked in more famous cities than most other people have visited. In this week's **A Life Worth Living (9.00 a.m. Radio 6)** Pat, who is retiring next month, talks to Sam Baker about a lifetime in journalism. Not to be missed.

You're Sam Baker. Make questions from these prompts.

• How long / work / as a foreign correspondent?
  How long have you been working as a foreign correspondent?

• How many different newspapers or magazines / work / for?

• How many different cities / live / in?

• Which / be / most exciting? Why / like / it so much?

• Which historic events / report / on?

• Which famous people / interview?

• Who / be / most interesting or difficult person / interview?

• How many books / write / in your life?

• Which city / live / in at the moment? How long / live / there?

• What / be / the strangest or funniest thing that / ever / happen / to you?

• What / be / your latest book about? How long / write / it?

• What / plan / do / when / retire?

Now think of two more questions to ask Pat Cook.

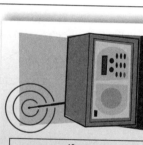

CLASS ACTIVITIES: Photocopiable

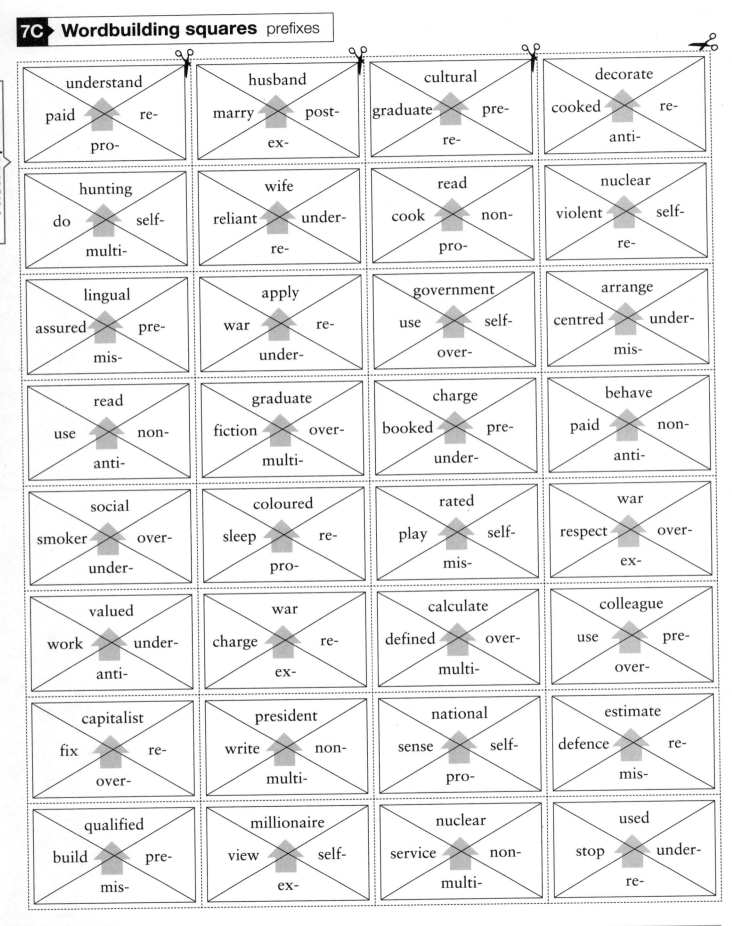

understand / paid / re- / pro-	husband / marry / post- / ex-	cultural / graduate / pre- / re-	decorate / cooked / re- / anti-
hunting / do / self- / multi-	wife / reliant / under- / re-	read / cook / non- / pro-	nuclear / violent / self- / re-
lingual / assured / pre- / mis-	apply / war / re- / under-	government / use / self- / over-	arrange / centred / under- / mis-
read / use / non- / anti-	graduate / fiction / over- / multi-	charge / booked / pre- / under-	behave / paid / non- / anti-
social / smoker / over- / under-	coloured / sleep / re- / pro-	rated / play / self- / mis-	war / respect / over- / ex-
valued / work / under- / anti-	war / charge / re- / ex-	calculate / defined / over- / multi-	colleague / use / pre- / over-
capitalist / fix / re- / over-	president / write / non- / multi-	national / sense / self- / pro-	estimate / defence / re- / mis-
qualified / build / pre- / mis-	millionaire / view / self- / ex-	nuclear / service / non- / multi-	used / stop / under- / re-

STUDENT A

You're a famous artist. You've just sold one of your pieces for (*how much?*) and you're getting ready for a big exhibition in (*where?*). However, life isn't perfect. **All the critics hate your work.** Why don't they realise how brilliant you are?

STUDENT B

You're a famous novelist. You write (*what kind of books?*) and at the moment you're writing a new novel about (*what?*). However, life isn't perfect. **You work on your own all the time** and you sometimes get extremely lonely.

STUDENT C

You're a famous singer. You've just finished a tour of (*where?*) and now you're recording a new album, which is coming out (*when?*). However, life isn't perfect. **Photographers follow you around every day,** which drives you crazy.

STUDENT D

You're a famous footballer. You play for (*which team?*) and at the moment you're getting ready for a big match this weekend (*against who?*). However, life isn't perfect. **The newspapers write about your private life all the time.**

STUDENT E

You're a famous fashion model. You've just come back from doing a show in (*where?*). However, life isn't perfect. **You can't eat the same food as everyone else.** You haven't had any (*what kind of food?*) for nearly six years!

STUDENT F

You're a famous comedian. You used to perform live in (*where?*) and at the moment you're making a TV series with (*who?*). However, life isn't perfect. **People ask you to tell jokes all the time** – but you're actually quite shy and serious.

STUDENT G

You're a famous tennis player. This year you've won (*which tournaments?*) and tomorrow you're making a new TV ad for (*which company?*). However, life isn't perfect. **You get so nervous before big matches** that you can't eat or sleep.

STUDENT H

You're a famous businessman/woman. You own (*which company?*). You've just been to the USA and tomorrow you're off to (*where?*). However, life isn't perfect. You're very stressed because **you're under so much pressure all the time.**

STUDENT I

You are a famous fashion designer. You've designed some amazing new (*what?*) and at the moment you're getting ready for a big fashion show in (*where?*). However, life isn't perfect. **Department stores keep stealing your designs.**

STUDENT J

You are a famous actor/actress. During the last few months you've been making the new Batman movie in (*where?*) with (*who?*). However, life isn't perfect. **You have to start filming at 6 a.m.** – and you hate getting up early!

STUDENT K

You're a famous TV presenter. At the moment you're presenting a show called (*what?*) on (*which channel?*). However, life isn't perfect. **People stop you in the street all the time.** Everyone thinks they know you, but they don't!

STUDENT L

You're a famous musician in a rock band (*which band?*). Today you've been rehearsing for your next big concert tour in (*where?*). However, life isn't perfect. **You have to be away from home most of the year** and you miss your family.

What did they wish?

a .... is a famous artist.

He/She wishes ....

b .... is a famous novelist.

He/She wishes ....

c .... is a famous singer.

He/She wishes ....

d .... is a famous footballer.

He/She wishes ....

e .... is a famous fashion model.

He/She wishes ....

f .... is a famous comedian.

He/She wishes ....

g .... is a famous tennis player.

He/She wishes ....

h .... is a famous businessman/woman.

He/She wishes ....

i .... is a famous fashion designer.

He/She wishes ....

j .... is a famous actor/actress.

He/She wishes ....

k .... is a famous TV presenter.

He/She wishes ....

l .... is a famous musician.

He/She wishes ....

30
You need to r _ _ _ _ the loan as soon as possible.

31
I hope to p _ _ / _ _ _ my mortgage in the next two years.

32

33
It's very hard to g _ _ / _ _ _ / _ _ debt if you're unemployed.

FINISH

29
When my uncle died, I c _ _ _ _ / _ _ _ _ quite a lot of money.

28
I'm afraid you get a very l _ _ / _ _ _ _ _ _ _ _ / _ _ _ on this account.

27
I don't have a credit card, so I always p _ _ / _ _ _ _ .

26
I'm thinking of t _ _ _ _ _ _ / _ _ _ a loan to buy a car.

25

20
I can't get any money out. I must be o _ _ _ _ _ _ _ _ .

21

22
If you don't have the money now, you can buy it on c _ _ _ _ _ _ .

23
The bank won't lend me money as I have a bad c _ _ _ _ _ / _ _ _ _ _ _ .

24
The mirror was scratched so they t _ _ _ £30 _ _ _ the price.

19
I never borrow money. I hate g _ _ _ _ _ _ into _ _ _ _ .

18
The total cost of the repairs c _ _ _ _ / _ _ £270.

17
HALF WAY

16
Thanks for the money. I'll p _ _ you _ _ _ _ soon, I promise.

15
I usually s _ _ _ _ _ about £100 a month _ _ food.

10
Prices of plasma TVs have been g _ _ _ _ / _ _ _ _ recently.

11
We've put a 10% d _ _ _ _ _ _ down on our new house.

12

13
I put money for my holiday into my s _ _ _ _ _ _ account.

14
I'm staying in tonight. I'm a bit s _ _ _ _ / _ _ / _ _ _ _ _ at the moment.

9
I'm going to i _ _ _ _ _ all my money _ _ the stock market.

8
My account will be in c _ _ _ _ _ as soon as I get paid.

7
£10 for a coffee?! You're trying to r _ _ me _ _ _ !

6
I'm s _ _ _ _ _ / _ _ / _ _ _ a new bike.

5
My uncle doesn't need to work. He's very w _ _ _ / _ _ _ .

START

1
If you need to borrow money, why not get a l _ _ _ from the bank?

2
Most people need a m _ _ _ _ _ _ _ if they want to buy a house.

3
There's a cashpoint. I'll g _ _ some money _ _ _ .

4
I pay quite a high i _ _ _ _ _ _ _ rate on my credit card.

Student A

figure out	vary	particularly
just	straightforward	obligatory
customary	acceptable	odd
offended	generally	dilemma
complicated	pursue	such as

Student B

find out	pursue	complicated
customary	precise	definitely
obligatory	additional	observe
odd	figure out	particularly
just	such as	acceptable

Student C

particularly	generally	dilemma
precise	offended	complicated
customary	figure out	observe
find out	additional	definitely
obligatory	straightforward	vary

Student D

straightforward	definitely	observe
just	vary	dilemma
acceptable	pursue	find out
additional	precise	such as
generally	odd	offended

to be attacked by a shark.	In restaurants in the UK you're	**expected** to leave a 10% tip.	Sally's fed up **with**
being taken for granted by her boss.	I think Rita really **wants**	**to be invited** to the wedding.	More than 20 people **have been**
kidnapped so far this year.	I was **the first** person	**to be interviewed.**	My boss told me that I **would** probably
be promoted in the next six months.	Help! My bag's just	**been stolen** by that man over there!	Many of the animals **have to**
be fed twice a day.	The staff will all **need**	**to be shown** how to use the new photocopier.	By the time I got there, most of the seats **had**
already **been taken**.	This factory **used to**	**be owned** by my ex-husband.	Last night two people **were**
arrested in connection with the robbery.	My six-year-old son **refuses**	**to be told** what to do.	These pills **must**
be taken three times a day with meals.	The travel agent says we're **going to**	**be met** at the airport.	Robert **hates**
being driven – he's a terrible passenger.	My car **is being**	**repaired** at the moment.	Juliet's terrified **of**
being left on her own.	Most people don't **like**	**being criticised.**	We suddenly realised that we **were**
being followed, so we started to walk faster.	I'll probably **end up**	**being asked** to organise my boss's leaving party.	I don't think people **can**
be expected to work every weekend.	Three of the suspects **are being**	**questioned** by the police at the moment.	He's **the third** tourist this year

Student A

Student B

face2face Second edition Upper Intermediate Photocopiable   © Cambridge University Press 2012   ⟨ Instructions p142

1 V7.2

Say two nouns for each of these adjectives.

economic   industrial   pollute

2 V7.2

Choose the correct words.

a The UK is a *capital/capitalist* country.
b My car is very *economic/economical*.

3 V7.3

What do these prefixes mean? Give one example for each prefix.

pro-   under-   multi-   non-

4 V7.3

What do these prefixes mean? Give one example for each prefix.

pre-   over-   re-   mis-

5 V7.3

What do these prefixes mean? Give one example for each prefix.

anti-   post-   ex-   self-

6 V7.4

What's the difference between having a *mobile phone contract* and *pay-as-you-go*?

7 V7.4

What do these 'on the phone' phrases mean?

get cut off
run out of credit
top up your phone

8 V7.8

What do these 'on the phone' phrases mean?

a mobile phone network
a landline
hang up

9 G7.1

Do we use simple or continuous verb forms to describe things that are:

a completed?   c temporary?
b unfinished?   d permanent?

10 G7.1

Which of these verbs are state verbs?

play   belong   travel   sit
dislike   study   deserve

11 G7.1

Which of these verbs are not state verbs?

envy   wait   adore   detest
believe   listen   understand

12 G7.2

Choose the correct verb forms.

I've *read/been reading* emails since 9.00. I've *replied/been replying* to about 30 so far.

13 G7.2

What's the difference in meaning between these sentences?

a I've been doing my homework.
b I've done my homework.

14 G7.2

Make questions with *How long* or *How many*.

a He's written three best-sellers.
b They've been living in the UK for two years.

15 RW7.1

Fill in the gaps in these phrases.

a Sorry, you're breaking ...... a bit.
b Sorry, it's a bad ....
c You'll have to speak ...... a bit.

16 V8.1

What are the opposites of these phrases?

be in credit
be short of money
put money into your account

17 V8.1

Which preposition?

invest money ...... something
spend money ...... something
pay cash ...... something
buy something ...... credit

18 V8.2

Fill in the gaps in these phrasal verbs.

a I've paid him ...... all the money I owed him.
b We finally paid ...... our mortgage.

19 V8.2

Fill in the gaps in these phrasal verbs.

a I've just taken ...... a loan so I can buy a new motorbike.
b I'm saving ...... for a holiday.

20 V8.2

Fill in the gaps in these phrasal verbs.

a When my grandfather died, I came ...... a lot of money.
b I think they're trying to rip us ....

21 V8.3

Say synonyms for these phrases.

work out   exact   especially

CLASS ACTIVITIES: Photocopiable

---

22 V8.3

Say synonyms for these words.

certainly   strange   differ

---

23 V8.3

Say synonyms for these words.

insulted   discover   usually

---

24 G8.1

Say these sentences again with I wish ... .

a I don't have a car.
b I have to work tomorrow.

---

25 G8.1

Rephrase these sentences with I wish ... .

a I'm not going on holiday next week.
b I can't swim.

---

26 G8.1

Correct these sentences.

a It's about time you go home.
b It's time go.

---

27 G8.2

Say these sentences again with I wish ... .

a I didn't pass the exam.
b I forgot my mum's birthday.

---

28 G8.2

Rephrase these sentences with should have.

a I didn't call John last night.
b I told Sue about the email.

---

29 RW8.1

Fill in the gaps in these phrases.

a I'm sorry ...... the noise.
b I'm sorry ...... waking you up.
c Don't worry ...... it.

---

30 V9.1

What is the difference between these words?

a a trailer, a soundtrack
b a review, a critic

---

31 V9.1

What is the difference between these words/phrases?

a a subtitled film, a dubbed film
b a remake, a sequel

---

32 V9.2

What do these adjectives to describe entertainment mean?

overrated   gripping   weird

---

33 V9.2

What do these adjectives to describe entertainment mean?

far-fetched   moving   hilarious

---

34 V9.3

Say eight homonyms in 30 seconds.

---

35 G9.1

Put these sentences into the passive.

a Somebody burgled my house last week.
b They're decorating my bedroom at the moment.

---

36 G9.1

Put these sentences into the passive.

a They've just arrested three men.
b Somebody was watching me.

---

37 G9.1

Choose the correct verb forms.

a I think the boss needs be/to be/being told.
b He enjoys be/to be/being photographed.

---

38 G9.1

Choose the correct verb forms.

a I'm worried about be/to be/being sacked.
b She was the first person be/to be/being asked.

---

39 G9.2

Fill in the gaps with as or like.

a Jane works ...... a waitress.
b It was ...... a bad dream.
c We had to use boxes ...... chairs.

---

40 G9.2

Fill in the gaps with so or such.

a The film had ...... a good plot.
b The play was ...... predictable.
c I've bought ...... many presents.

---

41 RW9.1

Fill in the gaps with one word.

a Have you got anything ...... this Saturday?
b Do you ...... going out tonight?
c I don't mind. It's ...... to you.

---

42 RW9.1

Fill in the gaps with one word.

a We could give that new club a ....
b I'd rather give that a ....
c I'm not ...... either way.

Find someone who ...	Name	Follow-up questions
1 _____ you ever _____ (have) your photo _____ (take) by a professional photographer?		Where? When? / still have the photo?
2 _____ you usually _____ (get) somebody _____ (check) your English homework for you?		Who? Where / learn English?
3 _____ you _____ (do) all your food shopping yourself?		How often / go food shopping? Which shops / go to?
4 _____ you ever _____ (have) an item of clothing _____ (make) especially for you?		What? Where? How much / cost?
5 If you were very rich, _____ you _____ (get) somebody _____ (cook) all your meals for you?		What else / get people / do for you?
6 _____ you _____ (choose) the colour of your bedroom walls yourself?		What colour? Who / paint / bedroom?
7 If there was a huge spider in your bathroom, _____ you _____ (get) somebody else _____ (remove) it?		Why / not / like / spiders? What else / scared of?
8 _____ you ever _____ (have) your palm _____ (read) ?		Who by? When? What / say?
9 _____ you _____ (get) your head _____ (shave) if somebody offered you £1,000?		/ do it for £100?
10 _____ you ever _____ (have) your portrait _____ (paint)?		Where? When? / look like you?

 face2face Second edition Upper Intermediate Photocopiable

1 I haven't seen none my friends from university for ages.

2 None of the lights worked because there was no electricity.

3 All of people in my office work very hard, but I don't really like none of them.

4 All of the rooms in my house is quite big, but none them are very tidy!

5 Both of my brothers live near me, but neither of them visits me very often.

6 No one in my family reads very much, but both of my kids love watching TV.

7 I've got all of his books, but I haven't read none of them.

8 Everyone in my family have got a mobile and all them text me quite a lot.

9 Both of my nephews will eat anything.

10 Sam bought both of these laptops last year, but either of them work any more.

11 I work hard every days, so I don't usually do nothing on Sundays.

12 I've got two digital cameras, but neither them don't work properly.

13 I've seen lots of documentaries on global warming and all of them say the same thing.

14 Tom's got five sisters, but neither of them live in the same town as him.

15 I know lots of Americans, but I've never met no one from Canada.

16 The guests ate all of food and anyone had a wonderful time.

Money left
£5,000

 Instructions p143

10D Love it or hate it adding emphasis

Student A

1 the Internet is What I about love
What I love about the Internet is

2 mobile phones The thing me about is annoys that

3 enjoy I One thing in hotels staying about is

4 like most about is weddings I The thing

5 the cinema is going to that me annoys One thing about

6 What the English language about I is like

7 is travelling that about me The thing by plane irritates

8 is depresses that about me the modern world One thing

9 living I What about is love town this in

Student B

a is me The thing about the Internet amazes that
The thing that amazes me about the Internet is

b I about What like most mobile phones is

c in hotels irritates What staying me about is

d that me The thing annoys is weddings about

e is I like the cinema about going to What

f the English language about One thing don't I is like

g really I by plane What enjoy is about travelling

h One thing the modern world I about is love

i living in me that about is The thing this town annoys

Instructions p144 © Cambridge University Press 2012 face2face Second edition Upper Intermediate Photocopiable 183

11A The photoshoot Future Perfect and Future Continuous

Student A: Photographer

You are a photographer for the fashion magazine *In Fashion*. You need to arrange a photoshoot with the famous singer, Kylie Houston. You need at least an hour for the photoshoot and you'd like to do it as soon as possible. **It is now 5.30 p.m. on Tuesday.** Look at your diary for the rest of the week. Phone Kylie's manager and try to arrange a suitable time.

8 Wednesday	**9** Thursday	**10** Friday
9.00–10.00 meeting with In Fashion photo editor	10.30 doctor	6.50 flight to London – arrive 7.35
11.30–1.00 do photoshoot (Kate Moss)	12.30 lunch meeting – Jack Harper (editor on new book?)	9.00–10.30 give lecture (London College of Photography)
1.15–2.15 lunch meeting with book publisher	2.00–4.30 do photoshoot (DKNY new collection)	11.15–12.45 do photoshoot (In Fashion model of the month)
2.30–4.15 give talk on fashion photography at Photo World conference	5.20 flight to Paris (arrive 6.05)	1.00 lunch (Kevin and Sophie)
5.45–7.30 do photoshoot (Stella McCartney's new collection)	7.30–10.00 Paris fashion show	2.00–3.00 editorial meeting
	10.00 dinner with event organisers – then party?	4.30–6.30 meeting with Gabriela about next week's photoshoots

Student B: Manager

You are the manager for the famous singer, Kylie Houston, and you organise all her appointments.
You have agreed that Kylie will do a photoshoot for the fashion magazine *In Fashion*. **It is now 5.30 p.m. on Tuesday.** Look at Kylie's diary for the rest of the week. When the photographer calls, try to arrange a suitable time for the photoshoot.

8 Wednesday	**9** Thursday	**10** Friday
8.00–9.00 private yoga class	8.00–9.00 breakfast meeting with video director	8.30–9.15 breakfast meeting with record company executives
9.30–12.00 record new single (Abbey Road studio)	9.00 travel to film studio (journey time: 45 minutes)	10.00–1.30 meeting with Pepsi marketing manager (TV ad?)
1.00–2.00 lunch with journalist from Rolling Stone magazine	10.00–12.00 film video for new single	12.30 check out of hotel
4.00–5.00 hairdresser	12.00 return to hotel	1.00 lunch with publicity manager
5.00 travel to Wembley Arena (journey time: 1 hour)	1.30–2.30 lunch with head of Paramount Studios (film project?)	2.00–3.00 record interview for TV show
8.00–10.30 Wembley concert	4.00–5.30 meeting about new clothing range KylieKlothes	4.30–6.30 shopping trip to Harrods
11.30 return to hotel	7.00–?? party at Madonna's!	6.30 travel to Heathrow (depart for New York 8.45)

PURE IN CRISIS

The relationship between Vicky Robinson and Mark Clarke, the founders of the hugely popular Pure range of skin care for women, seems to be going from bad to worse. The problems began last month when they were named Business Innovators of the Year at the UK Innovation in Business awards ceremony. After accepting the award, Vicky told the shocked audience that Mark had contributed nothing to the Pure range and did not deserve to share the award. Then last Thursday it was announced that Pure had bought Maxine Cosmetics, the cosmetics company owned by Mark's cousin, Maxine Drew. Vicky was not present at the press conference announcing the decision; according to Mark, she was on holiday in New York.

However, the problems between Vicky and Mark are not just about business. While the financial pages focus on rumours of serious money problems within Pure, the tabloids have been full of stories about Vicky's private life. At an emergency board meeting on Monday, Mark threatened to 'go public' about Vicky's personal problems, while Vicky accused Mark of stealing money from the company to pay off personal debts. According to other board members, the two partners haven't spoken to each other since that meeting.

In an attempt to put their sides of the story, both partners have agreed to be interviewed separately by *Business Weekly*. Read our exclusive interviews tomorrow – and then you can decide who's really telling the truth.

Journalist

You are going to interview Vicky Robinson and Mark Clarke separately.
Prepare at least 12 questions to ask them on these topics.

- Vicky's speech at the UK Innovation in Business awards ceremony
- what Vicky and Mark said to each other after the ceremony
- the decision to buy the cosmetics company Maxine Cosmetics
- Vicky and Mark's opinion of Maxine Drew, the ex-owner of Maxine Cosmetics
- Vicky's personal problems and how long they've been going on
- financial problems in the company and who's responsible for them
- if Mark has been stealing money from the company and what the evidence is
- whether the two of them will meet to discuss their problems

When you have finished, think of three more questions to ask Vicky and Mark.

While you are interviewing Vicky and Mark, make brief notes on their answers.

11C ▶ Business partners verb patterns (2): reporting verbs; reported speech

Vicky Robinson

You are going to be interviewed by a journalist from *Business Weekly*. Look at these things you want to say during the interview. Decide what you are going to say about each topic.

- Mark contributed nothing to the Pure skin care range. (Why did you decide to say this at the awards ceremony? What did you and Mark say to each other afterwards?)

- Mark never discussed buying Maxine Cosmetics with you. (Why not? What would you have said?)

- You think Mark's cousin Maxine is dishonest. (Why don't you trust her? What do you know about her past?)

- Mark claims that you have some personal problems. (Do you have any personal problems? If so, what are they? If not, why does Mark keep telling everyone that you have?)

- You admit there are financial problems in the company. (Why? Whose fault is it? What should be done about them?)

- You are certain that Mark has been stealing money from the company. (Why has he been doing this? What evidence do you have?)

- You want to meet Mark to discuss the situation, but only under certain conditions. (What conditions? Do you have a message for Mark?)

Mark Clarke

You are going to be interviewed by a journalist from *Business Weekly*. Look at these things you want to say during the interview. Decide what you are going to say about each topic.

- You came up with the idea for the Pure skin care range. (Why did Vicky decide to criticise you at the awards ceremony? What did you and Vicky say to each other afterwards?)

- You emailed Vicky in New York to tell her that you were going to buy Maxine Cosmetics. (Did you get a reply? If so, what did Vicky say? If not, why not?)

- You know that Vicky doesn't like your cousin Maxine. (Why not? What happened between them in the past? What's your opinion of her?)

- You know that Vicky has some serious personal problems. (What are they? How long have they been going on? What do you think Vicky should do about them?)

- You admit there are financial problems in the company. (Why? Whose fault is it? What should be done about them?)

- You have never stolen money from the company, but you did borrow some money earlier this year. (How much? Why? Have you paid it back yet? If not, why not?)

- You want to meet Vicky to discuss the situation, but only under certain conditions. (What conditions? Do you have a message for Vicky?)

Crime report

When **Lord William Breen** died recently, aged 107, he left his nephew, **Sir Thomas Breen**, a diamond worth £500,000 in his will. Last night Sir Thomas invited some of his family to his country house to show them the diamond. After dinner, he went to get the diamond from the safe in his study, but discovered that it had been stolen. He called the police, who searched all the guests and their bags. Nobody had the diamond. The suspects are: **Lady Mary Breen** (Sir Thomas's wife), **Henry Breen** (his younger brother), **Fiona** (Henry's wife), **Caroline** (Sir Thomas's cousin), and of course the butler, **Arthur**.

1
Sir Thomas put the diamond in the safe just before dinner. Only Sir Thomas, Lady Mary and Arthur know the combination of the safe.

2
Sir Thomas told Arthur last week that he couldn't afford to employ him any more. Arthur is sixty-seven and has no savings.

3
Sir Thomas's study is along a corridor between the dining room and the bathroom. He never locks the study door.

4
Lady Mary, Fiona and Caroline all went to the bathroom at different times during the meal.

5
Lady Mary is very unhappy in her marriage and is thinking of getting a divorce.

6
Arthur never left the dining room during the meal.

7
When Henry and Sir Thomas's father died 20 years ago, Sir Thomas inherited the house and all his father's money. Henry got nothing.

8
After the main course, Henry went into the back garden on his own to have a cigarette. He was gone for 10 minutes.

9
Sir Thomas's country house needs a lot of repair work. The work will cost £250,000. Sir Thomas only has £10,000 in the bank.

10
The whole family knows that Lady Mary is quite forgetful and that she keeps a notebook in her purse with all her important numbers in it.

11
Henry Breen has debts of over £300,000.

12
Lady Mary went to the bathroom between the first course and the main course. She left her purse on the right of the washbasin.

13
When the police checked the study, they found that the window was wide open.

14
Caroline Breen was Lord William Breen's only child. Caroline wasn't left anything at all in her father's will. When she found out, she was furious.

15
Fiona Breen runs an art gallery in London. She has many important clients from overseas. She also knows about her husband's debts.

16
Caroline and Fiona went to the bathroom at different times during the 10-minute break between the main course and the dessert.

17
After Sir Thomas had put the diamond in the safe, he locked the window of the study and put the key on the desk.

18
The police found the diamond under a bush 20 metres from the study window.

19
When Fiona went to the bathroom, she noticed that Lady Mary's purse was on the left of the washbasin.

20
Caroline Breen is left-handed.

Student A

A Guest for Tea

In 1987, a woman came home from work to find a TV van parked outside her house. A reporter took her around to her back garden to show her that an alien spaceship had crash-landed there. As she was recovering from the shock, the spaceship door opened and an alien walked out. Nervously she welcomed the 'visitor' to earth. Then – being British – she offered the alien a cup of tea. At this point the 'TV reporter' revealed that she was on a TV comedy show and the whole thing had been a hoax.

Lost on the Mountain

In November 2002, 19-year-old British tourist Louise Saunders set off to climb Mount Tyson in the rainforest in Queensland, Australia. She was wearing only a T-shirt and shorts, and the only 'food' she had with her was some chewing gum. Later that day she called a friend to say she was lost, but her mobile ran out of batteries before she was able to say where she was. Four days later she managed to walk to safety by following a stream down the mountain. She said she felt "very lucky to be alive".

Student B

Till Death Do Us Part?

In 1983 Fran Toto, from Pennsylvania, USA, tried to kill her husband, Tony, not once but eight times. However, all her various attempts to shoot, poison and blow him up failed. Then, after hiring two local men to shoot him – they missed his heart by two centimetres – Fran was finally arrested. Amazingly, Tony continued to live with her during the trial and after she had finished her four-year prison sentence she moved back in with her husband. "I love my wife," explained Tony. "We both made mistakes."

Lottery Loser

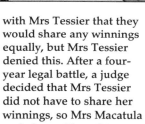

CORAZÓN MACATULA, a care worker from Winnipeg in Canada, always used to buy a lottery ticket for the woman she was looking after, Jean Tessier. Then, in March 2000, Mrs Tessier won $11.4 million on the lottery. Mrs Macatula claimed that she had a verbal agreement with Mrs Tessier that they would share any winnings equally, but Mrs Tessier denied this. After a four-year legal battle, a judge decided that Mrs Tessier did not have to share her winnings, so Mrs Macatula ended up with nothing.

Student C

A Costly Joke

In December 2005, British businessman Peter Aldred boarded a plane in Inverness, Scotland. As they were waiting to take off, a flight attendant asked him what was in his bag. "A bomb," joked Mr Aldred. The police were called immediately and asked all the passengers to get off the plane. Mr Aldred was arrested, but when his bag was searched, it was found to contain two toy Loch Ness monsters – presents for Mr Aldred's son. When Mr Aldred appeared in court, the judge sent him to prison for two months.

Time to Get Legless

In July 2000, Tony Higgins, from Redditch in England, was released from prison on condition that he wore an electronic tag on his leg, which would set off an alarm if he left his house between 7 p.m. and 7 a.m. However, the prison officer who attached the tag hadn't realised that Mr Higgins had an artificial leg. So every evening, Mr Higgins took off his false leg and went to the pub on crutches. He was only caught when police officers came round to his house to check up on him. The police moved the tag to his other leg.

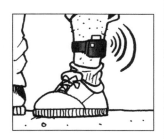

Vocabulary Plus

Instructions

There are 12 Vocabulary Plus worksheets (p194–p205). These worksheets introduce additional vocabulary. The topic of each Vocabulary Plus worksheet is linked to the topic of the corresponding unit in the Student's Book. There is an answer key at the bottom of each worksheet, which can be cut off if necessary. You will need to photocopy one Vocabulary Plus worksheet for each student.

- Use them as extra vocabulary input in class. We suggest you cut off the answer keys and check the answers after each exercise.
- Give them for homework for students to use on their own. You can either leave the answer keys on the worksheets so students can check the answers themselves or cut them off and check the answers at the beginning of the next class.
- When you have a mixed-level class give them to students who finish longer speaking activities early. They can begin the worksheets in class and finish them for homework if necessary. You can then give the worksheet for homework to the other students at the end of the class.

1 ▶ Academic subjects/professions p194

Language
chemistry/chemist, physics/physicist, biology/biologist, geology/geologist, psychology/psychologist, archaeology/archaeologist, history/historian, mathematics/mathematician, architecture/architect, mechanical engineering/mechanical engineer

When to use and time
Use any time after lesson 1B. 20–30 minutes.

Procedure

1 Students do the exercise on their own or in pairs. Check answers with the class (see answer key on worksheet). Drill the words chorally or individually, highlighting the pronunciation of *physics* /ˈfɪzɪks/ *psychology*, /saɪˈkɒlədʒiː/ and the stress on *mathematics*.

2 Students do the exercise on their own or in pairs. Check answers with the class. Point out the stress on *history/historian* and *mathematics/mathematician*. Students can then work in pairs and cover the list of professions. Students take turns to say a subject and ask their partner to say the correct profession.

3 Students do the exercise on their own before checking in pairs. Check answers with the class.

4 Students do the exercise on their own before comparing sentences in groups of three or four. Finally, ask each group to tell the class two interesting things that they have discussed.

2 ▶ Phrases with *get* p195

Language
get tired of, get a move on, get through, get lost, get hit, get hurt, get cross, get away with, get sacked, get round to, get down to

When to use and time
Use any time after lesson 2B. 20–30 minutes.

Procedure

1 Students do the exercise on their own before checking in pairs. Check answers with the class.

2 Students do the exercise on their own or in pairs. Point out that *get a move on* is used when the speaker is impatient. Check answers with the class. Students can then work in pairs and test each other on the phrases and definitions.

3 **a** Students do the exercise on their own before checking in pairs. Check answers with the class.
b Put students in groups. Students take turns to ask each other the questions in **3a**. Finally, ask students to tell the class one or two things they found out about other students.

3 ▶ Word pairs p196

Language
sick and tired, give or take, wait and see, peace and quiet, by and large, now and then, law and order, now or never, pros and cons, pick and choose, sooner or later, right and wrong

When to use and time
Use any time after lesson 3A. 20–30 minutes.

Procedure

1 Students read the column and answer the questions in pairs. Ask one or two pairs for their opinion.

2 Students do the exercise on their own or in pairs. Check answers with the class. Point out that in word pairs, the last word in the pair is stressed. Model and drill the phrases.

3 Students do the exercise on their own or in pairs. Check answers with the class.

4 ▶ Descriptive verbs p197

Language

wander, crawl, stagger, boast, groan, claim, peer, stare, spot, scratch, wrestle, grab

When to use and time

Use any time after lesson 4B. 25–35 minutes.

Procedure

1 Check students understand *sewer* and *colonies of alligators*. Students read the article and answer the question in pairs. Encourage students to give reasons for their answer. Check the answers with the class.

2 Students do the exercise on their own or in pairs. Check answers with the class. Model and drill the new words, paying particular attention to the pronunciation of *wrestle* /ˈresəl/, *crawl* /krɔːl/, *boast* /bəʊst/ and *groan* /grəʊn/. Students can then work in pairs and test each other on the words and definitions.

3 Students do the exercise on their own before checking answers in pairs. Check answers with the class.

4 **a** Students do the exercise on their own before checking answers in pairs. Check answers with the class.

b Put students into pairs or small groups. Students take turns to ask each other the questions from **4a**. Encourage students to ask follow-up questions if possible.

5 ▶ Geographical features p198

Language

a valley, a marsh, a glacier, a peak, a desert, a plain, a stream, a volcano, a waterfall, a cliff, the shore, a jungle

When to use and time

Use any time after lesson 5B. 20–35 minutes.

Procedure

1 Students do the exercise on their own or in pairs. Check answers with the class. Highlight the pronunciation of *glacier* /ˈglæsiə/ and *volcano* /vɒlˈkeɪnəʊ/.

2 Students work in pairs and do the crossword. Check answers with the class.

3 Students do the exercise on their own. Check answers with the class.

4 Students write a description on their own. When they have finished, put students in groups. Students take turns to read out their descriptions, leaving out the name of the country. The group tries to guess the name of each place.

6 ▶ Commonly confused verbs p199

Language

discuss/argue, borrow/lend, lose/miss, hope/expect, remember/remind, avoid/prevent

When to use and time

Use any time after lesson 6C. 20–30 minutes.

Procedure

1 **a** Students discuss the questions in pairs or small groups. Ask a few pairs to share their information with the class.

b Students do the exercise on their own before checking answers in pairs. Check answers with the class.

2 Students do the exercise on their own or in pairs. Check answers with the class. Students can work in pairs and test each other on the verbs and definitions.

3 Students do the exercise on their own before checking answers in pairs. Check answers with the class.

4 **a** Students do the exercise on their own before checking answers in pairs. Check answers with the class.

b Put the students in pairs. Students take turns to ask each other the questions in **4a**.

7 ▶ Words from other languages p200

Language

cuisine, marmalade, a siesta, kayaking, a chef, a ballerina, a chauffeur, sushi, a futon, pyjamas, karate, a yacht, a barbecue, a sauna, snorkelling, a delicatessen

When to use and time

Use any time after lesson 7B. 15–25 minutes.

Procedure

1 Students do the exercise by themselves or in pairs. Check answers with the class. Model and drill the words. Highlight the stress on *marmalade*, *siesta*, *ballerina* and *delicatessen*.

2 Students do the exercise on their own or in pairs. Check answers with the class.

3 Students do the exercise in pairs or groups. Check answers with the class.

4 **a** Students do the exercise on their own. Check answers with the class.

b Students work in pairs or groups. Students take turns to ask each other the questions.

8 ▶ British and American English
p201

Language

a (bank)note/bill, a chemist's/drugstore, a tap/faucet, a bank holiday/national holiday, the pavement/sidewalk, the motorway/freeway, a waistcoat/vest, a torch/flashlight, a queue/line, the underground/subway, a car park/parking lot, a mobile phone/cell phone, a block of flats/apartment building, a garden/yard

When to use and time

Use any time after lesson 8C. 20–30 minutes.

Procedure

1 Students do the exercise in pairs. Check answers with the class. Point out that in British English *a vest* is a type of underwear, often with no sleeves.

2 Students do the exercise on their own. Check answers with the class. Ask students which words helped them.

3 Students do the exercise on their own. Check answers with the class.

4 **a** Students do the exercise on their own before checking answers in pairs. Check answers with the class.

b Students work in pairs or in groups and take turns to ask each other the questions.

9 ▶ Compound nouns p202

Language

games arcade, fun park, Internet hit, documentary maker, film extras, table football, miniature basketball, cardboard boxes, sticky tape, car parts, scrapyard, college fees

When to use and time

Use any time after lesson 9C. 20–25 minutes.

Procedure

1 Check students understand *a craze for sth* and *flashmob*. Students read the article and answer the question in pairs. Check with the class.

2 Students do the exercise on their own or in pairs. Check answers with the class. Model and drill the words, asking students to note which compound nouns are stressed on the first word and which on the second (stress on first word: *games arcade, fun park, internet hit, documentary maker, film extras, sticky tape, car parts, scrapyard, college fees*; stress on second word: *table football, miniature basketball, cardboard boxes*). Students can test each other, taking turns to give definitions and provide the correct compound nouns.

3 Students do the exercise on their own before comparing in pairs. Check answers with the class.

4 **a** Students do the exercise on their own or in pairs. Check answers with the class.

b Students work in pairs or groups and take turns to ask each other the questions.

10 ▶ Nouns from phrasal verbs p203

Language

a setback, a walkout, a breakdown, a cutback, a letdown, a break-up, a breakthrough, a turnaround, a fallout, an outbreak, an uptake, a check-up

When to use and time

Use any time after lesson 10C. 20–30 minutes.

Procedure

1 Check students understand *pay dispute, representative, local health authority* and *union*. Students read the article and answer the questions in pairs. Check answers with the class.

2 Students do the exercise on their own or in pairs. Check answers with the class. Model and drill the words, highlighting that nouns from phrasal verbs are usually stressed on the first part of the noun.

3 Students do the exercise on their own before checking in pairs. Check answers with the class.

4 **a** Students do the exercise on their own before checking in pairs. Check answers with the class.

b Students work in pairs or groups and take turns to ask each other the questions.

11 ▶ Stress on nouns/verbs p204

Language
conflict, decrease, upset, export, import, produce, record, present, permit, rebel, suspect, transport, increase, contrast

When to use and time
Use any time after lesson 11B. 25–35 minutes.

Procedure

1 Focus students on the sentences and the pictures. Students do the exercise on their own or in pairs. Check answers with the class.

2 **a** Students do the exercise on their own or in pairs. Check answers with the class. Model and drill the words, highlighting the stress.

b Students do the exercise on their own or in pairs. Check answers with the class.

3 Students do the exercise on their own before checking in pairs. Check answers with the class. Point out that the verb and noun form of the word have the same spelling. Model and drill the words, highlighting the stress.

4 **a** Students do the exercise on their own. Check answers with the class.

b Students work in pairs or groups and take turns to ask each other the questions.

12 ▶ Idioms about feelings/ opportunities p205

Language
be on top of the world, get carried away, have a rough time, keep an eye on, stand a chance, be in two minds, get your act together, miss the boat, serve you right, be thrilled to bits

When to use and time
Use any time after lesson 12C. 20–30 minutes.

Procedure

1 Ask if students read their horoscopes and what signs they are. Students read the horoscopes and then answer the question. Check the answer with the class.

2 Students do the exercise on their own or in pairs. Check answers with the class. Model and drill each idiom. Highlight the pronunciation of *rough* /rʌf/ and *thrilled* /θrɪld/. Ask students to mark the stress on their worksheet.

3 **a** Students do the exercise on their own before checking answers in pairs. Check answers with the class.

b Put students in pairs or groups. Students then take turns to ask each other the questions. Ask students to tell the class one or two things they found out about other students.

1 ▸ Academic subjects/professions

1 Match pictures 1–10 to the subjects.

chemistry ☐ 3 physics ☐ biology ☐
geology ☐ psychology ☐ archaeology ☐
history ☐ mathematics ☐ architecture ☐
mechanical engineering ☐

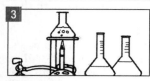

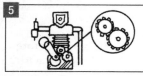

2 Complete the professions for each subject and mark the stress.

subjects	professions
chemistry	chem _ _ _
physics	physic _ _ _
biology	biolog _ _ _
geology	_ _ _ _ _ _ _ _ _
psychology	_ _ _ _ _ _ _ _ _ _ _
archaeology	_ _ _ _ _ _ _ _ _ _ _
history	histor _ _ _
mathematics	mathematic _ _ _
architecture	architect
mechanical engineering	mechanical engineer

3 Tick the correct sentences. Correct the sentences that are wrong by changing the words in bold.

A geologist

1 ~~An archaeologist~~ studies rocks and minerals.

2 **Psychology** is the scientific study of the way the human mind works and how the mind can change behaviour.

3 On average it takes six years to complete a degree in **architect** in the UK.

4 Mechanical **engineers** use **mathematics** every day.

5 Some **archaeology** think that Stonehenge was built over 4,000 years ago.

6 Albert Einstein completely changed the face of **physicist** in the 20th century, just as Charles Darwin was the most important evolutionary **biology** of the 19th century.

7 **Historians** disagree about who invented the telephone.

8 Many early **chemistry** tried to make gold in a process called alchemy.

4 Fill in the gaps with words from 2 so that the sentences are true for your country or for you.

1 _____ are very well paid in my country.

2 _____ don't make much money.

3 Many people who study _____ become teachers in the end.

4 I think _____ is one of the most interesting sciences.

5 Most _____ tend to be men.

6 I don't think _____ get enough recognition for the work they do.

7 At school/university I was reasonably good at _____ .

8 Many parents encourage their children to study _____ because they think it will lead to a good career.

9 I'd love to have a chance to study _____ .

10 If I had to study _____ , I'd leave college immediately!

11 I know someone who's a _____ .

---

1 physics 9; biology 4; geology 6; psychology 8; archaeology 2; history 7; mathematics 1; architecture 10; mechanical engineering 5
2 chemist; physicist; biologist; geologist; psychologist; archaeologist; historian; mathematician; architect; mechanical engineer **3** 2 ✓
3 architecture 4 ✓ 5 archaeologists 6 physics; biologist 7 ✓ 8 chemists

face2face Second edition Upper Intermediate Photocopiable © Cambridge University Press 2012 ⟨ Instructions p190

2 ▶ Phrases with *get*

1 **Read the story and put pictures A–D in order.**

My worst holiday job was one summer when I worked as a caddie* at a golf course. I used to **get tired of** being polite to unpleasant customers, especially one rude golfer who would shout "**Get a move on!**" whenever I walked too far behind him. One day, my car broke down on the way to work. I tried to phone my boss from the car, but couldn't **get through**. I got to work 30 minutes late and four people had already started playing. I took a shortcut across the course to catch them up, but I soon **got lost** in some trees. Suddenly out of nowhere I **got hit** on the back of the head – by the rude golfer's ball! When he came near me, instead of saying, "Are you OK?" he simply said, "Get out of the way!" and went to play his next shot. He wasn't worried about me **getting hurt** at all. I was starting to **get cross** by now so I picked up his ball and threw it into the middle of a nearby lake. Of course I didn't **get away with** it. The golfer complained to my boss and I **got sacked** straight away – but at least I finally **got round to** showing my true feelings.

Now I'm at university and I have my final exams in two weeks. However, I find it hard to **get down to** work, especially on nice sunny days like today. Maybe I'll go out and have a game of golf instead …

*caddie = a person who carries the equipment for someone who is playing golf

2 **Match the phrases in bold in the story in 1 to definitions a–k. Write the infinitive form of *get*.**

get = **start**

a start doing something that you have delayed
  get down to

b start doing something more quickly _____

get = **become**

c become bored or fed up with something
  _____

d become angry _____

e not know where you are _____

phrasal verbs with *get*

f do something that you have planned or wanted to do for a long time _____

g be able to talk to somebody on the telephone
  _____

h avoid punishment for doing something bad
  _____

the passive with *get*

i be hit _____

j feel pain _____

k be fired from a job _____

3 **a** **Fill in the gaps with the correct form of the phrases in 2.**

1 Did you ever *get away with* being naughty when you were a child?

2 Does it take you a long time to _____ answering your emails or do you do it straight away?

3 Would you _____ with your friend if he/she was extremely late?

4 When was the last time you tried to phone somebody and couldn't _____ for a long time?

5 Do you often _____ or do you have a good sense of direction?

6 Do you find it difficult to _____ work on a new project?

7 Did you ever _____ when you were doing sport at school?

8 If someone is always late for work or rude to customers, do you think they should _____ ?

9 Is there a film you never _____ seeing again and again?

10 When was the last time your country _____ by a big storm?

b **Answer the questions for yourself.**

---

3 ▶ Word pairs

1 Read the newspaper advice column. Do you think the columnist gives good advice? Why?/Why not?

Legal questions or problems? Or simply annoyed about something? Write to our lawyer Bob Mayfield for the best advice.

Dear Bob,
I really hope you can help me because I don't know who else to turn to. I'm being kept awake by students' parties in my street and I'm **¹ sick and tired** of the noise. It starts around 8.00 in the evening and goes on until 3.00 or 4.00 in the morning and it's been happening every night for two weeks now, **² give or take** a few nights. I don't like complaining (and frankly, I'm a bit embarrassed to go and knock on the door) so I decided not to do anything immediately but to **³ wait and see** if it was going to stop. But I can't stand it any longer! I'm desperate for a bit of **⁴ peace and quiet**. Please tell me if it's OK to call the police or if there is something else I can do to stop this awful noise.
Mr Jack Sargeant, Dublin

Dear Mr Sargeant,
Well, the good news is that there is something you can do, but it's not really a matter for the police. **⁵ By and large**, most people want good relations with their neighbours, so the first thing to do is to speak to the people concerned. Perhaps you can come to a reasonable agreement, for example, that they can have parties **⁶ now and then** but not every night. If that doesn't work, then most universities have a noise helpline. If you report the address responsible for disturbing the peace, the students will get a serious warning from their institution. Just let your neighbours know this is possible and in nine cases out of ten, the noise will stop.

Dear Bob,
I'm in a terrible dilemma and I hope you can help me. I went shopping with my six-year-old daughter yesterday and when we got home I noticed her pockets were full of sweets from the shop. As you can imagine, I was shocked and angry. I believe it's important to teach her about **⁷ law and order** but does that mean I should go back to the shop and tell them what she did? Will she get into trouble with the police? I mean, technically, that's shoplifting, isn't it?
Mrs Eileen Carter, London

Dear Mrs Carter,
I agree it's important to teach your daughter not to break the law and, given the situation, it's **⁸ now or never**. Why not go back to the shop and tell her to apologise for what she did and offer to pay the shop for the sweets out of her pocket money? There are **⁹ pros and cons** to this course of action: it will be a hard lesson for her, but you can't **¹⁰ pick and choose** real-life experiences like this one. It's very unlikely the shopkeeper will take it further, but **¹¹ sooner or later** your daughter will get into trouble if she doesn't learn the difference between **¹² right and wrong**.

2 Match word pairs 1–12 in the advice column in bold to definitions a–l.

a wait to discover what will happen __3__

b the advantages and disadvantages of a situation _____

c morally acceptable and unacceptable _____

d when you have to do something immediately _____

e a calm atmosphere _____

f when everything in a situation is considered together _____

g to take some things but not others _____

h very fed up with something _____

i when the rules of a country are being followed _____

j once in a while _____

k plus or minus _____

l some time in the future _____

3 Jack's speaking to his neighbour, Mark. Read their conversation. Choose the correct word pairs.

JACK Is it too much to ask for a bit of ¹*law and order /* (*peace and quiet*) in the evenings?

MARK No, of course not. We're really sorry about the noise, Mr Sargeant. But I think you'll agree that ²*by and large / give or take* we're actually quite good neighbours. I mean, we may have a party ³*sooner or later / now and then* but the rest of the time, we're studying, so we're as quiet as mice. That reminds me, I wanted to ask you if you could stop your dog barking during the day. It's difficult to study with all that noise.

JACK Ah, I'm sorry to hear that. Of course we can't ⁴*pick and choose / wait and see* our neighbours, can we? I suppose that ⁵*now or never / sooner or later* we're going to annoy each other!

MARK Would you like me to take your dog for a walk sometimes, Mr Sargeant? He must get ⁶*sick and tired / right and wrong* of being at home alone all day. I wouldn't charge much for the service.

4 ▶ Descriptive verbs

1 Read the urban legend about alligators living in the sewers of New York. Do you think any parts of the story are true? Why?/Why not?

It was once a fashion among New Yorkers on holiday in Florida to bring back baby alligators for their children to raise as pets. These infant alligators would **wander** freely around the New York apartments of their owners until eventually they grew up and were no longer attractive pets. At that point, their desperate owners flushed them down the toilet to get rid of them.

Some of these creatures managed to survive and breed in the dark Manhattan sewer system, so the story goes, producing colonies of giant alligators beneath the streets of New York City. Their descendants live down there to this day, **crawling** along the sewers, completely hidden from human eyes, apart from the rare heart-stopping moments when sewer workers find themselves **staring** directly into the eyes of a sewer alligator. In the 1930s, a retired sewer worker, Teddy May, **claimed** that he saw – and got rid of – a colony of alligators in the sewers. Further sightings include some teenage boys who went into a sewer in East Harlem for a dare. The boy in front was **peering** into the darkness when he **spotted** an eight-foot alligator. Encouraged by his friends, the boy **grabbed** the creature by the tail and **wrestled** with it. The alligator **scratched** the boy badly but didn't bite him. It then crawled away, leaving the boy – **groaning** in pain – to **stagger** away and join his friends. The boys, unharmed by the encounter, then **boasted** of their adventure to all their school friends, and so the story spread.

2 Match the words in bold in **1** with definitions a–l. Write the infinitive form of the verb.

ways of walking
a walk or travel around with no clear direction _wander_
b move slowly on your hands and knees _____
c walk as if you are going to fall _____

ways of speaking
d talk with too much pride about something you can do or have done _____
e make a long sound when you are in pain or unhappy _____
f say something is true although it has not been proved and may not be believed _____

ways of looking
g look at something with difficulty _____
h look for a long time with eyes wide open _____
i see or notice a person or thing, suddenly or when it is not easy to do so _____

ways of touching
j cut your skin slightly with something sharp _____
k fight somebody by holding them _____
l take something quickly and aggressively _____

3 Choose the correct word in these sentences.
1 I lost my map, so I ended up *wandering/staggering* around the town.
2 When the passengers heard that the plane was delayed, they all *groaned/claimed*.
3 I tried to *spot/peer* through the window, but it was so dirty I couldn't see a thing.
4 Many people disagree with *grabbing/wrestling*, but I think it's an entertaining sport.

4 a Fill in the gaps with the correct form of the verbs from **2**.
1 When was the last time someone _boasted_ about an achievement to you?
2 Have you ever been badly _____ or bitten by an animal?
3 How often do you _____ at a computer screen for a long time?
4 If a thief _____ your bag and ran away, would you chase after him?
5 How old were you when you stopped _____ and started to walk?

b Answer the questions for yourself.

VOCABULARY PLUS: Photocopiable

2 b crawl c stagger d boast e groan f claim g peer h stare i spot j scratch k wrestle l grab 3 1 wandering 2 groaned 3 peer 4 wrestling 4a 1 scratched 3 stare 4 grabbed 5 crawling

VOCABULARY PLUS:
Photocopiable

1 Match these geographical features to pictures 1–12.

a valley [11] a marsh ☐
a glacier ☐ a peak ☐
a desert ☐ a plain ☐
a stream ☐ a volcano ☐
a waterfall ☐ a cliff ☐
the shore ☐ a jungle ☐

2 Do the crossword.

```
3 P E A K
```

ACROSS

3 The pointed top of a mountain.

5 The land along the edge of a sea, lake or large river.

6 A tropical forest where trees and plants grow very close together.

8 An area of low land between hills or mountains, often with a river running through it.

9 Water dropping from a higher to lower point, sometimes from a great height.

10 A small, narrow river.

11 Ground near a lake, river or the sea, that tends to flood and is always wet.

DOWN

1 A large area of flat land.

2 An area often covered with sand or rocks, where there is very little rain and not many plants.

4 A high area of rock with a very steep side, often on a coast.

7 A large body of ice which moves very slowly.

8 A mountain out of which sometimes hot melted rock, gas and ash is forced.

3 Fill in the gaps with words from **1** in the singular or plural.

1 Iceland is covered by several large _glaciers_ .

2 Mauna Loa, in Hawaii, is the world's largest active _____ .

3 Although Tokyo is built on a large, flat _____ , the _____ of Mount Fuji can be seen from many parts of the city.

4 The city of Toronto is located along the _____ of Lake Ontario. There used to be a _____ there, but it was drained to make way for housing.

5 The source of the river Nile was difficult to find because of the many _____ that flow into it.

6 Singapore is famous for the Jurong Bird Park, an artificial _____ with thousands of different tropical trees and birds. Inside there is the world's largest man-made _____ , where water drops 30 metres into a large pool.

7 The Sahara is a very large, dry _____ , stretching across several countries.

8 The Loire _____ in France, named after the Loire river that runs through it, is home to many fine wines and beautiful castles.

9 The white _____ of Dover are about 100 metres high and are the first sight for many people coming to England by ferry.

4 Write a description of a country you've been to or would like to visit. Use the geographical features in **1**.

6 ▸ Commonly confused verbs

1 a Answer the questions.

1 What would you find most difficult about going to live abroad for three months?
2 How would you communicate with your family if you were in a different country?
3 What topics do you think are acceptable when talking to people you don't know well?

b Read the conversation and give Melek's answers to the questions in 1a.

KIM   So, are you excited about going to England?

MELEK Yes, I am. I **hope** I can find work after the course though.

KIM   Well, I **expect** it will be difficult, but I'm sure you'll find something.

MELEK I'm sure I will. I've **borrowed** some money from my parents, just in case.

KIM   That's lucky – that they're happy to **lend** you money, I mean.

MELEK Yes, they're great. You need to **remind** me about some of the things I shouldn't do in England.

KIM   You can **remember** what topics you shouldn't talk about when you meet people, can't you?

MELEK Yes, I know I should **avoid** talking about money, of course, and personal things like relationships. But weather's a good topic, right?

KIM   Yes, I'm afraid there's nothing you can do to **prevent** people talking about the weather. Just remember to agree when they complain!

MELEK Yes, and I must remember not to get too excited when I'm **discussing** things with people I don't know well or they'll think I'm angry!

KIM   Oh, I don't know about that. But don't **argue** loudly in the street – people hate that. Not that I can imagine you shouting at people!

MELEK Well, in Turkey it's quite normal, but I don't tend to raise my voice much; I only get cross with my family!

KIM   I suppose you're going to **miss** them?

MELEK Yes, it's going to be really hard not seeing them for months. But we'll talk on Skype most days, I expect. I'll have to buy a new mobile – you know I **lost** my phone the other day, don't you?

KIM   No! That's terrible. How did you lose it? …

2 Look at the verb forms in bold in the conversation in 1. Match verbs 1–12 to meanings a or b.

1 discuss	a	disagree with sb angrily
2 argue	b	talk about a subject with other people
3 borrow	a	give something to sb for a short time
4 lend	b	receive something from sb and give it back later
5 lose	a	no longer have sth
6 miss	b	feel sorry that sth or sb is not there
7 hope	a	think sth is likely to happen
8 expect	b	want sth to happen
9 remember	a	cause sb to remember sth
10 remind	b	keep a piece of information in your memory
11 avoid	a	keep away from sth
12 prevent	b	stop sth from happening

3 Choose the correct words.

1 When I *lend/* (*borrow*) a book from the library, I never *remember/remind* to take it back on time.
2 I try to *avoid/prevent* talking with my brother because we just end up *discussing/arguing*.
3 Melek is excited about working abroad, but she *expects/hopes* she will *lose/miss* her family.

4 a Fill in the gaps with the correct form of the verbs from 2.

1 What do you __hope__ to be doing in 10 years' time?
2 If you went to live abroad, what would you _____ from your country?
3 What's the best way to _____ misunderstandings when you're in another culture?
4 What _____ you of your childhood?
5 What's the best way to _____ teenage crime?
6 Would you _____ money to a friend in need?
7 When was the last time you _____ your keys?
8 Do you enjoy _____ politics?

b Answer the questions for yourself.

1b 1 Melek will find it difficult not seeing her family for months. 2 She'll communicate by Skype. 3 Money and relationships are not acceptable; the weather is acceptable. **2** 1b 2a 3b 4a 5a 6b 7b 8a 9b 10a 11a 12b **3** 1 remember 2 avoid; arguing 3 expects **4a** 1 miss 2 avoid 3 remind 4 reminds 5 prevent 6 lend 7 lost 8 discussing

7 ▶ Words from other languages

1 Match words 1–16 to pictures a–p.

> 1 cuisine [e] 2 marmalade ☐ 3 a siesta ☐ 4 kayaking ☐ 5 a chef ☐ 6 a ballerina ☐
> 7 a chauffeur ☐ 8 sushi ☐ 9 a futon ☐ 10 pyjamas ☐ 11 karate ☐ 12 a yacht ☐
> 13 a barbecue ☐ 14 a sauna ☐ 15 snorkelling ☐ 16 a delicatessen ☐

2 Complete the table with words from **1**.

sport	food	people	rest and relaxation
kayaking			

3 Guess which languages the words in **1** come from.

4 a Match the beginnings of these questions to the correct endings.

1 Do you usually buy cheese
2 What do you prefer on toast, jam
3 When you were a child, did you use to wear
4 Which country do you think has
5 Would you like to be driven round
6 When you go to the beach, do you ever go
7 Have you ever done
8 If you were a millionaire, would you
9 Would you like to work
10 Have you ever slept on a
11 Have you ever had a
12 Have you ever gone
13 What's your favourite food
14 Do you know anyone who wants to be a
15 Have you eaten Japanese food, such as
16 Do you ever have

a karate?
b snorkelling?
c buy a yacht?
d pyjamas?
e by a chauffeur?
f or marmalade?
g at a delicatessen?
h the best cuisine in the world?
i sushi?
j futon?
k a siesta after lunch?
l sauna?
m ballerina?
n kayaking down a river?
o to cook on the barbecue?
p as a chef?

b Answer the questions for yourself.

---

1 2l 3h 4c 5n 6a 7j 8p 9o 10g 11d 12k 13b 14f 15i 16m **2** *sport* karate; a yacht; snorkelling *food* cuisine; marmalade; sushi; a barbecue; a delicatessen *people* a chef; a ballerina; a chauffeur *rest and relaxation* a siesta; a futon; pyjamas; a sauna **3** 1 French 2 Portuguese 3 Spanish 4 Danish 5 French 6 Italian 7 French 8 Japanese 9 Japanese 10 Persian 11 Japanese 12 Norwegian 13 American Spanish 14 Finnish 15 German 16 German **4a** 2f 3d 4h 5e 6b 7a 8c 9p 10j 11l 12n 13o 14m 15i 16k

⟨ Instructions p191 ⟩

8 ▸ British and American English

1 Match British English words 1–14 to American English words a–n.

1	a (bank)note	a	a parking lot
2	a chemist's	b	a line
3	a tap	c	a vest
4	a bank holiday	d	an apartment building
5	the pavement	e	a cell phone
6	the motorway	f	the freeway
7	a waistcoat	g	a drugstore
8	a torch	h	a yard
9	a queue	i	a national holiday
10	the underground	j	a faucet
11	a car park	k	the sidewalk
12	a mobile phone	l	a bill
13	a block of flats	m	the subway
14	a garden	n	a flashlight

2 Read conversations 1 and 2. Are the people speaking British or American English?

1

BEN Hey, Jon! Where are you? The show starts in half an hour.

JON Sorry. I meant to get there earlier, but I'm caught in traffic on the freeway.

BEN Why didn't you take the subway? Anyway, give me a call when you get here.

2

SAM Jen? Our block of flats has had a power cut!

JEN Really? Are you OK?

SAM Yeah, I'm fine. I've got a torch in one hand, and my mobile in the other. But I can't cook! Could I come round for something to eat?

3 Read conversations 3 and 4 between the same people. Fill in the gaps using British or American English words from 1.

3

JON Hi Ben, it's me again. I'm on my way, but I just need to get some change for the parking meter as all I've got is a $100 ¹_____ . There weren't any spaces in the ²_____ .

BEN No surprises there. It is a ³_____ after all, and nobody's at work. I'm just in a long ⁴_____ in the ⁵_____ opposite the theatre picking up some pills.

JON OK, I'll meet you outside the theatre in five minutes. See you soon.

4

SAM You know, I've never experienced a power cut, not at home anyway. There was that one time on the ⁶_____ when all the trains just stopped. Everyone had to get out of the station and the police told us to wait in a ⁷_____ on the ⁸_____ until we could go down again.

JEN I remember one time when I was living on the 10th floor of a ⁹_____ and when we had a power cut, all I could hear was the sound of the kitchen ¹⁰_____ dripping. I was terrified!

4 a Rewrite these questions using British English.

tap

1 Do you usually drink water from the ~~faucet~~ at home?

2 Which famous people are printed on the bills in your country?

3 Do cyclists ride on the sidewalk in your country?

4 How many national holidays does your country have?

5 Do you enjoy driving on the freeway?

6 How do you feel about people who go straight to the front of a line?

7 Do you live in an apartment building?

8 How often do you use your cell phone?

9 Does anybody in your family wear a vest?

10 Do you ever take a flashlight when you go out at night?

b Answer the questions for yourself.

VOCABULARY PLUS: Photocopiable

1 Read the article. Why do you think Caine Monroy's penny arcade has been so successful?

Hollywood queues for boy's penny arcade

When a nine-year-old boy, Caine Monroy, built a [1]**games arcade** out of [2]**cardboard boxes**, [3]**sticky tape** and used [4]**car parts**, he hoped to charge his friends a few pennies to play [5]**table football** or [6]**miniature basketball**.

Instead, the arcade in his father's Los Angeles [7]**scrapyard** has inspired a craze for old-fashioned games and Hollywood agents are queuing up for the attention of its gap-toothed designer.

Few of Caine's friends thought much of his cardboard [8]**'fun park'** until last

month, when an 11-minute film called *Caine's Arcade* became an [9]**Internet hit**. It has now been viewed by almost ten million people.

The film was shot by Nirvan Mullick, a [10]**documentary maker** who discovered the arcade while shopping for a car part. Mullick organised a 'flashmob' of supporters who turned up on a Sunday afternoon to cheer on the boy and be [11]**film extras**. Mullick has set up a $25,000 fund for Caine's [12]**college fees**. Since then the arcade has been full of

customers, some travelling hundreds of miles so their children can spend a few minutes at play. A Hollywood agent said last week: "All the studios want to turn this into a film, like an *Alice in Wonderland* fantasy." As for Caine, he has ambitions: "It's cool that I have customers now, but ... next time I'm going to use bigger boxes."

2 Match the compound nouns 1–12 in **1** to definitions a–l.

a a short film which millions have watched online __9__

b non-actors who appear in films, often in crowd scenes _____

c a small-scale version of football in which two players control the players and the ball _____

d money to pay for higher education _____

e a person who makes factual films _____

f a fairground, with rides _____

g containers to store or transport objects _____

h an area full of games machines, usually indoors _____

i adhesive or glue on a roll used to join two surfaces together, such as paper _____

j an area used for unwanted possessions, such as cars _____

k a small-scale version of basketball _____

l items you buy to replace old items for your vehicle _____

3 Fill in the gaps with compound nouns.

1 It's great being a ___film extra___ . You stand around a lot, but it's fun watching all the actors.

2 I need to wrap this present. Have we got any _____ ?

3 We need to pack up these books. Can you ask the shop if they have any _____ ?

4 I don't see the attraction of _____ . People waste so much money on the machines.

5 I'm going to take my son to a _____ as soon as he's old enough to enjoy the rides.

6 My car mechanic buys old _____ from _____ and repairs cars really cheaply.

7 When I have nothing else to do, I watch the most popular _____ . They're usually hilarious.

8 I stopped studying at 18. Unfortunately, my family couldn't afford to pay _____ .

4 **a** Fill in the gaps with the second part of the compound nouns.

1 Do you enjoy watching Internet _____ with your friends?

2 How many different car _____ can you name?

3 Have you ever played table _____ or miniature _____ ? Did you enjoy it?

4 Would you like to get work as a film _____ ? Why?

5 When was the last time you went to a fun _____ or a games _____ ? What's your opinion of these forms of entertainment?

b Answer the questions for yourself.

---

2 b11 c5 d12 e10 f8 g2 h1 i3 j7 k6 l4 **3** 1 hits 2 parts 3 football; basketball 4 extra 5 park; arcade
7 Internet hits 8 college fees **4a** 1 hits 2 parts 3 football; basketball 4 extra 5 park; arcade

10 ▸ Nouns from phrasal verbs

1 Read the newspaper article. Why are the nurses angry? What might happen in the future?

ANGRY NURSES FUEL FLU EPIDEMIC FEARS

THERE WAS a ¹**setback** yesterday in the pay dispute when representatives of the nursing union staged a ²**walkout** during talks with the local health authority. Amanda Teale, spokesperson for the union, said that the ³**breakdown** in the talks was due to the local authority's refusal to accept that the nurses are underpaid. "Nurses have never been well off," Ms Teale said. "They've had to work longer hours since the ⁴**cutback** in staff last year. The authority's attitude is a serious ⁵**letdown** for all the nurses."

The health authority has always maintained that it cannot afford pay rises as it is already deeply in debt after the ⁶**break-up** of the area into smaller districts four years ago. "Unless there's a ⁷**breakthrough** soon, we'll have to consider going on strike," warned Ms Teale. "However, we're optimistic that there will be a ⁸**turnaround** in the authority's attitude."

The ⁹**fallout** from any strike will be far-reaching, as the region prepares itself for the ¹⁰**outbreak** of flu. Doctors expecting a rush in the ¹¹**uptake** of vaccinations say that patients wanting a routine ¹²**check-up** will have to wait much longer than usual if the nurses do go on strike.

2 Match words 1–12 in the article to definitions a–l.

a the failure of a discussion, relationship or plan ___3___

b a complete change in opinion or attitude _____

c something that delays or stops something else happening _____

d the rate of accepting something _____

e separation into different pieces _____

f an important development or discovery which solves a problem _____

g when people leave somewhere in protest _____

h a disappointment _____

i a reduction of something in order to save money _____

j the sudden beginning of something dangerous or unpleasant _____

k the unpleasant results of an action or event _____

l an examination by a doctor to make sure you are healthy _____

3 Choose the correct word.

1 That new film was a bit of a (letdown)/cutback.

2 My car is really reliable. I've never had a *breakdown/break-up*.

3 Doctors claim to have made *an uptake/a breakthrough* in the fight against lung cancer.

4 The success of the latest product has led to a big *turnaround/setback* in sales recently.

5 Political *fallout/check-up* is expected today after the deputy leader's resignation last night.

6 Employers fear that employees will stage a *walkout/uptake* if pay is reduced any further.

4 a Fill in the gaps with these words.

> ~~break-ups~~ outbreak cutback
> check-up setback

1 Does the media in your country pay too much attention to celebrity _break-ups_ ?

2 When was the last time you had a medical _____ ?

3 If you had to make a _____ in your spending, what would you give up?

4 When was the last time there was an _____ of disease in your country?

5 Have you ever suffered a _____ in your plans? If so, what did you do?

b Answer the questions for yourself.

1 The local health authority is refusing to give the nurses a pay rise. The nurses might go on strike. **2** b8 c1 d11 e6 f7 g2 h5 i4 j10 k9 l12 **3** 2 breakdown 3 a breakthrough 4 turnaround 5 fallout 6 walkout **4a** 2 check-up 3 cutback 4 outbreak 5 setback

Instructions p192   © Cambridge University Press 2012   face2face Second edition Upper Intermediate Photocopiable   **203**

11 ▸ Stress on nouns/verbs

1 Read these sentences. Tick the ones which are shown in pictures A–D.

1 The **conflict** between the two managers has led to a **decrease** in sales.
2 There was an **upset** in the stock market today when the number of **exports** in the last quarter was announced.
3 Due to cheaper **imports**, the country no longer needs to **produce** so much rice.
4 A&S Ltd. is going to **record** the ceremony, so that all their employees can watch the mayor **present** the chief executive with the Best New Business award.
5 The business **permits** trainees to wear what they like so they have no reason to **rebel** against company policy.
6 The police **suspect** that key evidence in the fraud case was left on public **transport**.
7 The **increase** in mobile phone contracts **contrasts** with the reduction in the number of people who use 'pay as you go'.

2 **a** Look at the words in bold in **1**. Which words are nouns and which words are verbs?

b Complete the rules with *nouns* or *verbs*.

1 Two-syllable _____ are usually stressed on the second syllable.
2 Two-syllable _____ are usually stressed on the first syllable.

3 Look at these words. Which are nouns and which are verbs?

1 rebel *n*   6 present   11 upset
2 permit   7 suspect   12 export
3 produce   8 transport   13 decrease
4 conflict   9 increase   14 import
5 record   10 contrast

4 **a** Fill in the gaps with the correct form of the words from **1** and **3**. Then mark the stress on each of these words.

1 How often do your views ___conflict___ with those of your colleagues or friends?
2 If you _____ a colleague or friend of dishonesty, what would you do?
3 How do you keep a _____ of your email correspondence?
4 Do you use public _____ to get to where you work or study? Why? / Why not?
5 Do you think the cost of living has _____ or _____ over the last few years in your country?
6 What does your country mainly _____ to other countries? What does it need to _____?
7 Have you ever applied for a special _____ to do something?
8 Would it _____ you if no one gave you a birthday _____?
9 Do you ever buy fresh _____ directly from a farmer?
10 Did you ever _____ when you were a teenager?
11 Do you like wearing bright colours that _____ with each other?

b Answer the questions for yourself.

---

1 A4 B1 C6 D5 **2a** 1 noun; noun 2 noun; noun 3 noun; verb 4 verb; verb 5 verbs; verb 6 verb; noun 7 noun; verb **2b** 1 verbs
2 nouns **3** 2 noun 3 noun 4 verb 5 noun 6 noun 7 noun 8 verb 9 verb 10 noun 11 verb 12 verb 13 verb 14 verb
4a 2 suspected 3 record 4 transport 5 increased; decreased 6 export; import 7 permit 8 upset; present 9 produce 10 rebel
11 contrast

VOCABULARY PLUS: Photocopiable

Horoscopes

VOCABULARY PLUS:
Photocopiable

Taurus (21 April–21 May)

Last month was a good month for Taureans romantically. You may **¹be on top of the world** right now, but you probably shouldn't **²get carried away** by your feelings. After a month of joy, you can expect to **³have a rough time** as you adjust to new realities. Remember to **⁴keep an eye on** your personal values, and if a new relationship is going to **⁵stand a chance** of lasting, it means you should be honest with yourself as well as your partner.

Gemini (22 May–21 June)

Geminis **⁶are** often **in two minds** when it comes to making decisions, and next month you'll be forced to make a couple of really big ones at work. Now is the time to **⁷get your act together**. If you delay you could **⁸miss the boat** and it would **⁹serve you right** for being so indecisive about a wonderful business opportunity. Be bold, and your colleagues will **¹⁰be thrilled to bits** by the success that you bring.

1 Read the horoscopes. Who will have the best month, Geminis or Taureans?

2 Match idioms 1–10 in **1** with definitions a–j.

a be extremely happy or healthy _1_

b be uncertain what to do ___

c be your own fault when something bad happens ___

d be too late to take an opportunity ___

e feel extremely pleased by the success of something

f watch or look after something or somebody ___

g start organising yourself so that you can be more effective ___

h become so excited that you find it hard to control what you say or do ___

i have an unpleasant period of time ___

j have a possibility ___

3 **a** Choose the correct idiom.

1 Are you *thrilled to bits*/*having a rough time* when someone says you look like a film star?

2 When was the last time you *served you right/ were on top of the world*?

3 When was the last time you *got carried away/ got your act together* and spent too much money?

4 If you *are in two minds/are on top of the world* about something, how do you decide?

5 Have you ever failed to *get your act together/ be on top of the world* in time to grab an opportunity and *stood a chance/missed the boat*?

6 Do you *keep an eye on/get carried away* by your bank account to avoid identity theft?

7 When you are *standing a chance/having a rough time*, who do you talk to?

8 Does your country *serve you right/stand a chance* of winning the next football World Cup?

9 Have you ever had to pay a fine? Did it *serve you right/keep an eye on you*?

b Answer the questions for yourself.

Extra Reading

Instructions

There are 12 Extra Reading worksheets (p213–p224). The aim of these worksheets is to provide extra reading practice of a variety of text types. The topic of each Extra Reading worksheet is linked to the topic of the corresponding unit of the Student's Book. There is an answer key at the bottom of each worksheet, which can be cut off if necessary. You will need to photocopy one Extra Reading worksheet for each student.

Use these worksheets as extra reading input in class. These instructions give additional communicative stages, background notes and other activities that you can include in each lesson. If you are using the worksheets in class, we suggest you cut off the answer keys and check the answers after each exercise.

Give these worksheets for homework for students to do on their own. You can either leave the answer keys on the worksheets so students can check answers themselves, or cut them off and check answers at the beginning of the next class. If you are checking the answers in the next class, you can also ask students to talk about the discussion questions at the beginning and end of each worksheet in pairs or groups.

1 ▶ The secrets of language p213

Genre and topic

A newspaper article about reasons for language diversity and survival.

When to use and time

Any time after lesson 1A. 20–25 minutes.

Procedure

1 Students answer the questions in pairs or groups. If you have a multilingual class, ask students from different countries to work together. Ask a few students to share their information with the class. If students are not studying in their own country, find out what they know about the country they are studying in.

2 a Focus students on the map and label and ask a few questions to check understanding, for example, *How many people live in Papua New Guinea? How many languages are spoken there?* Elicit the meaning of *linguistic diversity* (a wide range of languages) and *equator*. Students do the exercise in pairs.

Ask students to share any reasons they can think of, but don't ask them to comment on any of their ideas at this point.

b Students read the article then compare their ideas in pairs. Check answers with the class.

3 Students work in pairs and cover the article. Encourage them to discuss what the figures refer to from memory. After a few minutes, tell them to scan the article again to check their ideas. Check students are able to say the large numbers correctly and confidently.

4 Students discuss the questions in groups or as a class. If you have a multilingual class, ask students from different countries to work together. Ask a few students to share their opinions with the class.

> ### ⟨ EXTRA IDEAS ⟩
>
> - Write the word *evolution* on the board and elicit the meaning (history of (human) development) and word stress. Students scan the first paragraph of the article to find different forms of the word and identify the parts of speech. Check word stress in each form of the word.
>
>   > *evolved* = past verb form;
>   > *evolutionary* = adjective
>
> - Explain that the repetition of words and ideas through a long text helps to make it coherent. Give *evolution* as an example, then ask students which word is repeated most throughout the text (*language*). Students underline all the examples and forms of *language* they can find in the first three paragraphs, including pronouns. Check answers by asking how many references they have found, and what the pronouns refer to specifically.
>
>   > Para1: 3 (+ ellipsis = *more (languages)*)
>   > Para2: 5 (including *linguistic* and pronoun *they* = new languages)
>   > Para3: 8 (including *linguistic* and pronouns: *They use it* and *it's a way*; + ellipsis = *develops its own (language)*)

2 ▶ Supercentenarians p214

Genre and topic

Internet article about the diet and habits of the oldest people in the world.

When to use and time

Any time after lesson 2A. 25–30 minutes.

Procedure

1 Students discuss the questions in pairs or groups. Find out who knows the oldest people and encourage students to share information about them with the class.

2 **a** Students do the exercise on their own then compare answers in pairs. Encourage students to give reasons for their answers. Check students understand *full* in this context (when you can't eat any more) and *rubbed* (massaged with the fingers). Don't check answers at this stage.

b Students do the exercise on their own. Give them a time limit of about three minutes, then tell them to compare answers in pairs. Check answers with the class and ask a few students to give their opinions.

3 **a** Students do the exercise on their own or in pairs. Encourage them to scan the text, using the context to match words in the text with the definitions given. Check answers with the class, paying particular attention to the pronunciation of *longevity* /lɒnˈdʒevəti/, *centenarian* /sentɪnˈeəriən/ and *vastly* /ˈvɑːstli/.

b Check students understand *adventurous*, *disciplined* and *conscientious*. Students do the exercise in pairs. Ask students to give reasons for their answers, especially if there is disagreement among students.

4 Students discuss the questions in groups or have a class discussion. Students will probably be interested to know that at the time of writing, Jeanne Calment was the oldest woman to have lived, and Walter Breuning, the oldest man.

> **EXTRA IDEAS**
>
> • For homework, students write a paragraph about the oldest person (or any interesting old person) that they know, saying what they know about their life, habits and character. Students can swap texts in the next lesson or you can put them on the walls so students can read each other's.
>
> • Alternatively, students do research to find out who is the oldest living man or woman in their country. They should find out what they can about the person's habits and character, take notes and report back to the class in the next lesson.

3 ▶ Hacked! p215

Genre and topic

A magazine article about email hacking containing email correspondence.

When to use and time

Any time after lesson 3C. 25–30 minutes.

Procedure

1 Ask students if anyone knows of someone whose email account has been hacked and encourage them to give details to the class. If no one has a story, either give an example of your own or check understanding of what hacking involves before moving on to the hypothetical question. Students do the activity in pairs.

2 Check students understand *sheer (frustration)* (= total) and *scam* (= a trick to get money from people). Students read the article. Set a time limit of three minutes to encourage skim reading. Students answer the questions in pairs. Check answers with the class.

3 Students do the exercise on their own or in pairs. Check answers with the class.

4 Students discuss the questions in groups. Ask students to share interesting opinions with the class.

> **EXTRA IDEAS**
>
> • In pairs, students brainstorm a list of the things you can do to avoid hacking and other forms of identity theft. Compare ideas as a class and find out how many students follow the advice. (Examples: use different passwords for different accounts; include letters and numbers in your passwords; don't tell anyone your password or write it down; shred receipts with credit or debit card details, etc.)
>
> • For homework, students respond to the hacker's email request for £500 (students should convert the sum to their own currency). Students can read each other's email responses in the next lesson and compare them with their own. You need to use your judgement as to whether this would work with your class!

4 ▶ Strange but true p216

Genre and topic

Short tabloid newspaper stories about strange or amusing news events around the world.

When to use and time

Any time after lesson 4A. 25–30 minutes.

Procedure

1 You could set the context by asking students if and how they find out about news events (for example, the Internet, radio, TV or newspapers). If possible, tell students about an interesting or amusing story you've heard in the news recently, then ask students to share any news events they have heard about with the class.

2 **a** Focus students on the cartoons of the six stories. In groups, students predict what happened. Ask students to share their ideas with the class, but don't comment on their ideas at this stage.

b Students do the activity in pairs, then check their answers with another pair. Ask students to share the answers with the class and find out who predicted any of the stories correctly.

c Do the first item as an example. Students work in pairs and guess the meaning of the words and phrases from context. Check understanding and pronunciation as a class.

3 Point out that there are two or three answers for each question. Students read the stories again in detail and compare answers in pairs. Check as a class.

4 Students discuss their responses to the stories in groups. Ask students to share interesting information with the class.

> ⌐**EXTRA IDEAS**⌐
>
> • Students work in pairs. Tell them to cover the stories and focus on the pictures. Students take turns to retell one or two stories each, using only the pictures as prompts, helping each other where necessary. Encourage them to use as much new vocabulary as they can.
> • For homework, students find the short news stories in a free English-language daily paper if available or on the Internet. They should choose two or three interesting stories, take notes and check one or two items of vocabulary. Students share their stories as a warmer in the next class.

5 ▶ Clever animals p217

Genre and topic

Two magazine articles about clever animals.

When to use and time

Any time after lesson 5A. 30–35 minutes.

Procedure

1 Students discuss the questions in pairs or groups. If you have a multilingual class, ask students from different countries to work together. Ask a few students to share their information with the class. If students are not studying in their own country, find out what they know about people's attitudes to animals in the country they are studying in.

2 **a** Students work in the same pairs or groups. Focus on the two pictures and titles. Students guess what the animals can do. Ask students to share ideas with the class, but don't comment on their ideas yet.

b Set a time limit of three or four minutes to read both articles quickly. Check understanding of key words, for example *interpret, exceptional, drills, 'pretty' close, mimic, abstract* and *interaction.* Students check their answers, then discuss the question in pairs. Find out who thinks the dog is more intelligent, who thinks the bird is more intelligent, and why.

3 Point out that the questions refer to both articles. Students discuss the questions together before going back to the article to read in more detail. Students check answers in pairs. Check answers with the class.

4 Students do the activity in groups. Encourage students to give reasons for their opinions and to think of other examples of animal stories they have heard about or experiences they have had of animals themselves. Students share their opinions with the class. Extend this into a classroom discussion if students have strong opinions.

> ⌐**EXTRA IDEAS**⌐
>
> • Do **2b** (and **3** if you wish) as a jigsaw reading. Students work in pairs, with Student As reading about Chaser, and Student Bs reading about Alex to check their predictions. After reading, students work in A/B pairs and tell each other about the two animals' abilities. They then discuss which animal is more intelligent. Students discuss the answers to **3** in pairs, providing information for their own text, or they can read both articles for this stage.
> • There are a number of videos online of Chaser and Alex the Parrot. You could raise interest in the topic by showing clips from the videos at the beginning of the class and highlighting key vocabulary before students read the articles. Alternatively, show the videos after **3,** then ask students to discuss the question in **4**.

6 ▶ Tattoo p218

Genre and topic
A website covering different aspects of tattooing.

When to use and time
Any time after lesson 6C. 20–25 minutes.

Procedure

1 Students discuss the question in pairs or groups. Ask a few students to share their ideas with the class.

2 Ask students where they could find this text (on the Internet). Focus on the home page and the links by asking what information they could find in the website. Students do the exercise on their own, then compare answers in pairs. Check answers with the class.

3 Focus on the multiple-choice questions. Point out that there is only one correct answer. Students underline the relevant section of text for each question, then read the text again. Students do the activity on their own then compare answers in pairs. Check answers with the class, paying attention to the pronunciation of the character adjectives in question 5, and checking students remember the meanings.

4 Students discuss their attitudes in groups. If you have a multilingual class, ask students from different countries to work together. Ask a few students to share their information with the class. If students are not studying in their own country, find out what they know about attitudes to tattoos where they are studying.

> **EXTRA IDEAS**
>
> • Students imagine that a friend wants a tattoo and has asked for advice. In pairs, students decide what advice to give. Students work in new pairs and role play the situation, or if this is not appropriate for your class, students can compare their advice. For homework, tell students to look on one of the many websites about tattooing and compare their advice with the website. (Possible advice: research tattoo providers carefully for hygiene and professional service. Think carefully before getting a tattoo and take time to choose a design that won't date. Choose the place carefully to avoid issues when working or travelling in the future.)
>
> • If students are studying in another country, ask students to interview people they know of different ages to find out their attitudes towards tattooing. They can report back in the next class.

7 ▶ Robot baby p219

Genre and topic
An Internet article with postings about a robot baby designed to be helpful to the elderly.

When to use and time
Use any time after lesson 7C. 25-30 minutes.

Procedure

1 Students discuss the question in groups. If you have a multilingual class, ask students from different countries to work together. Ask several students to share information with the class. Make sure students are familiar with the idea of an 'old people's home', common in western countries and mentioned in one of the postings. This discussion will also give you an indication of how students will react to the article.

2 **a** Focus students on the photo and the title. Students predict what the baby can do in pairs. *Alternatively*, collect ideas from the class and put them on the board.

b Ask students where they would find an article followed by comments (on the Internet). Students read the article – but not the comments at this stage – then compare ideas about what Babyloid can do in pairs. Check answers with the class.

c Students read the three opening sentences taken from the comments below the article. They then read the comments and do the exercise on their own before comparing with a partner. If students disagree, tell them to decide which sentences are positive (3), neutral (1) and negative (2) and to find matching attitudes in the comments.
To help students, ask what *them* refers to in the first sentence of A (the elderly) and ask which of the missing sentences 1–3 cannot go first (3, because it is responding to another comment).

3 Students do the activity on their own or in pairs. Check answers with the class.

4 Give students a few minutes to prepare their responses alone. They work in groups to share their ideas. Find out how many students are positive, neutral and negative about Babyloid and encourage several students to give reasons for their opinions.

> **EXTRA IDEA**
>
> • If you have time, give students five to ten minutes to write their own postings in response to the article. Collect them in and redistribute the comments to different students. Students guess who wrote the comment, then check by asking that student some questions about their attitude to Babyloid. Depending on your class, this may set off some lively debate. Alternatively, students can write their comments for homework and read each other's in the next lesson.

8 ▸ Family fortunes p220

Genre and topic
A newspaper article about making money from funny family videos online.

When to use and time
Use any time after lesson 8B. 20–25 minutes.

Procedure

1 Do the activity as a class to find out what experience the students have of this popular pastime and what their attitude to it might be.

> **EXTRA IDEA**
>
> • If any of these videos, or similar ones, are available to view and you have access to the Internet, play one or two at the beginning of the class to raise interest in the topic and generate discussion material for **1** and **4**.

2 **a** Students read the article on their own, then work in pairs and discuss the meanings of the words in bold. Check understanding, paying particular attention to the pronunciation of *phenomenon* /fən'ɒmənən/ and *anaesthetic* /ænəs'θetik/.

b Remind students that they need to find evidence for the correct option in the text, so they will need to re-read relevant sections of the article carefully. Students do the activity in pairs. Check answers with the class.

3 Students do the exercise on their own, then compare answers in pairs. Check answers with the class.

4 Find out if any students have experience of uploading videos to a website and put them in different groups to discuss the question. Ask several students to share their opinions with the class.

> **EXTRA IDEA**
>
> • For homework, students can look for further funny family videos on the Internet. Encourage them to find English-speaking examples. They can then share the links with the class in the next lesson.

9 ▸ Street performers p221

Genre and topic
A blog interview about a life of street performing.

When to use and time
Use any time after lesson 9C. 15–20 minutes.

Procedure

1 Focus students on the blog and the photos. Check students understand *busking* (performing outside for money). Students discuss the questions in groups. Ask students to share interesting information with the class. Find out what the situation is as regards street performances in students' countries, i.e. are they accepted or illegal, how are the performers regarded, do people give money generously, etc.?

2 Students read the interview and do the exercise on their own, then discuss the answer in pairs. Point out that the question focuses on global understanding. Check students understand *spectacular* /spek'tækjələ/ (= an impressive performance), *hooked* (on sth) (= so attracted to sth that you want to keep doing it) and *steady job* (= stable, regular). Check answers with the class.

3 Remind students that there is no evidence in the text for a 'not given' statement and that 'false' statements contradict the text. Students read through the questions and discuss the answers with a partner, before going back to re-read relevant sections of the interview. Check understanding of *pointless* (= not worth doing). Check answers with the class.

4 Students discuss the questions in pairs or groups. Ask several students to share their ideas with the class.

> **EXTRA IDEAS**
>
> • Tell students to read through the interview once more. Students then cover the page and act out the interview in groups of three. The focus should not be on an exact reproduction of the text, but on capturing the purpose of the interviewer's questions, the gist of the responses, and on the pronunciation and fluency of the interaction.
>
> • Depending on where the students are studying, tell them to go out and interview one or more street performers to find out more about what they do and why. They can film the interviews or parts of the show on their cameras to make it more interesting, then report back to the class in a future lesson.

10 ▶ Changing times p222

Genre and topic

A newspaper article about the changing roles of men and women.

When to use and time

Use any time after lesson 10C. 20–25 minutes.

Procedure

1 Focus students on the pictures and open the discussion by asking how much time they spend doing the laundry. Students then discuss the questions in pairs or groups. In mixed classes, make sure you have men and women in each pair or group. Ask students to share interesting information with the class.

2 Students do the exercise on their own (as honestly as they can), before comparing with a partner. Find out how many students disagree with each other, but do not comment on their answers at this stage. Students then read the article to check their ideas.

3 **a** Tell students to read the sentences before going back to the article. Encourage them to underline the relevant information in the article as they read. This is good practice and will help them with the next exercise. Students compare answers with a partner, but do not check answers at this stage.

b Students do the exercise on their own or in pairs. Check answers for **3a** and **3b** with the class.

4 Students discuss the questions in groups. Ask students to share interesting information with the class.

┌─ **EXTRA IDEAS** ─────────────────────┐

- If students are not studying in their own country, or you have a multicultural classroom, this is a good opportunity to focus on cultural similarities and differences as regards roles of men and women at home and at work. Give students some time to note down the amount of time they and people they know spend on tasks focused on in the article. They can then compare the results in mixed groups with students from different countries. This will work better with more mature students.
- For homework, students conduct their own survey by interviewing people they know or other students to find out how much time they spend on the tasks focused on in the article. Students report back in the next class and see whether the results corroborate the above research or not.

└───────────────────────────────────────┘

11 ▶ Rags to riches p223

Genre and topic

A newspaper article about a Polish pianist's rise from cleaner to concert pianist.

When to use and time

Use any time after lesson 11A. 20–25 minutes.

Procedure

1 Students discuss the questions in groups. Ask students to share interesting information with the class. Find out how many students regularly go to concerts and what kind of music they like.

2 **a** Set a time limit of three minutes for students to read the article. Point out that the exercise requires students to order the events according to the article, not chronologically. Students do the exercise in pairs. Check answers as a class, but suggest non-Eastern European students replace *Kudajczyk* with *he* or it will take a long time! *Chopin* is pronounced /ˈʃəʊpæn/.

b Students scan the relevant paragraphs to find synonyms for the words. Pay particular attention to the pronunciation of *virtuoso* /vɜːtʃuˈəʊzəʊ/ and *enthralling* /ɪnˈθrɔːlɪŋ/.

3 Point out the options at the end of the six paragraphs and check students understand what to do. Students re-read the relevant paragraphs and do the exercise on their own before comparing with a partner. If students find this difficult, focus them on the context in the preceding paragraph.

4 Students discuss the questions in pairs. Ask one or two students to share their ideas with the class and find out if everyone agrees on the part luck played in the story.

┌─ **EXTRA IDEAS** ─────────────────────┐

- After **3**, tell students to cover the article and re-tell the story in pairs from the summary of events in **2**, adding as many details as they can remember. They should use the new vocabulary from the article, using the synonyms in **2b** as prompts.
- For homework, ask students to think of (and research if necessary) any other 'rags to riches' stories about people from their own countries. They can make notes about the person and report back in the next lesson. Alternatively, they can write an article about the person, using the Kudajczyk text as a model. Students can read each other's articles in the next lesson, or you can put them on the walls for students to read in their own time.

└───────────────────────────────────────┘

12 ▶ Inheritance p224

Genre and topic
Short magazine articles about unusual inheritances.

When to use and time
Use any time after lesson 12B. 25–30 minutes.

Procedure

1 Students discuss the questions in groups. Ask students to share information with the class.

2 **a** Focus students on the four pictures. Put students into pairs or small groups to predict who the money was left to. Find out different students' ideas for each story but do not comment on their ideas at this stage.

b Set a time limit of about four minutes for students to read the stories for gist. Students do the exercise on their own before comparing ideas with a partner. Check answers with the class.

c Students do the exercise on their own.

3 Focus students on the questions to check understanding and point out that there is more than one answer to two of the questions (4 and 7). Students discuss the questions in pairs before reading the text again in more detail to check their ideas. Check answers with the class, asking students to refer to the relevant sections of text if there are any queries about the answers.

4 Ask students if they know about any famous wealthy people who have refused to support their children financially or have given away most of their wealth to charities (for example, Bill Gates). Either continue to discuss the topic as a class, or students discuss in small groups. If you have a multilingual class, put students from different countries together. Find out if students have similar or different attitudes to each other.

> **EXTRA IDEAS**
> - Do **2b** as a jigsaw reading, with four students reading one article each, or two students reading two articles each. Students do the matching on their own, then retell their stories to their partners. Students can do **3** in the same way, providing information to their partners about the texts they have read.
> - As a follow up, students role play an interview between a lawyer and one of Luis Carlos's beneficiaries. Give students time to prepare their roles in pairs, referring to the text and their imaginations to provide details. They then swap pairs to role play the conversation. While students are working, monitor and take notes of language they use.

1 ▸ The secrets of language

1 How many languages are spoken in your country? How many languages do you speak?

2 **a** According to the map, in which countries or parts of the world are the most languages spoken? Can you think of any reasons for this?

b Read the article and complete the table.

Papua New Guinea	_____ languages	reasons for large number: 1 _____ 2 _____
the world	_____ languages	reasons for decline: 1 _____ 2 _____

3 Read the article again. Are these sentences true (T), false (F) or not given (NG)?

1 Scientists believe that about 500,000 languages are spoken in the world. *F*

2 People have probably been using language for nearly 200,000 years.

3 Most of the languages in Papua New Guinea are spoken inland.

4 A good climate means tribes do not need to communicate with other tribes in different places.

5 Language helps to identify tribal boundaries.

6 Languages spoken in warmer climates tend to use more consonants than vowels.

7 The remaining languages spoken by small groups are likely to die out in the future.

8 Pagel believes some languages are more effective than others.

4 Do you agree with Pagel that languages survive because they are 'lucky'? Can you think of other reasons why some languages are widely used? Which languages in the world today do you think are the most widely used and why?

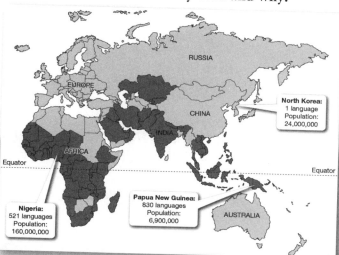

North Korea:
1 language
Population:
24,000,000

Nigeria:
521 languages
Population:
160,000,000

Papua New Guinea:
830 languages
Population:
6,900,000

Unlocking the secrets of language

It is one of the great puzzles of evolution but scientists are finally beginning to unlock the secrets of language. New research suggests that as many as 500,000 languages have lived and died since modern humans first evolved. Professor Mark Pagel, an evolutionary biologist, said: "It's reasonable to think we may have started speaking 160,000 to 200,000 years ago because that's when modern humans evolved. In that time about 500,000 languages will have developed – but there may have been many more."

The most surprising linguistic place is Papua New Guinea, which has 830 languages, making it home to one in eight of all the world's languages. "It's truly extraordinary," said Pagel. "There are places in the coastal regions of Papua New Guinea where you can find a new language spoken every couple of miles. I once met a Papuan man and I said to him, 'This can't possibly be true,' and he said to me, 'Oh no, it's not – they're far closer together than that.'"

One explanation suggested by scientists for this linguistic diversity is the climate, which makes it easy for small groups to grow their own food and survive. This means that more languages are successful as each tribe develops its own. "Tribal groups use language to mark their territories," said Pagel. "They use it to broadcast and advertise their identities – and to distinguish themselves from others. It's a way of drawing boundaries. Each language shows who is a member of the group and who isn't." For this reason about 60% of the world's languages are now found across equatorial Africa and the Pacific islands.

Climate also influences the way in which sound is used in language. According to Robert Munroe, an anthropologist, people in warmer countries use sounds that help them communicate outdoors such as vowels, which are easier to hear at a distance than consonants.

With around 7,000 languages currently in existence across the globe, there are fewer languages than ever before in history, with only about 20 languages covering almost the entire population of the world. The remainder are spoken by tribal groups of usually only a few thousand.

"Languages die out for political and geographical reasons," said Pagel. "Some languages just by accident get linked to successful societies and they drive those languages. Every language on Earth is equally good at being a human language. There are no languages that are superior to others. There are just lucky ones."

2 ▶ Supercentenarians

1 Who is the oldest person you know? What do you know about their life and character?

2 **a** Do you agree with the following statements?

1 There's no point in worrying about things you can't change.
2 You should stop eating before you are full.
3 A few cigarettes a day can help deal with stress.
4 People who deal well with stress live longer.
5 People should work for as long as they can.
6 Olive oil rubbed into the skin keeps you looking younger.
7 Men tend to live longer than women.

b Which statements in **2a** are true according to people in the text? Whose opinions are they?

> the writer   Jeanne Calment   Jean-Marie Robine
> Walter Breuning   Tom Perls

3 **a** Read the article again. Match the words in bold with these meanings.

1 old word for a record player _____
2 a great deal _____
3 a sudden illness which affects the brain and can cause death or paralysis _____
4 not affected by something _____
5 people who are over 100 _____
6 long life _____
7 missing, not taking part in _____
8 one of several things that cause or influence something _____

b Which three adjectives best describe Jeanne Calment or Walter Breuning?

> serious   adventurous   relaxed   disciplined
> independent   anxious   physically fit   conscientious

4 What can you learn from the people in the article? Whose lifestyle appeals to you most?

Supercentenarians: what can we learn from the oldest people in the world?

We are living longer than ever before. There are said to be about 75 people living (mostly women) who are 110 or older. Most of these people – known as supercentenarians – live in Japan, France, Italy, Britain and the USA.

Jeanne Calment (1875–1997) was born before the invention of the light bulb, the **phonograph**, the aeroplane and the automobile. She lived to the age of 122 in Arles, France, staying there her entire life. She ate more than two pounds of chocolate a week, drank port wine and rode a bicycle until she was 100. She believed her youthful appearance was due to the olive oil she rubbed into her skin and poured on her food. She also smoked from the age of 21 and only gave up her two-cigarette-a-day habit when she was 117; not for health reasons, a doctor said, but because she could no longer see well enough to light up and hated asking others to do it for her. Jean-Marie Robine, one of the authors of a book about Calment, said her great strength was her attitude to life. "I think she was someone who was **immune** to stress," he said. "She once said, 'If you can't do anything about it, don't worry about it.'"

Walter Breuning (1896–2011), from Minnesota, USA, lived to the age of 114. For the last 35 years of his life, he ate only two meals a day, **skipping** supper and limiting himself to a big breakfast of eggs, toast or pancakes and lunch. "I think you should push back from the table when you're still hungry," he said. He also ate a lot of fruit, drank plenty of water and a bit of coffee. "I drink a cup and a half of coffee for breakfast and a cup with lunch," he said. While he believed that his two-meal-a-day diet contributed to his **longevity**, Breuning also believed in hard work, and continued working until he was 99.

The Japanese are known for their longevity and, in particular, the Japanese island of Okinawa, with a population of a million, has around 900 **centenarians**. Older Okinawans eat an average of seven servings of vegetables and fruits daily, grain, tofu and soya products. In addition, Okinawans tend to eat until they are about 80% full. The Sardinians too are known for their long lives. Their Mediterranean diet, rich in olive oil, fish and red wine, differs **vastly** from that of the Japanese, but whatever they're doing, it's working.

Dr Tom Perls, an ageing specialist, says the secret to a long life is now believed to be a mix of genetics and environmental factors such as diet and exercise. His research recognises another **factor** that may protect people from illnesses such as heart attacks and **stroke**: "They seem to manage their stress better than the rest of us," he said.

3 ▶ Hacked!

1 Do you know anyone whose email account has been taken over by a stranger without permission (a hacker)? What happened? What would you do if this happened to you?

2 Read the article. What did Rowenna do to the hacker? What did the hacker ask Rowenna for?

The hacker who stole my email account and asked for sympathy

A hacker has been occupying my email account for the past week. And he or she may still be there. This person has been accessing my inbox, replying to messages, signing off with my nickname and refusing to let me email my contacts. In the weirdest twist, the hacker even started writing to me.

It started when my phone went crazy in the middle of a meeting. Some 5,000 contacts received an email from my account saying that I'd been held up at gunpoint in Madrid. According to the story, my mobile phone and credit cards had been taken and I was badly in need of money. There was a number to call to reach me at my hotel and an account had been set up in my name to send money to.

Suddenly there's a million things to do – stop your bank account; answer anxious calls; miss work deadlines; irritate bosses; reset all email-based passwords; forget to pay e-bills; upset friends who think you're ignoring them. At that point you realise that the email account is at the heart of the modern world. It's connected to just about every part of our daily life, and if something goes wrong, it spreads.

Out of sheer frustration, I sent an email to my occupied address, saying how I felt and asking for my contacts. Nine minutes later, I got this reply.

> **From: the hacker**
> **To: Rowenna**
> **8.42 a.m.**
> Can you send me £500?

3 Read the article again. Find five mistakes in this summary.

> Rowenna found out that someone had taken over her email account when she got a phone call from the hacker at home. The hacker had emailed her contacts to say she had been robbed in Spain and had asked for money to be sent to him there. With emails so central to Rowenna's life, she found it difficult to carry on as before without access to her list of contacts. She wrote to the hacker asking for her contacts back, and he replied asking for money, which Rowenna agreed to send. Finally, the police helped her to get her account back. In a final message, the hacker apologised to her.

4 Do you think it was a good idea for Rowenna to write to the hacker? Why?/Why not? What do you think should be done to help people in this situation?

To which I replied …

> **From: Rowenna Davis**
> **To: the hacker**
> **10.33 a.m.**
> 1) I literally don't have £500 to give you. I can't make any more money until I have access to my account back – I work freelance and all my work contacts are being held by you.
> 2) How would I know if I gave you any money that you'd actually send me my contacts anyway?
> 3) Do you ever feel even slightly bad about what you're doing?

> **From: the hacker**
> **To: Rowenna Davis**
> **10.38 a.m.**
> Sure I don't feel great, but I don't seem to have a choice, it's way better than robbing you on the streets. I give you my word, if you send me money, I will give you back access to your account with all your emails and contacts intact. If you can't send £500 at least £300 will do.

Apparently some 3,000 people reported such scams last year, but too few of these have been caught. The police haven't even returned my call. But I was lucky. The only reason I was able to regain access to my account was through chance – a friend of a friend works at Google. Even now, I'm not sure it's over. In one last message, addressed from myself just two days ago, the hacker wrote: "I see you got the account back. Sorry for the trouble."

Instructions p207

face2face Second edition Upper Intermediate Photocopiable **215**

2 Rowenna emailed the hacker. The hacker asked her for money (£500, then £300). **3** (1) the phone calls were from her contacts (2) at work; (3) the hacker asked for money to be sent to an account in Rowenna's name; (4) She refused to send the money; (5) a friend of a friend helped her – not the police.

4 ▶ Strange but true

1 Have you heard any strange or amusing stories in the news recently?

2 **a** Look at pictures 1–6. What do you think each story is about?

b Read the stories A–F. Match them to pictures 1–6.

c Choose the correct meaning, a or b, for these words/phrases.

1	gatecrashed	a jumped over a gate	(b)	entered without a ticket
2	harm	a damage	b	law breaking
3	did a good turn	a supported	b	did some clever tricks
4	above the law	a rules aren't important	b	rules don't apply to them
5	cutlery	a cups and plates	b	knives and forks
6	ignored	a insulted	b	paid no attention to
7	taking off	a becoming very popular	b	causing problems
8	toughest	a most challenging	b	most enjoyable
9	up for it	a able to do it	b	keen to do it

3 In which story or stories:

1 do people break the law?
___A___, _____, _____

2 does a new idea prove popular? _____, _____

3 does someone help people?
_____, _____

4 do people miss something they planned to do?
_____, _____

5 is there an unexpectedly positive outcome?
_____, _____

6 do people take things which do not belong to them?
_____, _____, _____

4 Which story do you find the most surprising? Why?

It must be true …

A A pair of newlyweds in the US spent their first night as man and wife behind bars after being caught stealing food for their wedding reception. Arthur Phillips, 32, and Brittany Lurch, 22, were caught wheeling a trolley carrying $600 of drinks and snacks from a supermarket. They were locked in separate cells while the party went ahead without them.

B A music fan **gatecrashed** a festival by dressing himself up in a police uniform that he'd taken from a police car. Daniel Tredinnick broke up a fight, called paramedics to treat an injured festival-goer and found a missing person before being arrested. "Strangely enough, he did more good than **harm**," said his lawyer.

C The mayor of Vilnius in Lithuania **did a good turn** for cyclists this week, when he used a Soviet-era tank to crush a Mercedes that was parked in a cycle lane. "That's what happens if you park your car illegally," said the mayor, before sweeping up the remains of the broken glass and riding away on a bicycle. Although this event was planned, mayor Arturas Zuokas insists he is serious about punishing owners of luxury vehicles who think they are **above the law**.

D Virgin Atlantic has released details of some of the strangest items that passengers have tried to check in at airports. One woman turned up at JFK Airport, USA, with family members carrying her bath. A couple who fell in love while on holiday in Grenada tried to bring back a bag full of sand and sea water as a souvenir. And staff had to turn away the passengers who tried to check in a dead cow, a car engine and a bag stuffed full of **cutlery** from a previous Virgin flight.

E A beggar has discovered that he gets more money if he is not there. Fed up with being **ignored** by passers-by, Nemanja Petrovic left his cap and his shoes on the street next to a sign reading 'Invisible Beggar'. When he returned, his cap was full of cash. "Now I just put down the sign and wait for the donations to roll in while I have a coffee," he said.

F A new sport is catching on: rabbit show-jumping. The contests originated in Scandinavia, and are really **taking off** in Germany, with 22 new clubs opening in the past year. The **toughest** course has 12 high jumps, up to 40cm in height, and three long jumps. "Not every rabbit is suitable," says breeder Karsten Schmid. "But if your rabbit is outgoing, he is probably **up for it**."

Copyright of The Week Ltd

2b A3 B5 C2 D1 E6 F4 2c 3a 4b 5b 6b 7a 8a 9b 3 1A, B, C; 2E, F; 3B, C; 4A, D; 5B, E; 6A, B, D

1 What are people's attitudes to animals in your country? What animals do you think are the most intelligent? Why?

2 **a** Look at the pictures and titles of two articles about clever animals. What do you think the two animals are able to do?

b Read the articles and check your answers. Which animal do you think is more intelligent? Why?

3 Read both articles again and answer the questions for Chaser and Alex.

1 Why did their trainers want to work with the animals?
2 What were they taught to do?
3 How were they trained?
4 How much time did they communicate with people every day?
5 Are they different from others of their kind, according to their trainers?

4 Do you think it's possible for animals to really understand what is being said? Why?/Why not?

The world's cleverest dog

Chaser, a border collie who lives in Spartanburg, in the USA, has the largest vocabulary of any known dog. The collie knows 1,022 nouns and can interpret a number of verbs, which shows us that dogs are able to learn far more than we had previously thought.

Chaser belongs to John W Pilley, who taught psychology at university for 30 years. Dr Pilley bought Chaser as a puppy in 2004 and started to train her for four to five hours a day in order to see whether he could repeat the success of Rico, another border collie who had been taught to recognise 200 objects by its owners. Dr Pilley would show Chaser an object and say its name up to 40 times, then hide the object and ask her to find it, while repeating the name all the time. She was taught one or two new words a day and proved to be an exceptional student. Unlike human children, she seems to love her drills and tests and is always asking for more. "She still demands four to five hours a day," Dr Pilley said. "I'm 82, and I have to go to bed to get away from her."

As for Chaser's abilities, Dr Pilley said that most border collies, with special training, "could be pretty close to where Chaser is." He added that it just takes a great deal of patience.

Alex the African Grey Parrot: a genius?

Parrots have been popular pets for thousands of years, largely due to their ability to speak. But the work of scientist Dr Irene Pepperberg with Alex, an African Grey, aimed to prove that a parrot can do much more than simply mimic language and sounds; it can actually understand and respond to language.

After buying him in a pet shop, Dr Pepperberg spent 30 years training Alex. He learned more than 100 words and was able to identify between different colours, sizes, shapes and materials. She used a range of simple questions, for example, "What matter?" to which Alex would reply, "Paper", "Wool", "Wood", etc. He even understood abstract questions; for instance, on producing four clicks, she would ask, "How many?" to which he replied, "Four." Although generally co-operative, Alex would frequently indicate that class was over by saying, "Wanna go back."

Alex had four to eight hours a day of interaction with humans and Dr Pepperberg claims that he had an understanding equal to that of a three-year-old child. But was Alex a genius or are other parrots capable of similar intelligence? Dr Pepperberg is now successfully repeating her experiments with another parrot, Einstein, to prove the intelligence of the species, not simply the individual. Alex's death at the age of 31 was reported in the *New York Times* and *The Economist* – unheard-of for an animal – but an appropriate celebration of the life of an extraordinary animal who was anything but a 'bird brain'.

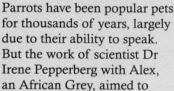

3 Chaser: **1** to repeat experiments with another border collie **2** recognise 1022 nouns and some verbs **3** showing and hiding objects **4** 4–5 hours a day **5** No.; Alex: **1** to prove that parrots can understand what they're saying **2** recognise and identify between different colours, sizes, shapes and materials **3** answering questions about objects and abstract information **4** 4–8 hours a day. **5** No.

EXTRA READING:
Photocopiable

6 ▸ Tattoo

1 Think of reasons why people might get a tattoo.

2 Read the information on a website about tattoos. Match each section 1–3 to a topic.

> attitudes   history   personal stories

The art of tattooing

With tattoos gaining in popularity around the world, there is a growing demand for information and advice.

1 In 1991, high up in the Alps and perfectly preserved by the ice, a mummified human body dating back 5,300 years was found. Known as Ötzi 'The Iceman', many believe that the dots, lines and crosses marking his skin are tattoos. There are 58 in total and they are believed to have been medicinal. If these are genuine, they represent the earliest known evidence of tattoos.

Others believe tattooing originates in Egypt, with tattoos found on Egyptian and Nubian mummies dating from about 2000 BC. As the Egyptian Empire spread, so did the art of tattooing and around this time it reached China.

Sailors travelling to exotic foreign lands began to collect tattoos as souvenirs of their journeys (for instance, a dragon showed that the sailor had served in China) and tattoo parlours sprang up in port cities around the globe. Tattooing was rediscovered by modern Europeans when exploration brought them into contact with Polynesians and American Indians. The word tattoo comes from the Tahitian word *tattau*, which means 'to mark'.

2 The meaning associated with tattoos has varied from people to people and place to place. However, tattooing has most often served as a sign of social status, as a mark of one's passage through life, or simply as a way to decorate the body.

For many people, tattoos have served as identification of the wearer's rank or status in a group. For example, the early Romans tattooed slaves and criminals. Tahitian tattoos served as rites of passage, telling the history of the wearer's life. Boys reaching manhood received one tattoo to mark the occasion, while men had another style done when they married.

In Borneo, women bore a symbol on their arms to represent their specific skills, thus increasing their chances of marriage, whilst tattoos worn around the fingers and wrist were said to prevent illness. The Polynesians employed tattoos to show status, tribal communities and rank. They carried this art to New Zealand where a facial tattoo, *moko*, was developed. Among the Maori, who raised tattooing to artistic heights, the practice served to distinguish between the social classes.

3 Leila was quite old when she got her first tattoo. "It was a 40th birthday gift, but it took me two years to make up my mind about what I wanted and where, so I was 42 by the time I got my tattoo. I settled on the Chinese symbol for tranquillity, a state I hope one day to achieve! The first time my mother saw it she said I'd regret it, but I absolutely love it and I know I always will. It's on my back so I forget it's there, but when I catch sight of it, it gives me pleasure. When friends see it, they're usually surprised and a little bit jealous. I enjoy that too!"

3 Read the website again. Choose the correct option, a, b or c, to complete the sentences.

1 From the evidence, it is safe to say Ötzi's body
   a was tattooed.   b contained markings.
   c is the earliest proof of tattooing.
2 Early tattoos
   a represented places visited.
   b were done after death.
   c became popular around the world.
3 Tattoos showed the wearer's status for
   a Tahitians.   b women in Borneo.   c the Maori.
4 People regularly had more than one tattoo in
   a Polynesia.   b Tahiti.   c Rome.
5 Based on her story, Leila can best be described as
   a calm.   b decisive.   c enthusiastic.

4 What are the attitudes of people you know towards tattoos? What do you think?

face2face Second edition Upper Intermediate Photocopiable   © Cambridge University Press 2012   ‹ Instructions p209

1 How are the elderly cared for in your country?

2 **a** Look at the title of the article and the picture of Babyloid, a robot baby. What do you think it can do?

b Read the article. Check your ideas.

c Read the comments below the article. Add missing sentences 1–3 to the three comments (A–C).

1 This may work but I think there are better solutions.

2 This is horrible, so insulting towards the elderly.

3 Obviously you have strong feelings on this but I am much less certain it is a 'bad thing'.

3 Read the article again. Find five mistakes in this summary.

> A robot baby called Babyloid has been developed in Japan by Professor Masayoshi Kanoh of Chukyo University. Babyloid looks and behaves like a baby and its purpose is to keep older people company by performing a series of infant functions. For example, its black eyes turn blue when it is sad and its cheeks turn red when it is happy. Babyloid responds to your voice and touch, may sleep when rocked and makes human baby sounds. In Kanoh's research, users engaged with the robot baby for over an hour at a time. People can buy Babyloid in Japan at a cost of 100,000 yen.

4 Imagine you decide to respond to the article by posting a comment. What would you say?

Fluffy baby robot helps to keep you company

It might just look like a large fluffy toy. But Babyloid, Japan's latest therapeutic robot baby, is also designed to help older people by keeping them company.

Towards the middle of its round, silicone face are two black dots that act as blinking eyes and a small opening that poses as a mouth and can produce a smile. The cheeks contain LED lights and turn red to signify when Babyloid is contented. Blue LED tears are produced when it is unhappy.

Developed by Masayoshi Kanoh, an associate professor at Chukyo University in Japan, Babyloid knows what's going on through its temperature, touch and light sensors. If you hold the crying Babyloid and rock it, it might – if you're lucky – fall asleep. Kanoh, who presented the latest version of Babyloid at a robotics conference in Japan last month, says the basic design – with a simplified, smiling face – was chosen "to avoid the creepiness a realistic baby face can have".

Babyloid can produce more than 100 different sounds. Kanoh is a father of three and he recorded the sounds of his youngest when she was an infant for the robot. During experimental studies at a retirement home, Kanoh found that users interacted with Babyloid an average of seven to eight minutes in a sitting with a total of 90 minutes per day, which helped ease depression.

The prototype model cost about 2 million yen (£16,500) but Kanoh hopes Babyloid can be available to consumers for 100,000 yen (£830) should it reach the market.

Comments

Mari on December 12, 12.37 p.m.

A ..... Can't we let them have relationships with real children rather than letting machines take care of them? What older people need is conversation and company, not electronic sounds.

Peter on December 12, 11.40 p.m.

B ..... I am the primary care-giver of my 84-year-old mother (at home with us), and my father, 85, is in a home. Mom has a stuffed animal which makes random sounds (purrs, sneezes and a kissing sound). This thing has given her more smiles than just about anything else in the last few years. At £830 this robot would be an expensive experiment, but I am sure much simpler and cheaper devices could be just as positive.

Anonymous on December 17, 7.28 p.m.

C ..... How about adopting a pet instead? Less money to buy, you'll save the life of the animal, and they're already proven to give the same results as these robots.

2c 1C 2A 3B 3 1 Babyloid doesn't look like a baby. 2 Its black eyes produce blue tears when it is unhappy. 3 Babyloid responds to temperature and touch, not voice. 4 Users engaged with Babyloid for seven or eight minutes at a time. 5 People can't buy Babyloid yet.

8 ▸ Family fortunes

1 Do you ever watch funny video clips online?

2 a Read the article. Match the words in bold to these meanings.

1 caught on, became extremely popular
2 non-serious accidents
3 biting
4 try to be like someone else you admire
5 extraordinary event
6 very quickly
7 waking up after an operation
8 profitable

b What is the writer's attitude towards this trend?

a He is surprised that it is so popular.
b People may not appreciate real-life experiences.
c He feels it may be changing parents' attitudes towards their children.

3 Read the article again and find out who:

1 wanted to be linked to *Charlie bit my finger*?
2 spent a lot of time watching life through a camera?
3 can make money from advertising in video clips?
4 is concerned about how some parents are spending their time?
5 filmed a child's medical problem?
6 was *Charlie bit my finger!* made for?

4 Do you think funny family videos are a good opportunity for making money? Why?

2,050,362

Online videos: how to cash in on your family

The old saying – never work with babies and animals – may have to be revised. A British parent revealed that he made more than £100,000 by posting an amusing video of his children online. Howard Davies-Carr was responsible for the online **phenomenon**, *Charlie bit my finger!*, a 56-second video clip of his baby son **chomping** down on his older brother's finger. The video was posted online in 2007 so that the children's godfather in Colorado could watch it but such was the charm and comedy of the clip that word soon spread and the video quickly **went viral** with nearly 400 million viewings. With advertisers keen to be featured alongside the clip, the website began sharing the profits with Davies-Carr under its 'partnership' deal.

The deal is a type of partnership between users who have posted videos online and the website. It monitors all uploads to its website, and if there is enough interest or it believes the video will go viral, it contacts the user who uploaded it to offer them the chance to make money. Advertisements placed on the page or embedded within the video clip can generate huge profits that are then shared between the user and the web company.

Inevitably, Davies-Carr's success story was **swiftly** followed by others. From the minute the news emerged that serious money could be made from funny family videos, cameras were raised in front of toddlers hoping to catch a similarly **lucrative** moment. David DeVore, who filmed his son **coming round from an anaesthetic** at the dentist, made almost £100,000 in the first year after uploading the video. Katie Clem, who filmed her daughter Lily's reaction to news of a family trip to Disneyland, earned more than £3,000 and five million views for her video, while Randy McEntee's film of his 17-month-old twin sons was viewed 50 million times.

In fact, browsing through the videos posted online, it appears that the next generation spend their whole time falling off swings, pulling the cat's tail, shoving teaspoons up their nose or falling asleep face down in chocolate pudding. It also suggests that for many a modern parent, life is experienced solely through the lens. After all, someone has to be filming all these comedy moments. Howard Davies-Carr admits that he had his nose pressed to the viewfinder all the time when his children were little, in the hope of a follow-up to his hit.

But what exactly was Davies-Carr – and those seeking to **emulate** his financial good fortune – missing in the anxiety to record his children's **mishaps**? Our contact with the world increasingly comes through a viewfinder. In the rush to record, are we forgetting how to interact with reality, even the most rewarding reality, like when our children do silly things? And when we have shot our film, rather than just boring our friends and neighbours with hours and hours of moderately funny – and not so funny – moments, we upload it on to a website in the hope that it goes viral and provides us with a pension.

---

9 ▶ Street performers

1 **What kind of performances can take place outside? What kind do you enjoy watching?**

2 **Read the interview. Choose the correct answer.**

The interviewer wants to know how:
a you become a street performer.
b street performing compares to other lifestyles.
c Mike learned fire juggling.

Interview in Istanbul: life on the road

Mike and Sibel live together in a van. They park wherever they feel like: beaches, mountainsides, fields. Sibel was employed as a manager in a five-star hotel in Istanbul in Turkey, but she gave up her job after meeting Mike. I interviewed them after watching Mike's fire show on Istiklal, a prime venue for street performers in Istanbul.

Nick: Why fire?
Mike: I've always been afraid of fire, actually. A couple of years ago I was working as a contact juggler and business wasn't great. Anyway, I saw this unbelievable fire act, a guy called Raul Mendoza, and I was immediately hooked! So I followed his act and practised, I don't know, eight, nine hours a day, then decided to give it a go myself. I was pretty nervous at first, but it really drew the crowds, so I carried on!
Nick: So, Sibel, when you met Mike, you had a job?
Sibel: Yes, I managed a hotel for five years. It was a good career for me.
Nick: So why did you leave?
Sibel: I fell in love! I broke up with someone after three years and I was sad, so my friends suggested we go into town to watch Mike, an American street performer, who was giving a fire show. You know, I was a very tough manager. But after

3 **Read the interview again. Are the sentences true (T), false (F) or not given (NG)?**

1 Mike's previous act was not successful.
2 Mike chose to work with fire to overcome fears.
3 Melek did not take her job as a manager seriously before she met Mike.
4 After meeting Mike, Melek felt her job was a waste of time.
5 According to Melek, being flexible about location is key to job security.
6 Mike enjoys the flexibility of his lifestyle.
7 Despite the lack of a monthly pay cheque, Mike maintains a regular way of life.
8 Mike and Melek would both like to stop travelling in the near future.

4 **Do you think you would enjoy the alternative lifestyle Mike and Melek describe? Why?**

I met Mike I became a much nicer person! And I found I couldn't do my job any more. I realised Mike's life was more beautiful than mine, more adventurous. In comparison, everything I did seemed pointless. But it was very scary to think of giving it all up.
Nick: And was it the right decision?
Sibel: You know, I felt like I'd been sleeping and then I woke up. I feel like now I have the opportunity to do whatever I want in life.
Nick: How do you deal with the insecurity of making a living from street performing?
Sibel: Actually, I disagree with the question! I mean, if ordinary people lose their job, they don't consider moving because they're not used to doing that. But if Mike cannot work here he will go to another place. People will always have time for street performers, so it's more stable, I think, than other jobs.
Mike: When you're receiving a pay cheque every month, everything happens on a schedule. That's a particular system that you get used to and rely on. This is a much looser system. The money comes in, but you don't always know when. Things are up and down, it could rain, there could be no money this day or that day, so you can't plan in the same way. It's a different lifestyle.
Nick: And what about the future?
Mike: Well, actually, we'd like to start a family so I'm keeping an eye out for a nice little farm in the mountains.
Sibel: Yeah, I do want to settle down and have children but there's no hurry! I have a lot of plans!

Instructions p210   © Cambridge University Press 2012   face2face Second edition Upper Intermediate Photocopiable   221

Changing times, changing roles

1 How long does it take you to get ready to go out? How much time do you spend on domestic chores every day?

2 a Choose the best options. Then read the article to check.

1 Getting ready to go out: Men take *more than/about/less than* an hour.

2 Deciding what to wear every day: Women spend *more time than/the same amount of time as/less time than* men doing this.

3 At work: Women spend *more time than/the same amount of time as/less time than* men in the workplace.

4 Domestic chores: Men today do *more than/the same amount as/fewer than* they used to.

5 Taking care of clothes: The average man devotes *more than 5 minutes/0 to 5 minutes/no time* to this.

b Find five new words or phrases in the article. Look them up in a dictionary.

3 a Where can you find this information? Match the sentences to the correct paragraph A–F.

1 The total number of days an average woman spends getting ready to go out. *C*

2 The time men and women spend at work.

3 Something that hasn't changed over the years.

4 How long it takes for women to get ready on an average day.

5 How much time men are spending on household chores every day.

6 A comparison of time spent on domestic chores by women over the past 30 years.

b Provide facts and figures for sentences 1–6 in **3a**.

1 *136*

4 Is there any information in the article that you find surprising? Do you think the information applies to men and women in your country?

A Who spends more time on their appearance, the man or woman of the house? According to new research carried out for a hotel chain, men spend six minutes longer a day getting ready to go out than women.

B On average, men spend 81 minutes a day on personal grooming, including cleansing, toning and moisturising, shaving, styling hair and getting dressed whereas women get hair, clothes and make-up done in just 75 minutes. Choosing an outfit is a time-consuming operation for men who want to look their best, taking them 13 minutes compared to 10 minutes for women.

C However, these results differ from a separate report which looks at the broader picture over a lifetime. The time women spend putting on make-up and getting ready works out at 3,276 hours while men only devote 1,092 hours to looking their best. In other words, women spend 136 days of their lives getting ready to go out. That's enough time for an astronaut to fly to the moon and back 22 times.

D The working woman spends 33.3 hours in paid employment compared with 38.4 hours for the average man in a job. But the findings suggest that the days of women carrying out a 'second shift' of work at home while men put their feet up may soon be over. This is easing the burden of cooking, cleaning and getting the children to bed, with women spending 40 minutes less on such tasks now than in the 1980s.

E By contrast, the average man of the house has increased the amount of time he devotes to domestic duties by more than 60% over the past 30 years, according to the results of surveys in 25 countries. The average man now spends two hours 28 minutes on domestic duties compared with the average woman's four hours 40 minutes. The gap remains big but the typical male is spending almost an hour more on domestic tasks now than in the 1970s.

F Finally, although a typical man now takes his time thinking about what to wear, he is still not washing and ironing his clothes. The average British male spends just four minutes a day on this.

Professor Jonathan Gershuny, director of the centre for time use research at Oxford University, said: "It's been a long time coming. The idea of what it is to be a man is changing. It wouldn't surprise me if men overtake women in total hours worked. But while men are doing more cooking and housework, they are doing no extra laundry whatsoever. I am guilty [of that] too."

11 ▶ Rags to riches

1 How often do you listen to live music? What kind of music do you most enjoy listening to?

2 a Read the article. Put the events in order.

- **a** Kudajczyk studied music in Poland as a child.
- **b** Kudajczyk is compared to a Polish composer.
- **c** Kudajczyk gave up his job as a cleaner.
- **d** Kudajczyk found cleaning work in a university.
- **e** A university employee heard him play the piano.
- **f** Kudajczyk found success as a concert pianist.
- **g** Lots of people at the university started listening to Kudajczyk's music.
- **h** Kudajczyk asked if he could use a piano.
- **i** Kudajczyk started to play for audiences.
- **j** Kudajczyk left Poland to live in Scotland. *1*

b Find words with the following meanings.

para 1: extraordinary
para 2: saw
para 3: amazed
para 7: delighting; started to do something he hasn't done before

3 Quotations a–c have been removed from the end of three paragraphs (see "..."). Match the quotations to the correct paragraph.

- **a** "But I hope to teach piano, or perhaps become a concert pianist in this country one day."
- **b** As he explains, "If it's about the piano, it has to be Chopin."
- **c** "I was terribly nervous playing my first concert of Chopin, but I'm getting used to it," he said.

4 How much do you think luck (both good or bad) played a part in Kudajczyk's story?

EXTRA READING: Photocopiable

From cleaner to concert pianist

1 When university cleaner Aleksander Kudajczyk put down his mop and bucket to practise on a grand piano he thought no one would hear him. Had he known of the camera in the corner of the room he would never have touched the instrument – and his virtuoso talent would have remained undiscovered.

2 Kudajczyk moved to Scotland from Poland hoping to find a job as a teacher. Instead, he was taken on as a cleaner in Glasgow University's School of Law, working four hours a day, starting at 6 a.m. On his rounds, he spotted a grand piano in the college chapel, and requested permission to play on it. ["..."]

3 What Kudajczyk did not know was that there was a webcam fitted to the chapel. One day, Joan Keenan, a secretary at the university, logged onto the webcam and was stunned by the beautiful sounds coming from it. She emailed dozens of friends, encouraging them to log on and listen. Soon, without knowing it, Kudajczyk was playing Chopin to an audience of hundreds of staff and students. ["..."]

4 The college persuaded Kudajczyk to perform in the chapel for two evenings during Glasgow's West End Festival, and he gave further performances while still working as a cleaner. ["..."]

5 Kudajczyk has certainly had a better time in Scotland than his idol, Chopin. In 1848, Poland's greatest composer accepted an invitation from a Scottish heiress to take refuge from the revolutions that were tearing Europe apart. His concert in Glasgow was a great success, but during his nine-month stay he fell desperately ill. A few months after returning to Paris, he died, aged only 39. ["..."]

6 Kudajczyk's gift for music had not passed unnoticed in his home town of Katowice, where he started playing piano at the age of four. He graduated from the town's Academy of Music, but found it difficult to earn enough money as a musician. "I came to Scotland because I wanted to settle down and make a living," Kudajczyk

said. "I found work, cleaning the law department in the university, then I practised when I could," he explained. ["..."]

7 Soon after being discovered, Kudajczyk was able to hang up his mop and bucket for the last time and achieve his ambition of earning a living from his music in Scotland. However, it is unlikely he ever believed he would become what he is today: a renowned concert pianist, enthralling audiences at sell-out performances around the world from the Scottish Islands to Australia and Indonesia. But Kudajczyk is not one to forget his roots; although he has occasionally branched out from Chopin, the Polish composer remains his favourite. ["..."]

2a 2d 3h 4e 5g 6i 7b 8a 9c 10f **2b** para 1: virtuoso para 2: spotted para 3: stunned para 7: enthralling; branched out from
3 a6 b7 c4

12 ▶ Inheritance

1 How easy do you find it to save money for the future? What do you do with money that you have saved? What will you do with it?

2 **a** Look at the pictures of four stories about unusual inheritances. Who do you think the money was left to?

b Read the stories and match them to pictures 1–4. Check your ideas.

c Find five new words or phrases in the article. Look them up in a dictionary.

3 In which story or stories:

1 has the beneficiary not received the inheritance?
2 did some beneficiaries die before receiving their inheritance?
3 did the person probably enjoy deciding who to leave his money to?
4 were the beneficiaries unrelated to the person leaving the inheritance?
5 were family members left out of the will?
6 did the money provide a luxury home?
7 were the beneficiaries not expecting to receive an inheritance?

4 To what extent should wealthy parents support their children financially when they become adults?

Unusual inheritances

A **LUIS CARLOS DE NORONHA CABAL DA CAMARA,** one of the few remaining Portuguese aristocrats, left his entire will to seventy total strangers. Luis Carlos was a childless bachelor when he died at the age of 42 so he was unusually free to dispose of his estate. This consisted of a 12-room apartment in central Lisbon, a house in the north of Portugal, a car and 25,000 euros ($32,000). Thirteen years earlier and in front of two witnesses, Luis Carlos had picked seventy names at random from a telephone directory. Amazingly, the lawyers were able to find every one of the 70 beneficiaries. It certainly came as a shock to them all when out of nowhere they were told about their inheritance. According to one of his friends, Anibal Castro Vila, Luis Carlos had a good sense of humour. "I am sure he just wanted to create confusion by leaving his belongings to strangers. It amused him."

B **TOMAS MARTINEZ,** a 67-year-old homeless man, ran away from police who had found him living on the streets of Santa Cruz, Bolivia. The police were bringing him news of an inheritance, but Mr Martinez did not wait to hear what the police had to say. Since then, the police, investigators and family members have been searching for Mr Martinez so he can claim the $6 million inheritance, but he has never been found. The money came to Mr Martinez from his ex-wife, Ines Gajardo Olivares, who had inherited the money herself from her family. She had obviously forgiven him for leaving her several years earlier.

C **WELLINGTON R BURT** was a rich timber merchant from Michigan, USA. He died in 1919 leaving a multi-million-dollar fortune, one of North America's largest at the time. However, he didn't leave his money to his children, or his grandchildren. His will stated that his inheritance should be distributed to his family, but only 21 years after his grandchildren's death. The millionaire's six children, seven grandchildren, six great-grandchildren and 11 great-great grandchildren all missed out on the inheritance, either because they were excluded by the will or because they didn't live long enough.

Now, 92 years later, it is finally being handed over to the 12 remaining family members, including three great-grandchildren, seven great-great grandchildren and two great-great-great grandchildren. The oldest beneficiary is 94 years old.

D **JONATHAN JACKSON OF OHIO, USA,** was an animal lover, that much is certain. When he died in around 1880, his will indicated that he thought it man's duty to protect the weak, including animals. In that spirit, he left his money to a cat charity for the creation of a cat house. This was not just any cat house, however. The cats had their own bedrooms, a dining room, an exercise area and a specially designed roof for easy climbing. For the more intellectual cats, Mr Jackson also requested a conversation room and an auditorium where they could listen to live music, played on the accordion.

2b A3; B2; C4; D1 **3** 1B 2C 3A 4A, D 5C 6D 7A, B, D

Study Skills

Instructions

There are four Study Skills worksheets (p228–p231). The aim of these worksheets is to help students become better and more independent learners. The worksheets are designed to be used in class, offering a change of pace and focus for both teacher and students. You will need to photocopy one Study Skills worksheet for each student.

1 ▶ Spelling rules: the final -e p228

Aim

To help students discover a spelling rule for verbs ending in -e and practise applying the rule.

When to use and time

Use any time after lesson 2C. 15–25 minutes.

Preparation

A class set of monolingual dictionaries would be useful.

Procedure

1 Check students understand *custom* /ˈkʌstəm/ and *courtship* /ˈkɔːtʃip/. Students do the exercise on their own before checking in pairs. Check answers with the class.

> 1 The marriages are rarely enforced.
> 2 A matchmaker. 3 Because some days are believed to be unlucky for wedding ceremonies.

2 Students do the exercise in pairs. Check answers with the class (see the words in bold in the answer key to **3**).

3 Give students time to read the flowchart and check they understand it. Do one or two words as examples with the class. Students then do the rest of the exercise in pairs. Check answers with the class.

> 1 arranged; arrangement 2 noted; noting; **notable**
> 3 noticed; noticing; **noticeable** 4 **enforced**;
> enforcing; enforceable; enforcement 5 disagreed;
> disagreeing; disagreeable; **disagreement** 6 involved;
> involving; **involvement** 7 encouraged; encouraging;
> **encouragement** 8 **agreed**; agreeing; agreeable;
> agreement 9 **believed**; believing; believable

4 Students do the exercise in pairs. Tell the students to use the flowchart in **3** to check the spelling of the word with the suffix. Check answers with the class.

> 2 amazing 3 making 4 tied 5 engagement
> 6 including 7 congratulating 8 remarkable
> 9 achievement 10 argument 11 disagreed

2 ▶ Mind maps p229

Aim

To raise awareness and provide practice of using mind maps as a way of taking notes quickly.

When to use and time

Use any time after lesson 5C. 20–30 minutes.

Procedure

1 Check students understand *shading* and *abbreviation*. Students discuss the questions in groups. Ask students to share interesting ideas with the class.

2 **a** Students do the exercise on their own. Explain there is more than one correct answer for some of the questions.

b Students compare answers in pairs. Check answers with the class.

> 1 History of English **Possible answers**
> 2 Old English; settlers 3 Eng. 4 500–1100 5 🔔

3 Students do the exercise on their own before checking in pairs. Check answers with the class.

> 2 around 3 lines and arrows 4 only key words
> 5 good idea 6 thick; thinner 7 Use 8 creative

4 **a** Check students understand *concept* /ˈkɒnsept/ and *root* /ruːt/. Students do the exercise on their own. Set a time limit and encourage students **not** to look up any other unknown words at this time.

b Students work on their own and draw mind maps.

c Students work in pairs and compare each other's maps. Students tell the class the best thing about their partner's map.

> **Possible answer**
>
>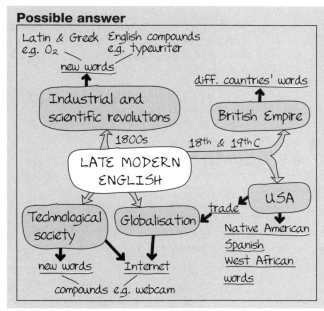

3 ▶ Silent letters p230

Aim
To help students identify silent letters that may cause confusion when spelling or pronouncing words.

When to use and time
Use any time after lesson 7C. 15–25 minutes.

Preparation
A class set of monolingual dictionaries.

Procedure

1 **a** Focus students on words 1–9. Students work in pairs and decide how to pronounce each word.

b Students decide which words in **1a** rhyme with words a–i. Check answers with the class.

> a7 b1 c8 d6 e5 f3 g2 h4 i9

2 Students do the exercise on their own before checking answers in pairs. Check answers with the class.

> doubt; walk; whale; castle; sign; hymn; receipt; guilt

3 Students do the exercise on their own or in pairs. Check answers with the class. Model and drill the words as necessary.

> would; psychology; honest; talking; Christmas; butcher; salmon; resigned; debt; listening; folk; guitar; calms; building; watch; hour; autumn

4 Explain to the class that silent letters usually have 'spoken partners' (letters which come directly before or after the silent letter, which have a sound when we say them). Use *would* as an example. Point out that it is useful to recognise some common patterns of silent letters with spoken partners.
Students work in pairs and complete the table. Check answers with the class. Point out that *psychology* and *Christmas* have two silent letters each and that 'ch' /tʃ/ is a single sound.

> 2 kn 3 bt 4 lk 5 lm 6 wh 7 ch 8 ho 9 st 10 tch
> 11 gn 12 ui 13 mn 14 pt 15 ps

5 **a** Students do the exercise on their own.

b Students work in pairs to check their answers. Check answers with the class. Model and drill the words.

> 2 whistle /ˈwɪsəl/ 3 honour /ˈɒnə/
> 4 psychiatrist /saɪˈkaɪətrɪst/ 5 catch /kætʃ/
> 6 knock /nɒk/ 7 stomach /ˈstʌmək/
> 8 design /dɪˈzaɪn/

c Students work in the same pairs to complete the table. Check answers with the class. Note that *whistle* and *psychiatrist* have two silent letters each.

> 2 knock 6 whistle 7 psychiatrist; stomach
> 8 honour 9 whistle 10 catch 11 design 12 biscuit
> 15 psychiatrist

4 ▶ Homonyms p231

Aim
To raise awareness of homonyms and to practise dictionary work.

When to use and time
Use any time after lesson 9C. 20–30 minutes.

Preparation
A class set of monolingual dictionaries.

Procedure

1 Focus students on pictures a–e. Tell students that each picture shows a different definition of the same word. Students work on their own or in pairs and match the pictures to the correct definitions. Check answers with the class.

> 1c 2a 3e 4b 5d

2 **a** Students read the text and answer the questions on their own. Check answers with the class. Then ask students whether they have seen any Laurel and Hardy films.

> They were both members of the cast of a silent film in 1918. Hardy died first.

b Students do the exercise in pairs. Before they start, ask students to copy the table onto a separate piece of paper. Tell students to find the definition in a dictionary that matches the words in bold in **2a** and complete definition 1 in column 1 in the table. Remind students that *n* = noun and *v* = verb. Check answers with the class.

> 2 have or use something at the same time as someone else 3 person or thing which is equal to another person or thing in strength, speed or quality 4 someone who admires and supports a person, sport, sports team, etc. 5 winning position during a race or other situation where people are competing 6 knot with two curved parts and two loose ends 7 small mistake

3 **a** Students do the exercise on their own. Check answers with the class.

> 2 match 3 slip 4 bow 5 stage 6 leads 7 shares

b Students work in pairs and read out the sentences that are true for them. Finally, ask students to tell the class two interesting things they have found out about their partner.

4 Students work in new pairs and complete definition 2 in column 2 in the table for each word in **3a**.

> 2 one of the equal parts into which the ownership of a company is divided and which can be bought by members of the public 3 sports competition or event in which two people or teams compete against each other 4 device that is used to move the air around 5 cause someone to do something 6 bend your head or body forward 7 escape

1 ▶ Spelling rules: the final -e

1 Read the article about arranged marriages in Japan. Then answer these questions.

1 What's the difference between Omiai and arranged marriages in other cultures?

2 Who offers advice to the young couple?

3 Why is the date of a wedding important in Japan?

OMIAI   お見合い

Omiai is the Japanese custom of **arranging** a marriage. It has made a **notable** comeback over recent years. However, there's a **noticeable** difference between *Omiai* and similar customs in other countries, in that the marriages are rarely **enforced** in Japan. If there is a big **disagreement** between the young couple during their courtship, the plans may be cancelled quickly. The **involvement** of a matchmaker is often part of the process. The matchmaker is usually a friend of the family who offers **encouragement** and advice for those first, important dates. Once the couple has **agreed** that they are serious about each other, they plan the date of the wedding very carefully, because in Japan some days are **believed** to be unlucky for wedding ceremonies.

2 Look at the words in bold in the article in **1**. Write the words in the correct place in the table.

	verb	-ed	-ing	-able	-ment
1	arrange		*arranging*	–	
2	note				–
3	notice				–
4	enforce				
5	disagree				
6	involve			–	
7	encourage			–	
8	agree				
9	believe				–

3 Work in pairs. Look at this flowchart for dropping the final -e. Use the flowchart to complete the table in **2**.

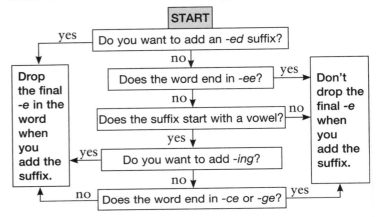

4 Read the article. Fill in gaps 1–11 with the correct form of the word and the suffix in brackets. Use the flowchart in **3** to help you.

A British couple [1]*celebrated* (celebrate+ed) an [2]_____ (amaze+ing) 80 years of marriage in 2005, [3]_____ (make+ing) it into The Guinness Book of Records for having the world's longest marriage. Percy and Florence Arrowsmith [4]_____ (tie+ed) the knot on June 1st 1925, after a brief six-week [5]_____ (engage+ment). The couple marked their anniversary with coffee and snacks amongst friends and family, [6]_____ (include+ing) their nine great-grandchildren. The Queen sent them a letter [7]_____ (congratulate+ing) them on their [8]_____ (remark+able) [9]_____ (achieve+ment). Asked about the secret of their successful marriage, Mrs Arrowsmith said, "Never go to sleep on an [10]_____ (argue+ment), always kiss each other, and hold hands every night before going to bed. When we have [11]_____ (disagree+ed), we never go to bed as bad friends." Mr Arrowsmith's answer was shorter, "The regular use of two words – yes, dear."

2 ▸ Mind maps

1 Work in groups. Discuss these questions.

1 Do you ever need to take notes? If so, when?

2 What note-taking techniques do you use to save time?

3 Do you use shading or different colours? Do you draw pictures or symbols? When? Why?

4 What kind of abbreviations do you use?

2 a Look at a mind map that a student drew at a lecture. Find examples of 1–5 in the mind map.

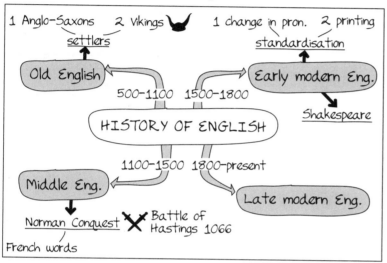

1 the main topic of the lecture _____

2 a heading and its subheading(s) _____

3 an abbreviation _____

4 information labelling an arrow _____

5 a picture or a symbol _____

b Work in pairs. Compare answers.

3 Read the advice about creating your own mind maps. Choose the correct words/phrases.

1 Put the main subject *at the top of/in the middle of* the page.

2 Write major subheadings in circles *directly below/around* the main subject.

3 Connect the main ideas with *punctuation marks/lines and arrows*.

4 Write *full sentences/only key words* so that you can write as much as possible.

5 It's a *bad idea/good idea* to include pictures and abbreviations.

6 Central lines should be *thick/thin*, becoming *thicker/thinner* as they move out from the centre.

7 *Use/Don't use* shading/different colours to highlight associations.

8 The mind map should grow in a *fixed/creative* way.

4 a Read the article about late modern English quickly. Decide which words you can use as headings and subheadings.

b Read the article again and draw a mind map. Personalise it in any way you like.

c Work in pairs. Compare and discuss your mind maps together.

Late modern English

The main difference between early and late modern English is in the number of words. Late modern English has a much larger vocabulary, mainly due to the rise of the technological society and the globalisation of the language.

The industrial and scientific revolutions from the 1800s created a need for many new words to fit the new concepts that were being discovered. These new words often came from Latin and Greek origins (e.g. *oxygen, protein*), while compounds from English roots were also sometimes used (e.g. *typewriter*). The tendency to create new compound words still continues today, especially in the field of computers and electronics (e.g. *webcam, download*).

The rise of the British Empire in the 18th and 19th centuries saw new words introduced to English from the many countries that Britain traded with. At the same time, Americans adopted many words from the Native American, Spanish and West African people they encountered. The globalisation of the language has continued in the 20th and 21st centuries, in part due to the USA's leading role in trade, and more recently through the widespread use of English on the Internet.

3 ▸ Silent letters

1 a Work in pairs. How do we say words 1–9?

1 fail	4 parcel	7 toe
2 fork	5 out	8 slim
3 delete	6 line	9 kilt

b Use your dictionary. Which words 1–9 in **1a** rhyme with words a–i?

a know ____	d sign ____	g walk ____
b whale ____	e doubt ____	h castle ____
c hymn ____	f receipt ____	i guilt ____

2 Work in pairs. Look at the words in **1b** again. Which letter is silent in each word? Complete the table.

silent letter	word with silent letter
k	*know*
b	
l	
h	
t	
g	
n	
p	
u	

3 Look at the words in bold and <u>underline</u> the silent letters from **2**.

1 I **would** like to study **psychology** because, to be **honest**, I like **talking** about emotions.
2 Every **Christmas** we buy a turkey from the **butcher** and a **salmon** from the market.
3 The banker **resigned** after he got his company into **debt**.
4 I really like **listening** to **folk** music, the sound of the **guitar calms** me down.
5 A Why is the **building** closed? My **watch** says it's still only 5.30.
  B It's September 22nd. We close an **hour** earlier in **autumn**.

4 Work in pairs. Look again at the words in bold in **3** and the words in **1b**. Which letter is silent and which is the 'spoken partner'? Use your dictionary and complete the first column of the table.

silent letter + spoken partner	example words
1 *ld*	would
2 ____	know, ____
3 ____	doubt, debt
4 ____	walk, talk, folk
5 ____	salmon, calm
6 ____	whale, ____
7 ____	psychology, Christmas, ____ , ____
8 ____	honest, hour, ____
9 ____	castle, Christmas, listen, ____
10 ____	butcher, watch, ____
11 ____	sign, resign, ____
12 ____	guilt, guitar, building, ____
13 ____	hymn, autumn
14 ____	receipt
15 ____	psychology, ____

5 a Look at these definitions. Fill in the silent letters.

1 bisc*u*it small flat cake that is dry and usually sweet
2 w__is__le make a sound by blowing air between your lips or teeth
3 __onour treat someone with special respect
4 __syc__iatrist doctor who treats mental illness
5 ca__ch take hold of something moving through the air
6 __nock hit a door with your hand to get attention
7 stomac__ part of the body where food is digested
8 desi__n drawing of a pattern or plan

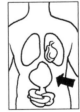

b Work in pairs. Check your answers to **5a**. How do you pronounce the words in **5a**?

biscuit /ˈbɪskɪt/

c Complete the second column of the table in **4** with the words from **5a**.

4 Homonyms

1 Look at these dictionary entries for *cast*. Match definitions 1–5 to pictures a–e.

> **1 cast** /kɑːst/ *noun* the actors in a film, play or show: *The director threw a party for the cast.*

> **2 cast** /kɑːst/ *verb* send light or shadow in a particular direction: *The tree cast a shadow over her face.*

> **3 cast** /kɑːst/ *verb* cast a look/glance/smile, etc. look/smile, etc. in a particular direction: *He cast a quick look in the rear mirror.*

> **4 cast** /kɑːst/ *verb* cast doubt/suspicion on sb/sth make people feel less sure about or have less trust in something or someone: *New evidence has cast doubt on the guilty verdict.*

> **5 cast** /kɑːst/ *verb* cast a/your vote vote: *All the votes in the election have now been cast and the counting has begun.*

2 **a** Read about Stan Laurel. How did he meet his partner, Oliver Hardy? Which partner died first?

Stan Laurel

Like many comics of the time, Stan Laurel started his career on the **stage**. He was born and raised in the north of England, but moved to California in 1910 and he **shared** an apartment with the young Charlie Chaplin. He first worked with Oliver Hardy as a member of the cast of a silent film in 1918. It soon became clear that they were a good **match** and the duo went on to make over 50 movies together, which were enjoyed by millions of **fans** around the world. In most of the films it was Hardy who took the **lead**, with Laurel, wearing his trademark **bow** tie, making many **slips** as he tried to follow his partner around. Laurel was devastated when Hardy died in 1957. Years later, when somebody asked Laurel, "Aren't you Oliver Hardy? What happened to the other one?" he replied, "Yes, I am. The other one went quite mad."

b Look at the words in bold in the text in **2a**. Complete column 1 of the table with the correct definition. Use your dictionary to help you.

word	definition 1	definition 2
1 stage	n *the area in a theatre where actors perform*	n *a period of development*
2 share	v	n
3 match	n	n
4 fan	n	n
5 lead	n	v
6 bow	n	v
7 slip	n	v

3 **a** Complete the sentences with the correct form of the words in the table in **2b**. Then tick the sentences that are true for you.

1 In my home we use an electric _____*fan*_____ during the summer.

2 I can't concentrate on studying if there's a football _____ on TV at the same time.

3 Unless I write things down immediately they easily _____ my mind.

4 In my country we usually _____ when we meet people for the first time.

5 Being a teenager is a difficult _____ in life.

6 Looking at the stars at night often _____ me to think about the meaning of life.

7 My financial advisor deals with my _____ .

b Work in pairs. Take turns to say your true sentences. Ask follow-up questions if possible.

4 Work in new pairs. Write a definition for each word in **3a** in column 2 of the table in **2b**.

© Cambridge University Press 2012

STUDY SKILLS: Photocopiable

Progress Tests

Instructions

The Progress Tests (p238–p261) are designed to be used after students have completed each unit of the Student's Book. Each Progress Test checks students' knowledge of the key language areas taught in the unit. The final exercise of each Progress Test also tests students' knowledge of language taught in previous units. It is helpful for students to have done the Review section at the end of each unit before doing a Progress Test. You can also encourage students to revise for the test by reviewing the relevant Language Summary in the back of the Student's Book and by doing exercises for that unit on the CD-ROM and in the Workbook. Note that Progress Tests 6 and 12 also contain a listening section.

- Allow students 40 minutes for Progress Tests 1–5 and 7–11, and 50 minutes for Progress Tests 6 and 12. You may wish to adjust this time depending on your class.

- Photocopy one copy of the test for each student. Students should do the tests on their own. You can either check the answers with the whole class at the end of the test or collect in the tests and correct them yourself. Keep a record of the test scores to help you monitor individual student's progress and for report writing at the end of the course.

- Progress Tests can also be given as homework for general revision.

Listening tests

There is a listening section in Progress Tests 6 and 12 only. The corresponding recording scripts (CD2 ▶ 21 and CD3 ▶ 34) are in the Answer Key for the tests. Focus on one section of the recording at a time. Allow students time to read through the questions for that section in the Progress Test before you start. Play that section of the recording without stopping and allow students to answer the questions. Then play that section of the recording again without stopping. Repeat this procedure for the other section.

Answer Key and Recording Scripts

▶ 1 ▶ Progress Test p238

1 2 in 3 up 4 at 5 rusty 6 few 7 by 8 in 9 have
10 word
2 2 fees 3 essay 4 graduate 5 tutor 6 lecture
7 student loan 8 undergraduate 9 postgraduate
10 scholarship 11 seminar 12 assignment
13 lecturer 14 professor 15 Master's (degree)
3 2 helping 3 study 4 making 5 taking 6 get 7 to buy
8 choose 9 to help 10 to drive 11 to like 12 to learn
13 doing 14 to tell 15 stay 16 talking

4 2 've never been 3 want 4 were advised
5 've been studying 6 're usually given 7 started
8 know 9 was reading 10 think 11 is getting
12 works 13 's having 14 've learned 15 were
16 told 17 started 18 'd never spoken
5 2 did 3 didn't 4 didn't 5 Were 6 was 7 do 8 's/has
9 hasn't 10 has 11 was 12 haven't 13 have 14 are
15 'm 16 don't 17 did 18 did 19 didn't 20 don't 21 do
6 2 come 3 's he like 4 what way 5 what exactly
6 sort of 7 's it going 8 for 9 with 10 as 11 else
12 for
7 3 ... refused to speak ... 4 ✓ 5 ... ended up eating
6 ✓ 7 ... the film had already finished. 8 ✓
9 ... plan to visit ... 10 ✓ 11 ... but mine did.
12 He's been riding ... 13 ... are you studying ...
14 I really like ... 15 ✓ 16 Lee regrets studying ...

▶ 2 ▶ Progress Test p240

1 2 She seldom walks from her flat to the city centre.
3 Once in a while Jan goes to visit her sister. / Jan goes to visit her sister once in a while. 4 Every so often I read the newspaper. / I read the newspaper every so often. 5 Most weeks he goes to the gym. / He goes to the gym most weeks. 6 Most of the time we have a healthy diet. / We have a healthy diet most of the time. 7 Tom rarely stays at work after 5.30. 8 Every now and again Alice sends me an email. / Alice sends me an email every now and again. 9 More often than not I do some work at the weekend. / I do some work at the weekend more often than not.
2 2 for 3 of 4 in 5 with 6 of 7 about 8 by 9 of 10 by
11 about 12 by 13 of
3 (2 marks each) 2 responsibility 3 preferable
4 conclusion 5 originally 6 criticism 7 weakness
8 convincing 9 really 10 recognisable 11 realistically
12 convinced
4 2 went 3 used to play/'d play 4 is always complaining/
always complains 5 used to have 6 will play/play
7 use to 8 tried 9 used to like/liked 10 'll have
11 wanted 12 will park/are always parking 13 use to
5 (2 marks each) 2 wasn't used to 3 'll/'d/could (ever)
get used to 4 're (slowly) getting used to 5 didn't use
to 6 Are (you) used to/Have (you) got used to 7 did
(you) use to 8 used to 9 's/is used to 10 hasn't got used
to/isn't used to 11 'm used to/'ve got used to/'ve been
used to 12 get used to
6 2 a good point 3 you mean 4 be right there 5 argue
with that 6 see the point of 7 you think so 8 got a
point there 9 still not convinced 10 your point
11 wouldn't say 12 suppose that's true
7 3 ... to get used to ... 4 ✓ 5 He needs ...
6 ... we saw ... 7 ✓ 8 ... remember meeting ...
9 ✓ 10 ... stopped playing ... 11 ... since we met,
hasn't it? 12 ... bilingual in 13 ✓ 14 I picked up ...
15 ... but I didn't.

3 ▶ Progress Test p242

1 2 robbery 3 rob 4 burglar 5 burgle 6 kidnapping 7 kidnapper 8 theft 9 steal 10 mugging 11 shoplifter 12 shoplift 13 bribery 14 vandal 15 vandalise 16 arsonist

2 2 with 3 sentenced 4 commit 5 fined 6 evidence 7 acquitted 8 court 9 guilty; sent 10 of 11 for

3 2 on 3 to; for 4 in 5 with 6 to; about 7 to; for 8 on 9 against 10 to 11 after; for 12 about 13 of

4 (2 marks each) 2 had; would (you) go 3 was/were able to; 'd/would go 4 didn't have; would (you) do 5 would buy; had 6 were; would (you) steal 7 found; would keep

5 (2 marks each) 2 'd/had seen; 'd/would have called 3 wouldn't have been; hadn't broken down 4 would (you) have got; hadn't lent 5 might have been; 'd/had taken 6 'd/had known; wouldn't have told

6 (2 marks each) 2 If I didn't enjoy working for this company, I'd look for another job. 3 Imagine your friends needed somewhere to stay, would you give them a room? 4 If we hadn't phoned, my parents would have been worried. 5 What would you have done if the police hadn't arrived? 6 I wouldn't go there again even if somebody offered me a free flight. 7 We'd have got there on time if we hadn't got stuck in traffic.

7 2 wouldn't mind 3 Would it help if 4 be wonderful if you could 5 would you like me to 6 be a great help 7 Why don't I 8 can manage 9 if you like 10 you don't mind 11 What if I 12 for offering

8 3 ✓ 4 Did you **hear** ... 5 ... so **judgemental** ... 6 ✓ 7 ... aware **of** ... 8 ... more **responsibly**! 9 He's **been** travelling ... 10 remember **to buy** ... 11 ✓ 12 The thief **stole** ... 13 ✓ 14 ... sick **of** working ... 15 ✓ 16 I didn't **use** to ...

4 ▶ Progress Test p244

1 (2 marks each) 2 run over 3 work out 4 knocked (me) out; come round 5 gone off 6 turned out 7 take off 8 ran away 9 making (it) up

2 2 blurb 3 plot 4 chick lit 5 browse 6 contents page 7 paperback 8 flick through 9 bestseller 10 literary genre

3 2 even though 3 apart from 4 instead of 5 as 6 whereas 7 However 8 despite 9 due to

4 (2 marks each) 2 I'm over the moon. 3 I'm scared stiff. 4 I'm starving. 5 I'm going out of my mind. 6 I'm speechless. 7 It costs a fortune. 8 It weighs a ton. 9 It takes forever. 10 It's a nightmare. 11 It's killing me.

5 2 decided 3 was driving 4 saw 5 stopped 6 got out 7 'd/had been running 8 didn't/couldn't remember 9 'd/had been lying ('d/had lain) 10 'd/had broken 11 helped 12 took 13 stayed 14 wanted 15 'd/had been waiting 16 told 17 had had 18 ('d/had) saved

6 2 which 3 who/that 4 which 5 - /that/which 6 which/that 7 who 8 whose 9 where 10 whose

7 2 fantastic news 3 bet 4 kidding 5 honest 6 believe it 7 on earth 8 be joking 9 wonder 10 I can imagine

8 3 ... a day **when** ... 4 ✓ 5 ... based **on** ... 6 If **he'd/he had taken** ... 7 ... were charged **with** ... 8 ✓ 9 ✓ 10 ... got used to **working** ... 11 ✓ 12 ... famous **for** ...

5 ▶ Progress Test p246

1 2 unsuitable 3 affectionate 4 outrageous 5 lucrative 6 eager 7 rewarding 8 enthusiastic 9 impressed 10 faithful 11 harmless 12 rare 13 addictive 14 fierce 15 weird 16 exotic 17 destructive

2 (2 marks each) 2 go ahead; catch up 3 fit in 4 talked ... into 5 pass by 6 put ... out

3 2a) 3b) 4a) 5a) 6a) 7b) 8a) 9b) 10a) 11b)

4 (2 marks each) 2 slightly 3 nowhere 4 nearly 5 less 6 deal 7 fewer 8 bit 9 twice 10 better 11 more and more 12 any

5 2 'm meeting 3 'll invite 4 isn't going to pass 5 'll be living 6 'll carry 7 won't be eating 8 'll definitely finish 9 will win 10 'll be swimming 11 're going to move

6 2 better 3 think 4 should 5 right 6 what 7 trying 8 meant 9 enough 10 how 11 argument 12 favour 13 point 14 never 15 thought 16 just 17 right 18 again 19 not 20 saying

7 3 ... if he **had** seen ... 4 ... **whose** parents ... 5 ✓ 6 ... a very **immoral** way ... 7 ✓ 8 ... couldn't work **out** ... 9 ... while I **was watching** TV. 10 ... in spite of the weather. 11 ... but I **do**. 12 ✓ 13 due **to** illness

CD2 ▶ 21 See p232 for Listening Test instructions.

1

a A   What did you give Jamie for his birthday?

   B   Well, um, he's been asking for a pet for ages. We were going to get him a dog, but he said that he really wanted a snake. The feeding would have been a bit of a problem, though – you know, live mice and so on. Anyway, um, my husband loves cats and they're, um, they're easy for kids to look after, so in the end that's what we got him.

b A   Hi, Joanne. Welcome back! Did you enjoy London?

   B   Yeah, it was great. The English are very nice, but they're, um, they're a bit different from people here.

   A   In what way?

   B   Well, er, they talk about the weather all the time – which isn't surprising, I suppose, as it changes every day. And they're, um, they're always saying 'please' and 'thank you', which I thought was very polite to begin with, but I, um, I got sick of it after a while.

   A   I've heard that nobody talks to strangers on the tube or anything.

   B   Yeah, that's right, but I didn't mind that. It was nice to be left alone, actually.

c A   From where I'm standing I've got a fabulous view of green hills, while just in front of me is one of the largest collections of tulips I've ever seen – and it's all the work of local resident, Jean Granger. You must be very pleased, Jean.

   B   Yes, I am, actually. When we, er, when we moved into the house three years ago, all we had was, um, a lawn and a couple of rose bushes. We love flowers, but it's, er, it's been a lot of hard work.

   A   I can imagine. But it's a magnificent display, better than any I've seen in a public park this year.

   B   Thank you.

d Hi Jenny, it's Philippa. Um, you know we'd arranged to go shopping in town this weekend? Well, I'm not sure that's such a good idea. It'll be difficult to park on a Saturday and, um, and the shops will be really crowded. As the weather's going to be so good, maybe it'd be nicer if we went for a walk by the river instead. Anyway, let me know what you think. I'm in a meeting till three, but give me a call any time after that. Bye.

e A   So how's the course going, Nick?

   B   Great, actually, I'm really enjoying it. At the beginning I wondered if we'd spend the whole time writing scripts and looking through a camera, but in fact we don't –

well, not yet anyway. We also have lectures on things like the history of the cinema, studying different periods and cultures, that sort of thing. It's really interesting, actually.

   A   That's good.

2

Hello everyone and thank you all for coming. I've spent the last two years studying a group of bottlenose dolphins off the east coast of Scotland. These dolphins live in an area of water called the Moray Firth, which is the most northerly part of the world where dolphins are known to live all year round. What's interesting is that if you compare them to bottlenose dolphins that live further south in, say, the Mediterranean, they're clearly bigger and fatter, probably because they need to survive in a much colder climate. Researchers who study the Moray Firth dolphins have also noticed another distinguishing feature, which is that they appear to have more injuries to their skin. Up until now, people thought this was because the dolphins live in difficult conditions in the water. However, some environmentalists now wonder whether the problems may be the effect of pollution in the sea and they're hoping to investigate this further.

Studying dolphins is difficult, as they spend so much time under water, and so my team have spent a lot of time analysing the different sounds that the dolphins make. The most common sounds are clicks which dolphins use for location, that is, they make these noises and then listen for echoes to come back from the seabed, boats, the fish they hunt or indeed other dolphins. So how do dolphins actually listen to these sounds? Well, they use a bone in the lower part of their mouth to receive the signals, which are then sent to the brain – a very clever adaptation.

Dolphins also make a range of sounds in order to communicate with each other. Researchers have noticed recently that each dolphin produces its own sound, which is known as a 'signature whistle'. I like to think of it as being similar to a person calling out his or her name. Interestingly, they also copy the signature whistle of other dolphins, although why they do this is not really understood. The dolphin also uses a special call when it finds a group of fish to feed on. Again, the reason for this call is unclear. Some researchers have suggested this sound may be used to confuse the fish, while others think that the first dolphin is calling for help in surrounding the fish before they start feeding. Another interesting thing we have discovered recently is that ...

1 (2 marks each) **a** 2 **b** 1 **c** 1 **d** 2 **e** 3

2 (2 marks each) **1** T **2** F These dolphins are **clearly bigger and fatter** than bottlenose dolphins in the Mediterranean. **3** T **4** T **5** F They **listen to** these sounds by using a bone in the lower part of the mouth. **6** T **7** F Researchers **don't agree** why dolphins make all the different sounds.

3 (2 marks each) **2** takes (me) seriously **3** take (my parents) for granted **4** taking responsibility **5** takes sides **6** taken any notice **7** 's taking advantage

4 (2 marks each) **2** Laid-back **3** Bad-tempered
4 Absent-minded **5** Strong-willed **6** Open-minded
7 Self-conscious **8** Easy-going **9** Big-headed
10 Narrow-minded **11** Level-headed **12** Self-assured
5 (2 marks each) **2** feeling **3** to pass **4** talking
5 cleaning **6** to change **7** travelling **8** make out
9 'll/will win **10** Finding **11** will promote
6 (2 marks each) **2** I'm really up against it at the
moment. **3** I was wondering if I could see you for a
moment. **4** I'm rather pushed for time at the moment.
5 I'm afraid I'm a bit tied up just now.
6 Sorry to bother you, but have you got a minute?
7 **3** ✓ **4** … stopped **working** …
5 If I **hadn't missed** … **6** ✓ **7** … twice as big **as** …
8 ✓ **9** … we'll **be walking** …
10 … everyone **had gone** home. **11** ✓
12 … went **off** … **13** … convicted **of** … **14** ✓

7 ▶ Progress Test p250

1 **2** realise **3** trust **4** envy **5** suspect **6** recognise
7 involve **8** respect **9** deserve **10** doubt
2 **2** industrial **3** capitalism **4** industry **5** producer
6 environmental **7** pollution **8** industrial **9** developers
3 **2** political **3** a capitalist **4** capitalist **5** an economist
6 economical **7** development **8** developing
9 investment **10** an industrialist **11** industrial
12 productive **13** manufacturing
14 an environmentalist **15** environmental
16 pollution
4 **2** overqualified **3** misunderstood **4** non-smoker
5 ex-colleagues **6** underrated **7** anti-government
8 multinational **9** redecorated **10** self-defence
11 preview **12** postgraduate
5 **2** voicemail **3** ring **4** landline **5** network/company
6 cut **7** top **8** run
6 (2 marks each) **2** does (that box) contain
3 don't know **4** Are (you) thinking **5** 's/is having
6 doesn't seem **7** smell **8** Do/Don't (you) wish
9 Do (you) think **10** 'm/am seeing **11** was listening
7 **2** 've visited **3** have known **4** 's been playing
5 's found **6** returned **7** 've been sorting out
8 has become **9** 's read
8 **2** reception **3** breaking up **4** phone **5** delay **6** ring
7 losing **8** line **9** speak up **10** catch **11** die
9 **3** … is very **economical**. **4** … deserves **to earn** … **5** ✓
6 … bound **to get** … **7** ✓ **8** ✓ **9** … spent ages
searching … **10** ✓ **11** What **will you** be doing …
12 **I'm** used to … **13** ✓ **14** … taking advantage **of**
you.

8 ▶ Progress Test p252

1 **2** on **3** for **4** in **5** into **6** off **7** in **8** on **9** in **10** of
2 (2 marks each) **2** ripped off **3** comes to
4 'll/will pay (you) back **5** taken (25%) off
6 came into **7** to save up **8** gone down
9 to pay off **10** taking out

3 **2** loan **3** mortgage **4** savings account **5** interest rate
6 deposit **7** credit rating **8** overdrawn
4 **2** precise **3** offended **4** vary **5** straightforward **6** odd
7 additional **8** pursue **9** dilemma **10** complicated
11 figure out **12** observe **13** particularly
5 **2** was/were **3** didn't have to **4** would tidy **5** 'll get/
gets **6** 'll have/have **7** weren't studying **8** had
9 to leave **10** did **11** wouldn't play/didn't play
6 (2 marks each) **2** hadn't eaten **3** booked **4** had
checked **5** 'd/would/could have helped **6** had sold
7 hadn't watched **8** hadn't increased **9** 'd/had spent
10 drunk
7 **2** for **3** realise **4** matter **5** no idea **6** that **7** didn't
mean to **8** forget **9** shouldn't have **10** alright
11 afraid **12** mind **13** can't believe **14** worry **15** sorry
about **16** some reason **17** no need
8 **3** I forgot **to cancel** … **4** ✓ **5** ✓
6 … **economic** development … **7** ✓ **8** I've **broken** …
9 How long **have you** been … **10** ✓ **11** **Talking** about
the weather … **12** … have you **visited**?

9 ▶ Progress Test p254

1 **2** costume **3** cast **4** soundtrack **5** remake **6** critic
7 sequel **8** subtitled **9** special effects **10** review
2 **2** scary **3** overrated **4** predictable **5** gripping
6 believable **7** hilarious **8** moving
3 **2** mind **3** case **4** state **5** point **6** handle **7** sense
8 mind **9** handle **10** state **11** sense **12** case
4 (2 marks each) **2** The missing child hasn't been
found. **3** He should be nominated for an Oscar.
4 I'd like my achievements to be remembered.
5 He can't stand being laughed at. **6** The awards will
be presented on Saturday. **7** The match had to be
cancelled because of rain. **8** The tiger escaped when
it was being taken to the zoo. **9** I used to be given
sweets (by my mum) if I was good. **10** He dreams of
being given a role in a film. **11** He was the first British
skier to be awarded a medal. **12** The cup final is being
shown live on TV.
5 **2** to be released **3** was marked **4** added **5** became
6 was controlled **7** have been achieved **8** expanded
9 are made/are being made **10** is needed **11** be found
12 was invented **13** predicted **14** decreased **15** went
16 have been attracted **17** 's/is hoped **18** continue
6 **2** such **3** so many **4** so **5** as **6** so much **7** like **8** as
9 so
7 **2** fancy **3** a try **4** easy **5** like **6** mind **7** about
8 feel up to **9** other time **10** up to **11** a miss **12** feel
13 bothered **14** the same **15** don't mind **16** up to
8 **3** ✓ **4** I'll pay you **back** … **5** ✓ **6** I wish he **wouldn't**
(**didn't**) leave … **7** It's time we **tried** … **8** … **I've** ever
seen … **9** ✓ **10** If only I **was/were** … **11** … have you
had … **12** ✓ **13** … **in** credit.

10 ▶ Progress Test p256

1 (2 marks each) 2 decorated 3 replaced 4 's/is putting
up 5 services 6 putting in 7 be dry-cleaned

2 (2 marks each) 2 breakdown 3 daydream
4 high-powered 5 downhearted 6 self-obsessed
7 widespread 8 good-humoured 9 attention span

3 2 prejudiced 3 abusive 4 disciplined 5 unruly
6 threatened 7 objective 8 biased 9 reasonable
10 resentful

4 (2 marks each) 2 got … to help 3 get/have … done
4 had … done 5 got/had … repaired 6 getting/having
… put in 7 get/have … fixed 8 get/have … replaced
9 getting/having … decorated 10 getting … to do
11 doing/going to do 12 getting … to come

5 2 both of 3 are 4 anything 5 either 6 house 7 are
8 gets 9 both of 10 Every 11 all of 12 is 13 anything
14 loves 15 Neither of 16 All of the

6 (2 marks each) 2 The thing that worries me about
him is that he works too hard. 3 What I admire about
him is his enthusiasm for everything. 4 One thing that
amazes me about him is that he can find the time.
5 What annoys me about my brother is that he never
answers my emails. 6 The thing I don't like about him
is that he doesn't listen properly. 7 One thing I love
about you is your sense of humour.

7 3 ✓ 4 … enjoys **being** looked after … 5 ✓ 6 … invest
some money **in** … 7 ✓ 8 … shouldn't have **told** …
9 … such **as** the Oscars. 10 … had to **be cancelled** …
11 ✓ 12 I wish I **didn't** have to … 13 If only **I'd/I
had gone** … 14 … work **as** a nurse … 15 … read the
review … 16 ✓

11 ▶ Progress Test p258

1 2 for 3 on 4 down 5 into 6 on 7 with 8 of 9 from
10 on 11 out

2 (2 marks each) 2 was made redundant 3 branches
4 working freelance 5 to set up 6 went bankrupt
7 making a loss 8 to make a profit 9 to expand
10 took over 11 run/'re running a chain

3 (2 marks each) 2 He denied breaking Erin's mobile
phone. 3 Fiona suggested visiting the art gallery.
4 The doctor advised Mr Lee to do more exercise.
5 She apologised for being late for class. 6 Alan
offered to give Jo a lift to the station. 7 I warned
Tina not to go into the park after dark. 8 He
admitted that he'd/he had stolen his cousin's laptop./
He admitted stealing his cousin's laptop. 9 Frank
accused Molly of lying to him. 10 Richard reminded
Kath to get some milk. 11 Harry threatened to call
the police if it happened/happens again.

4 2 logo 3 campaign 4 publicity 5 leaflet 6 launching
7 advertising 8 slogans

5 2 'll/will have completed 3 'll/will have retired
4 won't be working 5 'll/will be travelling 6 won't
have finished 7 will be lying 8 'll/will have arrived

6 2 … where John had put the scissors. 3 … him to
pick her up after work./… (him) if/whether he could
pick her up after work. 4 … (that) Val had already
borrowed £50 off him. 5 … to take my suit to the
dry cleaner's./… if/whether she could take my suit to
the dry cleaner's. 6 … when he was leaving.
7 … (that) he had to be home by ten o'clock.
8 … what she'd/she had been doing all morning.
9 … if/whether they were going to stay in a hotel.
10 … (that) he wasn't going to call them until
Sunday. 11 … to fix her computer./ … if/whether
he'd/he would fix her computer.

7 2 about 3 I'd rather 4 I wonder if 5 worth a try
6 we could do 7 such 8 what you're saying
9 should avoid 10 know 11 makes sense
12 sounds like 13 right in thinking 14 go over

8 3 … **in the middle of** … 4 ✓
5 … the best **headmistress/head teacher** …
6 … **loves** soap operas. 7 ✓
8 … to get someone **to help** you? 9 … **either** of …
10 … get my car **serviced** … 11 ✓
12 … needs **to be changed/needs changing.** 13 ✓
14 … about this house **is it's** … 15 ✓

12 ▶ Progress Test p260

CD3 ▶ 34 See p232 for Listening Test instructions.
1
Speaker 1
When you've been studying hard in college all week it's,
um, it's nice to do something different at the weekend.
My friends think I'm a bit odd, but I often just spend
a day in the flat doing boring things like, you know,
cleaning and washing. Strangely, this makes me feel
much more relaxed at the end of the weekend than I
would if I'd been, um, sitting watching TV or reading
the Sunday papers.

Speaker 2
I suppose I should do a few of the household things like
the washing and tidying up, but I prefer to spend time
outside doing jobs like mowing the lawn and cutting
the hedge, that kind of thing. It sounds like hard work,
but it's, er, actually, er, very relaxing. I need to get my
bathroom redecorated, but I keep, er, you know, putting
it off as I'm no good at DIY. One day, perhaps.

Speaker 3
I'm very busy during the week, what with working
and looking after the family, so, um, in the evenings
I just tend to fall asleep in front of the TV. Saturdays
are always very busy, and I usually, um, I, I usually go
and watch my boys playing football in the afternoon.
Sunday is my day, and you might think I'd have a lie-in
and read the papers. Actually, doing a bit of decorating
is my favourite way of relaxing. It's quite creative in its
way and I, um, I, I like making things look good.

Speaker 4

Weekends are my chance to switch off from work. I often get up early on Saturday and, you know, do some of the household jobs and get the shopping done. I, um, I hate doing that kind of thing, so it gets it out of the way. On Saturday evenings I usually invite some people round, and I enjoy experimenting with new ideas in the kitchen – that's how I relax, mainly. I'd like to grow my own fruit and vegetables, but I haven't got a very big garden.

Speaker 5

It's great having a weekend at home, particularly in the summer when I can, um, you know, just sit in the garden and do absolutely nothing. I used to be a keen tennis player, but now I don't even follow the sport on TV any more. My favourite way of spending Sunday morning is to, um, lie on the sofa with a big pile of papers and find some interesting articles to read while my partner prepares lunch for the family.

2

A Hello and welcome to the programme. My special guest today is sports therapist Karen Thomas.

B Hello.

A Karen, there's some recent research which has shown an alarming increase in the rate of sports injuries. Why are so many people, especially people over 30, taking up exercise these days?

B Well, um, of course, a lot of people in that age group are not new to exercise. They've been doing sport since childhood, and a lot of them, um, play for local teams and sports clubs. But many others are having a go for the first time because they, er, they want to keep their weight down and just generally keep fitter – possibly because they've got older relatives with serious health problems and, you know, they want to avoid getting those problems themselves.

A And who's likely to get more sports injuries – people who are new to exercise or people who've been training for many years?

B You're, um, you're expecting me to say the ones who've just started, aren't you? But actually, people who are used to exercising are actually more likely to have problems because they don't always remember that you have to look after your body. It's, um, it's just a case of being sensible. There's no need to, um, hire a personal trainer or buy a lot of expensive equipment or anything like that.

A The injuries that you see in the course of your professional life – how do people get them?

B Oh, all kinds of ways. For instance, quite a few ankle and knee injuries result from running. I'm not saying don't go running, but you shouldn't … er, it's not a good idea to run without doing a warm-up or some strengthening exercises first.

A So should, um, should we be worried about the increase in sports injuries?

B Well, we can't ignore it – but remember, most of the people I see have aches and pains and back problems because they never take any exercise. So we do need to take a balanced view about this.

A What about having the right footwear? How important is that?

B Mmm, very. Don't just, you know, rush out to the nearest high-street shop and get the first fashionable pair of trainers you see. Try to find a specialist shop where the staff are well-trained and professional, and know which shoe will be best for people with particular needs. And you don't have to get the most expensive pair in the shop either. Many, er, mid-price trainers are just as good.

A My last question, Karen – what sort of exercise do you recommend for someone like me who's never really done anything sporty since school?

B Well, um, I would say, whether you live in the country or the city, you can't beat getting out on the footpaths. Not jogging, not for a beginner – just getting those legs moving. Stepping out at a good pace for thirty minutes three times a week will, um, will do you more good than any number of hours sweating it out in the gym, in my opinion.

A Right, I'd better get exercising then! Thank you very much for coming in today, Karen.

B My pleasure.

1 (2 marks each) 1f) 2c) 3b) 4d) 5a)

2 (2 marks each) 1c) 2b) 3b) 4c) 5b) 6a)

3 2 fancy 3 quid 4 pop into 5 chill out 6 stressed out
7 trendy 8 mess up 9 mate 10 chuck out 11 loo
12 guy 13 pretty 14 bug 15 hassle

4 (2 marks each) 2 out (of the) blue
3 middle (of) nowhere 4 far (cry) from
5 keep (an) eye 6 slept (like a) log
7 recharge (my) batteries 8 piece (of) cake
9 pulling (your) leg 10 food (for) thought
11 break (the) ice

5 2 tons of 3 give or take 4 around 5 or so 6 tiny
7 -ish 8 vast 9 roughly / around 10 far longer
11 -odd / or so

6 (2 marks each) 2 might have crashed
3 can't have happened 4 must be
5 might have tried 6 must have fallen
7 must have been trying 8 might be giving
9 may have sent

7 (2 marks each) 2 needn't have gone/didn't need to go
3 wouldn't have bought 4 should have done
5 could have stayed

8 3 … warned me **not to talk** … 4 I'll have **finished**
… 5 ✓ 6 … having our kitchen **redesigned** … 7 ✓
8 No one **wants** … 9 ✓ 10 … denied stealing …
11 I don't want **either** of … 12 … was accused of …

Name ▶   Score [100]

1 Fill in the gaps with one word.

1 My ___first___ language is Spanish.
2 I'm quite fluent _____ Arabic now.
3 Did you pick _____ any Portuguese when you were in Brazil?
4 Sue's reasonably good _____ languages.
5 I did French at school, but it's a bit _____ now.
6 He knows a _____ words of Hungarian.
7 My boss can get _____ in German.
8 Joe is bilingual _____ French and English.
9 Anna can _____ a conversation in Polish.
10 Mum can't speak a _____ of Italian.

[9]

2 Write these words/phrases connected to education.

1 a written report saying whether a student is improving or not: a p*rogress report*
2 the amount of money you pay to go to a private school or a university: f_____
3 a short piece of writing on a particular subject: an e_____
4 somebody who has a first degree from a university or college: a g_____
5 a teacher who works with one student or a small group of students: a t_____
6 a talk on a subject, especially at university or college: a l_____
7 the money that a student borrows from a bank while at university: a s_____ l_____
8 somebody who is studying for their first degree at university or college: an u_____
9 somebody who has a first degree and is now studying for a higher degree: a p_____
10 money paid by a university, etc. to a student with ability, but not much money: a s_____
11 a class in which a small group of students discuss a particular subject: a s_____
12 a piece of work given to someone as part of their studies or job: an a_____
13 somebody who teaches at a university or college: a l_____
14 a teacher of the highest level in a university department: a p_____
15 an advanced university degree: a M_____

[14]

3 Fill in the gaps with the correct form of the verbs in brackets.

1 She loves __going__ (go) to the cinema.
2 He doesn't mind _____ (help) me.
3 I'd rather _____ (study) at home.
4 Could you stop _____ (make) that noise?
5 I remember _____ (take) my driving test.
6 I think you'd better _____ (get) some sleep.
7 Did you remember _____ (buy) some milk?
8 My dad made me _____ (choose) this course.
9 I stopped _____ (help) a girl who had fallen off her bike.
10 My older brother taught me _____ (drive).
11 Your sister doesn't seem _____ (like) me!
12 I encouraged him _____ (learn) Spanish.
13 Julie finished _____ (do) her homework.
14 I forced him _____ (tell) me his name.
15 I might _____ (stay) in tonight.
16 We avoided _____ (talk) to them.

[15]

4 Choose the correct verb forms.

My husband and I ¹(decided)/have decided to learn Chinese a year ago. We ²never went/'ve never been to China, but we ³want/'re wanting to go there next year. We ⁴advised/were advised to have lessons and we ⁵'re studying/'ve been studying with a private teacher for three months – we ⁶usually give/'re usually given some homework to do every week. I ⁷was starting/started mine after I got back from work last night. I ⁸know/'m knowing that my grammar isn't very good yet, but while I ⁹read/was reading my coursebook I recognised a lot of Chinese characters so I ¹⁰think/'m thinking my vocabulary ¹¹gets/is getting better. My husband often ¹²works/is working late so he can't study much, but he ¹³has/'s having a few days' holiday at the moment so he can do a bit more. Our teacher says that we ¹⁴'re learning/'ve learned a lot since September. We ¹⁵'ve been/were pleased when she ¹⁶was telling/told us that! Before we ¹⁷started/ had started having lessons we ¹⁸'ve never spoken/ 'd never spoken any Chinese at all!

[17]

© Cambridge University Press 2012   ⟨ Instructions p232

5 Fill in the gaps in this conversation with a positive or negative auxiliary. Use contractions where possible.

ANNA Hi, Paul! [1]___Did___ you go to that talk this morning?

PAUL Yes, I [2]_____ , but I [3]_____ enjoy it very much.

ANNA Oh, [4]_____ you? I'm glad I missed it then.

PAUL [5]_____ you working in the library?

ANNA No, I [6]_____ sleeping. I'm exhausted and I [7]_____ hate getting up early!

PAUL There [8]_____ been a lot to do this week, [9]_____ there?

ANNA Yes, there [10]_____ . You know, I [11]_____ going to try and finish my project this week, but I [12]_____ done anything yet!

PAUL Don't worry, neither [13]_____ I.

ANNA That makes me feel a bit better. By the way, [14]_____ you going to George's party next Saturday?

PAUL No, I [15]_____ not. Actually, I [16]_____ usually like parties much, although I [17]_____ enjoy that one we went to last month.

ANNA You mean Brian's? Yes, so [18]_____ I. I [19]_____ get home till 4 a.m.!

PAUL A lot of people find Brian a bit unfriendly, but I [20]_____ .

ANNA No, neither [21]_____ I. I think he's really nice.

PAUL Me too. Anyway, I must go. See you. [20]

6 Fill in the gaps in this conversation with these words/phrases.

> 's that   's it going   for (x 2)   what way   's he like
> come   sort of   with   as   what exactly   else

KEN Hi Jill. How are you?

JILL Not great, actually.

KEN Oh! Why [1]__'s that__ ?

JILL It's my course. I'm not enjoying it any more.

KEN How [2]_____ ? You loved it when you started.

JILL I know. I think it's the teacher really.

KEN Why? What [3]_____ ?

JILL He's a bit boring so I don't listen properly and then I don't do well in the coursework. I need to sort my life out a bit.

KEN In [4]_____ ?

JILL I don't know. Do something different.

KEN Like [5]_____ ?

JILL Join a study group and do some exciting things in my free time.

KEN What [6]_____ things?

JILL Acting, for example. I am studying drama, after all! By the way, did I tell you that I'm writing a play?

KEN Really? How [7]_____ ?

JILL Very slowly. I've had to do a lot of research into 20th-century politics.

KEN What [8]_____ ?

JILL My play's about a Canadian politician. In fact I'm going to Canada soon.

KEN Who [9]_____ ?

JILL My friend Jo. We're travelling around and visiting a few different places.

KEN Such [10]_____ ?

JILL Montreal, first of all. There's a film festival there.

KEN That sounds fun. Where [11]_____ are you going?

JILL Well, we're going hiking in the Rockies.

KEN How long [12]_____ ?

JILL Oh, about a month.

KEN Fantastic! [11]

7 Tick the correct sentences. Change the incorrect ones.

1 ~~I'm needing~~ *I need* a better computer.
2 I've been studying English for years. ✓
3 My brother refused speaking French.
4 I was driving home when he called.
5 We ended up to eat in a seafood restaurant.
6 She persuaded me to go to her yoga class.
7 When I arrived, the film already finished.
8 The way English is taught has changed a lot.
9 We plan visiting New York next year.
10 We stopped to get some petrol.
11 Jo's parents didn't go to college, but mine are.
12 He's riding his motorbike for three months.
13 What course do you study at the moment?
14 I'm really liking your new shoes.
15 You should tell your parents what happened.
16 Lee regrets study history at university. [14]

1 **Correct the word order in these sentences. There is sometimes more than one possible answer.**

1 I drink occasionally coffee.
  I occasionally drink coffee .

2 She walks from her flat to the city centre seldom.
  _____ .

3 Jan goes once in a while to visit her sister.
  _____ .

4 I read every so often the newspaper.
  _____ .

5 He most weeks goes to the gym.
  _____ .

6 We have most of the time a healthy diet.
  _____ .

7 Tom stays rarely at work after 5.30.
  _____ .

8 Alice every now and again sends me an email.
  _____ .

9 I more often than not do some work at the weekend.
  _____ .

[8]

2 **Choose the correct prepositions.**

1 I'm not very interested *of/in* politics.
2 Australia is famous *about/for* its beaches.
3 My mum is terrified *for/of* big dogs.
4 We were really disappointed *of/in* our hotel.
5 She was very satisfied *with/for* the course.
6 Were you aware *in/of* the problem?
7 I'm not sure *with/about* the colour of that tie.
8 Anna was shocked *for/by* the standard of driving.
9 I was very fond *of/about* music as a child.
10 I was fascinated *in/by* the local culture.
11 Is Tim excited *about/with* going to Japan?
12 My tutor was impressed *by/for* my exam results.
13 Frank is sick *of/with* driving to work every day.

[12]

3 **Fill in the gaps with the correct form of these words.**

> ~~improve~~ real (x 2) convince (x 2) weak origin
> recognise conclude prefer criticise responsible

1 I've seen a great __*improvement*__ in your work.
2 He needs to take _____ for his actions.

3 I think it would be _____ to buy a new car, not a second-hand one.

4 It's an interesting article but I don't agree with the writer's _____ .

5 We _____ planned to go to the USA, but in the end we went to Italy instead.

6 My only _____ of the restaurant is that the music was too loud.

7 If we change our minds, people will see it as a sign of _____ .

8 I didn't think his reason for being late was very _____ . Did you believe him?

9 Do you think he _____ meant it?

10 Despite wearing a hat and dark glasses, Madonna was immediately _____ to everyone.

11 Try to plan your time more _____ . You can't do everything in one day.

12 I wasn't sure it was the right thing to do, but in the end I was _____ by his arguments.

 [22]

4 **Look at these sentences. Are both verb forms possible? If not, choose the correct one.**

1 When I was young, I *used to be*/*'d be* very shy.
2 We *used to go/went* to Spain on holiday last year.
3 During the summer we *used to play/'d play* in the woods for hours.
4 My mother *is always complaining/always complains* about how much everything costs.
5 When Adela was younger, she *used to have/'d have* a pet rabbit.
6 Our kids *will play/play* their music too loudly – it drives me crazy!
7 My father didn't *use to/used to* like cooking.
8 Once I *used to try/tried* to write a novel, but I never finished it.
9 Uncle Harry never *used to like/liked* gardening.
10 Every day when I get home, I *'ll have/'m having* a packet of biscuits.
11 When I was a child, I *wanted/'d want* to be famous.
12 My neighbours *will park/are always parking* their car in front of my house!
13 What did you *use to/used to* do during the school holidays?

[12]

5 Fill in the gaps with the correct positive, negative or question form of *used to*, *be used to* or *get used to*. Sometimes there is more than one possible answer.

1 When I was younger, I ____used to____ eat a lot of burgers.

2 I grew up in the country so when I first came to London I _____ city life.

3 I don't think I _____ ever _____ speaking English all the time!

4 We've just moved to Australia, we _____ slowly _____ the different customs.

5 My grandparents _____ drive – they preferred to walk.

6 _____ you _____ living in such a hot country yet?

7 Where _____ you _____ live when you were at college?

8 The office _____ be very noisy, but it's much quieter now.

9 Nick works as a waiter in the evenings, so he _____ going to bed late.

10 John's only been in Germany a few days so he still _____ driving on the right.

11 Walking to work this morning was tiring because I _____ taking the bus every day.

12 I don't think I could ever _____ speaking a foreign language every day. [22]

6 Fill in the gaps in the conversation with these words/phrases.

| about that   be right there   wouldn't say |
| got a point there   suppose that's true   you think so |
| argue with that   see the point of   a good point |
| still not convinced   you mean   your point |

A I don't think children should eat fast food like burgers.

B Oh, I don't know ¹___about that___ . Surely, if it's not allowed they'll just want to eat it more, won't they?

A That's ²_____ , but fatty food is so bad for children.

B I see what ³_____ , but not if they only get a little bit now and then.

A You might ⁴_____ , Tim. I give my kids burgers or pizzas on Saturdays, but they eat healthy food quite happily all the other days, which is what all parents want.

B Well, I can't ⁵_____ . What about fizzy drinks?

A I let mine have what they like, you know, lemonade, cola. I can't really ⁶_____ forcing them to drink water all day. A bit of sugar gives them energy and it doesn't do any harm.

B Oh, do ⁷_____ ? Sugar makes children fat.

A I suppose you've ⁸_____ .

B Well, I'm ⁹_____ . My kids run about all day and they're not overweight.

A Yes, I see ¹⁰_____ . But what about all the chemicals they put in those drinks? Some of them are very bad for you, I think.

B Oh, I ¹¹_____ that. Most of that stuff is harmless. If it was dangerous, they couldn't put it in the drinks, could they?

A I ¹²_____ , actually. [11]

7 Tick the correct sentences. Change the incorrect ones.

         not
1 More often than ~~no~~ he gets to work late.
2 I've been to Italy twice in my life. ✓
3 It took me years to be used to the cold winters.
4 He ended up working as an English teacher.
5 He's needing some help with his homework.
6 Last week we've seen a great film on TV.
7 He's been working in that office since March.
8 I don't remember to meet him before.
9 They forgot to pick up the car from the garage.
10 He's stopped to play football professionally.
11 It's been a long time since we met, isn't it?
12 My father is bilingual at French and Spanish.
13 You'd better go or you'll be late.
14 I picked out some French on holiday.
15 Lots of people went to the lecture, but I wasn't. [13]

PROGRESS TESTS: Photocopiable

1 Complete the table with crimes, criminals or verbs.

crime	criminal	verb
looting	¹ *looter*	loot
² _____	robber	³ _____
burglary	⁴ _____	⁵ _____
⁶ _____	⁷ _____	kidnap
⁸ _____	thief	⁹ _____
¹⁰ _____	mugger	mug
shoplifting	¹¹ _____	¹² _____
¹³ _____	–	bribe
vandalism	¹⁴ _____	¹⁵ _____
arson	¹⁶ _____	–

☐ 15

2 Fill in the gaps with one word.

1 The police *arrested* three men last night.
2 Two boys were charged _____ vandalism.
3 She has been _____ to eight years in prison.
4 Why did he _____ such a terrible crime?
5 The thief was _____ £200.
6 The first witness gave _____ in the trial today.
7 The man was _____ of all charges and was allowed to go home.
8 He was taken to _____ for stealing a car.
9 The jury found the man _____ and he was _____ to prison for five years.
10 She's been convicted _____ a serious crime.
11 My cousin was arrested _____ shoplifting.

☐ 11

3 Choose the correct prepositions.

1 I'm shocked *of/(by)/with* what I read in the papers.
2 He always insists *on/in/at* driving the car himself.
3 I want to apologise *to/for/with* everyone *by/for/to* behaving so badly.
4 Our company has succeeded *on/with/in* making a profit in its first year of business.
5 I'm not sure I can cope *of/at/with* all the extra work I've got.
6 I complained *to/for/at* the manager *with/by/about* the terrible food.
7 She decided to apply *of/for/to* the same bank *for/to/after* a different job.

8 The film is based *of/in/on* a very successful novel.
9 There's a demonstration tomorrow to protest *against/for/about* the cuts in salary.
10 The coat I wanted to buy has been reduced *at/with/to* half price.
11 They've named the baby *for/after/of* the town she was born in.
12 Tony's parents never worry *for/with/about* money.
13 Maria managed to convince everyone *about/of/with* her innocence.

☐ 15

4 Complete these second conditional sentences with the correct form of the verbs in brackets.

1 If I *found* (find) a mobile phone on a train I *'d take* (take) it to the lost property office.
2 Imagine you _____ (have) the chance to travel for six months, where _____ you _____ (go)?
3 Assuming I _____ (be able to) go wherever I wanted, I _____ (go) to South America.
4 Supposing you _____ (not have) enough money to get home, what _____ you _____ (do)?
5 John _____ (buy) himself a sports car if he _____ (have) enough money.
6 If you _____ (be) really hungry, _____ you _____ (steal) some food?
7 If I _____ (find) a bit of money on the street, I think I _____ (keep) it.

☐ 12

5 Complete these third conditional sentences with the correct form of the verbs in brackets.

1 Emma *would have been* (be) terrified if she *'d been* (be) there when the thief broke in.
2 If I _____ (see) the accident, I _____ (call) the police.
3 We _____ (not be) late if the car _____ (not break down).
4 How _____ you _____ (get) home if Gary _____ (not lend) you his car?
5 Our journey _____ (might be) quicker if we _____ (take) the train.
6 If I _____ (know) it was a secret, I _____ (not tell) anyone.

☐ 10

6 **Put these words in the correct order. Add a comma if necessary.**

1 you / very / would / round / If / rich / the / were / you / world / go / ?
   If you were very rich, would you go round the world?

2 'd / for / If / I / working / this / enjoy / look / another / I / for / didn't / job / company .
   _____
   _____

3 friends / somewhere / stay / a / Imagine / give / your / to / room / needed / you / them / would ?
   _____
   _____

4 worried / hadn't / been / my / would / If / phoned / we / have / parents .
   _____
   _____

5 done / you / if / police / What / have / arrived / would / the / hadn't ?
   _____
   _____

6 free flight / I / wouldn't / even / me / there / if / offered / go / again / somebody / a .
   _____
   _____

7 hadn't / have / time / We / got / if / traffic / 'd / we / there / got / in / on / stuck .
   _____
   _____

   [ ]12

7 **Fill in the gaps in the conversation with these words/phrases.**

~~Let me~~   would you like me to   be a great help for offering   wouldn't mind   What if I   Why don't I you don't mind   be wonderful if you could Would it help if   if you like   can manage

A What's the matter, Jo? You look awful.
B I'm not feeling well and I've got people coming to stay.
A Oh dear, poor you. ¹ *Let me* help you get ready.
B Are you sure you ²_____ ?
A No, not at all. ³_____ I tidied the living room?
B Well, it'd ⁴_____ .
A Then ⁵_____ go to the supermarket for you?
B Thanks, that'd ⁶_____ .
A Have you got a list of the stuff you need?
B Yes, it's over there on the fridge.
A Oh yeah, I see. ⁷_____ cook dinner when I get back?
B No, that's OK. I ⁸_____ .
A What about the kids? I'll look after them this evening, ⁹_____ .
B That'd be fantastic. They'd love that – as long as ¹⁰_____ .
A No, of course not. ¹¹_____ collected them from school first?
B No, Fiona's doing that on her way home from college, but thanks ¹²_____.   [ ]11

8 **Tick the correct sentences. Change the incorrect ones.**

                                 criticism
1 He got a lot of ~~critical~~ for what he did.
2 My grandfather used to be a doctor. ✔
3 I can get by in Russian and Japanese.
4 Were you hearing all that noise last night?
5 I wish she wasn't so judgement about other people.
6 I go running in the park every so often.
7 I wasn't aware at the dangers.
8 You must try to behave more responsible!
9 He's travelling round Europe since July.
10 Did you remember buying some stamps? I need one for this letter.
11 Dave can't get used to working at night.
12 The thief robbed £2,000 from my bank account.
13 He's always leaving the front door open.
14 I'm really sick for working so hard.
15 I can't really see the point of going there.
16 I didn't used to enjoy going to school.   [ ]14

1 Fill in the gaps with the correct form of a phrasal verb.

1 Could you p_ass_ this message _on_ to the rest of your classmates?

2 When you drive around the farm, be careful that you don't r_____ _____ any chickens.

3 I couldn't w_____ _____ why everyone was looking at me.

4 I used to be quite good at boxing, but then one day somebody k_____ me _____ and I didn't c_____ _____ for about ten minutes.

5 We've just heard that a bomb has g_____ _____ near the airport.

6 I didn't really want to go to the wedding, but it t_____ _____ to be a lot of fun.

7 I always get really nervous when the plane is just about to t_____ _____ .

8 I was really scared so I r_____ _____ as fast as I could.

9 Don't worry, this isn't a true story, I'm just m_____ it _____ .

[18]

2 Write the words/phrases connected to books and reading.

1 a person who writes novels: a n_ovelist_

2 information about a book, written to attract interest: b_____

3 the story of a book, film, play, etc.: the p_____

4 a type of novel about women's lives today: c_____ l_____

5 walk around a shop, but without planning to buy anything: b_____

6 details of exactly what and where information can be found inside a book: the c_____ p_____

7 a book that has a cover made of thin card: a p_____

8 look quickly at the pages of a book, magazine, etc.: f_____ t_____

9 a book that is extremely popular with the public: a b_____

10 literature that has the same style or subject: a l_____ g_____

[9]

3 Complete the sentences with these connecting words.

~~because of~~ However despite instead of even though as due to apart from whereas

1 She didn't go for a walk _because of_ the rain.

2 We decided to go on the trip _____ it was terribly expensive.

3 He ate everything _____ the vegetables!

4 They decided to stay at home _____ going abroad this summer.

5 The concert in the park was cancelled _____ the singer was ill.

6 Dan loves jazz, _____ his girlfriend only likes classical music.

7 The style of the novel is simple. _____ , the ideas in it are quite complex.

8 They managed to climb to the top of the mountain _____ the thick snow.

9 Many trains were cancelled _____ problems on the railway.

[8]

4 Write these phrases used for exaggerating.

1 I'm very thirsty. _I'm dying for a drink_ .

2 I'm very happy. _____ .

3 I'm very frightened. _____ .

4 I'm very hungry. _____ .

5 I'm very worried. _____ .

6 I'm very shocked, surprised or angry. _____ .

7 It's very expensive. _____ .

8 It's very heavy. _____ .

9 It takes a very long time. _____ .

10 It's a very difficult situation. _____ .

11 It's very painful. _____ .

[20]

© Cambridge University Press 2012 ◁ Instructions p233

5 Fill in the gaps with the correct form of these verbs.

> ~~feel~~   tell   not remember   stop   have   decide
> wait   want   run   get out   take   drive   lie
> see   break   help   stay   save

I ¹ _was feeling_ bored one morning last week so I ² _____ to go to a nearby lake. While I ³ _____ there, I ⁴ _____ a man lying at the side of the road. I ⁵ _____ the car and ⁶ _____ to see if he was all right. The man explained that he ⁷ _____ along the road and then suddenly collapsed. He ⁸ _____ how long he ⁹ _____ there, but he thought that he ¹⁰ _____ his leg. I ¹¹ _____ him into the car and ¹² _____ him to the nearest hospital. I ¹³ _____ there because I ¹⁴ _____ to see if he was all right. After I ¹⁵ _____ for an hour and a half, the doctor came and ¹⁶ _____ me that the man ¹⁷ _____ a heart attack and I ¹⁸ _____ his life.

`[ 17 ]`

6 Fill in the gaps with *who, that, which, whose* and *where* if necessary. Put – if no word is needed.

A Wild Sheep Chase is the extraordinary novel ¹ _that_ brought its author, Haruki Murakami, to public attention. The book, ² _____ is set in Japan, begins simply enough. A young man ³ _____ works for an advertising agency gets a postcard from a friend. He decides to use the postcard, ⁴ _____ shows a photo of a country scene, for an advertisement ⁵ _____ his company is making. However, he doesn't notice that in the photo there is a sheep ⁶ _____ has a star on its back. This photo attracts the attention of a strange man in black, ⁷ _____ offers him a choice – find the sheep or lose everything. The search for the sheep takes the main character, ⁸ _____ name is never revealed, from Tokyo to the mountains of northern Japan, ⁹ _____ he has to face a number of dangers. Haruki Murakami, ¹⁰ _____ other books are available in English, is now one of Japan's best-known writers.

`[ 9 ]`

7 Fill in the gaps in the conversation with these words/phrases.

> ~~what~~   kidding   I can imagine   honest   believe it
> on earth   fantastic news   wonder   be joking   bet

A Guess ¹ _what_ ? My sister's going to have a baby!
B Oh, that's ² _____ .
A Yes, I'm so excited!
B I ³ _____ you are.
A And she's going to live in Hollywood next month.
B You're ⁴ _____ !
A No. I'm not surprised, to be ⁵ _____ . Her husband's an actor and he's always wanted to work in American movies.
B Are you going to visit them?
A Well, actually they've got me a job out there.
B I don't ⁶ _____ ! What ⁷ _____ are you going to do there?
A Work as an assistant at a film studio.
B You must ⁸ _____ ! Didn't you say you'd never work in the USA?
A Yes, I did, but this is too good a chance to miss. In fact, I've just booked my flight to LA.
B No ⁹ _____ you look so happy!
A I can't wait to get there!
B Yes, ¹⁰ _____ .

`[ 9 ]`

8 Tick the correct sentences. Change the incorrect ones.

1 The plane had taken off before we ~~were arriving~~ *arrived* at the airport.
2 I'm convinced that's the right decision. ✓
3 He arrived in London on a day where the buses were on strike.
4 He always insists on coming with us.
5 I didn't realise the film was based in a true story.
6 If he took his mobile phone last night, he could have called us.
7 The two men were charged for burglary.
8 Would it help if I drove you to the station?
9 If I met someone famous, I wouldn't know what to say.
10 We still haven't got used to work at weekends.
11 Where did you use to go to school?
12 This village is famous with its chocolate cakes.

`[ 10 ]`

PROGRESS TESTS: Photocopiable

1 **Complete these adjectives describing qualities.**

1 Painting these windows properly is very
   t _ime-consuming_ . It'll take me all weekend.

2 All my clothes are completely u_____ for
   my new job. I'll have to go shopping!

3 When it comes to pets, cats are not as
   a_____ as dogs.

4 I'm not surprised that Chris lost his job. His
   behaviour at the office party was o_____ .

5 You could try selling stuff on the Internet to raise
   the money. It can be very l_____ .

6 Why don't you ask Helen to help you? She's very
   e_____ to get involved.

7 Martin loves being a doctor. Although it's hard
   work, he finds it so r_____ being able to
   help people.

8 Maria's a great student. She really wants to learn
   and is so e_____ about the subject.

9 I was very i_____ with her performance.
   She was absolutely fantastic.

10 Sam's always been a f_____ friend. He
   would never do anything to hurt me.

11 Their dog barks a lot but you don't need to be
   frightened. He's completely h_____ .

12 There is only one place in the country you can see
   this flower. It's very r_____.

13 You mustn't spend so much time playing computer
   games. They can become a_____ .

14 I don't like going to their house because their dog
   frightens me. It's really f_____ .

15 I didn't understand that film. The story was
   strange; in fact, the whole thing was
   w_____ .

16 They paid a fortune for that bird. Apparently it's a
   very e_____ breed.

17 We're not allowed pets. The landlord says they're
   d_____ and will damage his property.

☐ 16

2 **Complete these phrasal verbs.**

1 Yumiko isn't very happy at the moment. Let's take
   her dancing to c _heer_ her u _p_ .

2 You can g_____ a_____ with the project without
   me. I'll c_____ u_____ when I get back from
   holiday.

3 Please decide what you want to do. I'll f_____
   i_____ with you.

4 He didn't want to go to the party but they t_____
   him i_____ it.

5 If you p_____ b_____ a shop on the way, can you
   buy some milk?

6 We won't stay the night. I don't want to p_____
   you o_____ .

☐ 12

3 **Read about wild cats. Look at the words/phrases
in bold in the article. What are they referring to,
a or b?**

WILD CATS

Cats walk on **¹their** toes, which enables **²them** to
run. The cheetah is the fastest of all big cats and
³it can reach a speed of 100km/h. Cheetahs run
using their sharp claws to grip the ground, and **⁴these** help
them to turn quickly. The colour and markings of the wild
cat's fur help to hide **⁵it** from other animals. Wild cats like the
leopard usually live in forests, while the tiger lives among tall
grasses, **⁶where** the stripes on its fur help to make it invisible.
Cats are good tree climbers, often dropping on other animals.
⁷They therefore need good balance and to be able to judge
distances. All cats also have highly developed senses. **⁸These**
enable them to hide and hunt efficiently. The most important
⁹ones are hearing and sight for **¹⁰they** frequently hunt at
dawn and dusk. When **¹¹doing** so, a big cat's sharp eyes and
sensitive ears give them an advantage over other animals.

1	a (cats)	b toes
2	a cats	b cheetahs
3	a another big cat	b a cheetah
4	a claws	b cheetahs
5	a the wild cat	b the wild cat's fur
6	a in tall grasses	b in forests
7	a other animals	b cats
8	a highly developed senses	b good balance and the ability to judge distances
9	a distances	b senses
10	a cats	b hearing and sight
11	a hiding	b hunting

☐ 10

4 Fill in the gaps with these words/phrases.

> ~~than~~ more and more any fewer deal bit
> nowhere twice nearly slightly less better

1 You're far more intelligent _than_ me.
2 My mother is 160 cm tall and I'm _____ taller – I'm 162 cm.
3 Our house is _____ near as big as yours.
4 That tulip isn't _____ as beautiful as this one.
5 He earns _____ money now that he's only working part-time.
6 This film is a great _____ more exciting than the one we saw last night.
7 I think there are _____ wild animals in the forest now due to hunting.
8 Let's buy this koi. It's a _____ cheaper than the other ones.
9 Your cat is enormous! It's _____ as big as my little one!
10 Come today – the sooner, the _____ .
11 People are getting _____ wasteful. They throw away a lot more than they used to.
12 The food in this restaurant isn't _____ better than it was last week.

> 22

5 Choose the correct verb forms.

1 I ('ll help)/'m helping you later, if you like.
2 I can't come this afternoon – I 'll meet/'m meeting my sister at 4.30.
3 Oh, is Jonathan back from his holiday? Then I 'll invite/'m inviting him to the party.
4 He hasn't been studying at all, so he doesn't pass/isn't going to pass his test.
5 This time next year we 're living/'ll be living in Australia.
6 Wait a minute. I 'll carry/'m carrying that suitcase upstairs for you.
7 We don't eat/won't be eating in that restaurant again. It's so expensive!
8 We 'll definitely finish/'re definitely finishing the project on time.
9 I think England will win/are winning the next World Cup.
10 This time tomorrow we 'll be swimming/'ll swim in the sea in the south of France!
11 They 're going to/'ll move house soon. They've found one they really like.

> 10

6 Fill in the gaps in this conversation with these words.

> ~~be~~ meant argument right not should what
> favour enough how again point think thought
> saying just never trying right better

A It'd ¹ _be_ much ² _____ if people went on holiday in their own countries.
B I'm not sure about that. I ³ _____ people ⁴ _____ have the ⁵ _____ to go on holiday wherever they want.
A No, that's not ⁶ _____ I'm ⁷ _____ to say. What I ⁸ _____ was planes are really bad for the environment.
B Fair ⁹ _____ , but I don't see ¹⁰ _____ we can stop people flying.
A Well, we could tax it more. One ¹¹ _____ in ¹² _____ of higher taxes is that it would reduce global warming.
B That's an interesting ¹³ _____ . I've ¹⁴ _____ really ¹⁵ _____ about that.
A I ¹⁶ _____ don't think it's ¹⁷ _____ that we can fly from London to Paris for £20. It's far too cheap.
B Yes, but then ¹⁸ _____ , if tourists stopped visiting places like Paris, a lot of businesses would close.
A No, that's ¹⁹ _____ what I meant. All I'm ²⁰ _____ is that people should pay the true cost of flying when they go on holiday.

> 19

7 Tick the correct sentences. Change the incorrect ones.

1 People are consuming more and ~~greater~~ ^{more} energy.
2 I've never been to the UK before. ✓
3 What would your boss have done if he would have seen you?
4 It's about a man who parents were secret agents.
5 Our present way of life is unsustainable.
6 That's a very unmoral way to behave.
7 He made up an excuse for arriving late.
8 I couldn't work over what he meant.
9 John arrived while I watched TV.
10 We enjoyed our trip in spite the weather.
11 Rick doesn't like swimming, but I like.
12 I'm dying for a drink.
13 The meeting has been cancelled due illness.

> 11

1 **CD2** 21 **Listen to five conversations. Choose the correct answers.**

a Listen to two friends talking. What kind of pet did Jamie get for his birthday?

1 a dog

2 a cat

3 a snake

b Listen to part of a radio play. What did Joanne find annoying about the English?

1 their polite way of speaking to people

2 their habit of talking about the weather

3 nobody talks to strangers on the tube

c Listen to part of a travel programme. Where are the speakers?

1 in a private garden

2 on a hill in the country

3 in a public park

d Listen to a woman leaving an answerphone message. Why has she called?

1 to change the time of a meeting

2 to suggest a different activity

3 to arrange a shopping trip

e Listen to two students talking. What subject is Nick studying?

1 history

2 photography

3 film studies   [10]

2 **Listen to John MacLeod, a marine biologist, giving a talk about dolphins. Are these sentences true (T) or false (F)?**

1 ☐ The dolphins that John has been studying live off the east coast of Scotland all year.

2 ☐ These dolphins are slightly smaller than bottlenose dolphins in the Mediterranean.

3 ☐ Some people think that the marks on the dolphins' skin might be caused by pollution.

4 ☐ Dolphins make sounds under water to find out what else is close to them.

5 ☐ They make these sounds by using a bone in the lower part of the mouth.

6 ☐ Dolphins have their own individual sound, which other dolphins sometimes copy.

7 ☐ Researchers agree why dolphins make all the different sounds.   [14]

3 **Fill in the gaps with the correct form of these phrases.**

> ~~take a long time~~   take advantage   take seriously
> take responsibility   take sides   take for granted
> take any notice

1 I usually *take a long time* to do my homework.

2 He never listens to my advice. I just don't think he _____ me _____ .

3 I never _____ my parents _____ . I think they're amazing and I often tell them so.

4 When he was released from prison, he finally started _____ for his actions.

5 Rachel never _____ when her children argue with each other.

6 That student has never _____ of what his teachers tell him to do.

7 Clive's been living in your house for weeks! I think he _____ of you.   [12]

4 **Complete the compound adjectives describing character.**

1 S*elf-centred* people are only interested in themselves.

2 L_____ people are very relaxed.

3 B_____ people are often annoyed or impatient.

4 A_____ people tend to forget things.

5 S_____ people are determined to behave in a particular way.

6 O_____ people are happy to accept ideas and ways of life different from their own.

7 S_____ people are shy and easily embarrassed.

8 E_____ people aren't easily upset, worried or annoyed by problems.

9 B_____ people think they are more important than they really are.

10 N_____ people don't want to accept new ideas or opinions different from their own.

11 L_____ people are calm and able to make sensible decisions in difficult situations.

12 S_____ people have confidence in their own abilities.

[22]

5 Fill in the gaps with the correct form of these verbs.

~~do~~ talk travel pass feel promote win make out change clean find

1 George may well _do_ a course in Arabic next year.

2 He went to the football match despite _____ very ill.

3 You're bound _____ the exam – you've studied so hard for it.

4 He tries to avoid _____ to people about his job.

5 Apart from _____ the kitchen, I've got nothing to do this weekend!

6 He's unlikely _____ his job this year. He's really enjoying it.

7 People _____ by train in England don't often talk to each other.

8 He couldn't _____ what was written on the envelope.

9 I dare say she _____ the competition – she's very lucky!

10 _____ information on the Internet is very easy.

11 I doubt if the managers _____ Brian. He's not very good at his job.

[20]

6 Put the words in these conversations in order.

1 A Sorry to disturb you.
  B now / really / I'm / right / busy / rather .
    I'm really rather busy right now.

2 A Is this a good time?
  B really / at / against / I'm / the / up / moment / it .
    _____

3 A was / could / you / a / wondering / I / moment / if / see / I / for .
    _____
  B Sorry, this isn't a good time.

4 A Are you busy?
  B at / I'm / pushed / moment / rather / for / the / time .
    _____

5 A Can I have a word?
  B just / afraid / tied / a / now / I'm / bit / up / I'm .
    _____

6 A to / but / Sorry / you / got / you / a / bother / minute / have ?
    _____
  B Yes, of course. How can I help?

[10]

7 Tick the correct sentences. Change the incorrect ones.

1 I might ~~taking~~ *take* my nieces to the beach.
2 I've never really thought about that. ✓
3 My sister is really terrified of flying.
4 Daniel has stopped work so hard.
5 If I didn't miss my bus this morning, I wouldn't have been late for work.
6 I'm not used to working with people.
7 His new house is twice as big than the old one.
8 That's the man who designed John's garden.
9 This time next week we'll walk round Paris.
10 By the time I left work, everyone went home.
11 We've named all of our children after their grandparents.
12 The bomb went out at 10.31.
13 He was convicted for arson and sent to prison.
14 Why on earth don't you listen to me?

[12]

1 **Write these state verbs.**

1 acceptable for a particular person or situation: suit_able_

2 understand a situation, sometimes suddenly: r_____

3 believe that somebody is honest and will not cheat or harm you: t_____

4 wish that you had somebody else's abilities, possessions, lifestyle, etc.: e_____

5 think or believe that something is true or probable: s_____

6 know somebody because you've seen them before: r_____

7 include something as a necessary part: i_____

8 have a good opinion of somebody because of their character or ideas: r_____

9 have earned something because of your good or bad actions or behaviour: d_____

10 think that something may not be true: d_____

[9]

2 **Fill in the gaps with the correct form of the words in brackets.**

Mumbai, previously known as Bombay, is the richest city in India. It is the ¹ _economic_ (economy) centre of India, generating 25% of its ² _____ (industry) output. Mumbai was the first Indian city to experience growth and changes associated with ³ _____ (capital) and has since become India's banking and finance capital. It is also home to the Bollywood film ⁴ _____ (industry), the largest film ⁵ _____ (product) in India.

However, Mumbai's success has led to enormous population growth, contributing to some serious social and ⁶ _____ (environment) problems. Air ⁷ _____ (polluted) from traffic and industry, for instance, pose a serious threat to quality of life in the city. In addition, the rapid ⁸ _____ (industry) development and enormous mass migration to the city have made it difficult for the city's urban ⁹ _____ (development) to plan ahead in this constantly changing city.

[8]

3 **Complete the table with nouns or adjectives.**

noun for a person	noun for a thing/idea	adjective
a politician	¹ _politics_	² _____
³ _____	capitalism	⁴ _____
⁵ _____	the economy	economic ⁶ _____
a developer	a developer	developed
	⁷ _____	⁸ _____
an investor	⁹ _____	–
¹⁰ _____	an industry	¹¹ _____ industrialised
a producer	a product	¹² _____
a manufacturer	¹³ _____	manufactured
¹⁴ _____	the environment	¹⁵ _____
a polluter	¹⁶ _____	polluted

[15]

4 **Complete the sentences with these words and a prefix.**

democracy decorated national rated view
qualified government colleagues understood
graduate defence smoker

1 Social networking sites are being used to organise __pro-democracy__ movements in some countries.

2 I think you're _____ for this job. We don't need a graduate.

3 He _____ the directions and ended up getting lost.

4 My brother feels much healthier since he became a _____ .

5 After I left the company I had a party for all my _____ .

6 I think the secretaries in this company are _____ . They do a great job.

7 The higher taxes have created a strong _____ feeling all over the country.

8 I don't think I'd ever like to work for a _____ organisation.

9 Trevor and Susannah have just _____ their bedroom.

10 A lot of people learn _____ because they want to be safe in the city.

11 I read a _____ of a documentary about China, which is on TV tonight. It sounds really interesting.

12 Anna finished her degree and is now studying for a _____ qualification. [11]

5 Fill in the gaps with the correct word.

1 Is there a _p a y p h o n e_ near here?
2 I left a message on his _ _ _ _ _ _ _ _ _ _ _.
3 I've changed the _ _ _ _ tone on my mobile.
4 I called your mobile and your _ _ _ _ _ _ _ _ _.
5 Which mobile phone _ _ _ _ _ _ _ _ are you with?
6 I'll have to phone him back. We got _ _ _ off.
7 I must remember to _ _ _ up my mobile.
8 My mobile has _ _ _ out of credit. [7]

6 Fill in the gaps with the correct form of these verbs.

> ~~have~~ think (x 2) contain smell wish
> not know see have not seem listen

1 My sister _has_ five children.
2 How many mobiles _____ that box _____?
3 I _____ how to use this machine.
4 _____ you _____ of getting an MP3 player?
5 It's her birthday today so she _____ a day off work.
6 The boss _____ to be in a good mood.
7 The flowers always _____ beautiful this time of year.
8 _____ you _____ you were still in bed on this cold morning?
9 _____ you _____ this is the right place?
10 I _____ Fran for a coffee at six.
11 I _____ to the radio when you phoned. [20]

7 Choose the correct verb forms.

1 Alan *'s been breaking/(s broken)* the window.
2 They *'ve been visiting/'ve visited* New Zealand several times.
3 Robin and I *have been knowing/have known* each other for years.
4 She *'s been playing/'s played* tennis since 8.30.
5 Graham *'s been finding/'s found* his car keys.
6 We've just *been returning/returned* from holiday.
7 I *'ve been sorting out/'ve sorted out* my tax all day. I should finish it tomorrow.

8 Since Sue retired her life *has been becoming/ has become* much more interesting.
9 Ian *'s read/'s been reading* five James Bond books. [8]

8 Fill in the gaps in the conversations with these words/phrases.

> ~~get~~ die losing reception delay line
> breaking up ring catch speak up phone

JEN   Sorry, I didn't ¹ _get_ any of that.
NICK The ² _____ isn't very good here.
SUE   Sorry Pat, you're ³ _____ a bit.
PAT   Would you like me to ⁴ _____ you back?
SAM   There's a bit of a ⁵ _____ on the line.
TOM   Do you want me to give you a ⁶ _____ later?
LYN   Sal, I keep ⁷ _____ you.
SAL   Sorry, it's a bad ⁸ _____ today.
LYN   You'll have to ⁹ _____ a bit. I can't hear you.
JO   Sorry, I didn't ¹⁰ _____ all of that.
ANN   I said my phone's about to ¹¹ _____ . [10]

9 Tick the correct sentences. Change the incorrect ones.

  is listening
1 John ~~listens~~ to music at the moment.
2 Two men were charged with burglary. ✓
3 Our new heating system is very economic.
4 He deserves earning more money.
5 She's got a pay-as-you-go mobile phone.
6 He's bound get promoted soon.
7 I'm a bit pushed for time at the moment.
8 Apart from visiting Paris, what else did you do?
9 He spent ages to search for information.
10 You shouldn't take any notice of him.
11 What you will be doing this time tomorrow?
12 I used to getting up early every day now.
13 I doubt we'll ever see each other again.
14 He's always taking advantage for you. [12]

1   **Fill in the gaps with the correct preposition.**

1 I put £1,000 <u>into</u> my account yesterday.
2 My brother is planning to buy his new computer _____ credit.
3 I always prefer to pay cash _____ food and things for the home.
4 My parents have agreed to invest some money _____ my business.
5 Alessandra got _____ debt when she bought a car.
6 I've heard that my sister-in-law Alice is extremely well _____ .
7 I don't believe it! For once I'm _____ credit at the bank!
8 My grandparents spent a great deal of money _____ their trip.
9 Mark's _____ debt again. He owes the bank thousands of pounds.
10 I'm afraid I'm a bit short _____ money at the moment.

[9]

2   **Fill in the gaps with the correct form of these phrasal verbs.**

| ~~put down~~   go down   rip off   take out   pay back |
| take off   pay off   come into   come to   save up |

1 Why don't you <u>put down</u> £10,000 now and pay the rest later?
2 You paid £200 for a ticket?! I think you were _____ .
3 And the total bill _____ £342.70. How would you like to pay?
4 Can I borrow £20? I promise I _____ you _____ next week.
5 I'm sorry, that's the lowest we can go. We've already _____ 25% _____ the price.

6 When Patrick died, his son _____ a lot of money.
7 I don't want to spend anything this weekend. I'm trying _____ for a holiday.
8 Prices of computers have _____ in the last few years.
9 Gary and Fiona have finally managed _____ all their debts.
10 We're thinking of _____ a loan so we can buy a new kitchen.

[18]

3   **Write these words/phrases connected to money.**

1 a bank account that you can get money from at any time: a c<u>urrent account</u>
2 an amount of money that is borrowed, often from a bank: a l_____
3 money you borrow to buy a house: a m_____
4 a bank account which earns a good rate of interest: a s_____ a_____
5 the amount of money charged by a bank, credit card company, etc. for borrowing money: an i_____ r_____
6 money that is given in advance as part of a total payment: a d_____
7 a measure of somebody's ability to pay back money: a c_____ r_____
8 when you have spent more money than is in your account: be o_____

[7]

4   **Write synonyms for these words.**

1 usually → <u>g e n e r a l l y</u>
2 exact → <u>p</u> _ _ _ _ _ _ _
3 insulted → <u>o</u> _ _ _ _ _ _ _
4 differ → <u>v</u> _ _ _
5 simple → <u>s</u> _ _ _ _ _ _ _ _ _ _ _ _ _ _
6 strange → <u>o</u> _ _
7 extra → <u>a</u> _ _ _ _ _ _ _ _
8 chase → <u>p</u> _ _ _ _ _
9 problem → <u>d</u> _ _ _ _ _ _ _
10 difficult → <u>c</u> _ _ _ _ _ _ _ _ _ _
11 work out → <u>f</u> _ _ _ _ _ _ / _ _ _
12 watch → <u>o</u> _ _ _ _ _ _ _
13 especially → <u>p</u> _ _ _ _ _ _ _ _ _ _ _

[12]

 face2face Second edition Upper Intermediate Photocopiable   © Cambridge University Press 2012   ⟨ Instructions p235

5 Fill in the gaps with the correct form of the verbs in brackets.

1 I wish I ___knew___ (know) how to save money!
2 I wish Rob _____ (be) here now.
3 I wish we _____ (not have to) go to work tomorrow.
4 If only Chris _____ (tidy) his room. It's in a terrible mess!
5 I hope he _____ (get) a new job soon.
6 I hope you _____ (have) a good time at the party tomorrow.
7 I wish you _____ (not study) so hard at the moment.
8 I wish the children _____ (have) more time to visit us this summer.
9 It's time _____ (leave) for the airport.
10 It's time you _____ (do) some exercise!
11 I wish the neighbours _____ (not play) their music so loudly all the time.

☐ 10

6 Fill in the gaps with the correct form of these verbs.

> go   not watch   sell   check   not increase
> spend   drink   not eat   book   help

1 I wish we ___'d gone___ to see him yesterday.
2 I wish I _____ all those sweets before lunch.
3 We should have _____ some tickets last week. The flight is full now!
4 If only John _____ his email last night.
5 If we'd known about the problem sooner, we _____ you with it.
6 My parents wish they _____ their big old house years ago.
7 I wish I _____ that terrible film last night.
8 If only the government _____ taxes so much last year.
9 Do you wish you _____ more time with your kids when they were young?
10 I shouldn't have _____ so much coffee today.

☐ 18

7 Fill in the gaps in these conversations.

> ~~really~~   no idea   no need   didn't mean to
> can't believe   shouldn't have   alright   worry
> forget   some reason   that   for   sorry about
> realise   matter   mind   afraid

A I'm [1] ___really___ sorry [2] _____ being so late. I didn't [3] _____ the time.
B It doesn't [4] _____ . The food isn't ready yet anyway.
A I had [5] _____ the traffic would be so bad.

A I'm sorry [6] _____ I was so bad-tempered this morning. I [7] _____ shout at you.
B Oh, [8] _____ about it.
A I [9] _____ said those things to you.
B That's [10] _____ . I could see that you were upset.

A I'm really sorry. I'm [11] _____ I've broken your camera.
B Never [12] _____ . It's an old camera anyway.
A I [13] _____ I dropped it. It was such a stupid thing to do.
B Don't [14] _____ about it. I've got another one.

A I'm [15] _____ the noise last night. I thought you were out for [16] _____ .
B There's [17] _____ to apologise. I had some friends round anyway.

☐ 16

8 Tick the correct sentences. Correct the mistakes.

1 This city sems very ~~pollution~~. *polluted*
2 I'm not used to cold winters. ✓
3 I forgot cancelling the appointment.
4 That was the most amazing film I've ever seen.
5 I think my phone's about to die.
6 We want to encourage economical development.
7 I'm thinking of going away this weekend.
8 Oh no! I've been breaking my glasses.
9 How long you have been living in Spain?
10 He's unlikely to be here before seven thirty.
11 To talk about the weather is common in the UK.
12 How many countries have you been visiting?

☐ 10

1 **Write these words connected to the cinema.**

1 a short extract from a film or TV programme, which is used as an advert: a t_railer_

2 a set of clothes worn by an actor in a film, play, TV drama, etc.: a c_____

3 all the actors in a film, play, TV programme, etc.: the c_____

4 the recorded music from a film which you can buy on CD: a s_____

5 a film that has the same story as one that was made earlier: a r_____

6 a type of journalist who gives his/her opinion about films, plays, etc.: a c_____

7 a film, book, etc. that continues the story of an earlier one: a s_____

8 when a film has a printed translation at the bottom of the screen: s_____

9 pieces of action in a film that are created on a computer: s_____ e_____

10 an article in a newspaper giving an opinion about a new film: a r_____

[9]

2 **Fill in the gaps with these adjectives.**

| ~~memorable~~ believable gripping predictable |
| moving overrated scary hilarious |

1 I think that *Titanic* was a very _memorable_ film.

2 Horror films are far too _____ for me. I can't get to sleep if I watch one.

3 A lot of people really admire Brad Pitt as an actor, but I think he's _____ .

4 That film was too _____ . It was obvious that he would end up marrying her!

5 I found that book absolutely _____ . I just couldn't put it down.

6 I only like realistic films. I think the plot should always be _____ .

7 That new comedy programme on TV is _____ . We couldn't stop laughing.

8 The final scene of the movie was so _____ it made me cry.

[7]

3 **Fill in the gaps with these homonyms. Use each word twice.**

| point sense handle mind state case |

1 You made a very good _point_ at the meeting.

2 I don't _____ answering some more questions.

3 Sandra's got a bad _____ of food poisoning.

4 Which is the largest _____ in the USA?

5 That's the most interesting _____ in the film.

6 I can't open the door – the _____ is broken.

7 These instructions don't make any _____ !

8 This book's about how the human _____ works.

9 I just can't _____ having lots of people to stay.

10 The poor man was in a terrible _____ .

11 She's got a very good _____ of humour.

12 Please put the guitar back in its _____ .

[11]

4 **Rewrite these sentences using passive verb forms.**

1 They show a new film every week.
A _new film is shown every week_ .

2 The police haven't found the missing child.
The missing child _____ .

3 They should nominate him for an Oscar.
He _____ .

4 I'd like people to remember my achievements.
I'd like my _____ .

5 He can't stand it when people laugh at him.
He can't stand _____ .

6 They'll present the awards on Saturday.
The awards _____ .

7 They had to cancel the match because of rain.
The match _____ .

8 They were taking the tiger to the zoo when it escaped.
The tiger escaped when _____ .

9 My mum used to give me sweets if I was good.
I used _____ .

10 He'd love someone to give him a role in a film.
He dreams of _____ .

11 No British skier had been awarded a medal before.
He was the first _____ .

12 They're showing the cup final live on TV.
The cup final _____ .

[22]

5 Fill in the gaps with the correct active or passive form of the verbs in brackets. There is sometimes more than one possible answer.

The History of Film

THE FIRST ever film [1] *was made* (make) in 1895 and the first commercially successful movie [2] _____ (release) was *The Great Train Robbery* in 1903. The end of the age of silent films [3] _____ (mark) by the

success of the first 'talkie', *The Jazz Singer*, in 1927, and the arrival of colour [4] _____ (add) to the popularity of the cinema. Between 1930 and 1945 the cinema industry in the USA [5] _____ (become) an entertainment factory which [6] _____ (control) by Hollywood studios. But since the 1940s the most significant advances in cinema [7] _____ (achieve) elsewhere. The British film industry [8] _____ (expand) after the war, but fewer films [9] _____ (make) in the UK today, mainly because the money that [10] _____ (need) to finance them can't [11] _____ (find) easily. In the 1980s the home video recorder [12] _____ (invent) and many people [13] _____ (predict) the death of the cinema. For a few years audiences [14] _____ (decrease) alarmingly and dozens of cinemas [15] _____ (go) out of business, but recently more people [16] _____ (attract) back to the cinema. It [17] _____ (hope) that this growth will [18] _____ (continue) and cinema can return to its golden age.

[ ] 17

6 Complete the sentences with these words/phrases.

such as   like   so (x 2)   so much   so many   as (x 2)   such

1 I love sci-fi films *such as* The Matrix.
2 That book has _____ an exciting story.
3 I can see why _____ people admire him.
4 The play was _____ good I saw it twice.
5 Daniel Craig is amazing _____ James Bond.
6 Why do some film stars make _____ money?
7 He looked _____ he'd run a marathon.
8 Let's use this box _____ a table.
9 It was _____ good to meet you again.

[ ] 8

7 Fill in the gaps in this conversation with these words/phrases.

on   other time   a miss   a try   don't mind
mind   like   feel up to   fancy   easy   feel
up to (x 2)   the same   about   bothered

A Have you got anything [1] *on* tonight?
B No, I haven't actually.
A Do you [2] _____ going out for a meal?
B That's a good idea. Where shall we go?
A I thought we could give that new French restaurant [3] _____ .
B I'm [4] _____ . Whatever you [5] _____ .
A Then afterwards I wouldn't [6] _____ going to a club. How [7] _____ you?
B I'm sorry, but I don't [8] _____ dancing tonight, I'm too tired. Some [9] _____ , perhaps. By the way, what are you [10] _____ on Saturday?
A Nothing special. Why?
B I was thinking of going to see *Hamlet* at the Playhouse.
A I'd rather give that [11] _____ , if you don't mind. We could go to the cinema instead.
B OK, do you [12] _____ like seeing an action film or a comedy?
A I'm not [13] _____ either way. It's all [14] _____ to me. But you prefer comedies, don't you?
B I really [15] _____ . It's [16] _____ you.
A OK. Let's decide at the weekend.

[ ] 15

8 Tick the correct sentences. Change the incorrect ones.

                in
1 The film is set ~~on~~ Istanbul.
2 I'm not aware of any problems. ✓
3 I wish the train had been on time yesterday.
4 Can I borrow £10? I'll pay you off tomorrow.
5 The play is based on a story by Kate Atkinson.
6 I wish he doesn't leave his clothes on the floor!
7 It's time we try a different restaurant.
8 This is the worst film I ever see in my life.
9 I've been trying to call you all day.
10 If only I would be ten years younger.
11 How long have you been having your car?
12 You're breaking up. I can't hear you.
13 My current account's hardly ever on credit.

[ ] 11

1 Fill in the gaps with the correct form of these verbs.

> ~~fix~~   put in   put up   dry-clean
> replace   service   decorate

1 Mr Jones *is going to fix* the broken fence next week.
2 It's about time we _____ the kitchen. The walls are looking rather dirty.
3 We had the boiler _____ last autumn. The old one was getting dangerous.
4 Dad _____ some new shelves in the living room at the moment.
5 Stef's very good with engines. He always _____ his car himself.
6 My husband's just finished _____ a new burglar alarm.
7 That suit should _____ as soon as possible. It's too dirty to wear again.   ☐ 12

2 Fill in the gaps by combining two of the words in the box to make a compound word.

> ~~draw~~ day span break dream humoured
> down attention self ~~back~~ powered down
> high wide good obsessed spread hearted

1 The cost of the product is its only __drawback__ .
2 My boss is off work. She's recovering from a nervous _____ .
3 I get my most creative ideas when I stare out of the window and _____ .
4 It's better for Tom to stay at home and look after the baby because Anne has such a _____ job.
5 She's feeling a bit _____ because she didn't get the job.
6 I think Simon's new girlfriend is rather _____ . She spent the whole night talking about herself!
7 Obesity is becoming more and more _____. Governments need to take serious action.
8 Lucy's mother is lovely. She's incredibly friendly and _____ .
9 The children don't have a long enough _____ for three-hour lessons.   ☐ 16

3 Write these adjectives connected to views and behaviour.

1 it is right to do or say something: f *air*
2 having an unfair and unreasonable dislike of someone or something: p_____
3 using rude and offensive words: a_____
4 obeying rules which control your behaviour: d_____
5 difficult to control: u_____
6 when you believe someone is going to harm you: t_____
7 based on facts rather than feelings or beliefs: o_____
8 unfairly preferring one person or group of people over another: b_____
9 fair and sensible: r_____
10 feel angry and upset because you think something is unfair: r_____   ☐ 9

4 Fill in the gaps with the correct form of *have* or *get* and the correct form of the verb in brackets. Sometimes there is more than one possible answer. In one gap, you don't need *have* or *get*.

When I was a child, my family lived in an old house which always needed work, but we never [1] __got__ anyone __to fix__ (fix) things. My dad liked doing everything himself, but he always [2]_____ me and my brothers _____ (help). I hated it, so now I always try to [3]_____ things _____ (do) by professionals who know what they're doing! Anyway, my husband Bill and I moved into this old cottage two months ago and we've already [4]_____ a lot of work _____ (do). Last month we [5]_____ the roof _____ (repair) and next week we're [6]_____ a new kitchen _____ (put in). Unfortunately, the boiler broke down this morning, so we haven't got any hot water at the moment! It's probably not possible to [7]_____ it _____ (fix) so we need to [8]_____ it _____ (replace) as soon as possible, which won't be cheap. Then there's all the decorating to be done. We were thinking of [9]_____ the house _____ (decorate) professionally, but it would have cost a fortune. I hate painting so I'll try [10]_____ my husband _____ (do) that. There's the garden to sort out too, but I love gardening so we're [11]_____ (do) that ourselves. Actually, I'm [12]_____ some friends _____ (come) and help, then we can have a party afterwards to celebrate all our hard work!   ☐ 22

5 Choose the correct words.

1 There's *no*/*none* milk in the fridge, I'm afraid.
2 I have two sisters and *either of*/*both of* them work as doctors.
3 Both dogs *is*/*are* taken for walks regularly.
4 I love food and I'll eat *all*/*anything*.
5 I haven't seen *neither*/*either* of my nieces for over a year.
6 Every *house*/*houses* in the street had a green door.
7 All of the teachers *is*/*are* women.
8 Each student *get*/*gets* a coursebook.
9 There were two different desserts and *both of*/*both* them tasted delicious.
10 *All*/*Every* member of the family was there.
11 She had six grandchildren and *all of*/*each* them went to university.
12 Every hat I try on *is*/*are* too small.
13 I haven't got *nothing*/*anything* to do tomorrow.
14 Everyone *love*/*loves* my mother's cooking.
15 *None of*/*Neither of* my parents smoke.
16 *All of the*/*Every* people in the room were shocked by what they heard.

[15]

6 Put the words in this conversation in the correct order.

A Hi, Joe. / had / I've / brother / just / with / lunch / your .
1 *I've just had lunch with your brother.*
B How was he? Did he look tired? The / that / about / is / works / him / hard / me / thing / he / that / too / worries .
2 _____
_____ .

A He looked fine, actually. What / about / his / is / I / enthusiasm / for / him / everything / admire .
3 _____
_____ .
B That's true. He's always got some new interest or other. One / time / about / thing / that / can / the / that / him / amazes / he / find / me / is .
4 _____
_____ .
A I know.
B What / me / that / my / about / answers / brother / is / emails / he / never / annoys / my .
5 _____
_____ .
A Yes, that must be annoying. The / don't / about / he / is / I / like / him / listen / thing / doesn't / that / properly .
6 _____
_____ .
B You're right, he doesn't. I've noticed that too.
A But you're a good listener, aren't you?
B Sorry? What did you say?
A Very funny! One / your / I / is / love / sense / you / humour / thing / of / about .
7 _____
_____ .

[12]

7 Tick the correct sentences. Change the incorrect ones.

1 The whole thing was ~~as~~ *like* a bad dream.
2 I've been sitting here for over an hour. ✔
3 It was such a boring film that I fell asleep.
4 My cat enjoys looked after by my neighbours.
5 We redesigned the garden ourselves.
6 I'd like to invest some money on property.
7 I wish he wouldn't shout at me all the time.
8 You shouldn't have tell him about it.
9 I like watching award ceremonies such the Oscars.
10 The meeting had to cancel because of a strike.
11 I've been saving up for a new computer.
12 I wish I don't have to go back to college next week.
13 If only I went to bed earlier last night.
14 My aunt used to work like a nurse.
15 Have you read the critic of that new play in *The Times*?
16 What are you up to on Sunday?

[14]

1 **Fill in the gaps with the correct preposition.**

1 My company exports tea __to__ the UK.
2 What do you do _____ a living?
3 We have a lot of work _____ this month.
4 I must stop chatting and get _____ to work.
5 I've just gone _____ business with a friend.
6 Tim never relaxes – he's always _____ the go.
7 It's been a pleasure doing business _____ you.
8 Gabi's been out _____ work for six months.
9 These toys have been imported _____ China.
10 Which project are you working _____ ?
11 They lost so much money they ended up going _____ of business.

☐10

2 **Fill in the gaps with the correct form of these words/phrases.**

> ~~work~~ work freelance go bankrupt set up
> make a loss take over run a chain branch
> expand make a profit be made redundant

Daniela Roberts used to ¹ __work__ for a bank, but she ² _____ eight years ago when the bank closed a number of ³ _____ around the country. Her husband, Ian, was a photographer, but he was fed up

with ⁴ _____ for lots of different newspapers. So they decided ⁵ _____ their own business – a pizza restaurant called Daniela's Pizza in their home town. The first year was very difficult and their company nearly ⁶ _____ , but after ⁷ _____ in the first year they managed ⁸ _____ in the next year. Soon the restaurant was so popular that they felt it was time ⁹ _____ the business. Two years ago they ¹⁰ _____ another restaurant, and now they ¹¹ _____ of restaurants all over the south of England.

☐20

3 **Write sentences 1–11 in reported speech. Use these verbs.**

> ~~promise~~ remind advise offer deny accuse
> suggest warn apologise threaten admit

1 "I'll definitely pay you back, Tim."
Wendy __promised to pay Tim back__ .
2 "I didn't break Erin's mobile phone."
He _____ .
3 "Why don't we visit the art gallery?"
Fiona _____ .
4 "You should do more exercise, Mr Lee."
The doctor _____ .
5 "I'm sorry I was late for class."
She _____ .
6 "I'll give you a lift to the station, Jo."
Alan _____ .
7 "Don't go into the park after dark, Tina."
I _____ .
8 "I stole my cousin's laptop."
He _____ .
9 "You've been lying to me, Molly."
Frank _____ .
10 "Don't forget to get some milk, Kath."
Richard _____ .
11 "I'll call the police if it happens again."
Harry _____ .

☐20

4 **Choose the correct words.**

1 I did a course in (advertising)/adverts.
2 Can you draw me the company's new logo/slogan?
3 How much do you want to spend on the advertising budget/campaign?
4 I see that Jim Carrey's new film is getting a lot of good advertising/publicity.
5 Excuse me, can I give you this leaflet/free sample to read?
6 We're designing/launching the new range of children's clothes on May 1st.
7 Fast food companies spend a lot of money on advertising/publicity.
8 Most slogans/logos are less than six words long.

☐7

5 Put the verbs in brackets in the correct form of the Future Continuous or Future Perfect

1 What _will_ you _be doing_ (do) at this time tomorrow evening?

2 By the end of next year he _____ (complete) his pilot's training.

3 I hope that I _____ (retire) long before I reach 70.

4 I certainly _____ (not work) here in 10 years' time!

5 I'm afraid that Roberta can't see you on Friday morning. She _____ (travel) to a conference in the south of France then.

6 I _____ (not finish) decorating the house by the end of the week.

7 This time next week Christopher and Adela _____ (lie) on a beach in Goa.

8 Do you think your cousins _____ (arrive) by the end of this week?

[7]

6 Complete these reported statements, questions and requests.

1 "Have you got time for a coffee, Maria?"
He asked Maria ____if she had time for a coffee____ .

2 "Where did you put the scissors, John?"
She wanted to know _____ .

3 "Can you pick me up after work?"
Peter's wife asked _____ .

4 "You've already borrowed £50 off me, Val."
He pointed out _____ .

5 "Could you take my suit to the dry cleaner's?"
I asked her _____ .

6 "When is he leaving?"
She wanted to know _____ .

7 "You must be home by ten o'clock."
Bob told his son _____ .

8 "What have you been doing all morning?"
Jack asked her _____ .

9 "Are we going to stay in a hotel?"
Sandra asked him _____ .

10 "I'm not going to call them until Sunday."
Kevin explained _____ .

11 "Will you fix my computer?"
Gillie asked Richard _____ .

[10]

7 Fill in the gaps in this conversation with these words/phrases.

> ~~got an idea~~   worth a try   we could do   makes sense
> sounds like   go over   I wonder if   know   such
> should avoid   I'd rather   right in thinking   about
> what you're saying

A What are we going to do about the presentation?

B I've ¹_got an idea_ . How ²_____ asking Jack?

A Personally, ³_____ we didn't ask him. He wasn't very impressive last time.

B ⁴_____ it'd be a good idea to ask Sally.

A Yes, that's ⁵_____ . She knows the market and she's very keen.

B One thing ⁶_____ is ask George to help her.

A I'm not sure that's ⁷_____ a good idea. They're, um, not exactly friends, are they?

B So ⁸_____ is that they don't get on very well.

A Exactly.

B OK, so maybe we ⁹_____ asking them to work together.

A I ¹⁰_____ ! Why don't you give her a hand, Pat?

B Yes, that ¹¹_____ . You're really good at presentations and you know the audience.

A That ¹²_____ a good idea.

B OK, if you like. Am I ¹³_____ that the presentation is only half an hour?

A Yes, and it's just before lunch.

B So, can we just ¹⁴_____ the conference plans again?

[13]

8 Tick the correct sentences. Change the incorrect ones.

1 Everyone needs to ~~do~~ a living. _make_

2 They've been living there for years. ✓

3 I'll be on the middle of a meeting at three.

4 One thing I love about Paul is his smile.

5 She's the best headmaster I've ever met.

6 Everyone in my family love soap operas.

7 I'm having a new boiler put in next week.

8 Are you going to get someone help you?

9 I haven't seen neither of these films.

10 I get my car service every year.

11 The plot was so far-fetched.

12 This tyre needs being changed.

13 I don't feel up to going out tonight.

14 What I like about this house it's close to the park.

15 I've got such a lot of things to do.

[13]

1 **CD3** ▶ **34** Listen to five people talking about things they like doing at the weekend. Match speakers 1–5 to activities a–f. Use each letter once only. There is one extra letter which you don't need to use.

1 Speaker 1 ____   a relaxing with the Sunday papers
2 Speaker 2 ____   b doing some DIY
3 Speaker 3 ____   c doing some gardening
4 Speaker 4 ____   d preparing a meal for friends
5 Speaker 5 ____   e watching sport on TV
                 f doing routine jobs at home

☐ 10

2 Listen to a radio interview with Karen Thomas, a sports therapist. Choose the correct answers.

1 Recent research has shown that the number of sports injuries has ...
  a gone down. b stayed the same. c gone up.
2 Karen says that more people over 30 are taking up exercise because they ...
  a want to join a sports club. b want to lose weight.
  c have serious health problems.
3 Karen thinks people are more likely to get injured if they ...
  a have just started exercising. b have been exercising for years. c hire a personal trainer.
4 Most of the people she sees have physical problems because they ...
  a go running. b need to lose weight.
  c don't exercise at all.
5 Karen advises people who want new sports shoes to ...
  a buy fashionable trainers.
  b go to a shop with well-trained staff.
  c get the most expensive pair they can afford.
6 She thinks the best exercise for people who haven't done any before is ...
  a walking. b going to the gym. c jogging.   ☐ 12

3 Write these colloquial words/phrases.

1 stupid or silly: c_razy_
2 find somebody attractive: f_____
3 a British pound: a q_____
4 go somewhere for a short time: p_____ i_____
5 relax: c_____ o_____
6 worried and anxious: s_____ o_____
7 fashionable: t_____
8 do something wrong or badly: m_____ u_____
9 a friend: a m_____
10 throw something away: c_____ o_____
11 a toilet: a l_____
12 a man: a g_____
13 quite, but not extremely: p_____
14 annoy or worry somebody: b_____
15 something that is annoying because it causes problems or is difficult to do: a h_____

☐ 14

4 Complete the idioms in these sentences.

1 Thanks for the card. It really _made_ my _day_ .
2 I had no idea I was going to get promoted – it came completely _____ of the _____ .
3 My parents live in the _____ of _____ . It takes an hour to drive to the nearest shop!
4 I love living in New York, but it's a _____ cry _____ the small village where I grew up.
5 Sarah, I've lost my watch. Could you _____ an _____ out for it when you're tidying up?
6 I was so tired when I went to bed last night that I _____ like a _____ .
7 I've been working so hard recently. I'm going to the countryside for a week to _____ my _____ .
8 That exam was a _____ of _____ . I got every question right.
9 No, don't worry, he was only _____ your _____ . You shouldn't take him seriously.
10 That documentary on global warming certainly gave me _____ for _____ .
11 When everyone arrives, let's play some party games to _____ the _____ .

☐ 20

5 Fill in the gaps with these words/phrases. There may be more than one possible answer.

> ~~in excess of~~   give or take   tons of   or so   -ish
> tiny   around   roughly   vast   -odd   far (+ -er)

1 My cousin's company made profits _in excess of_ £100,000 in their first year of business.
2 We'll have _____ food for the party so you don't need to bring anything.
3 It takes twenty minutes to drive to my house, _____ a minute or two.
4 Let's leave the house _____ eight in the morning.
5 They said the book would get here in a day _____ .
6 The house looks great. There was only a _____ bit of work to be done.
7 Shall we invite people round for seven_____ or is that too early?
8 They ate a _____ amount of food!
9 She thinks it's _____ three days' work but it's difficult to be sure.
10 That job took _____ _____ (long) than I expected.
11 There must have been forty_____ teenagers at my son's party. It was crazy.   [10]

6 Read this conversation. Choose the correct modal verbs and fill in the gaps with the correct form of the verbs in brackets.

A I'm so worried. James flew to Canada today and he hasn't phoned.
B It's a long journey. He ¹(must)/can't _be_ (be) tired.
A Or his plane ²can't/might _____ (crash).
B Don't be silly. That ³must/can't _____ (happen). It would have been on the news.
A Yes, you're right. But why hasn't he phoned?
B What time is it in Canada now?
A Er, about three in the morning, I think.
B That's it, then. He ⁴can't/must _____ (be) asleep.
A Yes, of course. I suppose he ⁵can't/might _____ (try) to text me when he landed, but perhaps his phone doesn't work over there.
B Isn't that James's mobile on the floor?
A Oh no! It ⁶must/can't _____ (fall) out of his pocket when we were having breakfast.

B And look, there are seven text messages for him from someone called Bill.
A Oh dear, that's his boss. He ⁷must/may _____ (try) to get hold of James about something important.
B Do you know why James has gone to Canada?
A Er, he ⁸might/can't _____ (give) a talk at a conference, but I'm not sure.
B Have you checked your computer? He ⁹may/can't _____ (send) you an email.
A Yes, that's good. I hadn't thought of that.   [16]

7 Fill in the gaps with the positive or negative forms of these verbs and the correct form of the verb in brackets.

> would   need   should   could

1 I don't know whether he _would have studied_ (study) harder in another school.
2 We _____ (go) to the airport because Gina's boyfriend had already picked her up.
3 He _____ (buy) that house if he'd known that the roof leaked.
4 I know I was wrong. I _____ (do) what you told me, but I didn't.
5 We _____ (stay) longer at the party last night, but we decided to leave early.   [8]

8 Tick the correct sentences. Change the incorrect ones.

1 She managed ~~passing~~ *to pass* her driving test.
2 I slept like a log last night. ✓
3 He warned me to not talk to them.
4 I'll have finish by the time you get home.
5 They finally persuaded Joe to help them.
6 We're having our kitchen redesign next month.
7 At midday I'll be driving to the hotel.
8 No one want to come to the cinema with me!
9 They replaced the window themselves.
10 Peter denied not stealing my mobile.
11 I don't want neither of my parents to come.
12 My brother was accused for shoplifting.   [10]

Acknowledgements

Chris Redston would like to thank: Claire Nielsen-Marsh for updating the Teacher's Notes and editing the rest of this book; Theresa Clementson for writing the Extra Reading Worksheets and updating the photocopiable materials; Andrew Reid for taking the book through proofs; Greg Sibley for managing the face2face Second edition project with such efficiency and good humour; Hilary Mead for her help with the photos; Gillie Cunningham for all her excellent work on the second edition of the Student's Book; and everyone at eMC for the book design. He would also like to offer particular thanks to his wonderful fiancée Adela Pickles for putting up with book-writing guy for another three years and to Skipper the Bunny for all the late-night running around, bunnyflops and binkies.

The authors and publishers are grateful to the following contributors:
emc design: text design and page make up
Hilary Luckcock: picture research

The authors and publishers acknowledge the following sources of copyright material and are grateful for the permissions granted. While every effort has been made, it has not always been possible to identify the sources of all the material used, or to trace all copyright holders. If any omissions are brought to our notice, we will be happy to include the appropriate acknowledgements on reprinting. Puzzles on p. 178 made at www.puzzle-maker.com; NI Syndication Limited for the text on p. 202 adapted from 'Hollywood queues for boy's penny arcade' by John Harlow, *The Sunday Times*, 06.05.12. Copyright © NI Syndication Limited; NI Syndication Limited for the text on p. 213 adapted from 'Lost in evolution - 500,000 languages gone and counting' by James Gillespie, *The Sunday Times*, 11.12.11. Copyright © NI Syndication Limited; Guardian News and Media Ltd for the text on p. 215 adapted from 'How an email hacker ruined my life and then tried to sell it back to me' by Rowenna Davis, *The Observer*, 16.10.11. Copyright © Guardian News & Media Ltd 2011; The Week for text A, B, C, D, E, F on p. 216 adapted from 'It must be true…I read it in the tabloids', *The Week*, 03.09.11, 09.07.11, 06.08.11, 07.05.11, 01.10.11, 30.04.11. Copyright © of The Week Ltd; New Scientist for the text on p. 219 adapted from 'Fluffy baby robot helps keep you company' by Yuriko Nagano, *New Scientist*, 12.12.11. Copyright © 2011 Reed Business Information UK. All rights reserved. Distributed by Tribune Media Services; Telegraph Media Group Limited for the text on p. 220 adapted from 'YouTube pays families £100,000 as funny videos go viral' by Sarah Rainey, *The Telegraph*, 13.11.11, for the text on p. 220 adapted from 'YouTube dads always have their finger on the button' by Jim White, *The Telegraph*, 15.11.11. Copyright © Telegraph Media Group Limited 2011; Professor Jonathan Gershuny for the quote on p. 222 from 'British men sharing the burden of household chores' by Richard Alleyne, *The Telegraph*, 31.07.11. Reproduced with permission of Professor Jonathan Gershuny; The Independent for the text on p. 223 adapted from 'From a cleaner to a concert pianist, the Polish immigrant who hit the right note in Britain' by Andy McSmith, *The Independent*, 07.12.07. Copyright © The Independent 2007.

English Pronunciation in Use Elementary by Jonathan Marks, Cambridge University Press, 2007 for the diagram on p24 and *English Pronunciation in Use Intermediate* by Mark Hancock, Cambridge University Press, 2012 for the diagrams on p20, p22, p30, p40, p44, p46, p48. Reprinted with permission.

Photo acknowledgements

The publishers are grateful to the following for permission to reproduce copyright photographs:

Key: l = left, c = centre, r = right, t = top, b = bottom

P148: Getty Images/Jimmy Chin; p196: Shutterstock/P T Images; p197: Shutterstock/Jo Crebbin; p199: Masterfile; p202: www.cardboardchallenge.com; p203: Shutterstock/PhotoCreate; p214(L): Press Association/AP; p214(R): Press Association/Michael Albans/AP; p215: Shutterstock/Hugo Felix; p217(L): istockphoto/happyborder; p217(R): Alex Foundation; p218(TL): istockphoto/LesByerley; p218(BL): Thinkstock/istockphoto; p218(R): Superstock/Blaines Harrington/age fotostock; p219: Rex Features/Masayoshi Kanoh; p221: Fotolia/dan talson; p222(T): Shutterstock/Lilyana Vynogradova; p222(B): Corbis/Superstock; p223: Ross McDiarmant; p228: Alamy/Gunter Marx; p231: Getty Images/Hulton Archive/MGM Studios; p239: Corbis/Pixland; p246: istockphoto/Mark Wilson; p248: Shutterstock/kristian; p251(L): istockphoto/Jennifer Morgan; p251(R): istockphoto/Linda & Colin McKie; p252: istockphoto/Paul Gardner; p255: Ronald Grant Archive.

Front cover photos by Shutterstock/Andresr (TCL); Shutterstock/Konstantin Sutyagin (BR)

The publishers would like to thank the following illustrators: Fred Blunt (Meiklejohn Illustration Ltd); Kate Charlesworth; Mark Duffin; Dirty Vectors; Andy Hammond (Illustration); Graham Kennedy; Joanne Kerr (New Division); Naf (Meiklejohn Illustration Ltd); Dave Russell.

Corpus
Development of this publication has made use of the Cambridge English Corpus (CEC). The CEC is a computer database of contemporary spoken and written English, which currently stands at over one billion words. It includes British English, American English and other varieties of English. It also includes the Cambridge Learner Corpus, developed in collaboration with the University of Cambridge ESOL Examinations. Cambridge University Press has built up the CEC to provide evidence about language use that helps to produce better language teaching materials.

English Profile
This product is informed by the English Vocabulary Profile, built as part of English Profile, a collaborative programme designed to enhance the learning, teaching and assessment of English worldwide. Its main funding partners are Cambridge University Press and Cambridge ESOL and its aim is to create a 'profile' for English linked to the Common European Framework of Reference for Languages (CEFR). English Profile outcomes, such as the English Vocabulary Profile, will provide detailed information about the language that learners can be expected to demonstrate at each CEFR level, offering a clear benchmark for learners' proficiency. For more information, please visit www.englishprofile.org